ORIGINS *of* LIFE

FAZALE RANA & HUGH ROSS

ORIGINS

of

LIFE

BIBLICAL AND
EVOLUTIONARY MODELS
FACE OFF

NAVPRESS®
BRINGING TRUTH TO LIFE

OUR GUARANTEE TO YOU

We believe so strongly in the message of our books that we are making this quality guarantee to you. If for any reason you are disappointed with the content of this book, return the title page to us with your name and address and we will refund to you the list price of the book. To help us serve you better, please briefly describe why you were disappointed. Mail your refund request to: NavPress, P.O. Box 35002, Colorado Springs, CO 80935.

The Navigators is an international Christian organization. Our mission is to reach, disciple, and equip people to know Christ and to make Him known through successive generations. We envision multitudes of diverse people in the United States and every other nation who have a passionate love for Christ, live a lifestyle of sharing Christ's love, and multiply spiritual laborers among those without Christ.

NavPress is the publishing ministry of The Navigators. NavPress publications help believers learn biblical truth and apply what they learn to their lives and ministries. Our mission is to stimulate spiritual formation among our readers.

ISBN 1-57683-344-5

Cover design by Jonathan Price, Reasons To Believe
Cover illustration by Aaron Garcia
Creative Team: Nanci McAlister, Rachelle Gardner, Kathy Mosier, Pat Miller

Some of the anecdotal illustrations in this book are true to life and are included with the permission of the persons involved. All other illustrations are composites of real situations, and any resemblance to people living or dead is coincidental.

Unless otherwise identified, all Scripture quotations in this publication are taken from the HOLY BIBLE: NEW INTERNATIONAL VERSION® (NIV®). Copyright © 1973, 1978, 1984 by International Bible Society. Used by permission of Zondervan Publishing House. All rights reserved.

Rana, Fazale, 1963-
  Origins of life : biblical and evolutionary models face off / Fazale
Rana and Hugh Ross.
     p. cm.
Includes bibliographical references (p.   ).
  ISBN 1-57683-344-5
  1. Life--Origin. 2. Creationism. I. Ross, Hugh (Hugh Norman), 1945-
II. Title.
  QH325.R36 2004
  576.8'3--dc22

                          2003017389

Published in association with the literary agency of Alive Communications, Inc.,
7680 Goddard St., Suite 200, Colorado Springs, CO 80920.

Printed in the United States of America

1 2 3 4 5 6 7 8 9 10 / 08 07 06 05 04

FOR A FREE CATALOG OF NAVPRESS BOOKS & BIBLE STUDIES,
CALL 1-800-366-7788 (USA) OR 1-416-499-4615 (CANADA)

For
Amanda, Whitney, Mackenzie,
Jose, and Olga Rana
and
Joel and David Ross

CONTENTS

Authors' Note   9
Acknowledgments   11
Introduction: In Pursuit of My Passion   13

PART I: THE MYSTERY UNFOLDS

1. Questions, Questions—Always Questions   21
2. Are There Any Answers?   29
3. Putting Creation to the Test   35
4. The Naturalistic Approach   47

PART II: THE FACTS OF LIFE

5. An Early or Late Appearance?   63
6. A Slow or Sudden Arrival?   81
7. Where's the Soup?   93

PART III: FROM THE BOTTOM UP AND TOP DOWN

8. The Search for Chemical Pathways   109
9. Look! Only One Hand   123
10. The Codes of Life   135
11. Beneficial Boundaries   143
12. Life's Minimum Complexity   159

PART IV: LOOKING FOR LOOPHOLES

13. Extreme Life   171
14. Life on Mars?   183
15. Europa and Beyond   197
16. Life, Seeded on Purpose   205

PART V: A MODEL FOR LIFE

17. Solving the Mystery   211

Epilogue   223
Appendix A: Biblical Creation References   227
Appendix B: Carbon-12 Enrichment in Photosynthesis   229
Notes   231

Glossary of Terms   269
Index   277
About the Authors   297
About Reasons To Believe   299

FIGURES AND TABLES

Figures

5.1 Stromatolites in Shark Bay, Australia   65
6.1 Cratering Intensity for the Inner Solar System   83
6.2 Before, During, and After the Collision Event Between
Earth and a Mars-Sized Planet   88
9.1 Chiral Molecules   123
10.1 The Different Levels of Protein Structure   137
11.1 Transmission Electron Micrograph of Biological
Membranes   144
11.2 The Molecular Structure of a Typical Phospholipid
with a Schematic Representation of Its Structure
Superimposed upon It   145
11.3 Tail-to-Tail Assembly of Phospholipid Molecules to
Form a Bilayer   146
11.4 The Different Ways Proteins Interact with
Phospholipid Bilayers   147
11.5 Structures of Different Phospholipid Aggregates   153
11.6 Different Bilayer Structures Formed by Phospholipids 155
14.1 Martian Meteorite ALH84001   184
14.2 Tiny Martians?   188
14.3 Outflow Channels and Valley Networks on Mars' Surface 192
15.1 Galileo Spacecraft Image of Europa's Surface   198

Tables

4.1 "Textbook" Description of Life's Origin   48
4.2 Origin-of-Life Scenarios   50
12.1 Organisms with the Smallest Genomes   161
12.2 Probabilities That Proteins Could Come into Existence
Simultaneously   164
12.3 Bacterial Components Displaying Organization   167

AUTHORS' NOTE

We would like to welcome you to this book. Whether you accept creation or evolution or just don't know what to think about the origins of life, we invite you to join us on a fascinating investigation of the scientific evidence. We are Christians. But we are also scientists who know what it's like to seek after truth, painstakingly follow wherever the evidence leads, and arrive at a conclusion based on what seems most reasonable. The clues provide a challenging trail, but following them will take us to an amazing destination—the origins of life.

Fazale Rana & Hugh Ross

ACKNOWLEDGMENTS

This book represents the sacrifice and hard work of many people, not just the authors. We want to thank our wives, Amy Rana and Kathy Ross, and our children, for their love and encouragement and for understanding when this book project took "priority" over family matters.

We want to acknowledge all who are part of the Reasons To Believe team (staff and volunteers) who tirelessly dedicated themselves to this book as if it was their own labor of love. Thank you Kathy Ross, Patti Townley-Covert, Tani Trost, and Joe Aguirre for expert editorial guidance (and more). Thank you Jonathan Price and Phillip Chien for designing the tables and many of the figures to enhance the book's clarity. Thank you Sandra Dimas, Jody Donaldson, Marj Harman, and Colleen Wingenbach for preparing the manuscript and taking care of all the little chores that must be done during a book.

We want to thank scholars Kenneth Samples, David Rogstad, Timothy Boyle, Walter Bradley, Russell Carlson, and Guillermo Gonzalez for critical peer review. Your input was invaluable. We assume responsibility for any errors found herein.

Thanks also to our friends at NavPress for their commitment to this project and for their belief in our work at Reasons To Believe. Thank you Eric Stanford, Rachelle Gardner, Kathy Mosier, and Terry Behimer.

Finally, we want to thank Lee Hough at Alive Communications for his encouragement, friendship, and practical advice.

INTRODUCTION:
IN PURSUIT OF MY PASSION

The mystery of life's origin intrigues many people, including me. Graduate courses helped me develop a strong appreciation for life's chemistry when I was in the doctoral program at Ohio University during the mid-1980s. Like a hungry man with a stack of pancakes set in front of him, I devoured books and journal articles that weren't even required reading. I wanted to know how life originated. How could the chemical systems that carry out life's fundamental processes come into existence? How did biochemistry begin? Though not part of my formal course work, these questions motivated me to look for answers at every opportunity.

Origin-of-life researchers explained that complex chemical mixtures on early Earth organized themselves into the first living entities in a gradual stepwise fashion. But to me, this process of chemical evolution seemed unconvincing and inadequate to produce the cell's vastly complex, highly sophisticated, and tightly orchestrated molecular systems. Based on my training, I knew that chemical systems could self-organize, but the organization displayed by biochemical systems differs qualitatively from the regular and repetitive order possessed by crystals and other types of molecular aggregates that form spontaneously.

The best scientists typically experience difficulty getting a few chemicals in a flask to do what they want, even when they expend enormous effort and rely on the past work of others. Whenever I worked through the evolutionary pathways suggested by origin-of-life researchers, I always came back to the same question: How could random physical and chemical events yield the amazingly elegant, highly integrated biochemical systems found inside living cells?

I could envision realistic chemical pathways that on occasion, by chance, could yield molecules with useful properties for living systems. But isolated chemicals don't constitute life. Numerous complex molecules—

each carrying out a specific but limited function—work in concert to form biochemical systems. In turn, numerous biochemical systems interact in an orchestrated fashion to support the activities of even the simplest cells. A molecule's function contributes to life processes only in the context of the entire ensemble of systems. In other words, for life to emerge, its biochemical systems must come into existence all at once, not step by step.

My suspicions of what biochemist Michael Behe years later described as "irreducible complexity"[1] led me to conclude that life's beginning involved more than chemical and physical processes alone. I reasoned that life's beginning must spring from activity beyond the natural.[2] Inability to express clearly and defend my convictions made me reluctant to speak of them to my fellow graduate students or the faculty in the chemistry department. Fear that I would not be taken seriously as a scientist kept me quiet.

Who Is the Creator?

Convinced that a creator must exist, in private I pondered his identity. Initially I thought all the different religions led to the same truth—that life's author revealed himself to humanity in different ways, at different times. Religious pluralism appealed to me because I saw overlapping truth-claims among the world's great religions.[3]

Being raised by parents of differing beliefs contributed to my view. My father, a Muslim born in India, was not a strict adherent to Islam, but with personal and private faith he prayed and read the Qur'an every day. He also carried a prayer book with him wherever he went. Meanwhile, my mother was a nonpracticing Catholic. She and my father agreed to disagree on religious matters. They provided a sound ethical upbringing for my brother and me, but no religious training. In our home evangelical Christians were generally considered uneducated, unintelligent, and gullible.

As a young person, I never disbelieved in God; I just never considered God in anything I did. Education was the supreme value in our home. My parents considered any grade lower than an A to be a sign of failure. My father, a nuclear physicist, worked as a research scientist in private industry and as a university professor. My mother earned degrees in math, physics, and education. Together, they encouraged my brother and me to pursue careers in science or medicine.

At West Virginia State College, I discovered my passion for chemistry and biochemistry. I embraced the evolutionary paradigm, and the professors I looked up to were ardent evolutionists. Some of the faculty members in the biology department worked hard to combat young-earth creation science, which at that time threatened to infiltrate the educational system. The men and women I most admired taught me to reject supernatural explanations for the world, and I responded to their tutelage.

Before beginning graduate studies at Ohio University, I fell in love with a young woman named Amy and we became engaged. During this time, Amy began to take her Christian faith seriously. Though I accepted her decision to pursue religion, I didn't accept the beliefs she shared with me. Embracing a form of universalism made me more comfortable.

But, before Amy and I married, the pastor who officiated at our wedding challenged my pride as a scientist. He persuaded me to read the Bible by reasoning that a scientist should be willing to seek truth no matter where it may be found and to follow wherever it leads. The thrust of this point made me decide that I should at least examine Christianity. For the first time in my life, I seriously read and contemplated the Bible.

I was well into my graduate studies at Ohio University by now, and each evening after completing my work, I sat down at my lab bench to read Scripture. After paging randomly the first few evenings, I finally settled on the book of Matthew. The Christmas story piqued my interest because I had never before read firsthand from the Gospels about Christ's birth. From that passage, I moved on to the Sermon on the Mount where Jesus admonishes His disciples to avoid a superficial appearance of goodness, and challenges them to pursue right attitudes as well as right behavior.

The way Jesus taught—His authority and revolutionary message—amazed me. He conveyed a message regarded by most of humanity as true yet one that no human being can actually live out (at least on his or her own). Through what I now consider to be supernatural insight, I recognized Jesus Christ as the Son of God. The high standards Jesus holds up for His followers forced me to recognize my inability to keep them—and forced me to recognize my need for a Savior.

The elegance of life's chemistry had already led me to recognize a creator's existence. Reading the Bible led me to embrace Christianity. Jesus was the Creator I had discovered inside the cell. With no felt need for a "crutch," I came to faith in Christ as a scientist in search of truth.

Rather than look for ways to integrate my newfound faith with my studies and scientific career, I chose to keep those two areas of my life neatly compartmentalized. The Genesis 1 creation account seemed to square generally with the scientific record of Earth's and life's history, and to a large degree that satisfied me. Yet I could not adequately reconcile the details of Genesis 1 with the scientific record. Because of this, my faith was tentative and I chose to keep it private. I did not feel comfortable discussing a Christian perspective with laboratory colleagues.

The Investigation Begins

Several years after my conversion to Christianity (and after completing my studies and starting a career in private industry), I read a few creation science books out of mild curiosity. These volumes turned my casual interest into deep concern. Their contents, riddled with scientific errors, frustrated me. Instead of providing a scientific basis for Christianity, these works linked the Bible's truth with scientifically inaccurate ideas.

My first exposure to creation science jarred me into appreciating why so many scientists lack openness to Christianity. It also motivated me to undertake a serious study of the relationship between science and the Bible.

This pursuit connected me with several works by astronomer Hugh Ross. To my pleasant surprise, he successfully demonstrated how nature's record, embodied in the latest scientific discoveries, integrates with the Bible. His careful scholarship impressed me. I was also interested to learn that he had gone through a personal search for truth not so different from my own.[4]

Overjoyed to discover a researcher who could explain how science and Christianity intertwined, I enthusiastically began sharing my new insights with scientists and laypeople alike. I was even more excited to find new points of connection on my own each week as I read about the latest discoveries in scientific journals. My quest to understand how life originated began in earnest.

With information accruing at a rapid pace, aided by amazing technological advances, scientists should be well on their way to resolving the impossibilities I had perceived in the textbook scenarios for life's beginnings. Fifteen years of new discoveries (since my graduate school days) ought to have made the case for a natural start to life stronger, if indeed life arose on its own. If, on the other hand, the years of intensive research in chemistry and physics had yielded little or no real progress toward explaining the origin of life, then perhaps my conclusions as a graduate student had been right. The thought carried huge ramifications, and yet it seemed to me that origin-of-life science was in fact floundering in its attempt to identify a naturalistic process that could reasonably be said to have produced the first life forms.

A few years ago, I started working with Hugh Ross at Reasons To Believe (RTB). This interdenominational organization provides research and teaching on the harmony of God's revelation in the words of the Bible and the facts of nature. Since then, I have been able to focus more intensively than ever on scientific evidence as it bears on the origin-of-life issue. And now we've combined Hugh's astrophysics and my biochemistry research to produce this book. Herein we offer a new model—the RTB Model—to explain life's origin.

About This Book

This is not a book about evolution per se. That is, it is not about the theory by which life accumulates changes over time, so that simple, early organisms change over eons into more complex, advanced ones. It is not about the entire history of life on Earth either. Rather, this book has a narrower, yet crucial, focus. And it is within this context that the RTB Model is presented. This book is about the origin of life — the first appearances of living organisms on Earth. We address such questions as: What was first life like? When did it appear on Earth? How did it get here?

Many thought-provoking books on the origin of life have been written from a naturalistic perspective in recent years. And, many books have been written on the larger topic of evolution from either a pro or a con position. But to the best of our knowledge, many years have passed since a scientifically reputable book has been written specifically about the origin of life from a Christian perspective. The last such book was *The Mystery of Life's Origin* by Charles B. Thaxton, Walter L. Bradley, and Roger L. Olson (Lewis & Stanley, 1984). Although an outstanding work for its time, origin-of-life science since then has advanced considerably, in the process becoming a multidisciplinary enterprise that encompasses chemistry, biochemistry, geology, planetary science, and astronomy. Our objective is to bring the discussion up to date.

The material unfolds in what we hope is a helpful way. The first quartet of chapters sets the stage for all that follows. *Chapter 1* summarizes the history of origin-of-life science, giving special attention to the current state of frustration among naturalistic scientists. *Chapter 2* examines reasons scientists resist supernatural explanations for the origin of life. *Chapter 3* presents our biblically based and scientifically testable creation model (called the RTB Model) for life's origin. *Chapter 4* summarizes the evolutionary models for the origin of life. In both chapter 3 and chapter 4, predictions are developed that logically emanate from both classes of models. At this point, the models are ready to face off!

Next, a group of three chapters pursue the natural-history approach to life's origin. They examine what scientists know about conditions on Earth at the time life first appeared. *Chapter 5* considers how early in Earth's history life showed up. *Chapter 6* investigates whether life appears suddenly in the geological record or instead appears gradually. Finally, *chapter 7* looks at the evidence for amino acids and other building blocks of life in the environment of early Earth.

We then move into several chapters on the bottom-up and top-down approaches. (A bottom-up approach considers how life could have started in a way that would lead to life as we know it today. A top-down approach looks at present-day life and works backward to consider how it could have gotten to this point.) *Chapter 8* evaluates the pathways that biochemists have suggested for nonliving materials to organize themselves into living entities. *Chapter 9* explores how natural processes might account for homochirality—a lining up of molecules with similar configurations that mark living cells. *Chapter 10* uses a review of protein research to consider how information-bearing molecules could have first formed. *Chapter 11* depicts the details of cell membranes and imagines their origin. Those chapters all use a bottom-up approach. *Chapter 12*, though, follows a top-down approach by employing the new science of genomics to consider the most minimal form of life and what it might have taken to produce such life.

The next batch of chapters looks at the more exotic theories of origins that provide new directions in origin-of-life research. *Chapter 13* asks whether extremophiles (hardy microbes that thrive in severe conditions) could have arisen on early Earth as first life by natural means. *Chapter 14* questions whether there's any evidence that our neighbor planet Mars has ever harbored life, or seeded Earth with life. *Chapter 15* goes on to look at whether other places in space (such as Jupiter's moon Europa, Saturn's moon Titan, or some extrasolar planet) could serve as a life-origination site. Then *chapter 16* evaluates the most exotic theory of all—the idea that aliens on a distant planet seeded early Earth with life. Summaries at the ends of *chapters 5* through *16* show how the RTB Model fares against the naturalistic models when faced with the scientific evidence. The headings for these sections, *Putting the RTB Model to the Test* and *Evaluating the Evidence,* make them easy to identify.

Chapter 17 suggests why life might have appeared on Earth so early. Finally, the *epilogue* wraps up the investigation by returning to the core issue of why all this matters on a personal level, just as it did to me on my own origin-of-life journey.

A word of encouragement: For readers with little background in science, the analyses of research findings that appear in this book may at times seem hard to slog through. We wish it could be easier. The problem is that science can really be complicated. While we've done our best to make it understandable, we don't want to oversimplify, because those who expect a high level of proof deserve to get it. But even if you do not easily grasp all the details, look for the underlying point. By the end of each chapter, concepts should become clear. And don't hesitate to check the glossary at the back of the book for difficult terms. Now, the mystery behind the origins of life unfolds.

Fazale Rana

Part I

THE
MYSTERY
UNFOLDS

CHAPTER 1

QUESTIONS, QUESTIONS — ALWAYS QUESTIONS

Almost every individual recognizes that humanity is a part of the web of life on this planet. People want to know where life came from, in order to have a better sense of place in the universe. The search for life's origin thus becomes no dispassionate journey but a pilgrimage filled with significance. This trek draws each person onward with the nagging need to answer the ultimate question: What is the meaning of existence?

In search of answers for life's origin, there are two general directions from which to choose—evolution and creation. Each of these concepts raises a multitude of questions. The goal of this book is to bring the answers to some of these questions into clearer focus and to let the known scientific facts determine which theory better solves the mystery behind life's beginning. The ultimate purpose is to discover the truth.

Evolution, derived from naturalism (the belief that the physical universe comprises all reality), is the better known and preferred theory in many circles. To some, it seems the only possible pathway to knowledge of life's start. And certainly this concept has a long and distinguished history, counting among its advocates many of modern history's greatest thinkers. But whether this idea makes the most sense, based on what is known about the initial appearance of life, remains to be seen.

Can evolution's theory of abiogenesis (the birth of life from nonlife) be demonstrated as true? If abiogenesis lacks scientific support, then evolutionary theory stands by blind faith alone. For biology to be framed in naturalistic terms, scientists must demonstrate the continuum from a prebiotic mixture of chemicals through the most complex life forms. However, if something more than nature, namely the supernatural, was involved in life's origin, then the door is open for viewing biological phenomena from a creation perspective.

The history behind the current state of origin-of-life science begins the investigation.

A Brief History

Scientific explanations for the origin of life have a colorful history over the last 150 years.[1] Along the way, this discipline has taken a number of remarkable twists and turns.

Darwinism. Biology moved with full force into the materialistic arena in the late 1850s with the publication of Charles Darwin's *The Origin of Species*. Darwin and those who accepted the essence of his ideas no longer regarded species as the fixed product of divine creative activity. Rather, Darwinists viewed species as evolving from one form into the next strictly through natural mechanisms—inheritable variation operated on by natural selection. They believed that all life throughout Earth's history stemmed from a single form or a few original forms.[2]

Darwin did not address the origin of life directly until more than a decade after publication of his now famous book. His theory dealt only with life's transformation once it existed. In 1871 he advanced the bold idea that life could have emerged on Earth through chemical processes involving ammonia, phosphates, and other inorganic materials.

Darwin's contemporaries, such as T. H. Huxley and Ernst Haeckel, suggested similar pathways to the first life form. Haeckel, one of Darwin's leading German supporters, proposed the existence of ancient creatures that occupied an intermediate position between life and nonlife. Haeckel called these predecessors to life "monera" and thought them to be formless lumps of gel with the capacity for reproduction. Shortly after Haeckel advanced his hypothesis, Huxley provided observational support for the idea. He detected gelatinous lumps in ocean-floor mud and interpreted them as moneran remains.[3]

The protoplasmic theory of the cell—the idea that the cell consists of a wall surrounding a nucleus and homogeneous jellylike protoplasm—made the early naturalistic explanations of abiogenesis seem plausible.[4] As early as the 1830s biologists Matthias Schleiden and Theodor Schwann, working independently, advanced the theory that all life is composed of units called "cells." Observational capacity at that time limited biologists' view of the cell to three features: the cell wall, the nucleus, and the protoplasm.

When biologists and chemists focused attention on the protoplasm in the 1850s, they began to envision chemical routes that could possibly produce what they believed to be the single ingredient of the cell's protoplasm. For example, German chemist Edward Pflüger suggested that simple carbon- and nitrogen-containing compounds on early Earth underwent a series of transformations to produce the single complex molecule comprising cellular protoplasm.

By the end of the nineteenth century, with the rise of the new field of biochemistry, the protoplasmic view of the cell waned. Scientists recognized that the cell's protoplasm is a chemically complex system. This complexity became apparent with the discovery of enzymes in the cell's protoplasm, capable of catalyzing a large number of chemical reactions. With the demise of the protoplasmic model, the earliest ideas about abiogenesis came to an end. At the same time, chemical studies indicated that Huxley's "moneran" remains were simply chemical artifacts — calcium sulfate precipitate caused by alcohol addition to mud samples.[5]

Panspermia. In the late nineteenth century, an entirely different approach to the origin-of-life question became popular. Many scientists began to regard life, like matter, as eternal. This idea left no room for a creator. It embraced materialism and circumvented the question of a beginning by regarding life as always present in the universe. Scientists referred to this concept as panspermia — "everywhere life's seeds."[6]

Proponents of this theory viewed life as qualitatively different from matter, yet considered it an inherent part of the universe. Panspermia gained legitimate support from the prevailing view that the universe is eternal and infinite. Also integral to the concept was the recognition that biological organization is far too complex to emerge by the random processes that comprise abiogenesis.

Many prominent scientists of the time, such as Lord Kelvin, Hermann von Helmholtz, and Nobel laureate Svante Arrhenius, argued vigorously for panspermia. Research efforts involved identifying mechanisms that could transport life throughout the universe. Life's origin on Earth equated to life's first arrival under survivable conditions. Kelvin and von Helmholtz thought that meteorites transported the first life forms to Earth. Arrhenius suggested that naked bacterial spores, or spores associated with dust particles, prevailed throughout the universe. He proposed the idea that radiation pressure from stellar systems propelled the spores through interstellar space.

Panspermia lost its appeal in the early twentieth century as cosmologists began to recognize from Einstein's theory of general relativity and Edwin Hubble's observations of space's expansion that the universe had a beginning. Other experiments showed that ultraviolet radiation kills bacterial spores. Because this deadly ultraviolet radiation permeates interstellar space, bacteria could not have survived interstellar journeys. The evidence seemed to be turning against panspermia.

Neovitalism. Given the vast complexity of life and the complicated problems with abiogenesis and panspermia, most scientists of the early 1900s gave up trying to discover how life originated. Life's beginning was considered a profound mystery.

Other scientists began to argue for a special "life force." A scientific minority emerged that gave attention to this concept, termed neovitalism. One leading proponent, Hans Driesch, argued that the hypothesized life force mysteriously propagated from one generation to the next and that the origin-of-life question stood beyond reach.[7]

The Oparin-Haldane hypothesis. Reacting to this neovitalism, Russian biochemist Alexander I. Oparin and British geneticist J. B. S. Haldane independently provided a detailed hypothesis for abiogenesis in the 1920s. Though initially rejected by much of the scientific community, the Oparin-Haldane hypothesis became the chief organizing principle in origin-of-life research through the 1970s, and in some form it persists today.[8] Oparin and Haldane were the first to propose the mechanism for life's origin as part of a detailed scientific model.

That model presented stepwise pathways from inorganic systems on primordial Earth to the emergence of Earth's first living entities. They postulated an early atmosphere devoid of oxygen and dominated by reducing gases—hydrogen, ammonia, methane, and water vapor. Within this gas mix, energy discharges formed prebiotic molecules that accumulated in Earth's oceans to form a primordial soup. Chemical reactions then led step by step to the first life forms.

Oparin and Haldane differed regarding the intermediates to life. Oparin viewed the transitional molecular system as protein aggregates, whereas Haldane regarded life's intermediate as a large self-replicating molecule.

Not until the 1950s did anyone offer significant experimental verification for the Oparin-Haldane hypothesis. Stanley Miller, a student of Nobel laureate Harold Urey at the University of Chicago, performed the now famous spark-discharge experiments, launching the origin-of-life research program as a formal scientific discipline.[9] His experiments produced amino acids and other organics by passing an electrical discharge through a gas mixture devoid of oxygen, and his success inaugurated a series of similar experiments by other scientists.[10] Results seemed to continually validate Oparin's and Haldane's ideas. Giddy with Miller's accomplishment, many scientists predicted the origin-of-life problem would be solved in the next few decades.[11]

Chemical analysis of a meteorite that fell in Murchison, Australia (in 1969) further fueled the optimism and sense of accomplishment within the origin-of-life research community. Scientists looked to the Murchison meteorite and others like it as a proxy for the chemistry operating on early

Earth because they are from the era when the solar system formed. The organic compounds found in the Murchison meteorite resemble in quantity and type those formed in laboratory simulation experiments.

Excitement grew as researcher Sidney Fox achieved the next important milestone in the 1970s.[12] Fox and his lab group coaxed amino acids to condense, forming "proteinoids." Some of these compounds — closely related to proteins in structure — possessed the ability to catalyze, or assist, chemical reactions. Fox and his coworkers observed that under certain conditions proteinoids aggregated to form microspheres. These microspheres superficially resemble cells.

Disappointment

While earlier studies focused on finding chemical routes that produced life's molecular building blocks, scientists in the mid-1980s and 1990s began to assess the operation of these chemical pathways on early Earth. Their research seemed to turn up more dead ends than fruitful avenues to study. They also started probing the geochemical and fossil records of Earth's oldest rocks — data that establish time constraints for beginning-of-life scenarios. In addition, researchers began applying information theory to the origin-of-life dilemma and started to understand life's minimal complexity. Problems grew increasingly insurmountable. The thrills of the early decades of research gave way to growing frustration and pessimism.

Currently, scientists stand no closer to understanding life's beginning than they did when Stanley Miller conducted his first experiments fifty years ago. Though some scientists assert that the research is in its infancy, significant resources have been brought to bear on the origin-of-life question over the past five decades. To date, no real answers have emerged. Rather, a misguided approach has essentially stalled the research program.

Best-selling author Paul Davies makes this point in his book *The Fifth Miracle:*

> When I set out to write this book, I was convinced that science was close to wrapping up the mystery of life's origin. . . . Having spent a year or two researching the field, I am now of the opinion that there remains a huge gulf in our understanding. . . . This gulf in understanding is not merely ignorance about certain technical details; it is a major conceptual lacuna.[13]

Davies' statements likely surprise most people, including scientists. From popular media reports, one would think researchers have all but finalized the explanation for life's beginning. But such is not the case.

Davies explains why this mismatch persists between public perception and stark reality:

> Many investigators feel uneasy about stating in public that the origin of life is a mystery, even though behind closed doors they freely admit that they are baffled. There seems to be two reasons for their unease. First, they feel it opens the door to religious fundamentalists and their god-of-the-gaps pseudoexplanations. Second, they worry that a frank admission of ignorance will undermine funding.[14]

So scientists are keeping quiet and searching for new directions in which to proceed. Their behind-the-scenes frustration became evident (to these authors) at the combined meetings of the International Society for the Study of the Origin of Life and the International Conference on the Origin of Life, held both in 1999 at the University of California, San Diego, and in 2002 in Oaxaca, Mexico (hereafter referred to as ISSOL 1999 or ISSOL 2002).[15] This joint scientific meeting, held every three years, attracts leading origin-of-life investigators from around the world and serves as a platform for them to share and discuss their latest findings.

The atmosphere at such gatherings typically crackles with anticipation as participants gather to hear about new discoveries and breakthroughs. However, at both of these last two ISSOL events, a grim mood laced with desperation prevailed. Participants acknowledged that some fifty years of well-funded investigation have led to one barricade after another. The old intractable problems remain as new ones come to light.[16]

Origin-of-life investigators have successfully discovered many plausible chemical routes, from simple compounds to biologically important compounds. Yet for other critical biomolecules no pathways are known—in fact, they may not exist. For those molecules with identified synthetic routes, in many cases their chemical pathways would likely be blocked by early Earth's conditions. Origin-of-life researchers cannot identify any location on primordial Earth suitable for production of prebiotic molecules. Those studying the problems cannot explain how the uniform "handedness" (homochirality) of amino acids, nucleotides, and sugars could emerge in any so-called prebiotic soup.

Data from the geological, geochemical, and fossil records all place impossible constraints on naturalistic scenarios. Life arose rapidly and early in Earth's history—as soon as Earth could possibly support it. Origin-of-life researchers recognize that life had no more than tens of millions of years to emerge. Life also appeared under amazingly harsh conditions—conditions that would not allow life to survive, let alone originate.

Earth's first life was complex chemically, though simple morphologically (that is, in its form). Consistent with this, investigators have discovered that life in its most minimal form requires an astonishing number of proteins that must be spatially and temporally organized within the cell.

"Déjà vu All Over Again"

History seems to be repeating itself. Just as the first Darwinists gave up on the earliest versions of abiogenesis, so scientists today are abandoning long-cherished pillars of the naturalistic origin-of-life paradigm. Many now speculate that life may have originated somewhere other than on Earth.

In the face of this challenge, the science community is turning once again to the panspermia idea to explain life's first appearance on Earth. However, the panspermia of the twenty-first century differs from that of the nineteenth. Originally, panspermists viewed the universe as eternal and viewed life as qualitatively different from matter. Today scientists consider the universe to have had a beginning in time and they see life and matter as indistinguishable at a chemical level.

Some neopanspermists merely transfer the life-origin problem to another body in the solar system (Mars, for example). They posit that materials ejected from the surfaces of these other solar system bodies could have served as the vehicles that delivered life to Earth, or perhaps life originated in a nearby star system and traversed interstellar space as spores or on interstellar dust grains, similar to Svante Arrhenius's mechanisms.

A few researchers, influenced by astrophysicists such as the late Fred Hoyle and Chandra Wickramsinghe, adopt a form of panspermia virtually identical to that of the nineteenth century. They reject big-bang cosmology and regard the universe as eternal. Also, they see biological complexity as too great for abiogenesis. Infinite time, infinite matter, and infinite life become the only way around this dilemma. Yet—amazingly—most panspermia proponents today view life's beginning as a reasonably likely occurrence.

The appeal to panspermia offers only a short reprieve for the naturalistic paradigm. Mounting scientific evidence underscores the unlikelihood that life could emerge on any planet (or other body) in Earth's solar system or travel through interstellar space. As today's panspermists rediscover the obstinate problems associated with panspermia, they will likely be forced to abandon these ideas again.

Recognizing the problems with origin-of-life scenarios on Earth and with both interplanetary and interstellar panspermia, some scientists have begun to espouse a radical version of the concept—*directed* panspermia. First suggested by Nobel laureate Sir Francis Crick and origin-of-life researcher Leslie Orgel, this approach explains life's first occurrence on Earth as the work of aliens who sent an unmanned ship to Earth, seeding it with life.[17]

Like the neovitalists of the early 1900s, other scientists recognize the problems of chemical evolution and panspermia and appeal to a yet undiscovered law of physics or life principle to explain life's beginning.[18] But another alternative may make more sense.

The dead ends that continually stymie researchers need not yield the same confusion and frustration experienced by scientists at the beginning of the last century. A radical new approach based on new findings may begin to provide solutions to the intractable problems.

CHAPTER 2

ARE THERE ANY ANSWERS?

C an the mystery surrounding the origin of life ever be solved? Science writer John Horgan doesn't think so. According to this dismal perspective, investigators who pursue answers to life's beginning engage in *ironic science*—an enterprise that has more in common with literary criticism than with science.[1] Researchers in such an endeavor can only offer points of view, opinions, and speculations. They can espouse exotic ideas that may be fashionable or fall out of favor, but their concepts will never be fully confirmed or rejected through testing.

But what if the ironic-science perspective is wrong? Perhaps the mystery behind life's start *is* solvable. The problems that multiply with each new discovery and the so-called irony of origin-of-life research may not reflect unknowable questions after all. They may merely signify a failed paradigm.

Most of the scientific community examines origin-of-life questions exclusively within a naturalistic framework. But if trying to explain life's beginning by natural processes alone is a misdirected approach, then the puzzles facing researchers would be expected. Each new discovery will increase the perplexity. Ideas offered to explain life's start will become more exotic and unrealistic, making science appear more and more speculative, or ironic. This trend has been in evidence for more than twenty years.

Resistance to Change

What reasonable alternatives exist for investigating and analyzing the scientific clues? In the broadest sense, the only way to account for life's beginning apart from naturalism is one that allows for transcendent causation, or supernaturalism. But without a testable scientific model for creation, scientists understandably balk at this notion. So even though the evidence fits awkwardly within the naturalistic paradigm and at the same time points beyond the physical realm, the scientific community by and large rejects this supernatural approach. Yet is supernaturalism really so alien to science?

Most investigators would rather confront the problems and frustrations of naturalistic models than consider any explanation for life's start that lacks scientific credibility, especially when it involves a divine Creator. Both Nobel laureate Sir Francis Crick and physicist and best-selling author Paul Davies make this point. In *The Fifth Miracle* (1999), Davies concedes "science rejects true miracles. Although biogenesis strikes many as virtually miraculous, the starting point of any scientific investigation must be the assumption that life emerged naturally, via a sequence of normal physical processes."[2]

Nearly twenty years earlier, Sir Francis Crick made the identical point. He asserted in his book *Life Itself* that an honest man recognizes that life's origin appears to be "almost a miracle, so many are the conditions which would have had to be satisfied to get it going."[3] Yet Crick rejects consideration of any supernatural basis. Rather, as one of the originators of directed panspermia (the theory of the seeding of life on Earth by an alien intelligence), Crick prefers to consider life's birth as a lucky accident in which the virtually miraculous did occur, if not on Earth, then somewhere in the universe. Science philosopher and historian Iris Fry maintains that Crick and Leslie Orgel advanced their idea in part to call attention to the insurmountable problems facing the origin of life on Earth.[4]

Philosophical reasons strengthen the resistance to considering life's origin through creation. In *The Triumph of Evolution and the Failure of Creationism,* well-known paleontologist Niles Eldredge captures this concern.[5]

> We humans can directly experience that material world only through our senses, and *there is no way we can directly experience the supernatural.* Thus, in the enterprise that is science, it isn't an ontological claim that a God . . . does not exist, but rather an epistemological recognition that even if such a God did exist, there would be no way to experience that God given the impressive, but still limited, means afforded by science. And that is true by definition [italics in original].[6]

Eldredge and many others believe that science does not and cannot address questions beyond the natural realm. They argue that science can neither prove nor disprove God's existence. Therefore, when probing the origin-of-life question, science by definition confines the answers to natural-process explanations, regardless of what the data indicate.

In general, the scientific community considers science and religion to be different enterprises.[7] They consider religious ideas, including creationism, to be based on unsubstantiated faith. Scientific ideas (that is, statements about the physical and biological world), on the other hand, are testable. Moreover, scientific statements have necessary consequences—logical outcomes that lead to predictions. If future scientific discovery comports with these predictions, the statements describing the natural realm gain credibility. If future scientific advance contradicts the predictions, then scientists tend to cast the statements aside and pursue other ideas.

While no idea in science escapes irreverent challenges, religious beliefs are often considered sacred, beyond challenge. Because of this reasoning, scientists will not allow supernatural explanations for life's origin or any other phenomenon at the high table of scientific debate, nor in the science classroom. They see creation as an untestable concept.

Eldredge adds to the explanation of why religion does not belong at the table:

> Creation science isn't science at all. Creation scientists have not managed to come up with even a single intellectually compelling, scientifically testable statement about the natural world. . . . Creation science has precious few ideas of its own—positive ideas that stand on their own, independent of, and opposed to, counter opinions of normal science.[8]

He extends this line of reasoning:

> There is as little substance in scientific creationists' treatment of the origin and diversification of life as there is in their treatment of cosmological time. They pose no novel testable hypotheses and make no predictions or observations worthy of the name. They devote the vast bulk of their ponderous efforts to attacking orthodox science in the mistaken and utterly fallacious belief that in discrediting science . . . they have thereby established the truth of their own position. . . . [T]hey impugn the integrity and intelligence of thousands of honest souls who have had the temerity to believe that it is both fitting and

proper to try to understand the universe, the Earth, and all its life in naturalistic terms using only the evidence of our senses to evaluate how truthful an idea might be.[9]

In this, Eldredge identifies yet another contributor to scientists' rejection of creationism. The sole content of the case for God's supernatural role in bringing about life has been an attack on the evolutionary model. Many Christians think that by pointing out the many problems confronting origin-of-life researchers, they have proven the case for biblical creationism. The scientific community finds this negative approach repugnant, and rightfully so.

Scientists do not eschew criticism of their ideas. Indeed, the scientific enterprise thrives on criticism and challenges to proposed ideas. But science involves more than just critiquing ideas. At its best, science includes proposing ideas, hypotheses, models, and theories and advancing them through observation, experiments, and theoretical work. Once an idea is on the table, scientists make predictions and suggest tests, giving shape to future research efforts. The goal is to understand and explain nature. Scientific ideas are public ideas presented to the scientific community at large. These ideas are accepted, modified, or rejected in light of existing data and new discoveries.

For their part, religious devotees, including Christians, have tended to shield their ideas from scientific testing. By doing so, they have kept supernatural explanations for life in the realm of theology. No wonder most scientists have little use for religious notions about life's origin. Without testable ideas, they cannot see how supernatural explanations might advance understanding.

Nevertheless, an either-or approach to the origin question represents a false dichotomy. What if supernatural activity can be detected? What if such explanations fall within science's domain and lead to scientific advance? While the legitimate concerns of scientists merit careful consideration, so does the possibility that faith (as the Bible defines it) rests on evidence and not on blind devotion.

Room for Another Approach

The Bible states that God reveals Himself through nature.[10] If this is true, then scientists should be able to identify God's fingerprints in nature—if indeed God brought about life's origin. Though scientists may not be able to experience this supernatural being as visibly and tactilely as they do their spouses and children, they can, in principle, recognize the effects of God's activity by examining the material realm directly with their senses.[11]

Philosopher Stephen C. Meyer points out that science frequently engages in this type of investigation.[12] Science routinely deals with phenomena that are not directly observable, such as forces, fields, and subatomic particles. Scientists infer the properties and monitor the effects of unobservables indirectly by examining observable macroscopic phenomena and effects directly with their senses.

Science also possesses the capacity to investigate intelligent causes. Archaeologists study artifacts produced by human intelligence. Anthropologists study the bipedal primate fossil record to discriminate between stones intelligently shaped into tools and those formed by the forces of nature. The search for extraterrestrial intelligence (SETI) is a search for signatures in the cosmos that reflect the existence of aliens living in another star system. Crick and Orgel's directed panspermia appeals to intelligent activity to explain life's first appearance on Earth—an idea they demonstrate to be testable.[13] By extension, life's appearance on Earth by a supernatural, extra-universal Intelligence should also be detectable and testable.

Prohibiting an appeal to the supernatural places a false restriction on science's capability. By limiting available scientific explanations to material explanations alone, naturalists hinder science's capacity to discover truth. The goal is no longer to discover the most plausible explanation but rather to identify a more or less naturalistic explanation. If a Creator exists and has intervened in the natural realm, His activity (in principle) should be detectable by inference from what a researcher can verify directly with his or her senses. Science, in that way, can probe the supernatural. Still, if Christians wish to define science as allowing for supernatural explanations, then they bear the burden of showing how this approach can form a reputable scientific program—one that leads to scientific advance through testing and predictions.

Models advocating supernatural intervention in nature must be testable and must generate predictions that have the capacity to guide the discovery process. The case for the supernatural origin of life does not have to find its sole support as a default position once the failure of natural-process explanations has been demonstrated.

If the mystery that surrounds the origin of life is ever to be solved, the focus of investigation must extend beyond the intractable problems facing the naturalistic paradigm. Legitimate scientific concerns must be taken seriously. A testable supernatural model may be advanced if evidence supporting the model can be demonstrated. The next chapter shows how such a model is being built and how its predictions are being tested.

CHAPTER 3

PUTTING CREATION
TO THE TEST

The RTB testable creation research model program represents a new approach to the creation/evolution controversy. This endeavor offers the means to eliminate some of the impasses associated with the life-origin debate and responds to significant concerns raised by scientists.[1] Investigators on both sides of the issue—naturalists and supernaturalists—can work toward resolving the controversy without rancor by allowing their models to compete side by side for explanatory and predictive supremacy. The model that successfully predicts future discoveries and accommodates unexpected results stands as the best and most credible explanation for the beginning and characteristics of the universe, life, life's major groups, and humanity. The best hypothesis is balanced between complexity and simplicity, is coherent, corresponds to the facts, and avoids presumptions—and thus has true explanatory power.

The proposed creation model derives its framework from the biblical description of God's creative activity. The process of building this model is ongoing. Refinements continue taking place as new information and insight becomes available. The model begins with the collation of data from all relevant Scripture passages, not just Genesis 1 and 2. Once collected, the statements touching on God's creative activity are integrated and interpreted according to established techniques for interpreting the Bible. All plausible interpretations are evaluated for internal consistency. The interpretation that best fits the biblical data is then recast in scientific terms, rendering the Bible's creation account testable.

Biblical statements about God's creative activity can be subjected to experimental validation, like any scientific hypotheses. Further, they can lead to predictions of future scientific discoveries because the statements imply necessary physical consequences and logical outcomes. This approach evaluates the harmony between the Bible's record and nature's record. It also makes the study of creation a scientific endeavor.

Creation is a testable idea that can fall within the domain of science. The RTB Model's predictions define the features scientists would expect to see in the record of nature if the model has validity. Although biblical text inspires the model's tenets and constraints, within its confines the model finds considerable freedom for adjustments and fine-tuning as scientists and theologians make new discoveries.

As a whole, the RTB creation model encompasses the entire multifaceted realm of nature, thus necessitating the ongoing approach. Though spoken of as the "RTB Model" throughout this book, the details presented here apply to only one specific portion of it—the origin-of-life portion. Future works will examine other aspects of the larger RTB creation model.

Biblical Sources

Defining the limits of a scientific creation model according to the biblical text can be compared to the way many Americans determine what type of income tax deductions they should take. Some take standard deductions provided by the Internal Revenue Service because it makes filing taxes quicker and easier. This approach typically yields a minimal reduction of taxes. Others take time to understand the tax code. They methodically itemize deductions and receive the ultimate reward in their tax refund.

In much the same way as the first type of person approaches filing a tax form and gets minimal benefit from it, a superficial reading of a scriptural passage yields only some information and understanding central to the passage. This type of Bible study, though easy and straightforward, often leaves valuable details unrecognized—details that can enrich the reader's understanding of the passage. In some cases, important theological concepts might be overlooked or missed entirely.

Developing a more comprehensive understanding of a biblical passage requires disciplined application of hermeneutical principles—rules that govern Bible study. The scholar and layperson alike receive a tremendous return when they focus detailed attention on:

- the original language, carefully weighing the meaning of words and phrases
- the immediate as well as the wider context of the passage
- imagery and symbolism
- the literary genre of the text in question
- information and insight from other biblical passages and from nonbiblical sources
- historical circumstances

Theologians call this the historical-grammatical method.[2] Because of the multifaceted and complex nature of Scripture, a sound model of creation can be achieved only through a thorough study of both the major creation accounts and the isolated passages that make reference to God's creative work (see Appendix A).

When it comes to life's origin, even a cursory reading of Genesis 1 or of other relevant verses leaves no room for doubt that life emanates and finds its ongoing sustenance through God's direct intervention. Beyond this point, many questions remain. At what point does the Bible describe God's work to create Earth's first life? Does the Bible even mention the origin of life, as the scientific community understands it (that is, the emergence of simple single-cell organisms from a nonliving chemical mixture)?

A testable creation model for the origin of life requires answers to these questions. A superficial glance at Genesis 1 seems to place life's first appearance on day three. Genesis 1:11 describes God as commanding the land to produce vegetation. Prior to day three, God's creative activity apparently focused on transforming Earth from its primordial state into a planet ready to receive the animal and human life to be introduced on days five and six.

This understanding of Genesis 1 is widespread. In fact, Paul Davies used this interpretation to title his book *The Fifth Miracle*.[3] Davies enumerates the appearance of vegetation on the land as the fifth miracle in Genesis 1, with the creation of the universe, light, atmosphere, and dry land as the first four miracles.

This interpretation is not unreasonable. The first explicit mention of life's creation in Genesis 1 comes in the day-three passage. However, careful study of the text with close attention to the original language (Hebrew) suggests that God created the "seeds" of life before land plants appeared. Comparing various Bible passages to establish the correct context supports this concept. And shared imagery in those passages further develops the picture of God's creative activity or preparation *prior to* the six creation days.

Earth's Initial Conditions

Genesis 1:2 states, "Now the earth was formless and empty, darkness was over the surface of the deep, and the Spirit of God was hovering over the waters." This passage describes primordial Earth as it awaits its destiny—transformation into a suitable cradle for human life. Genesis 1:2 builds upon the opening declaration that "God created the heavens and the earth." As the text transitions from verse 1 to verse 2, the focus shifts from the cosmos to the early earth.[4] The reference frame also shifts. Genesis 1:2 says that the Spirit of God hovered above primordial Earth's surface. This clue means that the subsequent description of early Earth (and the stages of its trans-formation) comes from the vantage point of an observer just above the sur-face of the waters, looking up at the sky and across the horizon, describing the details as they would have appeared from that perspective.[5]

The first testable assertions with respect to life appear in this verse, as the author describes early Earth's initial conditions. The *New International Version* translation says that primordial Earth was "formless and empty." In English, and to some extent in the original Hebrew, these words indi-cate that the early earth awaited God's transforming work, the time when it would be fit for life and filled with life.

The Hebrew phrase *tōhû wabōhû*, translated as "formless and empty," appears only a few times in the Old Testament. *Tōhû* occurs more fre-quently on its own. Depending on the context, *tōhû* can mean "nothing" or "vanity;" however, it is frequently used as a parallel for "desert" and "wilderness" (see Deuteronomy 32:10). Bible scholar Victor P. Hamilton points out in his commentary on Genesis that this word lacks a true English counterpart and is perhaps best translated as "empty wasteland."[6]

According to Bible scholar Henry H. Halley, Genesis 1:2 describes pri-mordial Earth's surface as "*a seething desolate mass,* covered with boiling waters."[7] *Bōhû* occurs only two other times in Scripture, each time with *tōhû.* Jeremiah 4:23 says,

> I looked at the earth,
> and it was formless and empty;
> and at the heavens,
> and their light was gone.

Isaiah 34:11 says,

> God will stretch out over Edom
> the measuring line of chaos
> and the plumb line of desolation.

Both passages echo the imagery of Genesis 1:2.

Science confirms the desolate condition of early Earth. In fact, scien-tists refer to this period of Earth's history (from 4.5 to about 3.9 billion years ago) as the Hadean Era, after Hades (Greek for hell). The desolation persisted to some degree beyond the 3.9-billion-year mark, even into the era after Earth had cooled sufficiently for oceans to form. The impact events (asteroid and comet crashes) that contributed to the hellacious con-ditions continued with some frequency until about 3.5 billion years ago.

Even though the impactors diminished in size and the collisions decreased in frequency, on occasion they still released enough energy to convert Earth's oceans to steam and decimate any surface or subsurface life.

New scientific advances on the details of the Hadean Era and its importance to the origin-of-life question are discussed in chapter 6. Remarkably, in Genesis 1:2, the phrase *tōhû wabōhû* accurately depicts the harsh conditions of early Earth discovered by twentieth-century scientists. These conditions represent a starting point in God's transformation of Earth.

> This is what the LORD says—
> he who created the heavens,
> he is God;
> he who fashioned and made the earth,
> he founded it;
> he did not create it to be empty [*tōhû*],
> but formed it to be inhabited.
> —Isaiah 45:18

Genesis 1:2 indicates that an observer, *if* located on Earth's surface, would also experience darkness as one of Earth's initial conditions. Scientists agree.[8] Both theoretical and observational research done by astronomers indicates that any planetary system forming in the Milky Way galaxy would have possessed large quantities of gas, dust, and debris in its interplanetary space as its planets coalesced. These same studies also show that when the planets were forming, opaque (or nearly opaque) atmospheres shrouded them. The early solar-system debris, together with Earth's dense atmosphere, would have blocked the Sun's light from reaching early Earth's surface. Science confirms that an observer on early Earth would be confronted with darkness in every direction.

An observer would also note that Earth's entire surface was submerged below oceans. The biblical text implies that initially no permanent landmasses were present. Psalm 104:5-6 also describes primordial Earth's surface as covered entirely with water.

> He set the earth on its foundations;
>   it can never be moved.
> You [God] covered it with the deep as with a garment;
>   the waters stood above the mountains.

This creation psalm poetically echoes Genesis 1. The passages within it correspond to the creation-day events delineated in Genesis 1.[9] Though Psalm 104 is not structured as a strict chronology, the psalmist's descriptions of God's creation miracles convey a sense of progression and purposefulness as God transforms Earth for the sake of different life forms.[10] The text implies that God established the planet's core, mantle, and crust before cloaking Earth in oceans.

Scientific orthodoxy holds that early Earth's oceans became permanent around 3.9 billion years ago, and for the first third of Earth's history thereafter, oceans dominated its surface.[11] During this time, if any land existed, it would have been sparsely distributed, limited to volcanic islands that protruded from beneath Earth's oceans.

Then about 3 billion years ago, driven by tectonic activity and volcanism, significant continent building began. Over the course of the next 500 million years, exposed landmass dramatically increased from less than 3 percent of Earth's surface area to about 29 percent. At this time continental land growth slowed, due to decreases in erosion and tectonic and volcanic activity. Currently, the land on Earth's surface remains steady at this level as land formation and erosion forces roughly balance.

The biblical suggestion of God's involvement in covering Earth with oceans and later forming continents also receives some scientific confirmation. More than a few astronomers express surprise that the Earth has oceans at all.[12] They point out that little water should have associated with early Earth initially, given its proximity to the Sun (93 million miles). As the solar system formed, most of Earth's light volatiles, including water, should have escaped to outer space. Other astronomers take the opposite point of view. Given that water constitutes up to 20 percent of carbonaceous chondrite meteorites, if Earth formed from these or similar materials, it would have been a water world with surface waters hundreds of miles or kilometers deep—no dry land, no marine or land mammals.

The Hovering Spirit
Against the backdrop of Earth's initial conditions, Genesis 1:2 narrates that "the Spirit of God was hovering over the waters" of Earth's surface.[13] God did not just create the earth and leave; He was present and involved with the course of the planet's development.

Because Deuteronomy 32:9-11 shares much of its imagery with Genesis 1:2, it sheds light on the interpreter's understanding of God's activity on the early earth.[14] Found within the Song of Moses, the Deuteronomy passage depicts the Creator as "hovering over" His people (the nation of Israel) as He brought them through the desolate wilderness:

The LORD's portion is his people,
    Jacob his allotted inheritance.
In a desert land he found him,
    in a barren and howling waste.
He shielded him and cared for him;
    he guarded him as the apple of his eye,
like an eagle that stirs up its nest
    and hovers over its young,
that spreads its wings to catch them
    and carries them on its pinions.

In Deuteronomy 32:11, the Hebrew verb translated "hovers," *rāḥap,* is the same verb used in Genesis 1:2 to express what the Spirit of God was doing. In fact, Genesis 1:2 and Deuteronomy 32:9-11 are the only two passages of Scripture that use this verb. Some translations render *rāḥap* as "brooding." As a mother eagle broods over her young, so too the Spirit of God nurtured and protected the burgeoning nation Israel. Deuteronomy 32:10 uses the word *tōhû* for the desolate land that the Israelites wandered through. In this barren wasteland God brought forth the new nation of Israel, and in this empty desert land God sustained His people.

Transposition of this imagery (and theological significance) to Genesis 1:2 implies that the Spirit of God brooded over the primordial Earth to nurture and protect something precious and fragile. In this context God appears to be hovering over the seeds of life and supernaturally acting to protect that life as it awaits transformation of its home from the initial state of *tōhû wābōhû.*

Bible scholar John Rea suggests another correlation with this imagery from the New Testament.

> It is highly significant that the concept of God's *hovering* presence occurs in the angel's birth announcement to Mary: "The Holy Spirit will come upon you, and the power of the Most High will overshadow [*episkiasei*] you" (Luke 1:35). The conception of Jesus is the first act of the new creation.[6] . . . By this common figure of the hovering and overshadowing presence of God's Spirit, *the original creation,* the creation of God's covenant, the nation of Israel, and the new creation in Christ are linked together.[15]

The RTB Biblical Creation Model

The shared imagery and theological connection of the Luke, Deuteronomy, and Genesis passages suggest that God worked on early Earth to bring forth life's "seeds," much as God used Jacob's "seed" to bring forth the nation of Israel. Recasting this understanding of Scripture in scientific terms leads to the portion of the RTB testable creation model for life's beginning. In the broadest terms, the model ascribes life's origin to God's direct creative activity soon after the time of Earth's formation, more specifically to the time of the oceans' formation, prior to complete transformation of Earth's atmosphere from opaque to translucent. This explanation for life's start establishes a scientific framework that carries logical consequences and outcomes. The first predictions (delineated and explained in the following text) provide the means to evaluate the model's validity. The chief predictions that logically arise from Genesis 1:2 also help define the RTB Model and represent some of its most important features. This is true for any scientific model.

The testable creation model's framework constrains it. Yet this framework contains sufficient flexibility for further development and refinement through additional research in both theological and scientific arenas. Enough space exists underneath the umbrella of this approach to advance variants of the model. This significant point means that the model stands poised to stimulate further research that can lead to scientific advance and new understanding of existing conundrums. Plenty of opportunity remains for controversy and debate—the chief ingredients of scientific progress. For example, the biblical text and the RTB Model allow the freedom for scientific investigation to establish the exact time frame for Earth's formation and life's first appearance.

If scientific research indicates that life appeared long after Earth's formation, or if the earth formed within the past few thousand years, the proposed RTB Model is incorrect. Scientific measurements of Earth's antiquity and life's early appearance belong to the model's structure. This approach allows the opportunity to debate Earth's age and the precise timing of life's appearance while leaving the room to refine the model's details in response to new discoveries. In every respect, this approach to the origin-of-life question conforms to sound scientific methodology.

It is important to recognize that scientific predictions do not necessarily constitute prophesy, rather they logically flow from the model's tenets. Once proposed, a model does not have to await future discovery for its evaluation. Often the data required to initially assess a prediction's validity already exists.

THE RTB MODEL'S PREDICTIONS

The RTB biblical creation model for the origin of life sets forth the following central ideas and predictions:

1. Life appeared early in Earth's history, while the planet was still in its primordial state. The backdrop for the origin of life in Genesis 1:2 was an early Earth enveloped entirely in water and as yet untransformed by tectonic and volcanic activity. This tenet anticipates the discovery of life's remains in the part of the geological column that corresponds to early Earth.

2. Life originated in and persisted through the hostile conditions of early Earth. Genesis 1:2 describes early Earth as *tōhû wābōhû,* an empty wasteland. This model maintains that God nurtured the seeds of Earth's first life, perhaps re-creating these seeds each time they were destroyed. This model predicts that science will discover life's first emergence under the hellish conditions of early Earth.

3. Life originated abruptly. If God created the first life on Earth through direct intervention, one can reasonably assume that life appeared suddenly, seemingly out of nowhere. This model predicts that the planetary and geological record will demonstrate life's emergence in a narrow, if not instantaneous, time window.

4. Earth's first life displays complexity. If a Creator brought life into existence, first life should display significant complexity. Therefore, the RTB Model predicts that fossil and geochemical remains will indicate that Earth's earliest life forms display complexity.

5. Life is complex in its minimal form. Life in its simplest form should also display considerable complexity. An inherent minimal complexity reasonably indicates that life has been intelligently crafted.

6. Life's chemistry displays hallmark characteristics of design. Systems and structures produced by intelligent agents typically possess characteristics that distinguish them from those produced by natural processes. These properties serve as indicators of design. They will be apparent in biochemical systems of the cell if the biblical Creator is responsible for life.

It stands beyond this book's scope to describe in suitable detail the cell's chemical features that reflect design. A comprehensive case for biochemical design will appear in a future work. For now, the epilogue summarizes some of these characteristics and points to the relevant scientific literature. The point can be made that current biochemical knowledge satisfies this prediction.

7. First life was qualitatively different from life that came into existence on creation days three, five, and six. The third creation day describes the creation of plants (*zera'*, *'ēs*, and *p*ᵉ*rî* in the Hebrew). The fifth creation day discusses the creation of marine invertebrates and fish, marine mammals, and birds. The sixth creation day includes the creation of specialized land mammals.[16] These multicellular advanced plants and animals are qualitatively different from the first life forms created on primordial Earth.

8. A purpose can be postulated for life's early appearance on Earth. The RTB Model bears the burden of explaining why God would create life so early in Earth's history and why (as well as when) He would create the specific types of life that appeared on primordial Earth. While God would be free to create life for nonutilitarian purposes, discernible reasons should exist for God's bringing life into existence under the violent conditions of early Earth—conditions under which life could not persist and would presumably need to be re-created.

The eight predictions mentioned follow logically from RTB's creation model for life's origin. Some predictions are specific to the Genesis 1:2 implication of life's origin; others would be part of any model that appeals to a Creator to explain life's existence. The list of predictions is incomplete and the appropriateness of some of the predictions may be debated. The same can be said for any scientific model. Future discussions will become an important part of the model's development and refinement. Nevertheless, the cited predictions strongly emphasize this book's main premise—*the creation of life can be tested.* The scientific consideration of creation plays a pivotal role in the establishment of a new paradigm for life's origin.[17]

Subsequent chapters discuss the latest scientific advances and discoveries in origin-of-life research. These discoveries provide a basis for evaluating the creation model. They also refine the model and fill in some missing details. For example, scientific studies on the early solar system and early planetary conditions not only test the biblical description of Earth's conditions at the time that life first appeared on Earth, but also provide details regarding the early Earth not included in Genesis 1:2. The fossil and geochemical records provide key details on the early history of life—details that distinguish Earth's first life, its metabolic properties, and the timing of its appearance.

Research that addresses these questions also directly tests predictions made by the RTB Model. Molecular biologists now have the capability to sequence and manipulate genomes—the entire genetic content—of microorganisms. This technology puts researchers in hot pursuit of life's fundamental requirements and its minimal complexity. As scientists define life's minimal features, this creation scenario for life's origin is directly tested. Moreover, biochemists and biophysicists are studying the cell's inner workings at the atomic level. For the first time, details are being revealed that put these scientists in a position to identify hallmark features of design in the cell's inner workings, if they exist.

Competing Models

A model that finds agreement with scientific research may not necessarily represent the best explanation. Any proposed model must compete against alternative explanations and demonstrate superiority. The biblical creation model for the origin of life must do a better job of explaining the scientific data for life's beginning than do naturalistic scenarios, if it is to be adopted as a viable explanation for life's origin.

The scientific community, which rejects any explanation that invokes the supernatural, maintains that an evolutionary approach to life's beginning is justified by those instances in which the naturalistic scenario matches the scientific record. The validity of the evolutionary models is seldom called into question, even when new discoveries run counter to the paradigm. Rather, such findings are regarded as indicators that the problem is more complicated than originally conceived. The naturalistic paradigm, although problematic, can never be rejected in a landscape restricted to just one class of models.

Scientists frequently pit one model against others in the quest to explain phenomena in nature. Part of the scientific enterprise involves selecting the best model from among competing models. The scientific community does this in two ways. The first approach involves comparing competing models for best overall fit with the data and the greatest capacity to explain all the results. The second approach attempts to identify experimental results or observations that can be true for only one model. These discriminating tests effectively identify erroneous ideas and push them aside. These two approaches work in a complementary manner and are not mutually exclusive. Scientific advance takes place most efficiently when these two methods are used hand in hand.

Both approaches apply to the model this book presents. The RTB Model for life's beginning stands side by side with naturalistic scenarios in an attempt to determine which model best accounts for life's origin. Head-to-head comparison becomes possible because both models make predictions. The biblical creation model and the evolutionary scenarios for life's start are compared with the scientific record to determine which model best accommodates the available data. At the same time, observations and experimental results are identified that discriminate between the two models—tests that, in effect, have the power to eliminate a model from contention.

Before such an evaluation can take place, however, the textbook description for the evolutionary origin of life must be summarized along with some of its most important and prevalent variations. Chapter 4 outlines the naturalistic set of models and sets forth its predictions.

CHAPTER 4

THE NATURALISTIC APPROACH

An octopus is a fascinating creature. Its "arms" extend in many different directions and appear to function with a measure of independence even though its head demonstrates some central control. In many ways, the evolutionary explanation for life's origin resembles that complex animal. Instead of one simple scenario, many possibilities unfurl in several different directions.

These ideas for life's beginning, prolific in number and complexity, at times appear to have no relationship at all to one another. Yet, like octopus arms, regulated by the head, all naturalistic models share some "controlling" central features, including natural pathways for:

- synthesis (combining) of prebiotic (pre-life) molecules
- concentration of prebiotic molecules
- formation of life's building blocks
- assembly of building block molecules to form complex biomolecules
- development of self-replication
- emergence of metabolism (the physical and chemical processes continuously going on in living organisms and cells)
- aggregation of biomolecules to form protocells (a primitive cell)
- evolution of protocells into true cells

Because of its widespread familiarity and clear illustration of naturalism's central features, the following summary of the "textbook" explanation for life's origin serves as a starting point. With a strong influence by the Oparin-Haldane hypothesis of the early twentieth century,[1] this description represents the octopus head from which all the different origin-of-life models currently in vogue emanate and extend. This overview assists in developing a list of predictions that flow logically from such models.

The Textbook Case

The concept of life's evolution as taught in public schools begins shortly after Earth's formation, when conditions differed markedly from conditions today.[2] These environmental features have prompted evolutionary biologists over the years to postulate that gases such as water vapor, ammonia, methane, carbon monoxide, carbon dioxide, and nitrogen made up primordial Earth's atmosphere. Equally important to this backdrop is an assumed lack of atmospheric oxygen. Such an atmosphere, called a reducing atmosphere, could sustain the formation of *small* prebiotic molecules, such as hydrogen cyanide, formaldehyde, and so forth, under high-energy conditions. Through the years, origin-of-life researchers have suggested various high-energy sources as catalysts for the formation of these prebiotic molecules. The list of potential energy sources includes lightning, ultraviolet radiation, solar and volcanic heat, cosmic rays, and ionizing radiation from radioactive decay.

According to the textbooks, these prebiotic molecules, once formed, accumulated in Earth's oceans over vast periods of time to make up the legendary primordial or prebiotic soup.[3] Within this chemical soup—again, over long periods of time—the prebiotic molecules reacted to form more complex molecules, such as amino acids, sugars, fatty acids, purines, and pyrimidines. These molecules, in turn, functioned as building blocks for more complex molecules that eventually led to the biomolecules (DNA, RNA, and proteins) found in cells today.

Early Earth's Atmosphere → Simple Prebiotic Molecules (aq) → Prebiotic Soup
Energy   *Energy*

Prebiotic Molecules → Biomolecules → Protocells
Condensation Reactions   *Aggregation*

Protocells → Simple Cells → LUCA*
Time   *Time*

*Last Universal Common Ancestor

Table 4.1: "Textbook" Description of Life's Origin

This scenario continues with the eventual production of a self-replicating molecule. The increasing concentration of complex molecules in the prebiotic soup supposedly prompted their aggregation to form protocells. These entities possessed partial cellular properties and served as the predecessors for the first true cells. The first cells that emerged as random chemical and physical events caused the self-replicators to transfer their self-replicating capability to the protocells. Evolutionary processes (for example, natural selection) are said to have transformed the protocells, gradually increasing their capacity to self-replicate and to carry out various metabolic processes. As this occurred, the protocells gained complexity.

Finally, these protocells yielded an organism, referred to as the last universal common ancestor (LUCA). Presumably LUCA resembled modern-day prokaryotes, like bacteria and archaea (archaeabacteria). These single-celled organisms, about one micron in diameter, lack a nucleus and other internal cell structures. Supposedly LUCA, the root of the evolutionary tree of life, then evolved to yield life's three major domains: eubacteria (true bacteria), archaea (single-celled organisms superficially resembling bacteria but biochemically different), and eukarya (plants, animals, and fungi).

The Updated Explanation

Today, the origin-of-life research community has moved beyond the Oparin-Haldane hypothesis and the standard textbook description for life's start.[4] New discoveries and acknowledged problems with the Oparin-Haldane explanation prompted this movement (though unfortunately many schools and texts have yet to catch up with the research). Table 4.2 summarizes the various naturalistic origin-of-life scenarios currently under consideration and highlights some of the complex relationships that exist among the different models.[5]

Origin-of-life locations. While the textbook description for life's origin focuses exclusively on a terrestrial location for life's emergence, a significant number of investigators have begun to look elsewhere in this solar system—and beyond—for life's beginning, or at least for the origin of prebiotic molecules. These scientists postulate the independent origin of life (or life's molecules) at extraterrestrial locations, and mechanisms to transport life or biotic compounds to Earth. For the proponents of this concept (known as panspermia), life (or life's building blocks) arrived on Earth from an extraterrestrial location.

Investigators propose two forms of panspermia: nondirected and directed. Nondirected panspermia appeals to natural mechanisms to transport life (or life's molecules) to Earth once it has originated elsewhere in the universe.[6] It falls into two categories: (1) interplanetary, which looks to bodies within Earth's solar system, such as meteorites, comets,

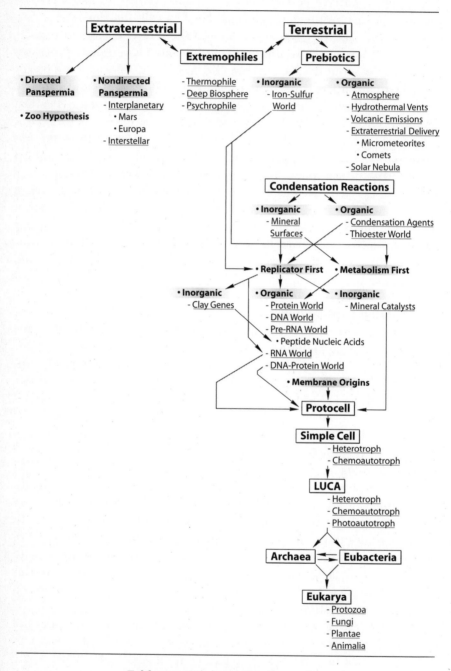

Table 4.2: Origin-of-Life Scenarios

Mars, or Europa (one of Jupiter's moons), as a source of Earth's first life; and (2) interstellar, which hypothesizes the transport of life or life molecules to Earth (and elsewhere, perhaps) from other star systems.

Directed panspermia is a radical form adopted by a minority of origin-of-life scientists. These scientists maintain that an intelligent alien race transported life to Earth.[7] Proponents of directed panspermia typically express their belief that intelligent life is abundant in the universe. Based on this abundance, they infer that an alien race could have acquired the necessary technology to seed Earth with life.

Both the newly launched Astrobiology Institute at NASA (National Aeronautics and Space Administration) and the Origins Program are rapidly propelling panspermia to the forefront in origin-of-life research.[8] The two groups' shared goal is to explain life's origin, not only on Earth, but also throughout the universe. With funding from NASA, they search for life within Earth's solar system and beyond.[9] With this financial support comes the emphasis on life's existence beyond Earth and, consequently, research that bears directly on panspermia mechanisms and models.

Much of the research emphasis for extraterrestrial origin-of-life models centers on identification and characterization of life transport mechanisms between planetary bodies and stellar systems. Still, extraterrestrial explanations must, at some point, account for life's emergence. In this area, extraterrestrial explanations rely on and overlap with models that seek to explain life's origin on Earth. Panspermia is addressed in chapters 14 through 16. The remainder of this chapter focuses on terrestrial models.

Prebiotic formation. All naturalistic origin-of-life scenarios, whether extraterrestrial or terrestrial, require a source of prebiotic compounds. The Oparin-Haldane hypothesis considered chemical reactions in Earth's atmosphere as the chief way to generate prebiotic molecules. Some researchers still pursue atmospheric reactions as the source of prebiotics.[10] Others, prompted by recent discoveries about early Earth's atmosphere, explore different mechanisms for prebiotic molecule production.

A small group of origin-of-life researchers speculates that early Earth's volcanoes served as a source of prebiotic molecules.[11] These investigators exchange the gases of the atmosphere for gases emitted by volcanoes as the starting materials for prebiotic molecule synthesis. They hypothesize that reducing gases made up the volcanic emissions on early Earth, and argue that volcanic lightning ignited the spark that catalyzed reactions within the volcanic gases to produce prebiotic compounds.

One of the more popular alternative locations for prebiotic synthesis in recent origin-of-life thought is deep-sea hydrothermal vents.[12]

Presumably the gases released at these vents reacted with the assistance of metal ions and sulfide to produce prebiotic compounds. The discovery of microbes that inhabit these environments, considered to be some of the oldest organisms on Earth, further fuels this line of thinking.[13]

Closely related to the idea of hydrothermal production of prebiotic materials is the iron-sulfur world model proposed and advocated almost exclusively by German patent lawyer and chemist Günter Wächtershäuster.[14] Wächtershäuster asserts that pyrite played a central role in producing the first prebiotic compounds and the earliest metabolic pathways. Pyrites accumulate at the edge of deep-sea hydrothermal vents as iron(2) sulfide reacts with hydrogen sulfide. According to this depiction, energy released from pyrite formation and the pyrite surfaces drives prebiotic molecules to form from carbon monoxide and hydrogen gas emitted by the sea-floor vents.

Along a different line, some investigators propose an extraterrestrial source for prebiotic compounds.[15] (This differs from panspermia in that only the components necessary for life are said to come from an external source.) Extraterrestrial delivery of prebiotic materials rivals the deep-sea hydrothermal vent models in popularity among those researching the origin of life. Comets, micrometeorites, and interstellar dust particles are the proposed delivery vehicles bringing prebiotic compounds to Earth.[16] Those who advocate an extraterrestrial delivery of prebiotic compounds point to the detection and recovery of a wide class of organic compounds from meteorites as evidence supporting their hypothesis.

Condensation reactions. Once prebiotic compounds (such as amino acids, sugars, and nucleotide bases) assemble and accumulate to form either global or localized "primordial soups," the stage is set for the next phase of life development. In this phase, prebiotic compounds react with one another to form more complex molecules that eventually result in important biomolecules, including proteins and nucleic acids (RNA and DNA). These biomolecules consist of chainlike structures that form when smaller subunit molecules link together. Chemists refer to reactions thought to have produced complex biomolecules on early Earth as "condensation reactions."

When condensation reactions take place, the reactants collectively lose two hydrogen atoms and an oxygen atom in the form of a water molecule. For example, if two glycine molecules (amino acids) condense, the product is diglycine and a water molecule. Because water is a by-product, condensation reactions are thermodynamically prohibited in an aqueous environment, such as a prebiotic soup. As a way to get rid of the problematic liquid, most origin-of-life explanations appeal to localized evaporation of the soup or to the depositing of prebiotic compounds (through tidal actions), such as on the shores of volcanic islands. Under dehydrating conditions, the condensation reactions become energetically feasible. But even though thermodynamically allowed under arid conditions, condensation reactions still require assistance. Some theorists speculate that the reactions that generated prebiotic molecules also yielded another class of compounds called "condensing agents."[17]

These condensing agents participate in chemical reactions by removing a water molecule from the reactants and adding the water molecule to their structural makeup. Because of this property, condensing agents drive condensation reactions. Investigators maintain that if condensing agents were present in the prebiotic soup and were codeposited with other prebiotic compounds in locations where the soup evaporated, these compounds could, in principle, facilitate the formation of more complex biomolecules.

Support for these kinds of scenarios comes from lab experiments that demonstrate the ready production of condensing agents (for example, cyanamide, cyanogen, cyanoformamide, cyanate, diaminomaleonitrile, trimetaphosphate, and pyrophosphates) under conditions that conceivably simulate early Earth's environment. Other experiments show that these condensing agents promote the initial steps of protein and nucleic acid (DNA and RNA) formation from amino acids, sugars, and nucleotide bases, respectively.

The appeal to condensing agents found its way into more traditional explanations. In contrast, more current explanations appeal to mineral surfaces as the catalyst for condensation reactions.[18] Mineral surfaces have chemical characteristics that allow them to bind organic molecules, which would include prebiotic compounds. These surfaces also have properties that make them ideally suited to assist chemical reactions.

Origin-of-life researchers proposed that mineral-assisted formation of complex biomolecules from prebiotic precursors could, theoretically, occur either at locations where the prebiotic soup evaporates or within the aqueous environment of the prebiotic soup. Because prebiotic compounds can adsorb (collect in condensed form on a surface), minerals found in the prebiotic soup could bind and sequester prebiotic compounds and promote repetitive condensation reactions before the complex biomolecules became unbound from the mineral surface. In support of this idea, researchers have used clays (kaolinite, montmorillonite) to drive the condensation of amino acids to form, in turn, protein precursors (peptides) and short RNA chains from activated nucleotides.[19]

Nobel laureate Christian de Duve offers a different mechanism, the thioester world model, to account for the formation of complex biomole-cules.[20] Thioesters are sulfur-containing compounds having high-energy sulfur-carbon chemical bonds. Cells use high-energy thioesters to store and provide the chemical energy needed to form fatty acids.

Presumably, thioesters could form in sulfur-rich environments such as hydrothermal vents. Thioester derivatives of prebiotic compounds (for instance, amino acids) readily react with other amino acids to form con-densation products because of the chemical instability of the high-energy thioester bond. This reaction could possibly occur under both dry and watery conditions.

Emergence of Self-Replication and Metabolism

Regardless of where prebiotic compounds arose or how they condensed to form more complex biomolecules, all naturalistic origin-of-life scenarios next seek to identify self-organization pathways capable of generating two of life's key biochemical features: self-replication and metabolism. From a molecular standpoint, self-replication describes the capacity of a complex molecule to guide its own reproduction, typically by serving as a template that directs the assembly of chemical constituents into molecules that are identical to it.

Metabolism defines the entire set of chemical pathways in the cell. The foremost of these involve the chemical transformation of relatively small molecules, pathways that (1) generate chemical energy through the con-trolled breakdown of fuel molecules like sugars and fats; and (2) produce (in a stepwise fashion) the building blocks needed to assemble proteins, DNA, RNA, and cell membrane and cell wall components. Life's metabolic pathways often share many molecules. This sharing causes the cell's meta-bolic routes to interconnect and form complex webs.

An intramural debate exists within the origin-of-life community at this point. One group argues that self-organization started with metabo-lism (the metabolism-first model), whereas the other insists that life stemmed from self-replicators (the replicator-first model).

Metabolism first. Metabolism-first proponents maintain that mineral surfaces catalyzed the formation of a diverse collection of small molecules that, with time, evolved to form an interconnected series of chemical reac-tions. Once in place, these interrelated chemical reactions formed the basis for the cell's metabolic systems.[21] These chemical networks eventually became encapsulated to form protocells complete with a form of protome-tabolism. Some metabolism-first scenarios, like the iron-sulfur world, even suggest that minerals (for example, pyrite) became encapsulated along with the protometabolic networks and thereby served as life's first catalysts.

According to the metabolism-first idea, once protometabolic systems were established, they spawned self-replicating molecules.

Replicator first. The replicator-first enthusiasts propose the emergence of a naked replicator that later became encapsulated along with the precursor molecules needed to sustain its activity. Metabolism subsequently emerged as a means to support the production and turnover of the replicator's building blocks and ultimately its self-replicating activity.

The main focus of the replicator-first research program is to determine the original replicator's identity. Early on, the replicator-first community debated whether DNA or proteins served as the first replicators. The controversy sparked what origin-of-life researchers call the chicken-and-egg problem.[22] This conundrum refers to the complete interdependence that proteins and DNA have on one another when it comes to their synthesis and biochemical roles in the cell. DNA stores within its molecular structure the total information that the cell needs to function. DNA replication produces duplicate copies of this information and transmits it to the next generation as part of the reproductive process.

Even though scientists refer to DNA as a self-replicating molecule, its synthesis, and hence its replication, requires a suite of proteins. In other words, proteins replicate DNA. On the other hand, proteins, which play a role in practically every cell function, depend upon DNA for their production because DNA contains the information that the cell's machinery uses to synthesize proteins. Without DNA, the cell cannot produce proteins. Because of this interdependence, origin-of-life explanations must account for the simultaneous appearance of DNA and proteins. As yet, no one has envisioned a scenario that involves either class of molecule apart from the other.

The RNA World and Its Alternatives

Other origin-of-life researchers find the resolution to this chicken-and-egg problem in RNA. This chainlike molecule shares many structural similarities with DNA. It assumes the role of an intermediary in protein formation by conveying the information stored in DNA to the cell's protein-making systems.

Many scientists think that RNA was the premier replicator, predating both DNA and proteins.[23] According to this model, called the RNA-world hypothesis, RNA took on the contemporary biochemical function of both DNA and proteins by operating as a self-replicator that catalyzed its own synthesis. According to the RNA-world hypothesis, numerous RNA molecules with a wide range of catalytic activity emerged through time. RNA-world biochemistry centered exclusively on RNA. Through more time, the

RNA world transitioned to an RNA-protein world and finally gave way to contemporary biochemistry with the addition of DNA to the cell's arsenal. As the RNA world transitioned to the DNA-protein world, RNA's original function became partitioned between proteins and DNA, with RNA assuming its current intermediary role. The RNA ancestral molecules presumably disappeared without leaving a trace of their primordial existence.

The RNA world has its roots in the late 1960s when Francis Crick, Leslie Orgel, and Carl Woese suggested there must have been a primitive cellular system based on RNA.[24] In the mid-1980s the discovery of RNA molecules with enzymatic activity (called ribozymes) propelled the RNA-world hypothesis to prominence.[25] Since then, several researchers have produced in the lab a number of ribozymes that engage in a range of potential biological activities.[26] For many researchers, this success further adds credibility to the RNA-world explanation.

The RNA-world hypothesis may well be the most prominent and promising idea in the origin-of-life arena. Much of the latest research focuses on identifying chemical routes to produce prebiotic compounds and identifying condensation reactions that have the potential to lead to RNA.

Nevertheless, difficulty in making RNA building blocks motivates some origin-of-life researchers to look beyond the RNA-world hypothesis for the first replicator. They are revisiting the possibility that either DNA or proteins filled that role. These revitalized DNA- and protein-world scenarios find support in new studies that demonstrate DNA's capacity to catalyze (to a limited degree) chemical reactions, and proteins' ability to self-replicate.[27]

Other investigators still hold to the RNA-world hypothesis, but incorporate an additional stage in the origin-of-life pathway that precedes the RNA world. Proponents of these pre-RNA-world interpretations search for self-replicating molecules structurally simpler and more stable than RNA. One leading candidate for the first replicator is a class of protein-DNA hybrids called peptide-nucleic acids (PNA).[28] PNA's backbone resembles a protein's, and PNA side groups are the same as those found in DNA and RNA. In principle, PNA may possess the characteristics necessary to self-replicate.

Emergence of Protocells
One of life's defining features is the presence of a membrane that surrounds the cell and segregates its contents from the external environment. In addition to defining life's boundaries and forming internal cell compartments, cell membranes play a central role in energy production and a supporting role in a variety of biochemical processes. For example, cell

membranes regulate the transport of materials into and out of the cell.

The formation of presumably primitive and, later, contemporary cell membranes represent key stages in the emergence of the first protocells. Over the years, researchers have given only limited consideration to cell membrane origins. One reason for this attention deficit is the implicit assumption that once cell membranes' components are present in a watery environment, they readily and spontaneously self-assemble and self-organize.[29] Scientists regard cell membrane origins as essentially an automatic step in various origin-of-life scenarios. They maintain that primitive cell membranes, once formed, could have readily encapsulated self-replicators and protometabolic pathways. How? Through dehydration-hydration cycles that occurred when prebiotic soup evaporated, or through tidal action along shorelines of volcanic islands.

The central problem researchers face, as they attempt to account for cell membranes and the consequent emergence of the first protocell, is determining the source of the self-assembling prebiotic compounds that formed these primitive membranes. Some researchers point to prebiotic compound production on early Earth, while others suggest that extraterrestrial delivery made the molecules available.[30]

The Last Universal Common Ancestor

Once protocells arose, origin-of-life researchers theorize that natural selection took over to transform these prelife forms into simple cellular entities. Cellular evolution occurred, they say, as random chemical and physical changes generated modified protocells with increased metabolic efficiency and improved reproductive efficacy.

Some scientists think that the first cells were heterotrophs. That is, these cells consumed preexisting organic compounds from the prebiotic soup to provide the energy and raw materials needed to sustain primitive cellular activities. The chief difficulty with a heterotroph-first model is overconsumption of the organic matter. Without a means to replenish the raw materials needed to sustain a heterotrophic lifestyle, these first cells would exterminate themselves.

Other origin-of-life investigators suggest that the first cells were autotrophs. Autotrophs generate energy and biomolecules from simple inorganic materials in the environment. Two types of autotrophs are known: photoautotrophs and chemoautotrophs. Photoautotrophs capture solar energy, whereas chemoautotrophs harvest chemical energy from materials in their environments. Because of photoautotrophs' added metabolic complexity, most researchers do not consider them the best candidate for the first cells. Rather, they assert that chemoautotrophic pathways arose along with the protocells' other biochemical systems. The chemoautotroph-first model alleviates the overconsumption problem but places a significant additional demand on the origin-of-life scenario, because it requires the emergence and evolution of complex chemoautotrophic pathways before chemoautotrophic life is possible.

Once simple cells took hold, researchers assert, these cells evolved to produce the last universal common ancestor (LUCA). Some scientists see LUCA as a single cellular entity, while others view LUCA as a community of cells that coevolved and coalesced to form the root of the evolutionary tree of life.[31]

Once established, the theory goes, LUCA diversified to yield life's major domains. According to the standard evolutionary model, LUCA cleanly diversified, yielding to eubacteria and archaea domains. These two domains consist of prokaryotes that are indistinguishable in form yet fundamentally different at the biochemical level. The textbook model is being revised as origin-of-life investigators discover what seem rampant transfers of large amounts of genetic material between bacteria and archaea after diverging from LUCA.[32] This exchange of genetic material causes the base of the evolutionary tree of life to take on a complex, web-like pattern.

Naturalistic Predictions

Given the number of possible scenarios under consideration by the scientific community and the complex relationships among these models, developing a consistent set of predictions from them hardly seems possible. The challenge is heightened by the fact that predictions are often closely tied to a model's details. Nevertheless, from the shared features of these evolutionary theories come nine general predictions:

1. Chemical pathways produced life's building blocks. For natural processes to explain life's beginning, investigations must identify plausible chemical routes that could generate life's building-block molecules (amino acids, purines, pyrimidines, sugars, fatty acids, and so on).

2. Chemical pathways yielded complex biomolecules. Once life's building-block molecules formed, plausible chemical routes and processes must have existed for them to condense into the molecular entities that ultimately led to the complex biomolecules central to the cell's structural and functional components. These biomolecules include DNA, RNA, proteins, and membrane and all cell wall components.

3. The chemical pathways that yielded life's building blocks and complex molecular constituents operated in early Earth's conditions. Not only must origin-of-life models identify plausible chemical routes that yielded life's molecules, but these routes also must have operated under early Earth's conditions and generated sufficient material to allow life to evolve.

4. Sufficiently placid chemical and physical conditions existed on early Earth for long periods of time. This prediction is a necessary corollary to the previous one. While the production of prebiotic compounds required high-energy conditions, these conditions could not persist for long without destroying the very molecules they formed. Fragile complex biomolecules like DNA, RNA, and proteins are particularly susceptible to breakdown by water and to breakage by mechanical, shear stresses.

5. Geochemical evidence for a prebiotic soup exists in Earth's oldest rocks. Regardless of the source of prebiotic compounds, if a prebiotic soup existed on early Earth as a necessary preamble to life's origin, then evidence for it should be discovered in the oldest layers of Earth's geological column. (Of course, this prediction need not be a part of models in which life originates beyond Earth.)

6. Life appeared gradually on Earth over a long period of time. The transition from the prebiotic starting materials thought to have been present on early Earth, through a prebiotic soup to the first cellular entities, would require many chemical steps. Some of these steps proceed slowly, while others seem highly unlikely. Given these facts, life's emergence should have required a long time to unfurl once Earth's conditions could feasibly support life.

7. The origin of life occurred only once on Earth. This prediction stands as a corollary to the previous one, especially considering the number of steps required to generate first life from nonliving chemical entities and the low probability of some of the steps. In other words, it was such a lengthy, unlikely process that it could at most have happened just once.

8. Earth's first life was simple. Given the arduous process required to generate the first life forms, it follows that life as it first appeared on Earth must have been simple, both in terms of its chemical makeup and its morphology, or form.

9. Life in its most minimal form is demonstrably simple. Life's minimal complexity describes the fewest number of different biomolecules that must have simultaneously co-occurred for life to originate. For a realistic probability of emergence through natural processes, life's most minimal form must have been relatively simple.

With these predictions in place, the focus of this book shifts from descriptions of the models for life's beginning to examination of the scientific data. The following chapters survey the latest and most important scientific advances in life-origins research.[33] Within this survey lie the means to test the predictions and thereby to comparatively evaluate the RTB and the naturalistic origin-of-life models.

Part II

THE
FACTS
OF LIFE

CHAPTER 5

AN EARLY OR LATE APPEARANCE?

Greenland, a Danish province, is the world's largest island.[1] Though fifty times larger than Denmark, it has only a fraction of the population. No wonder. A permanent ice cap covers most of Greenland's inland plateau. Such extreme cold discourages habitation. During the summertime, Greenland's southwestern coast, home to most of the island's population, warms only to 50 °F (10 °C). While the climate keeps most people away, recent geological discoveries have attracted scientists—particularly those interested in the origin of life.

Earth's oldest rocks—about 3.8 billion years old—were discovered near Greenland's capital, Nuuk, by geologists.[2] Scientists may never discover rocks much older. Prior to about 3.85 billion years ago, early Earth had not yet cooled sufficiently to form a solid crust and oceans as permanent features.[3]

These rocks are currently being investigated along with deposits greater than 3.3 billion years old in the Warrowana Hills of northwestern Australia and the Barberton Mountain Land of eastern South Africa for clues about life's early history. To uncover these "facts of life" scientists probe the fossil and geochemical records contained in the sediments of the ancient rocks. Such studies provide direct insight into the timing of life's appearance on Earth, and an indirect view into the characteristics of first life. These important details can be used to evaluate both RTB's model for life's supernatural beginning and the naturalistic scenarios asserting the spontaneous generation of life from nonlife.

A Startling Discovery

Over the past twenty years, scientists have amassed a large and diverse collection of fossil evidence for life's early appearance on Earth. Evidence compiled from the rock formations in Australia and South Africa dates between 3.3 and 3.5 billion years in age.[4] Researchers are amazed to find these ancient rocks. Many forces (erosion and plate tectonics in particular) work together over time to destroy them. The older a rock deposit, the less likely its survival.[5]

Three-billion-year-old rocks that contain fossils are even more difficult to find. Those surviving tectonic activity and erosion can still undergo metamorphosis caused by the heat and pressure of burial. Sediments experience a 35 to 55 °F (20 to 30 °C) increase in temperature for every 6.2 miles (10 kilometers) of depth as they move closer to Earth's hot mantle. The pressure from burial also generates hotter temperatures. This intense pressure and heat alters the fossilized remains to such an extent that they are destroyed.

The only two locations where ancient rock deposits experienced only limited geological metamorphosis are the Pilbara Supergroup, west of the Great Sandy Desert in western Australia, and the Swaziland Supergroup in eastern South Africa.[6] Remains recovered from these ancient deposits indicate that a variety of microorganisms existed as Earth's first life. Because all are simple, single-celled microbes that lack internal cell structures, such as a nucleus, scientists classify them as prokaryotes. This classification encompasses the bacteria and archaea domains of life. These realms superficially resemble each other but differ fundamentally at a biochemical level. Life's third domain (eukarya) includes the single-celled protozoans and the familiar complex multicellular fungi, plant, and animal kingdoms. Organisms that belong to eukarya didn't appear until much later in Earth's history.

The fossils discovered in Australia and South Africa are not like those familiar to most people. Instead of two-dimensional imprints or three-dimensional solids of skeletal remains, fossils of ancient life fall into two categories: macroscopic stromatolites (fossilized bacterial mats) and microscopic cellular remnants of microorganisms.

Layered Life

Shark Bay, located nearly seven hundred miles (1,100 kilometers) north of Perth along Australia's desolate west coast, has come to symbolize the wonder of the origin of life. The hypersaline conditions of Shark Bay's lagoon make it unfit for most life. Stromatolites pepper the bay's shoreline waters. At first glance, these unusually hard, rocky, dome-shaped structures appear to be lifeless geological features. However, closer inspection of the layers reveals that they teem with life. Produced primarily through the activity of cyanobacteria (blue-green algae), stromatolites contain a vibrant and complex community of microorganisms.[7]

When cyanobacteria grow under ideal conditions, they form dense macroscopic mats. Requiring sunlight to survive, they grow on surfaces, forming sheetlike colonies, and secrete mucilage. This substance forms a slippery gel-like matrix that allows the cyanobacteria to glide toward sunlight. Cyanobacteria often exist in chainlike filaments of cells. These filaments form when the cyanobacteria undergo cell division but not cell separation. The cyanobacteria filaments intertwine in the mucilage matrix to form a network that imparts structure to the mats.

Figure 5.1: Stromatolites in Shark Bay, Australia

These shoreline boulders are actually built up by cyanobacteria and teem with microorganisms. (Photo courtesy of Digital Vision)

Cyanobacteria grow best in shallow water environments where sunlight readily reaches the matlike colony of cells. Near a shoreline, tidal action deposits sediment on the mats. The seawater also leaves carbonate deposits on the sediment's surface. These deposits cause the mat to have rocklike characteristics. When the sediment and carbonate deposits become thick enough to block sunlight, the cyanobacteria migrate to the sediment's surface. There they establish a new mat community. Repeated over and over again, these processes yield large stromatolites—structures composed of numerous stacks of thin layers.

A complex community of microorganisms lives within these structures. Cyanobacteria reside primarily in the upper stromatolite layers, where they can access sunlight. They need the blue and green light wavelengths for photosynthesis. This activity helps them generate oxygen, which enables them to extract energy from organic compounds. Other microbes (aerobes) share the upper layers with cyanobacteria and use the oxygen to consume organic materials and debris also generated by the cyanobacteria. Green sulfur and purple bacteria—microbes that use red and near infrared wavelengths, respectively, for photosynthesis—make their living just below the upper layers. This region, referred to as the undermat, is oxygen-depleted. The low oxygen environment makes an ideal location for green sulfur and purple bacteria, which need sunlight to thrive but are poisoned by oxygen. Green sulfur and purple bacteria share the undermat with another collection of microbes called facultative anaerobes. These organisms can thrive in either the presence or absence of oxygen. Their capacity to use oxygen allows them to scavenge this molecule and protect the green sulfur and purple bacteria that cannot tolerate oxygen.

Rich assortments of microorganisms also thrive beneath the undermat. These microbes are oxygen-intolerant and consume organic remains left behind by cyanobacteria, green sulfur, and the purple bacteria. Methane-generating and sulfate-reducing single-cell archaeans also live alongside the oxygen-intolerant bacteria consumers.

Revealing a Rarity

Numerous shallow water environments could theoretically sustain the formation of stromatolites; however, these environments usually house invertebrates that graze upon the cyanobacterial mats as soon as they form. Stromatolites can't develop. But extremely salty conditions make Shark Bay unsuitable for these predators. In their absence, cyanobacteria form thriving communities. Detailed characterization of modern-day stromatolites give paleontologists a rare and valuable view into the life that existed in Earth's distant past.

Stromatolite fossils. For the last 550 million years, stromatolites have been largely absent. That is, they scarcely developed after complex, multicellular invertebrates—cyanobacteria consumers—first appeared in Earth's oceans. Prior to this time stromatolites flourished in Earth's shallow water environments. These structures, similar in appearance to the ones found in Shark Bay, dominate the fossil record in deposits ranging from about 600 million to 2.8 billion years of age.[8] They correspond to the time in Earth's history when continental landmasses, and hence shallow water environments, first appeared. Because of their stonelike characteristics, stromatolites left behind a clear record of their existence.

Although infrequently, geologists and paleontologists do find stromatolite fossils in rocks older than 2.8 billion years of age.[9] In all, scientists have recovered roughly two dozen stromatolite fossils older than 2.8 billion years.[10] Deposits from western Australia dated between 3.4 and 3.5 billion years old; others from eastern South Africa dated between 3.3 and 3.5 billion years old; and still others from Zimbabwe were found to be 3.5 billion years old.[11] These 3.5-billion-year-old deposits indicate that cyanobacteria and the complex, symbiotic microbial interactions found in stromatolites existed just 350 million (or 0.35 billion) years after Earth's oceans became permanently established.

Are they authentic? A few geologists and paleontologists have challenged the biological authenticity of the stromatolite fossils dated as 3.3 to 3.5 billion years old. Their skeptical response to ancient stromatolites' biogenicity (biological origin) comes from three areas of concern: (1) the relatively rare occurrence of stromatolites older than 2.8 billion years; (2) the absence of microbial fossils in the oldest stromatolite remains; and (3) the identification of possible inorganic mechanisms that can produce stromatolite-like features. (For example, they view the macroscopic wavy layers as inorganic frauds that happen to resemble stromatolite remains.)[12]

Paleontologists who advocate the authenticity of the oldest stromatolite fossils and defend their biogenicity have addressed these concerns.[13] The rare occurrence of stromatolites in rock deposits greater than 2.8 billion years in age makes sense, they argue. Between 3.9 and 2.8 billion years ago, shallow water environments were uncommon on Earth, limited to the shore regions of sparsely distributed volcanic islands.[14] In all likelihood, violent tectonic activity during that time destroyed most stromatolite fossils.

The absence of microfossils is also readily explained. Stromatolites younger than 2.8 billion years old don't contain microfossils either, and researchers don't question their biogenicity. Ancient stromatolites resemble their undisputed younger brothers and the modern-day specimens from Shark Bay so closely as to support their authenticity.

The ancient stromatolites are too large and irregular to be products of inorganic processes, and the geological data indicate that they were deposited in shallow water environments. Though the case has yet to be established beyond all doubt, the weight of evidence tips the scales in favor of the stromatolites' biogenicity.

Miniature fossils. Though microfossils associated with ancient stromatolites have not been found, researchers have recovered bacterial fossils from geologically older layers in both western Australia and east South Africa.[15] Paleontologists (fossil hunters) focus their search for ancient microfossils in carbon-rich cherts (rocks) composed of micro-crystalline silica. The fine-grained silica indicates that these rocks have not experienced fossil-damaging metamorphosis.[16] The high carbon con-tent signifies that organic materials and biological remains were code-posited with the silica. When silica deposits formed in Earth's early history, they began as a gel-like substance surrounding and impregnating microbial cells. As the silica slowly crystallized, it preserved the cells with remarkable detail. Once the silica hardened, the cherts became watertight, permanently entombing the microfossils.

Threadlike microfossils (with a morphology similar to cyanobacteria) have been detected in cherts recovered from the Kromberg Formation, dated at 3.3 billion years old, and the Hooggenoeg Formation, dated at 3.4 billion years old, both part of the Swaziland Supergroup.[17] Breaks in the fil-aments define individual cells. The microfossils are associated with organic kerogen (organic tars), stacks of thin sheets that appear to be stromatolite remnants. One research team noted microfossils that show microbes undergoing cell division.[18] Recently an international team reexamined these cherts.[19] The scientists observed spherical, "sausage-shaped," and fil-amentous bacterial fossils. They also uncovered evidence of fossilized biofilms. The variety of fossil forms, presumably deposited under similar conditions, reflects a complex microbial ecology and confirms the authen-ticity of the microfossils discovered in earlier studies.

A team of paleontologists headed by UCLA scientist J. William Schopf uncovered microfossils (resembling cyanobacteria) in the Pilbara Supergroup, dated older than 3.47 billion years in age.[20] In all, eleven different forms have been recovered from the western Australian cherts. Scientists regard these microbial remains as the oldest-known fossils. The variety of forms again suggests a complex microbial ecology on early Earth. The recovery of microfossils from the site that also yielded stromatolite remains further supports the interpretation that both have biological origins.

Phony fossils? A scientific team from the United Kingdom led by Martin Brasier recently challenged the authenticity of the oldest microfos-sils recovered from western Australia.[21] According to Brasier's team, further analysis suggests that the microscopic shapes in the cherts are pseudofos-sils—carbon deposits generated by an unusual chemical process that occurred under hydrothermal conditions. These scientists also maintain that the cherts lacked a shallow water environment—a condition that cyanobacteria require. However, it is important to note that these researchers do not challenge life's early appearance. Rather, they dispute the identification of the microfossils recovered from the Pilbara Supergroup cherts as the *oldest* fossils, and they question the rapid emergence of cyanobacteria and complex photosynthetic processes.

In spite of the challenges leveled against their biological origin, the data amasses in favor of authenticity. Isotope analysis of the carbon associated with the individual microfossils shows a carbon-12 enrichment.[22] This enrichment reflects a biological, rather than an inorganic, origin for the carbon deposits. The magnitude of carbon-12 enrichment equals that measured for the undisputed microfossils recovered from the Gunflint Formation in Canada (2.1 billion years old) and the Bitter Springs Formation in Australia (dated at 850 million years old). In addition, laser Raman microscopic analysis of individual microfossils confirms their authenticity.[23] This technique provides a chemical "fingerprint" of the carbon associated with the individual microfossils. As with the carbon-12 measurements, the Raman signature from the Pilbara Supergroup matches that of undisputed microfossils.

At ISSOL 2002 (an international conference on the origin of life attended by the authors) J. William Schopf, the paleontologist credited with the discovery of the oldest microbial fossils, and Martin Brasier, the scientist who challenged Schopf's discovery, presented back-to-back papers.[24] Despite Brasier's skepticism, Schopf's case remained convincing. Further work will help settle this controversy. The scientific community waits with anticipation for the results that will soon come from applying a microscopy method (atomic force microscopy) to microfossils recovered from the northeastern Australian rock formations.[25] Application of this technique, pioneered by Schopf's team, provides detailed images of microfossil cell walls. Detecting cell walls in the oldest microfossils will prove their authenticity. Recently a team from the Polish Academy of Sciences demonstrated that the microfossil features that led Brasier's team to question the oldest microfossils' authenticity result from thermal alteration. This bodes well for the biogenicity of the oldest microfossils.[26]

In the midst of this controversy, French and Japanese scientists working independently discovered microfossils in the Australian rock deposits dated older than 3.47 billion years. These microfossils manifest the same variety of forms as those recovered from South African deposits. This finding indicates that a diversity of microbes existed in Australia by about 3.5 billion years ago. Both teams reevaluated the geological setting of the cherts. This work indicates the possibility that these microfossils may represent microbes that occupied deep-sea hydrothermal vents—microbes other than cyanobacteria.[27]

Life's Chemical Remains

Fossils are not the only evidence in the geological record for biological activity in Earth's distant past. Occasionally, when an organism dies, its organic remnants escape total decomposition and continue their association with geological deposits. With time, these organic remains undergo chemical transformation driven by the heat and pressure that are part of geological processes. Familiar biomolecules convert into nondescript kerogen, graphite, and other carbonaceous deposits.

The chief geochemical evidence for life on early Earth comes from carbon-12 and nitrogen-14 isotope enrichment of (1) bulk kerogen, and (2) microscopic carbonaceous deposits recovered from rocks dated between 3.3 and 3.8 (or more) billion years old. Geochemists and paleontologists also consider sulfur-32–enriched sulfide deposits as an important independent marker of microbial activity on early Earth. Isotopes are alternate forms of the same type of atom with different atomic weights. For example, carbon has two stable isotopes, carbon-12 and carbon-13, and one unstable (radioactive) isotope, carbon-14.

Each of the major types of geochemical evidence for life in the era approaching 4 billion years ago will be considered in turn.

Isotopes as life's signatures. When living organisms use inorganic material to build biomolecules or extract energy from the environment, they preferentially use the lighter isotopes of that material. This process, called isotope fractionation, adds carbon-12 (and nitrogen-14 under some conditions) to the biomass. (See Appendix B.)

Scientists have developed a technique (comparing carbon-12 enrichment to certain inorganic standards) for measuring the carbon-12/carbon-13 isotope fractionation caused by living systems.[28] The different carbon-fixing metabolic processes found in nature cause a carbon-12 enrichment over a characteristic range of values.[29]

Investigators consider carbon-12 isotopic excess found in carbonaceous compounds in geological deposits to be an important indicator that the carbon-containing materials are the residue of past life. Moreover, the extent of the carbon-12 enrichment provides an important clue as to the type of metabolic pathways that produced the carbonaceous deposits.[30]

Discoveries yield dividends. Researchers recovered kerogen from the same rock formations in Australia (Pilbara Supergroup) and South Africa (Swaziland Supergroup) that yielded stromatolite fossils and cellular microfossils. Isotopic analysis of bulk kerogen from both locations shows carbon-12 enrichment sufficient to indicate life's presence on Earth between 3.3 and 3.5 billion years ago.[31] These measurements also strongly suggest that this early life possessed photosynthetic capability. The isotopic profile of these ancient kerogen deposits nicely dovetails with the presence of stromatolite remains — also indicative of photosynthetic activity — and microfossils that resemble photosynthetic cyanobacteria.

Bulk kerogen and graphite deposits recovered in western Greenland from the oldest known rocks (dated even older than 3.7 billion years) also show carbon-12 excess. After studies of the isotopic profile observed in these deposits, researchers affirmed that the carbon-12 enrichment represents life's signature.[32]

Apatite's appetite for graphite. More recently, a scientific team used new technology to conduct a highly detailed isotopic analysis of carbonaceous materials from Greenland's ancient rock deposits. Ion microprobe analysis allowed these researchers to measure the isotopic profile of individual graphite grains entombed in apatite (an inorganic salt) crystals.[33]

These scientists argue that the apatite "coffin" protects the graphite's carbon from isotope exchange caused by metamorphic activity, specifically by its intense heat and pressure. Initial measurements dated the rock containing the apatite grains at 3.86 ± 0.01 billion years old.

The isotopic enrichment noted for these pristine graphite grains measure in a range expected for life remains but exceeds the values expected for photosynthetic microbes. It falls within the range expected for methanotrophic (methane-using) organisms.[34] Moreover, the scientists who conducted the isotope studies regard the association of the graphite grains with apatite as another meaningful indicator of life's remains. The apatite possibly represents the transformed remains of organic phosphates. This class of chemical compounds includes important biomolecules such as DNA, RNA, ATP, and sugar phosphates (key and abundant metabolic intermediates).[35]

Searching the setting. Researchers hold little hope that microfossils will be recovered from the rock formations of western Greenland. The extreme geological alteration of these rocks should have destroyed any delicate microfossils ever associated with the oldest known rocks. Fossils would provide important and independent confirmation of life's existence prior to 3.8 billion years ago. Their discovery would provide additional clues to the types of life present on Earth at that time. Microfossils would generate insight into the biological activity and metabolic characteristics of this early life.

Although researchers lack fossil facts, they can gain additional understanding about ancient organisms from studying the geological record and deciphering information about the environmental setting at the time the rock deposits formed. Careful evaluation of the geological features of western Greenland rock formations has recently yielded such information.[36] The data suggests that Earth's oldest rocks formed in shallow water environments along the coastal area of a volcanic island. The primary source of the rocks seems to have been volcanic weathering products. This type of environment readily supports stromatolite formation and the activity of cyanobacteria. Indirectly, the geological record indicates that life on Earth 3.8+ billion years ago may well have been photosynthetic—or at least this remains a possibility.

Lost apatite? Although apatite-entombed graphite seems to provide convincing evidence for life—perhaps photosynthetic life—on Earth at greater than 3.8 billion years ago, controversy still surrounds the conclusion. Two independent scientific teams, one from Japan and the other from Canada, have challenged the authenticity and age of the apatite crystals.[37] The team from Japan claims that while the iron formations that co-occur with the apatite crystals themselves date at greater than 3.8 billion years old, the crystals date at only 1.5 to 1.6 billion years old. The Japanese researchers maintain that these crystals formed and encased the graphite granules when the rocks underwent their last major metamorphic event.

The Canadian scientists, like the Japanese, challenge the date of the apatite-graphite complexes. They also question the likelihood that the apatite-protected graphite granules could have survived more than 2 billion years of metamorphic heat and pressure intact. In their opinion, the apatite crystals and their contents could not have been originally present in the rock deposits at the time they formed, but instead were introduced some time later in the rock formations' complex history.

A date for life's appearance on Earth before 3.8 billion years ago troubles the Canadian researchers for another reason. If life existed this early, then it must have survived what is called the late heavy bombardment. This event occurred between 3.8 and 3.9 billion years ago when, according to one popular theory, a gravitational perturbation in the solar system caused objects in the Edgeworth-Kuiper belt to pelt the inner solar system. Astronomers believe that Earth experienced over seventeen thousand collisions during that period. Such impacts would have destroyed any and all life. A thorough description of the late heavy bombardment and of its implications for both the RTB Model and naturalistic origin-of-life scenarios appears in the next chapter. Even a cursory review of the details surrounding the late heavy bombardment shows why the Canadian researchers find the overlap between this dramatic event in Earth history and life's earliest appearance incomprehensible.

In spite of the seemingly impossible appearance of life at the time of the late heavy bombardment, the scientific team that originally made the isotopic measurements of the apatite-encased graphite granules still maintains the authenticity of the samples. They assert that the apatite must be original to the deposit because it is associated with rock that has no intrinsic capacity to form apatite during metamorphosis. This team also redated the samples and determined their age to be greater than 3.83 billion years.[38]

More recently, scientists from Sweden and George Washington University raised new questions about the validity of the apatite-graphite signature for early life.[39] They offered evidence that the banded iron formations (BIFs) of western Greenland (where the apatite crystals were found) are not BIFs at all (see "Banded Iron Formations," page 75). Rather, they formed during much later metamorphic events. If the supposed BIFs did not really result from sedimentary processes, then it is unlikely the graphite comes from life that codeposited in those sediments. However, these scientists lacked an explanation for graphite granules' carbon-12 enrichment.

Other researchers from the United States and Norway also recently cast doubt on the geochemical evidence (from western Greenland) for early life.[40] They demonstrated that carbonates in these rock formations with associated graphite granules were introduced well after the rock was deposited. If so, the graphite granules are secondary features. Based on laboratory chemical studies, these scientists maintain that carbon-12 enrichment occurred via inorganic processes catalyzed by iron(2) during carbonate infusion into the rocks. This team also showed, based on bulk measurements, that some of the carbon-12 enrichment represents "contamination" from recent life.

For now, the authenticity of the apatite-graphite complexes remains a point of contention. Future work will determine whether the apatite crystals and their contents are indicators of life's existence on Earth 3.86 billion years ago or earlier. In the midst of this controversy, however, one should note that *none of the scientific teams challenges the 3.8-billion-year-old existence of life on Earth*. The dispute simply surrounds the authenticity of the apatite-encased graphite granules as the residue of early life. All the critics acknowledge other compelling geochemical signatures for life in the ancient rock formations of western Greenland.

Recently a geologist from Greenland recovered graphite globules within sedimentary rocks from a different rock formation (Garbenschiefer Formation). Initial results show a carbon-12 enrichment within a range indicative of photosynthetic life.[41] A team of Japanese scientists also found that 3.8-billion-year-old microscopic graphite granules encased in quartz deposits (in western Greenland) display carbon-12 enrichment consistent with early life on Earth.[42] As the data accumulates, scientists gain confidence that life, perhaps even photosynthetic life, existed on Earth at least as far back as 3.7 billion years ago and quite likely even 150 million years prior to that. The controversy that surrounds individual pieces of potential evidence is healthy and important. It forges the way for the origin-of-life community to make advances in its capacity to detect life's signature in the geochemical record.

Nitrogen numbers nailed down. Carbon-12 enrichment is not the only isotopic signature for life. Nitrogen isotopes also serve as a geochemical marker for biological activity.[43] In the presence of significant atmospheric oxygen, organisms that fix nitrogen preferentially incorporate the heavy nitrogen isotope, nitrogen-15, into their biomolecules (relative to atmospheric nitrogen). Kerogens that are derived from organic compounds biologically produced under high oxygen conditions typically display a nitrogen-15 excess.[44] On the other hand, biologically driven nitrogen fixation in a *low* oxygen (anoxic) environment enriches the biomass in the light nitrogen isotope, nitrogen-14.[45]

Nitrogen isotopic analysis provides independent corroboration of life's early appearance on Earth. Kerogens isolated from South African and western Australian rocks dated between 3.4 and 3.5 billion years old show a nitrogen-14 enrichment indicative of life's remains.[46] These same kerogen samples showed a carbon-12 enrichment that also supports this conclusion. The combined carbon-12 and nitrogen-14 enrichment confirms life's presence prior to 3.5 billion years ago. Attempts to detect a nitrogen isotopic life signature in older rocks from western Greenland so far have yielded inconclusive results.[47]

While the scientific community readily agrees that the nitrogen isotopic evidence reflects biological activity in Earth's distant past, limited agreement exists as to the type of metabolic processes at work. One interpretation regards the nitrogen-14 enrichment as evidence for microorganisms that engage in anoxygenic photosynthesis (photosynthesis that takes place in low oxygen conditions), whereas the other posits that chemoautotrophic microbes (organisms that use chemical energy to drive cell processes) caused the nitrogen isotope fractionation.

Sulfur-32: Less is more. The biological activity of some microbes (referred to as sulfate-reducing bacteria) causes fractionation of sulfur isotopes.[48] Sulfate-reducing microorganisms preferentially use sulfur-32 (the light sulfur isotope) at the expense of sulfur-34 when sulfate is reduced to hydrogen sulfide. This preference produces sulfur-32–enriched hydrogen sulfide, which in turn interacts with iron in the surrounding sediments to produce pyrite.

Recently recovered sulfide deposits from 3.5-billion-year-old rocks located in northwestern Australia that date about 3.5 billion years in age are enriched in sulfur-32.[49] These sulfide deposits are associated with organic carbon residue. Taken together these results indicate a biological origin for the sulfide deposits. The sulfide deposits further indicate that not only were photosynthetic bacteria present on early Earth, but so too were sulfate-reducing bacteria.

Iron, layer upon layer. The geochemical evidence for early life is not limited exclusively to the chemical residue from dead organisms. Biochemical interactions among living systems, the presence of inorganic materials in the organisms' immediate surroundings, and atmospheric conditions all carry wide-scale impact. This impact becomes most noticeable when the organisms achieve broad geographical distribution and operate for a geologically significant period of time. An organism in Earth's environment leaves telltale markers in the geological record. These markers serve as a chemical signature for life's existence and its metabolic characteristics.

Banded Iron Formations

Unusual iron ore deposits exist in sedimentary rocks older than 1.8 billion years. These iron deposits, called banded iron formations (BIFs), alternate with chert (silica) layers.[50] Deposits of this type don't form today. Geologists believe that BIFs developed at a time in Earth's history when high levels of dissolved iron and silica existed in the oceans. Silica deposited in ocean sediments formed the chert layers. Geologists believe that the iron ore "bands" formed when oxygen generated by photosynthetic organisms reacted with the dissolved iron to form hematite and magnetite.[51]

The alternating BIF layers suggest to geologists that the iron deposits formed seasonally as periodic nutrient upswells from the ocean floor delivered nutrients to cyanobacteria in shallow water environments. These freshly delivered nutrients allowed the cyanobacteria to flourish, which led to a temporary increase in oxygen output followed by iron oxide deposition onto the backdrop of silica sediments. Seasonal deposits of iron also increased during the summer when warm temperatures encouraged cyanobacterial growth.

An alternative explanation involves the anoxygenic photosynthetic purple bacteria in BIF production. These microbes convert iron carbonate into iron oxide during photosynthesis.[52]

The geochemical remains of both oxygenic and anoxygenic photo-synthesis, banded iron formations (BIFs), appear in the geological record from 3.8 to about 1.8 billion years ago.[53] The oldest of such remains appear in Earth's oldest rock formations, in western Greenland.[54] BIFs also show up in the rock formations of western Australia and South Africa dating between 3.4 and 3.5 billion years old. These formations provide another independent line of geochemical evidence for early life on Earth and strongly imply that photosynthetic microbes were indeed present.

The Weight of Evidence

The fossil and geochemical data recovered from some of the world's oldest geological formations consistently tell the same story. Life was present early in Earth's history. Prokaryotic microorganisms were firmly entrenched on Earth at 3.7 billion years ago. The record for ancient life may well date beyond this to 3.8+ billion years in age.

While some of the individual details stir controversy among scientists, the preponderance of evidence does not. Origin-of-life researchers universally acknowledge life's existence on Earth prior to 3.5 billion years ago. Several lines of fossil (stromatolites and microfossils) and geochemical (carbon-12, nitrogen-14, and sulfur-32 isotope enrichment and BIFs) research all independently point to life's presence on early Earth. Additionally, much of the evidence works together to substantiate life's ancient existence. For example, stromatolites, microfossils that resemble various types of cyanobacteria, BIFs, and carbon-12–enriched kerogen not only indicate microbial activity but also reveal the type of validation scientists expect in the geological record if indeed photosynthetic bacteria were present early in Earth's history. For origin-of-life researchers, the conclusion is inescapable: early Earth teemed with a variety of microbial life forms.

The fossil and geochemical records not only indicate the timing of life's appearance on Earth but also provide a means to assess the biochemical and metabolic properties of that life. Investigators now realize that Earth's first life, while morphologically simple, was biochemically complex. The cyanobacteria likely present on Earth 3.5 billion years ago appear to have been identical to the cyanobacterial forms on Earth today.[55] Cyanobacteria are some of the most biochemically complex microbes known to microbiologists.

The fossil chronology indicates that by 3.5 billion years ago complex microbial ecosystems were already in place. As described earlier, the presence of stromatolite remains in the geological records of western Australia and eastern South Africa imply that bacteria capable of both oxygenic and anoxygenic photosynthesis must have existed along with aerobic and anaerobic heterotrophs—creatures that feed on organic materials produced by other organisms. The diverse collection of microfossils recovered from Australian and South African rock formations also signify complex microbial communities. Microbial ecologies on early Earth were not limited to surface microbes, but they may also have included deep-sea hydrothermal vent communities as displayed by microfossils in hydrothermally influenced sediments.

Biologists who view life's diversity from an evolutionary perspective conclude that the existence of cyanobacteria on early Earth means that nearly all bacteria groups must have evolved by 3.5 billion years ago and that prokaryote diversity was fully established by that time.[56] The rationale for this conclusion is the placement of cyanobacteria in the evolutionary tree. These microbes are considered the most recently evolved and advanced bacterial groups. Naturalistic origin-of-life scenarios must account not only for life's early appearance but also for life's diversification in a time frame of less than 400 million years.[57]

An abundance of data indicates that cyanobacteria and other photosynthetic microbes existed by 3.5 billion years ago. Cyanobacteria employ oxygenic photosynthesis—photosynthesis that occurs in the presence of oxygen and produces oxygen as a byproduct. Other types of photosynthetic microbes use a form of anoxygenic photosynthesis that cannot operate in oxygen's presence. Recent work by two independent scientific teams indicates that if evolution generated photosynthesis, anoxygenic photosynthesis emerged before the oxygenic version.[58]

The results of the two studies show that naturalistic origin-of-life scenarios depend on the existence of anoxygenic photosynthesis well before 3.5 billion years ago since the fossil and geochemical evidence places cyanobacteria and oxygenic photosynthesis on Earth 3.5 billion years ago. The carbonaceous residues uncovered from rock deposits in Greenland display a carbon-12 enrichment that is consistent with the operation of either oxygenic or anoxygenic photosynthesis.[59]

Microfossils and sulfur-32 enriched sulfide deposits, along with the carbon-12 and nitrogen-14 enriched kerogen and graphite globules, indicate that chemoautotrophic organisms—organisms that use chemical energy extracted from the environment to power cell activities and make organic materials—existed on early Earth along with photosynthetic microbes. The geochemical record is fully compatible with complex biochemical pathways that sustain methanogenesis and sulfate-reduction. In the words of the research group that discovered the oldest evidence for sulfate-reducing microbes in the geological record, "Sulphate reduction is a complex metabolic process requiring advanced membrane-bound transport enzymes, proton motive force generation by ATPase and other charge separation proteins and the genetic regulation of protein synthesis through DNA and RNA."[60]

Neither photosynthesis nor chemoautotrophic metabolic activities can stand alone. A complex ensemble of supporting biochemical processes must operate simultaneously. This list of essential processes includes protein synthesis and biochemical pathways that produce cell-membrane and cell-wall components. Because Earth's first life must have possessed the full capability to produce all the chemical building blocks needed for cell activity (autotrophism), biochemical pathways for synthesizing amino acids, nucleotides, sugars, and fatty acids must have been in effect. In addition, metabolic pathways that degrade these compounds must have operated in Earth's first life. Finally, these life forms had reproductive potential, and therefore DNA replication and cell replication machinery (or its equivalent) must have been in place.

The fossil and geochemical record, along with the recognition that Earth's first life is no different qualitatively from photosynthetic and chemoautotrophic microbes alive today, strongly intimates that a remarkable degree of biochemical complexity appeared simultaneously with life's first occurrence on Earth. This conclusion is consistent with recent discoveries about life's minimal complexity, which are discussed in chapter 12.

Putting the RTB Model to the Test

The RTB biblical origin-of-life creation model makes several predictions that can be evaluated by the fossil and geochemical data coming from Earth's oldest geological formations. One defining prediction (#1) is that life appeared early in Earth's history, while the planet was still in its primordial state. This concept flows from the setting of Genesis 1:2, which describes primordial Earth. The fossil and geochemical evidence indicates clearly that life early in Earth's history was diverse and extensive, consistent with the model.

The RTB Model also predicts (#4) that if the Creator revealed in the Bible brought life into existence, then Earth's first life should display complexity. Here again, the fossil and geochemical evidence indicates that first life was metabolically complex even though it was morphologically simple. Again, the model meets the criteria.

Prediction 7 states that first life was qualitatively different from life that came into existence on creation days three, five, and six. This proves to be the case. Single-celled prokaryotes were the first life forms on Earth. Based on both cellular and biochemical distinctives, scientists classify prokaryotes into separate domains (eubacteria and archaea) distinct from the realm of plants and animals (eukarya).

Research advances from detailed studies of Earth's oldest fossil and geochemical evidence align with a biblical account for life's start and provide substantial validation of the RTB Model. The question remains as to how these same discoveries comport with naturalistic predictions for life's origin.

Evaluating the Evidence

Though origin-of-life researchers readily acknowledge life's early entrance onto Earth's stage, they find it remarkable and totally unexpected. Naturalism's proponents would not have predicted the early appearance of such complex life forms. Origin-of-life investigator J. William Schopf makes this point quite plainly in *The Cradle of Life,* where he says, "No one had foreseen that the beginning of life occurred so astonishingly early."[61]

Elsewhere in his book, Schopf details the problem that complex early life presents for naturalistic explanations:

> No one has publicly disagreed with my interpretation of the Apex fossils. But privately, some would prefer I were mistaken, since they (and I, too) would prefer a simpler evolutionary story, one that told us these oldest fossil organisms were capable only of primitive ways of living and that advanced metabolic lifestyles evolved much later. But the evidence seems strong, and what one might "prefer" shouldn't matter.[62]

Natural processes alone offer no explanation for the data found in the fossil and geochemical record.

In the next chapter, the comparative evaluation continues. The fact of life under question this time is: Could life have evolved slowly over a long period of time, as evolutionary theory requires, or did it suddenly appear?

CHAPTER 6

A SLOW OR SUDDEN ARRIVAL?

I n 1966, Carl Sagan wrote a piece of evolutionary doctrine that still appears in textbooks.

> There is an elaborate apparatus involving messenger RNA, adapter RNA, ribosomes, and a diversity of specialized enzymes. . . . We cannot imagine these complex and specific accessory molecules to have arisen spontaneously in the primitive environment. The apparatus for the transcription of the genetic code must itself have evolved slowly, through billions of years of evolution.[1]

Sagan believed that the period during which prebiotics assembled themselves into Earth's first organism must have covered an extremely lengthy time span. While he referred to billions of years, the assemblage of prebiotics at most extended from the origin of the planet until life's first appearance in the fossil record. In the 1960s few researchers imagined just how short this time was. Earth's origin has since been dated to 4.566 ± 0.002 billion years ago.[2] Fossils extend back 3.5 billion years.[3]

This time frame would seem to give nature over a billion years for abiogenesis (the emergence of life from nonlife). But does it? This calculation supplies the theoretical boundaries on that time. Given a choice between an upper limit, the mean, and a lower limit for the period when life first formed, naturalists understandably choose the upper limit. Undergraduate and high school textbooks reflect this choice without clarification or explanation. Rarely can even a graduate-level text be found that questions whether the time frame for life's start could be shorter than the maximum theoretical boundary.

Nevertheless, the assumption that prebiotics existed from Earth's beginning, in a medium suitable for assembly into an organism, seems less and less likely as researchers learn more about early Earth. And the lack of fossil evidence prior to 3.5 billion years ago does not automatically prove that no life existed before that time. Geochemical evidence for life's presence, for example, likely extends as far back as 3.83 billion years (see chapter 5). Isotope ratio measurements for carbon establish that life was abundant on Earth at least as far back as 3.8 billion years.

An Inhospitable Early Earth

The Sun's burning history made early Earth violently hostile to life's origin and potential survival. The Sun formed from the gravitational collapse of a gas cloud. At times during the collapse phase, gas and dust were sucked into the Sun; at other times gas and dust escaped to outer space. Different nuclear reactions switched on and off at different times within the emerging star.[4] During its infancy (lasting 50 million years), the Sun's luminosity was highly unstable.[5] For the next 500 million years, solar ionizing radiation (in particular, x-rays) persisted at a level 50 times higher than at present.[6]

Astronomers draw these conclusions about the hostile radiation activity of the early Sun from theoretical models, and observations of young solar-type stars confirm them.[7] The extreme variability of the infant Sun's luminosity and the intensity of the young Sun's ionizing radiation are only two of several reasons why life likely could not have survived on Earth until at least 3.9 billion years ago.

Accurate measurements of impact craters on Mars, Mercury, the Moon, and asteroids establish that life-destroying collisions frequently pummeled the earth between 4.5 and 3.5 billion years ago, with the most intense episodes occurring between about 3.8 and 4.0 billion years ago. With high-resolution imaging from orbiting satellite missions, NASA astronomers can accurately determine the degree to which these craters have eroded. Looking at a given body's atmosphere, rotation rate, ambient interplanetary dust, meteorites, and solar ultraviolet radiation, astronomers can determine the date of a collision event. The size and shape of the crater tells them the size of the collider.

In addition to learning from these craters that planetesimals (miniature planets) and asteroids pounded the entire inner solar system during its first billion years, NASA astronomers have confirmed that the degree of damage suffered by each body was proportional to its mass, as Newton's laws of motion predict. Earth, the most massive of the inner solar system bodies, suffered the greatest damage from these impactors.

Intense research during the late 1980s examined the implications of this damage for early life. Three different interdisciplinary teams concluded that

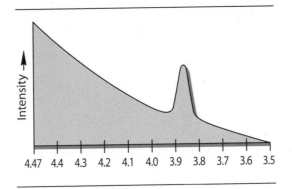

Figure 6.1: Cratering Intensity for the Inner Solar System

Large asteroids and comets pummeled the entire inner solar system (Mars, Earth, the Moon, Venus, and Mercury) between 4.5 and 3.5 billion years ago. The cratering intensity declined exponentially throughout that era except for a brief episode known as the late heavy bombardment that occurred between 3.8 and 3.9 billion years ago.

(Presented by Marc van Zuilen in his lecture on July 1, 2002, at ISSOL 2002, Oaxaca, Mexico, June 30-July 5, 2002 abstract #16)

until 3.85 billion years ago, Earth suffered many dozens of "sterilization events."[8] For each of these events, one or more giant colliders smashed into Earth, releasing enough energy to melt Earth's surface. No liquid water, solid rocks, conceivable life forms, or even basic prebiotic molecules could have survived anywhere on the seething planet during such collision episodes. Water would have taken at least three thousand years to begin condensing after such a collision event.[9]

Geologists refer to this epoch as the Hadean era, with obvious reference to Hades.[10] The conditions of this era explain why no Earth rocks or marine deposits older than about 3.85 billion years have ever been located.[11] Violent collisions lasted until 3.5 billion years ago, explaining why no earlier fossils (and few older rocks) have been found.

Lunar rocks help illuminate the details of the last great sterilization event. Combining accurate radiometric dates (dates based on the decay of radioactive isotopes) of thirty-one meteorites that had come to Earth from the Moon with the analysis of Moon rocks recovered from the Apollo program, astronomers verified that an intense bombardment of the Moon's entire surface occurred 3.9 billion years ago.[12] This barrage lasted for about 100 million years.[13] The lack of any impact melt in lunar rocks older than 3.9 billion years supports this conclusion. Earth's greater gravitational cross section would have made the simultaneous assault on Earth about thirty times more intense. Scientists have estimated that the total accumulation of extraterrestrial material upon Earth's surface during this event added up to an average of 200 tons per square yard over the entire surface of Earth.[14]

Recently, four Australian geologists uncovered terrestrial evidence for this period, called the late heavy bombardment. They found an anomalously low abundance of the tungsten-182 isotope in metamorphosed sedimentary rocks from deposits dating from 3.7 to 3.8 billion years ago in west Greenland and northern Labrador.[15] This low tungsten-182 isotope abundance, never observed in strictly terrestrial rocks, is consistent with that of deposits heavily contaminated by meteorites (all meteorites have a low abundance of this isotope). High nickel and chromium abundances, characteristic of iron and chondritic (rocky, carbon-rich) meteorites, add further confirmation.

During this last bombardment, comets (with a mass about 75 percent frozen water) and asteroids (which contain less water but are perhaps more numerous) may have contributed slightly to Earth's water supply. This extra water would have instantly converted to steam on impact, condensed, and amplified the water cycle. It also would have affected the carbonate-silicate cycle.[16] The enhancement of both of these cycles proves essential for sustaining life, especially in the long term.

The Carbonate-Silicate Cycle

The carbonate-silicate cycle describes the process whereby basaltic crustal rocks, through plate tectonics and exposure to dense liquid water, are gradually transformed into silicates. Because silicates are lighter than basalts, they float above the basalts. In time, the silicates rise high enough to break the water's surface.

As exposed silicates make contact with a strong water cycle, rain acts as a catalyst to transform them and atmospheric carbon dioxide into carbonates and sand. This gradual removal of carbon dioxide—a powerful greenhouse gas—from the atmosphere helps compensate for the increasing luminosity of the Sun. (A smaller, but crucial, part of the compensation takes place through organisms' converting water and carbon dioxide from the atmosphere into sugars, starches, and fats that are then buried and converted into fossil fuels.) In this manner, and through regulating silicate erosion with just-right plants at just-right times, the surface temperature of Earth is maintained at a level necessary for life's survival.[17]

Narrow Time Window

The discovery and confirmations of life on Earth as far back as 3.8 billion years shrink the maximum time window for life's origin from 1,070 million years to 770 million years. With at least many dozens of bombardments, or sterilization events, taking place between 4.5 and 3.9 billion years ago (the last being particularly catastrophic), the window shrinks to no more than 100 million years.

The latest assessment of the date for the late heavy bombardment sets it at 3.85 billion years ago.[18] This calculation closes the window for life's origin even more tightly—to less than 50 million years. How much less depends on how quickly this barrage subsided to a level that permitted the existence of life. It also depends on confirmation of the geochemical evidence for life as old as 3.83 billion years. Regardless, given that the late heavy bombardment lasted for about 100 million years, life appeared on Earth in a geological moment. The instant permanent rocks formed, life burst forth.

Zircons, Lenses to the Past

Origin-of-life researchers Christopher Wills and Jeffrey Bada once expressed the frustration of geologists and geophysicists that the Hadean era remained so long off limits for research. They said, "Scientists would cheerfully sell their souls to get a glimpse of the missing 700 million years of the geological record."[21] What kept the era out of observers' reach was the lack of relics with melting points high enough to endure the heat generated by impact events and hard enough to resist the extreme erosions, pressures, and metamorphisms in Earth's crust.

Such relics from this time period between the formation of Earth (4.57 billion years ago) and the first appearance of rocks (3.85 billion years ago) were once deemed nonexistent, if not impossible to locate. But they have now been found. And though valuable, these tiny zircon crystals can be obtained without a scientist's selling his or her soul.

A zircon crystal remains unaffected by any base or any acid (except the rare hydrogen fluoride). With a hardness measure of 7.5 (compared with steel's at 5.5 and diamond's at 10.0), zircon crystals withstand erosion. A melting point above 2,000 °F (1,100 °C) enabled them to remain intact through the melting of at least some host rocks. While life and rocks could not survive the extremes of the Hadean era (and diamonds had not yet formed), a few tiny flakes of zircon crystals did. These crystals provide an unprecedented look into Earth's history prior to the late heavy bombardment.

Zircons make excellent geochronometers. When forming, they

Impact Reseeding

Could life have survived one of the sterilization events in Earth's early history by orbiting the planet for a while before returning to Earth? It's one intriguing possibility.

When a body strikes the earth with enough force to sterilize all life on the planet, some of the material in Earth's crust gets ejected into interplanetary space. Although the length of time this matter spends traveling through space ranges greatly (up to millions of years), eventually some of this matter lands on Venus, Mars, and other planets in the solar system. A significant fraction of the ejected matter returns to Earth, with return travel times measured in thousands of years.

Recently three astronomers estimated that if a sterilizing impactor about 190 miles in diameter hit Earth, an ejected rock larger than about 40 feet in diameter that contained at least ten thousand cells of *Bacillus subtilis* and *Deinococcus radiodurans* per kilogram would still house one surviving organism three thousand to five thousand years later.[19] During that length of time, Earth's crust could have cooled sufficiently for life once again to survive. Therefore, the idea that life could have been reseeded on Earth following a sterilization event via the return of ejected matter is at least a possibility.

This kind of possible reseeding does not extend the time of life's origin. However, it may minimize the number of independent origins of Earth's hardiest life. The scenario requires bacteria much more complex than ordinary bacteria. Organisms as hardy as *Bacillus subtilis* and *Deinococcus radiodurans* survive due to complicated biochemical capacities and intricate DNA repair mechanisms.[20] Thus the origin of such species on early Earth is chemically much less plausible than it would be for ordinary bacteria.

trap small amounts of uranium, thorium, and lead. Uranium-238 and thorium-232 decay into different isotopes of lead and other products with half-lives of 4.46 and 14.1 billion years, respectively. (A half-life is the time it takes for one-half of an element to decay.) Therefore, by carefully measuring the ratios of uranium-238 to lead-206 and thorium-232 to lead-208 in zircons, geophysicists can accurately determine their age. Extremely high-temperature events do not disturb these ratios, making zircons especially helpful.[22]

Given the ratio of oxygen-18 to oxygen-16 within the ancient crystals, they reveal that between 3.9 and 4.4 billion years ago Earth's crust

The Greatest Frustration Event

The late heavy bombardment that occurred 3.85 billion years ago was not Earth's greatest impact event. The Apollo space mission and other evidence revealed that a far greater collision took place just prior to 4.47 billion years ago.

From the Apollo lunar rock samples, astronomers established the Moon's age as 4.47 billion years old.[27] The same lunar rocks indicate a crust chemically distinct from Earth's. Laser reflectors placed by Apollo's astronauts verify the Moon's slow and steady spiral away from Earth. Celestial mechanics' calculations on the collision event have determined that the Moon was a mere 15,000 miles away when it formed.[28] Today, the moon is about a quarter of a million miles away.

The Moon's composition, smaller density, and younger age indicate that the Moon did *not* form at exactly the same time as Earth. The Moon's movement away from Earth and the slowing of Earth's rotation imply some kind of collision event more than 4 billion years ago.[29] Only one scenario fits all the observed Earth-Moon dynamics and parameters: a body about the size of Mars (nine times the mass of the Moon and one-ninth the mass of Earth) struck Earth — neither a glancing nor a head-on blow but something in between — and was absorbed for the most part into Earth's core.[30] The impact blasted almost all of Earth's original atmosphere into outer space. The shell or cloud of debris from the collision orbited Earth and eventually coalesced to form the Moon.

This remarkable event rescued Earth from a life-suffocating atmosphere and resulted in a replacement atmosphere thin enough and with the right chemical composition to permit the passage of light to Earth's surface. At the same time, Earth's mass and density were boosted enough to retain (by gravity) a large quantity of water vapor for billions of years. The elevated iron content of Earth's crust permitted an abundance of ocean life, which in turn allowed advanced land life.[31]

The collision also played a major role in salting Earth's crust with a larger abundance of radioisotopes, the heat from which drives most of Earth's exceptionally high rates of tectonics and volcanism.[32] These activities were critical for sustaining the carbonate-silicate cycle that is essential for life. The result of this impact was that Earth's rotation rate gradually slowed so that a wide variety of lower life forms could survive long enough to later sustain advanced life forms. Eventually, the collision resulted in Earth's just-right rotation axis, a stable tilt that protects the planet from climatic extremes that would extinguish advanced life.[33]

melted, solidified, and remelted more than once.[23] Liquid oceans also formed, evaporated, and reformed more than once.[24] For brief episodes during that half-billion-year period, at least some continental crust existed, with landmasses periodically rising above the level of liquid water.[25] This ancient zircon evidence is consistent with Earth's suffering intermittent bombardment from the time the Moon formed 4.47 billion years ago until 3.85 billion years ago.[26] The evidence indicates that Earth did not remain continuously hellish throughout the Hadean era.

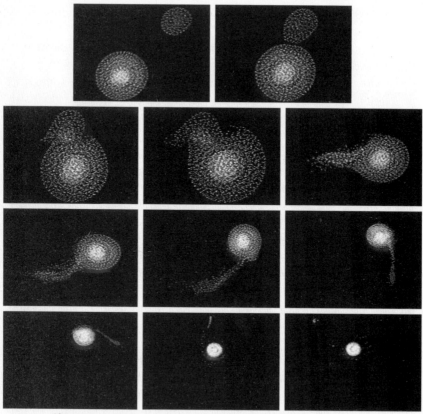

**Figure 6.2: Before, During, and After the Collision Event
Between Earth and a Mars-Sized Planet**

(Photo courtesy of A. G. W. Cameron, Ph.D., Donald H. Menzel Research Professor Emeritus of Astrophysics, Harvard University College of Astronomy)

Finding Enough Time

Naturalistic origin-of-life scenarios find some help for this extreme time challenge in calculations published by Antonio Lazcano and Stanley Miller in 1994.[34] These calculations indicate that cyanobacteria might have evolved from a prebiotic soup within a 10-million-year time span. Their work also identifies six steps for life's origin:

(1) formation of prebiotic compounds
(2) assembly of the first self-replicating molecules
(3) emergence of RNA molecules
(4) transition from an RNA world to the DNA-protein world
(5) emergence of starter proteins
(6) emergence of gene duplication and divergence

In addition to these steps at least two more must exist:

(7) assembly of a workable membrane to protect and feed the RNA, DNA, and/or protein molecules
(8) positioning of all the molecular components in the correct locations with respect to one another

Lazcano and Miller produced a crude estimate of the time needed for the first and sixth steps. They gave no estimate of the time required for steps two through five. Nor has any researcher since the publication of Lazcano and Miller's paper derived any estimates of how long these intermediate steps might have taken.

Knowing that life vitalized in less than a few million years and convinced that the assembly of the first organisms occurred through strictly natural processes, naturalism's proponents simply presume that the unknown rates for steps two through five (and the unknown rates for parts of steps one and six) must be extremely rapid. Their conclusion constitutes circular reasoning.

Rapid Breakdown of RNA

All models for life's origin at some point involve the building and operation of RNA molecules. Thus the stability of nucleotide building blocks that comprise RNA molecules and the stability of the RNA molecules themselves provide an independent measure of the maximum time span for any naturalistic life origin.

The stability of both nucleotides and RNA molecules depends on temperature. At the time of life's origin, Earth was likely hot. Early Earth's atmosphere, loaded with greenhouse gases (carbon dioxide and/or methane), generated surface temperatures between 158 and 194 °F (70 and 90 °C). And with gases like these in the atmosphere, little temperature variation over Earth's surface could occur.[35] Earth at that time had no isolated cold spots.

Nucleotide building blocks are known to fall apart quickly at warm temperatures. Origin-of-life specialist Matthew Levy recently demonstrated the problem. His experiments showed that all four of RNA's nucleotide building blocks degrade at warm temperatures in time periods ranging from nineteen days to twelve years.[36] These extremely short survival rates for the four RNA nucleotide building blocks suggest why life's origin would have to be virtually instantaneous—all the necessary RNA molecules would have to be assembled before any of the nucleotide building blocks decayed.

Levy also chilled naturalistic *cold* origin-of-life possibilities. He established that at water's freezing point, cytosine (one of the nucleotide building blocks) decomposes in less than 17,000 years.[37] At any possible temperature, the origin of life must take place quickly. Astronomer Donald Goldsmith noted in his book *The Hunt for Life on Mars,* "Since complex molecules tend to be fragile, 'Use them or lose them' may be the general rule about the chances that they will lead to living creatures. It could be that unless life appears on a planet within a few thousand years, . . . it will not arise at all."[38]

Putting the RTB Model to the Test
The Hadean conditions of early Earth as the backdrop for life's origin fit with the declaration in Genesis 1:2 about God's Spirit brooding over a primordial Earth described as *tōhû wabōhû*—an empty wasteland. Thus, prediction 2 of the RTB Model appears to be fulfilled. Furthermore, life's rapid emergence on Earth is exactly what one would expect if the first organisms were designed, built, and enlivened by a transcendent Creator. And that fulfills prediction 3. RTB's model, as a result, appears strengthened by the latest knowledge about life's sudden appearance.

Evaluating the Evidence
All the evidence converges on one conclusion: life appeared suddenly on Earth, probably on several occasions. Comments from researchers show how severely the rapid origin of life on Earth challenges naturalistic explanations.

In 1996, when it first became evident that life had left its mark in Greenland before 3.8 billion years ago and had significantly altered the oceans' and atmosphere's chemistry, marine biologist John Hayes reviewed the discovery for the prestigious science journal *Nature*. He acknowledged that life must have begun "with breathtaking rapidity."[39] Paleontologist Peter Ward and astronomer Donald Brownlee echoed this conclusion in their book *Rare Earth:* "Ancient life existed at Isua [Greenland], and perhaps, elsewhere on Earth, as early as 3.8 billion years ago, [*sic*] it leads to a striking conclusion: Life seems to have appeared simultaneously with the cessation of the heavy bombardment. . . . This seems like an awfully short period of time for the first life to evolve."[40] Niles Eldredge, cofounder (along with the late Stephen Jay Gould) of the punctuated equilibria hypothesis for the evolution of life, recently wrote, "In the very oldest rocks that stand a chance of showing signs of life, we find those signs—those vestiges—of life. Life is intrinsic to the Earth!"[41]

Speculations of extremely variable conditions during the Hadean era make the naturalists' paradigm for life's origin more difficult. Instead of needing to explain one unlikely event, their model must explain multiple, independent unlikely origin-of-life scenarios (with the possible exception of super-hardy species of bacteria). While the last of these events clearly took place with extreme rapidity, any earlier possible origins of life would also require completion in brief periods of time given the frequency of ongoing large impact collisions.

How do naturalists explain life's sudden appearance? Eldredge declines to speculate on why life is intrinsic to Earth. However, Stuart Kauffman, a chaos and complexity theoretician and founding member of the Santa Fe Institute, offers his ideas on the nature of this unknown physical property: "Life is an expected, emergent property of complex chemical reaction networks. . . . Catalysis is ubiquitous. . . . The formation of collectively autocatalytic sets of molecules suddenly becomes almost inevitable."[42]

In an attempt to account for the inevitable, sudden formation of autocatalytic sets of molecules, Kauffman proposes the operation of a "fourth law of thermodynamics." He hypothesizes "a law in which the diversity and complexity of the universe naturally increases in some optimal manner."[43] This optimal increase, however, directly contradicts the second law of thermodynamics. According to that law, *all* natural systems manifest entropy (increasing disorder, decay, and degradation of complexity) with time. This second law is so exhaustively confirmed that physicists routinely use it as a screening device for hypotheses and immediately reject any proposed model of a natural phenomenon that violates it.[44]

The absence of any supporting observational or experimental evidence also renders a premise invalid. In the case of the fourth law of thermody-namics, no such evidence can be cited.

Hubert Yockey, who founded the discipline that applies information theory to molecular biology, concluded after years of research that "life is consistent with the laws of physics and chemistry but [is] not derivable from them."[45] He adds, "I have no scenario to explain the origin of life."[46] Concerning the search for the origin of life from nonliving matter, Yockey has deduced that the persistent failures to solve the puzzle simply arise from the fact that "there is no solution."[47] He expresses agreement with the renowned theoretical physicist Niels Bohr that "life is to be accepted as an axiom."[48] In other words, life is a given. Just as the laws of logic, the principles of mathematics, and the existence of matter and energy cannot be attributed to any natural process or explanation, so too the origin(s) of life simply must be accepted as the starting point of all biological scientific research and analysis.

Though the sudden appearance of life contradicts their models (prediction 6—life should have appeared gradually on Earth over a significant period of time), naturalists acknowledge that life did indeed appear suddenly. The possibility that life may have emerged multiple times also defies explanation by their model (prediction 7—the origin of life should have occurred only once on Earth). So does the appearance of first life under the hostile conditions of early Earth (prediction 4—sufficiently placid chemical and physical conditions must have existed on early Earth for significant and enduring periods of time). However, other challenges may prove more daunting yet.

CHAPTER 7

WHERE'S THE SOUP?

The words *alphabet soup* conjure up visions of the ABCs swimming in consommé. Yet, when scientists talk about a prebiotic soup, technical terms define the content and make the soup much more difficult to describe. The assumption that a vast pool of concentrated prebiotic molecules on early Earth must have brewed for a very long period of time serves as the popular explanation for life's origin. But, what ingredients did such a prebiotic soup contain? Or did one even exist?

Examining scientific clues for a prebiotic soup leads to another essential "fact of life." According to the naturalistic explanation, the waters of the world were filled with amino acids, sugars, and others compounds that are the building blocks for life. New research evidence now permits a look back in time to see which of these building blocks might have been available in the legendary prebiotic soup—if one actually existed.

Life's Basic Ingredients
Organisms derive the necessary intricacy for metabolism and reproduction from four sets of complex molecules: proteins, nucleic acids (DNA and RNA), polysaccharides, and lipids. These complex molecules are made from specific sequences of about fifty different relatively simple (typically a dozen to a few dozen atoms each) carbon-based molecules (amino acids, nucleotides, fatty acids, and sugars). Carbon, oxygen, nitrogen, hydrogen, sulfur, and phosphorus are predominant among these simple molecules. While not the only ingredients of the hypothesized prebiotic soup from which the first life forms presumably emerged, these sets of carbon-based molecules are the most important.

The Phosphorus Problem

One of the rarest light elements, phosphorus has an abundance in the Sun of only 200 parts per billion.[1] As small as that proportion seems, it is still higher than the average abundance found anywhere else in the universe—except Earth, which is an unusually phosphorus-rich planet. The phosphorus abundance in Earth's surface ocean waters is 1.5 parts per billion.[2] Earth's crust—the most phosphorus-rich source known—contains 1,000 parts per million.[3] Still, this "high" number indicates rarity.

The short supply of phosphorus poses a significant problem for a naturalistic origin of life because so much of this ingredient is required to make replicator molecules. Phosphates are part of the backbone of both DNA and RNA. A phosphate molecule must accompany every nucleoside in them. Possible precursors to DNA and RNA molecules would seem to require similar phosphate richness. Without life molecules (already assembled and operating), no known natural process can harvest the amounts of phosphorus necessary for life from the environment. All the phosphate-rich deposits on Earth are produced by life.

Of the 112 known chemical elements, only carbon possesses a sufficiently complex chemical behavior to sustain living systems.[4] Carbon readily assembles into stable molecules comprised of individual and fused rings and linear and branched chains. It forms single, double, and triple bonds. Carbon also strongly bonds with itself as well as with oxygen, nitrogen, sulfur, and hydrogen. In other words, *life molecules must be carbon-based.*

Some researchers think boron and silicon may be possible life-support elements. Boron can form complex compounds, but these compounds have only limited stability, and boron is rare in the universe. Silicon belongs to the same chemical group as carbon and should display similar chemical properties. This once prompted the speculations of alien life based on silicon. But while silicon does form rings and chains, these structures lack the stability and range of complexity found in carbon-based compounds. For example, protein analogs made with silicon form chains no longer than one hundred "amino acids" in length. The silicon bond is much weaker than the corresponding carbon bond, and unlike carbon bonds, it is susceptible to oxidation. These properties account for the differences in chemical behavior of carbon and silicon.

No element but carbon can form the chemical basis for life.[5] This fact places limitations on the quest for molecules that would have made up a prebiotic "soup."

Searching for the Store

Two types of evidence persuade most origin-of-life scientists that prebiotics were plentiful on early Earth: (1) laboratory simulation experiments, and (2) the fact that meteorites, comets, and interplanetary and interstellar grains look like places where the right ingredients might be found. How strong is this evidence and does it build a case for evolution or creation?

Prebiotics in the lab. Beginning in the mid-1950s, origin-of-life investigators began "cooking up" several important prebiotic compounds under a variety of laboratory conditions simulating those of early Earth.[6] For example, several of the twenty amino acids used by cells to construct proteins have been synthesized in a simulated prebiotic soup. So, too, have the nucleotide bases—adenine, guanine, cytosine, and uracil. However, adequate prebiotic synthesis for numerous key biomolecules has yet to be achieved. Included in this list are the amino acids arginine, lysine, and histidine and several enzyme cofactors.

While individual laboratory conditions could conceivably represent those of early Earth, many prebiotic ingredients mutually exclude one another. For example, two nucleotide bases (adenine and guanine) require freezing conditions for their synthesis, while two other nucleotide bases (cytosine and uracil) demand boiling temperatures.[7] For all four building blocks to take shape at the same time, the prebiotic soup must simultaneously freeze and boil.[8]

All laboratory simulation experiments require painstaking *design* and care on the part of the researchers to produce measurable quantities of either amino acids or nucleotide bases. Moreover, the yields are always small. Little progress has been made toward finding the right mixtures. Yet the mere fact that laboratory experiments generated *any* preorganic compounds has been enough for most origin-of-life researchers to conclude that a source for life's naturalistic origin is established.[9]

Prebiotics from space debris. Contributing to this optimism was the discovery of various simple preorganic compounds, including a few amino acids, in carbonaceous chondrites (a subclass of meteorites). But only the Murchison meteorite contained any of the nucleotide bases— guanine, adenine, and uracil—and then only at very low abundances. Cytosine has not yet been detected.

This optimism has been squelched somewhat by ongoing analysis of these meteorites. The soluble organic compounds found in them, especially the amino acids, proved much less abundant than in the lab experiments.[10]

The Murchison meteorite, the one with the highest amino acid abundance, contained less than fifteen parts per million of the amino acids found in proteins.[11] And the simplest of these, glycine, made up 40 percent of the total.

The Tagish Lake meteorite, a carbonaceous chondrite recovered and analyzed just one week after its fall on a frozen lake in Canada (therefore, the meteorite least likely to have been contaminated by Earth's organic material), contained from twenty times fewer (by one measurement) to a thousand times fewer (by another measurement) amino acids per unit volume than the Murchison meteorite.[12] It must be noted that meteorites can absorb airborne contaminates in as little as one week. So Earth life may have tainted even the Tagish Lake meteorite.[13] Nevertheless, the sheer quantity of meteorite impacts on Earth previous to 3.5 billion years ago prompts many origin-of-life researchers to consider meteors as a significant source of ingredients for the prebiotic soup.

Comets also contributed their contents to Earth prior to 3.5 billion years ago. In fact, the quantity of carbon and carbon compounds brought to Earth by comets is about a hundred times greater than whatever quantity might have come via meteorites.[14] No amino acids have been found in any comet, but astrochemists have discovered more than twenty carbon compounds.[15] Carbon monoxide, carbon dioxide, and water comprise about 99 percent of the total comet mass. In a few comets, hydrogen cyanide and formaldehyde constitute as much as 1 percent of the comet mass. The total combined abundance of the other fifteen carbon compounds comes to less than 0.1 percent.

The discovery of hydrogen cyanide in comets has excited origin-of-life chemists. Under controlled laboratory conditions researchers are able to produce amino acids and nucleobases from hydrogen cyanide and other simple molecules. However, comets passing through Earth's atmosphere heat up. As scientist Stanley Miller pointed out, heating hydrogen cyanide to temperatures just a little above 212 °F (110 °C) hydrolyzes (chemically reacts with water) hydrogen cyanide to formate, bringing it to a chemical dead end for the production of biologically useful compounds.[16]

By far the greatest quantity of extraterrestrial carbon material delivered to Earth's kitchen came through microscopic grains of interplanetary and interstellar dust. These grains dumped more than a hundred times as much carbon material on Earth as comets did—and about 40,000 times as much as meteorites.[17]

For more than thirty years astrochemists have been studying interstellar clouds where these grains are abundant. They have yet to positively detect any amino acids in such clouds (only a tentative and disputed identification of glycine in 1994), but more than 120 carbon compounds—

including two alcohols, two aldehydes, a ketone, and even some simple carbon rings and chains—have been discovered.[18] This finding seems to indicate the possibility that amino acid formation can occur because ultraviolet radiation and cosmic rays bombarding the icy grains provide abundant opportunities for chemical processing, and as long as the grains are kept at temperatures below –420 °F (–250 °C), the chemical products can be preserved for a long time.

Recently, two different research teams attempted to simulate the physical and chemical conditions of interstellar ice grains in the laboratory. One team irradiated an ice film made from water (80 percent) plus methanol, ammonia, and hydrogen cyanide (20 percent) held at –433 °F (–258 °C). These scientists found three amino acids—glycine, alanine, and serine—in the post-irradiation residue.[19] Glycine was the most abundant at 0.5 percent concentration.

The second team irradiated an ice mixture consisting of water (30 percent) plus methanol, ammonia, carbon dioxide, and carbon monoxide (70 percent) at –438 °F (–261 °C). After irradiation, they found sixteen amino acids, of which six are biologically significant.[20] Like the first team, they discovered that glycine was by far the most abundant amino acid produced.

Three new findings, however, have neutralized the excitement these experiments raised over the possibility of amino acid production. Five astronomers from the Leiden Observatory, NASA Ames Research Center, and the SETI Institute performed laboratory tests of amino acid stability under ultraviolet photolysis (light strong enough to induce a chemical reaction).[21] They determined that "amino acids are highly susceptible to UV photodestruction even under exposure to UV photons of relatively low energy."[22] Given that strong ultraviolet radiation permeates both interstellar and interplanetary space, they concluded that amino acids could not survive in icy grains or on the surface layers of asteroids, comets, and meteorites. In their words, "amino acids have not been detected [in interstellar and interplanetary grains] because they are destroyed before they can accumulate in the gas phase."[23]

A second study by Curt Mileikowsky and his colleagues confirms the destruction of amino acids and other possible organics in interstellar and interplanetary grains.[24] This team determined that galactic cosmic radiation penetrates up to about thirty-nine inches of solid material in meteorites and comets, destroying all organics in the process. Therefore, any amino acids or other building blocks of life that may form in interstellar or interplanetary grains or in molecular clouds would promptly be destroyed.

In a third study, Daniel Glavin and Jeffrey Bada of the Scripps Institute showed that if amino acids were somehow contained in interstellar or interplanetary grains, the heat of atmospheric entry would destroy them.[25] For all possible early-Earth atmospheres, such grains would be heated to at least 1,020 °F—a temperature high enough, according to Glavin and Bada's experiments, to incinerate all amino acids (with the possible exception of glycine).

The quality of the carbon compounds arriving on Earth relative to life chemistry varies considerably among the three sources (dust, comets, and meteorites). But, what do their quantities reveal?

From an Out-of-This-World Pantry

In 1992 Christopher Chyba and Carl Sagan attempted to estimate the total delivery to Earth of carbon compounds over the period from 4.4 to 3.0 billion years ago. They noted an exponential decrease from about a million tons per year to about 4,000 tons per year during that period.[26] Narrowing the focus from carbon compounds to amino acids from credible sources (comets and meteorites), delivery estimates can be calculated as ranging from 2,000 tons per year (4.4 billion years ago) to one ton per year (3.0 billion years ago). Limiting delivery to *proven* sources of amino acids (meteorites), 20 tons of carbon compounds arrived annually 4.4 billion years ago and 20 pounds arrived every year at around 3.0 billion years ago.

Only a tiny percentage of these carbon compounds—a few amino acids and even fewer nucleotide bases—are biologically significant. Assuming that the quantity of significant material was as abundant as that in the most amino acid- and nucleotide-base-rich carbonaceous chondrite yet measured (the Murchison meteorite),[27] the delivery totals would have ranged from 60 tons per year to 480 pounds per year if calculated from all cosmic sources. If calculated from credible sources of amino acids and nucleobases, the total would have ranged from 240 pounds per year to 2 ounces per year. If calculated from *proven* sources of amino acids, the range would have been just 38 ounces per year to 0.019 ounces per year. At 3.8 billion years ago, when life suddenly appeared on Earth, the annual delivery rate of amino acids would have been 2,400 pounds (for all possible sources), 4 pounds (for credible sources), and 0.06 ounces (for proven sources).

Jeffrey Bada argued recently for a slight upward adjustment of these extraterrestrial delivery rates.[28] Meteorites from that ancient era would have been exposed to significantly less radiation than meteorites falling upon Earth since then.[29] Based on his figures, the quantities should be increased to 2,800 pounds, 5 pounds, and .07 ounces, respectively.

Other researchers promote adjustment of the figures in the opposite direction. They believe the various fragments of the Murchison meteorite were seriously contaminated by organic materials at the impact sites.[30] They would argue for basing calculations of extraterrestrially delivered amino acids and nucleosides on the significantly less contaminated Tagish Lake meteorite. In that case, the delivery rates at 3.8 billion years ago would be less than 140 pounds, 2 ounces, and 0.0035 ounces per year from the respective sources. However, if the larger object from which the Tagish Lake meteorite broke off was smaller than the thirty-nine-inch (one meter) cross-sectional limit for protection from galactic cosmic radiation, no amino acids or nucleobases would have survived.

From these calculations, scientists can derive a reasonable best-case scenario. Assuming half of all meteorites delivered to Earth 3.8 billion years ago were carbonaceous chondrites as rich in amino acids and nucleosides as the Murchison meteorite, and assuming that half of the carbonaceous chondrites come from a depth of thirty-nine inches (one meter) or more relative to the surface of the parent body, a little less than .02 ounces of biologically significant amino acids would have been delivered globally per year.

To put this quantity into perspective, only half a gram of biologically significant amino acids would have been sprinkled into the world's oceans each year in the era when life appeared. Even if this delivery rate were somehow accumulated without any destruction for the maximum possible time between the last great sterilization event and the first proven appearance of life (a span of about 30 million years), the concentration of amino acids in the ocean covering the whole surface of Earth would be less than a hundredth of a quadrillionth of a gram per cubic centimeter.

Carl Sagan once compared Earth's early oceans to a thin French consommé. In retrospect, his statement (unintentionally) insulted the French soup. Even the purest water on Earth today has a higher concentration of amino acids—by a factor of a hundred million—than what could possibly have been deposited from outer space into Earth's oceans before life originated.

In short, while extraterrestrial production of some prebiotic compounds does occur, the contribution of these materials to a prebiotic soup on Earth appears negligible. So does atmospheric synthesis of prebiotics.

An Empty Cupboard

More traditional scenarios for the origin of life expect atmospheric chemistry to explain the formation of prebiotic molecules. Under these scenarios, Earth's earliest atmosphere was thought to consist of reducing gases (gases rich in hydrogen, such as molecular hydrogen, methane, ammonia, and water vapor). Lab experiments demonstrate that under these conditions some prebiotic compounds may form.

Recent advances now indicate, however, that Earth's earliest atmosphere was not reducing but neutral, consisting of nitrogen, carbon dioxide, carbon monoxide, and water vapor.[31] Even in the complete absence of molecular oxygen, this atmosphere could not have sustained the production of prebiotic molecules.[32] Prebiotic molecular synthesis can occur in this type of atmosphere only if high levels of hydrogen gas are included.[33] Because molecular hydrogen escapes to outer space because of its low molecular weight, it most likely escaped early Earth's atmosphere rapidly.[34] This atmosphere simply could not have supported the chemistry needed to form prebiotic compounds. From this perspective, lab experiments are irrelevant to the origin-of-life question.

In an attempt to keep the primordial soup idea viable, Stanley Miller and collaborators recently appealed to atmospheres based on carbon monoxide as a possible matrix for the production of prebiotic materials.[35] According to this alternative scenario, carbon monoxide, not carbon dioxide, was present in the primordial atmosphere. Miller and his team maintain that this would have been the case if the early earth's crust was in a more reduced state than today and if cool temperatures prevailed on the planet's surface. These researchers also think that comets may have delivered carbon monoxide to early Earth.

Miller's team showed that laboratory gas mixtures comprised of carbon monoxide, nitrogen, and water produce organic compounds, including amino acids, when bombarded with high-energy protons (a component of cosmic rays). On the surface, this seems to indicate that if carbon monoxide was present in the primordial atmosphere, cosmic rays could stimulate the production of primordial soup ingredients.

Still, this account has questionable relevance for the production of prebiotic compounds. It is not certain that carbon monoxide was ever present in the primitive atmosphere. Even if carbon monoxide were introduced through cometary delivery or through the outgassing of the crust, it would have limited residence time in the atmosphere. Carbon monoxide readily reacts with photochemical products of water to produce carbon dioxide. In other words, water vapor in Earth's atmosphere removes carbon monoxide. Also, because the carbon monoxide chemical bond is so stable, only the high-energy components of cosmic rays can break it apart—a necessary step to start the process down the chemical routes to prebiotic materials. But the flux of cosmic rays to Earth is not great enough to produce sufficient levels of prebiotic materials to keep up with their subsequent chemical decomposition in the primordial soup.

The Oxygen-Ultraviolet Paradox

Oxygen's presence, either in the atmosphere or dissolved in oceanic or subterranean water, shuts down prebiotic chemistry pathways. Even minute amounts of oxygen will prevent prebiotic chemistry.[36]

Recent work indicates low but significant levels of molecular oxygen on early Earth. Romanian physicist Ivan Draganic points out that between 3 and 4 billion years ago the intensity of radiation from radioactive decay of uranium, thorium, and potassium-40 must have been much greater than today's.[37] This radiation, when passing through pockets of water on Earth, converts water into molecular oxygen and reactive oxygen species such as hydrogen peroxide and the short-lived superoxide and hydroxyl free radicals. These compounds are highly reactive and destroy organic molecules. The presence of radiation means a continual production of oxygen and reactive-oxygen species occurred in any body or layer of Earth's water. Some of that oxygen remained dissolved in the water. The rest escaped to accumulate in the atmosphere. Continuous oxygen production means Earth's kitchen never cooked a prebiotic soup to life. Other work, utilizing sulfur isotope composition of sulfide deposits included in ancient diamonds, indicates that only limited oxygen existed on early Earth.[38] The sulfur isotope could only occur if the early atmosphere consisted of low oxygen levels and experienced chemically destructive wavelengths of ultraviolet radiation.

Ironically, oxygen's absence would also have turned off prebiotic chemistry. Without oxygen in Earth's atmosphere, there would be no ozone layer, and ultraviolet radiation from the Sun, bright stars, and supernova eruptions would have penetrated to Earth's surface and through the upper ocean and lake layers. Such intense ultraviolet radiation breaks apart the chemical bonds of prebiotic molecules. Therefore, either way, in the presence of oxygen or in the absence of oxygen, the soup is ruined because prebiotic molecule formation is stymied.

Even though carbon monoxide atmospheres can generate prebiotic compounds under plausible early Earth conditions, the yields would have been too low to be meaningful because of the stability of the carbon-oxygen bond and the requirement of highly specific atmospheric conditions and compositions. Miller and his coworkers eloquently demonstrated the conditions necessary for carbon monoxide to play a role in the generation of prebiotic materials, yet failed to show that these conditions would be relevant to early Earth.

A Possible Supplier?

With the atmospheric chemistry of early Earth unable to support prebiotic molecule production, some origin-of-life investigators suggest a couple of other geological mechanisms that perhaps could have produced the building blocks of life. Might prebiotic molecules have been spewed forth from volcanoes or from underwater vents?

Volcanoes. Some researchers have suggested that volatile compounds released from Earth's mantle through volcanic emissions provided the reducing gas mixtures needed to form prebiotic compounds.[39] It's true that, today, the earth's crust exists in an oxidized state. As a result, gas exhalations from volcanoes consist primarily of water, carbon dioxide, and sulfur dioxide. This oxidizing gas mixture cannot support prebiotic molecule synthesis. But was that the case when life appeared?

Using chromium minerals as markers, studies of ancient volcanic materials indicate that volatiles released from Earth's mantle 3.6 billion years ago were identical to today's volcanic emissions—oxidizing, not reducing.[40] It seems likely that such emissions were the same as those released 3.8 billion years ago and earlier.

Underwater vents. Deep-sea hydrothermal vents are popularly considered the possible sites for prebiotic molecule synthesis and life's origins. These vents are the only places on Earth with the necessary hydrogen-rich and (supposedly) oxygen-free chemical environments to facilitate the production of amino acid and/or nucleotide molecules (the building blocks of proteins, DNA, and RNA). Laboratory experiments simulating a hot, chemically harsh environment modeled after deep-sea hydrothermal vents indicate that amino acids, peptides, and other biomoleculars can form under such conditions.[41]

However, a team led by Stanley Miller has found that at 660 °F (350 °C), a temperature that the vents can and do reach, the amino acid half-life in a water environment is only a few minutes. (In other words, half the amino acids break down in just a few minutes.) At 480 °F (250 °C) the half-life of sugars measures in seconds. For a nucleobase to function as a building block for DNA or RNA it must be joined to a sugar. For polypeptides (chains of amino acids linked together by peptide bonds but with much lower molecular weight than proteins) the half-life is anywhere from a few minutes to a few hours. RNA molecules themselves hydrolyze (render themselves useless) within minutes at 480 °F (250 °C) and within just seconds at 662 °F (350 °C). These results led Miller and his team to conclude that the same vent conditions that can produce amino acids and/or nucleotides also destroy them.[42] In other words, molecular decomposition outstrips composition at hydrothermal vents, making vents more damaging than helpful.

It is possible that some biomolecules could survive after production in deep-sea hydrothermal vents. A fraction of biomolecules produced in superheated water would make their way to cold water only a few seconds after leaving the hydrothermal vent's chimney. It remains unclear at this time if the amount of prebiotics formed could achieve levels significant for naturalistic origin-of-life scenarios.

Researchers at Penn State and SUNY Stony Brook identified another problem with prebiotic formation at deep-sea hydrothermal vents: ammonia production.[43] For prebiotic molecules to be synthesized at deep-sea hydrothermal vents, ammonia must be present. Ammonia serves as a key starting material in the synthesis of amino acids and other biologically important nitrogen-containing compounds. However, researchers recognize that ammonia did not exist at appreciable levels on early Earth. For prebiotic synthesis to occur, ammonia must form at the hydrothermal vents. In principle, ammonia could form there from nitrogen via a route that involves hydrogen sulfide or another route involving iron(2) sulfide. Laboratory experiments, however, show that the hydrogen-sulfide-mediated route yields too low a level of ammonia to sustain prebiotic compound formation, and the iron(2) sulfide reaction occurs too slowly.

Deep-sea hydrothermal vents not only make poor candidates for life molecule synthesis but also serve to frustrate prebiotic synthesis anywhere in their vicinity. In fact, they eliminate that possibility anywhere in Earth's oceans. As Miller's team pointed out, the current density of hydrothermal vents is such that all the water in the oceans is destined to circulate through the vents over the course of 10 million years. When life originated on Earth 3.8 billion years ago, the density of hydrothermal vents would have been much higher than at present, reducing the circulation time to much less than 10 million years. Any possible success in the assembly of life molecules anywhere in Earth's oceans would have been largely lost as those molecules passed through the vents.

Deep-sea vents, then, just like volcanoes, Earth's early atmosphere, and other suggested sources, appear inadequate to produce the hypothetical prebiotic soup. Of even greater significance is the fact that now scientists have direct ways of testing whether the prebiotic soup existed at all.

Direct Evidence
Geochemists have developed two powerful tools for measuring the quantity of prebiotics on ancient Earth. One uses carbon. The other uses nitrogen. Both lead to the same conclusion.

Carbon ratio. Carbonaceous substances (the decay products of once-living organisms) manifest a distinctly lower ratio of carbon-13 to carbon-12 than do the same carbonaceous substances that chemically developed from inorganic compounds. Therefore, careful measurements of the carbon-13 to carbon-12 ratio in ancient deposits yield the quantity of prebiotics present on ancient Earth.

The surprising result of carbon-13 to carbon-12 ratio measurements of carbonaceous deposits is that all such deposits formed from the remains of once-living organisms. None of the deposits formed from prebiotic material.[44] The researchers who made some of the most extensive carbon-13 to carbon-12 ratio measurements concluded, "No known abiotic process can explain the data."[45]

With this accumulation of data, the primordial-soup hypothesis evaporates. Given the measurable abundance of life on Earth 3.8 billion ago, a primordial soup—if it existed—would be geochemically obvious. Origin-of-life researcher Hubert Yockey points out, "The significance of the isotopic enhancement of 12c [carbon-12] in the very old kerogen in the Isua rocks in Greenland is that there never was a primordial soup and that, nevertheless, living matter must have existed abundantly on Earth before 3.8 billion years ago."[46]

Nitrogen ratio. A second geochemical tool, nitrogen isotope ratios, now provides independent confirmation that no primordial soup ever existed on (or in) Earth. The first of these confirmations comes from nitrogen-15 to nitrogen-14 ratio analysis. The same ancient carbonaceous filamentous microstructures in which researchers read the carbon-13 to carbon-12 ratio signature for postbiotic decay (as opposed to prebiotic origin) also reveal a nitrogen-15 to nitrogen-14 ratio indicative of a biogenic origin.[47]

Another confirmation arises from calculations of ammonia abundances. For any kind of primordial soup or mineral substrate to yield a chemical pathway for the development of complex life molecules, significant quantities of ammonia must be present. Laboratory simulation experiments, lacking significant quantities of ammonia, consistently fail to produce any amino acids. Several studies of the nitrogen-15 to nitrogen-14 ratio in ancient kerogens (carbonaceous deposits) show that while there may have been some ammonia in Earth's atmosphere at the time of life's origins 3.8 to 3.5 billion years ago, the quantities would have been inadequate to sustain the prebiotic chemical pathways necessary for life's spontaneous origin.[48]

The answer is in: There was no prebiotic soup on the menu billions of years ago when life began.

Putting the RTB Model to the Test

This "fact of life"—the absence of a prebiotic soup and the building blocks of life—makes no difference to the RTB origin-of-life model. The Creator God of the Bible could have manufactured life with or without a primordial soup.

Evaluating the Evidence

The existence of some kind of primordial soup is foundational for all naturalistic models for life's origin on Earth. Indeed, the hypothesis of a primordial soup arises from the assumption that life originated by a naturalistic means. With the evidence that no prebiotic soup ever existed on Earth and the evidence that life appeared on Earth early and quickly, naturalists have turned their attention to outer space (see chapters 14-16).

Research over the past fifty years has failed to produce a viable explanation for self-assembly of prebiotic compounds on or in Earth. Putting that problem aside and assuming somehow that prebiotic starting material existed, could this material assemble into complex biomolecules? The next three chapters address this question.

Part III

From the
Bottom Up
and
Top Down

CHAPTER 8

THE SEARCH FOR
CHEMICAL PATHWAYS

I n most university chemistry labs, graduate students clad in long, white lab coats stand before a maze of tubing and glassware, working diligently. They check and recheck the apparatus, making slight adjustments each time something comes to mind that might ensure the desired results. Curiosity motivates this difficult and often tedious work, along with a hope for the moment when they will achieve an important breakthrough—a discovery that might even result in worldwide recognition.

That dramatic moment arrived for twenty-three-year-old Stanley Miller in 1953. While he was performing his now legendary spark-discharge experiments, a small quantity of amino acids appeared in the glass apparatus. Miller's notable place in the scientific community was secured. Articles detailing his findings appeared in the *New York Times* and the *New York Herald Tribune. Life, Newsweek,* and *Time* also featured his work.[1]

Miller's discovery propelled him to fame. A possible prebiotic source for amino acids intrigued people everywhere. Nearly twenty years after its initial presentation, the Oparin-Haldane hypothesis appeared to be confirmed.

Even today, the discovery of a new chemical route to a crucial life molecule receives widespread media attention and draws public interest because it satisfies an important requirement for evolution. In the naturalistic approach to the origin of life, a bewildering series of chemical reactions must transform relatively simple gas molecules into a complex chemical blend (the so-called prebiotic soup). Then, within the soup, reactions among the building-block molecules of life must occur in a stepwise fashion to form increasingly complex biomolecules. This process, according to the models, leads to the production of metabolism, self-replicators, and complex information-rich molecules that form the cell's structures and carry out its processes. Therefore, the

---

Stanley Miller's Discovery

In his famous experiment (conducted under the auspices of his adviser, Nobel laureate Harold Urey), Stanley Miller circulated methane, ammonia, hydrogen gas, and water through a glass apparatus in which electric discharges were provided by a Tesla coil. After running the experiment for one week, a thick chemical layer built up on the water's surface. Miller stopped the spark discharges and tested for the existence of amino acids. Finding none, he rearranged his glass apparatus and tried again. This time he found significant quantities of the two simplest amino acids, glycine (2.1 percent) and alanine (1.7 percent). No significant quantities of other amino acids were found. Twenty years later, Miller was surprised to find that the second run of his 1953 experiment still held the record for the highest yield of amino acids in any prebiotic laboratory experiment.[2]

---

world anticipates the attempts made to identify and explain plausible chemical reactions for each step of this complex and arduous pathway.

This bottom-up endeavor to solve the mystery of life's start has met with some success. Chemical reactions that could have produced a portion of the necessary makings for a prebiotic soup have been defined. Scientists have also identified reasonable chemical processes that could have yielded the cell's metabolic systems and information-rich self-replicators.[3] This fulfills naturalistic predictions 1 (chemical pathways produced life's building blocks) and 2 (chemical pathways yielded complex biomolecules).

However, merely to identify chemical routes that can lead to life's molecules is not enough. These pathways must also meet prediction 3 and have the capability to operate efficiently under the conditions of early Earth.

The thrill of researchers' success in identifying plausible synthetic routes to the ingredients of the prebiotic soup must be tempered by the growing recognition that early Earth's conditions would have thwarted prebiotic compound production. As discussed in the previous chapter, the composition of Earth's primitive atmosphere could not have accommodated the production of prebiotic molecules, and the harsh conditions of hydrothermal vents would have destroyed any prebiotic compounds produced at those locations. The absence of residues from a prebiotic soup in Earth's oldest rocks and the lack of a solution to the oxygen/ultraviolet paradox independently support this conclusion. Many, if not all, the chemical pathways discovered that could conceivably form prebiotic compounds, and hence the prebiotic soup, must be considered irrelevant, given the current data on early Earth's environment.

Satisfaction Guaranteed

The recognition that Earth's conditions are important dictators of chemistry leads to a set of straightforward, unyielding principles—a type of chemical logic that establishes the requirements for life's emergence from simple chemical compounds through natural means. In addition to identifying reactions that can produce key prebiotic components, the following criteria must be met:

- Starting materials for chemical reactions must be present on early Earth.
- Starting materials must occur at the right concentrations.
- Energy sources and/or catalysts must be present to drive prebiotic reactions.
- Chemical products formed by these reactions must remain stable and sufficiently concentrated long enough for subsequent chemical steps to be effected.
- Chemical interference by other prebiotic compounds must not occur.

Flawed Reasoning

Even a cursory survey of the scientific literature over the last fifty years makes it clear that bottom-up work on the origin-of-life question largely ignores these chemical principles.[4] Researchers conduct laboratory prebiotic experiments under carefully controlled, pristine conditions designed to maximize the success of the experiment rather than evaluate the likelihood that a chemical process could operate on early Earth. They carefully control the temperature, the pH, and the concentrations and ratio of reactants. They also select energy sources and conditions that promote prebiotic reactions but avoid destruction of chemical products once they form. These are unrealistic conditions for primordial Earth.

In laboratory research, prebiotic reactions are stopped before chemical breakdown occurs. Chemists are well aware that once a synthesis is completed, the products must be removed from the reaction in time or they will be destroyed. Researchers often exclude materials from prebiotic simulations that were present on early Earth, materials that would disrupt the reactions taking place in the lab. By making sure everything works in their favor, these investigators have achieved a pseudo-success.

Three significant examples of unrealistic results—laboratory production of cytosine, ribose, and high-energy phosphate—illustrate how the proposed prebiotic reactions on early Earth fail to meet important chemical requirements.[5]

Cytosine. One of the molecular components of nucleic acids (DNA and RNA), cytosine assumes an important place in both RNA-world and pre-RNA-world origin-of-life models (this posits that RNA or some RNA precursor chemically evolved before proteins and DNA). Cytosine, a pyrimidine, is a six-membered ring composed of four carbon atoms and two nitrogen atoms. Along with other ring compounds, such as adenine, guanine, thymine, and uracil, cytosine repeatedly extends from the chain-like backbone of DNA and RNA. The nitrogen-containing rings sequenced along DNA or RNA provide the chemical information that determines biochemical function.

Chemists have discovered two possible pathways that produce cytosine. One route involves a reaction between cyanoacetylene and cyanate, and the other reaction begins with cyanoacetaldehyde and urea.[6] These four compounds represent essential ingredients of early Earth's supposed prebiotic soup.

Chemist Robert Shapiro demonstrated, however, that the two chemical routes lack any relevance.[7] He points out the unlikelihood that cyanoacetylene, cyanate, cyanoacetaldehyde, and urea existed at sufficient levels on primordial Earth to effect the production of cytosine. Even if they had occurred at appropriate levels, interfering chemical reactions would have quickly consumed these compounds before cytosine could form. Cyanoacetylene rapidly reacts with ammonia, amines, thiols, and hydrogen cyanide. Cyanate undergoes rapid reaction with water. In the presence of water, cyanoacetaldehyde decomposes into acetonitrile and formate. When cytosine does form, it rapidly decomposes. At room temperature and with a neutral pH, cytosine breaks down, losing half its molecules in 340 years. At 32 °F (0 °C), its half-life is 17,000 years—still too short a time for cytosine to be part of the supposed first self-replicator.[8]

To date, scientists have failed to produce cytosine in a spark-discharge experiment, nor has cytosine been recovered from meteorites or extraterrestrial sources.[9] Because meteorites (and other extraterrestrial materials) serve as a proxy for early Earth's chemistry, the absence of cytosine in these sources would seem to affirm Shapiro's conclusion.

Shapiro also critically analyzed prebiotic simulation experiments that produced the DNA and RNA component adenine.[10] As with cytosine, he showed that adenine formation on early Earth (by currently recognized prebiotic routes) could not reasonably have occurred, for many of the same reasons.

Recent work by James Cleaves and Stanley Miller uncovers an additional problem.[11] Nucleobases readily react with formaldehyde and acetaldehyde, compounds most certainly present on early Earth, to form both small molecule derivatives and large intractable molecules.

Even under mild conditions, these reactions take place so rapidly that they would preferentially occur at the expense of reactions that could lead to RNA. Thus, if nucleobases could form, competing reactions would likely consume them.

Ribose. The five-carbon sugar ribose, like cytosine, is an important component of RNA. (The closely related sugar deoxyribose takes ribose's place in DNA structure.) Ribose repeatedly alternates with phosphate to form RNA's backbone. This sugar also serves as the attachment point for cytosine, uracil, guanine, and adenine. Ribose production on early Earth stands as a central requirement for all origin-of-life scenarios that pass through an RNA world.

The only known plausible prebiotic route to ribose (and all sugars) is the Butlerow reaction (also known as the formose reaction).[12] This reaction begins with the one-carbon compound formaldehyde, which readily forms in spark-discharge experiments. In the presence of an inorganic catalyst (calcium hydroxide, calcium oxide, alumina clays, and so on), formaldehyde reacts with itself and resultant products to generate sugars containing two, three, four, five, six, or more carbon atoms.

Though this route to ribose and other sugars exists, most researchers question its applicability to the origin-of-life scenario.[13] Numerous side reactions dominate formose chemistry. As a consequence, this reaction yields over forty different sugar species with ribose as a minor component. If this reaction did operate on early Earth, it could never have yielded enough ribose to support an RNA world. This reaction's lack of chemical selectivity would have frustrated the RNA world. Laboratory formose reactions are free of contaminants that would likely be present on early Earth. Ammonia, amines, and amino acids, for example, react with formaldehyde and the products of the formose reaction.[14] These side reactions would have consumed key reactants and frustrated the formation of ribose and other sugars.

As with cytosine, decomposition negatively affects ribose formation. Sugars decompose under alkaline and acidic conditions and are susceptible to oxidation. Even within a neutral pH range, sugars decompose.[15] At 212 °F (100 °C), under neutral conditions, ribose's half-life is seventy-three minutes. At 32 °F (0 °C), ribose has a half-life of forty-four years. Deoxyribose, the sugar component of DNA, likewise possesses limited stability even under neutral conditions.

The instability of sugars is reflected by their virtual absence in meteorites. Despite media fanfare to the contrary, the only sugar to be recovered from a meteorite is dihydroxyacetone (a three-carbon sugar), and this compound was found in extremely low abundance.[16] The other compounds discovered in meteorites (sugar alcohols and sugar acids) are structurally distinct from sugars and irrelevant to the origin of life.

High-energy phosphate compounds. Phosphate groups assume an integral role in the linkages that form the backbone of DNA and RNA. They also comprise the head-group region of key cell membrane components (phospholipids).

In addition to their structural importance, phosphates also serve a critical role in the cell's metabolic processes. Phosphate chains, called polyphosphates, form a relatively unstable high-energy chemical structure in which the cell's metabolic systems store energy. The breakage of these high-energy phosphate bonds releases energy used by the cell to power its operation. All organisms continuously produce and consume massive amounts of ATP (adenosine triphosphate) and similar compounds in which polyphosphate groups are constituents. Many researchers speculate that more primitive prebiotic polyphosphate compounds played a similar role to ATP during the origin-of-life process and later evolved into ATP. Because high-energy compounds that could transfer phosphate groups to the RNA and DNA backbones were essential to the RNA and DNA-protein world scenarios, a phosphate source must have been present on early Earth.

Researchers propose several possible prebiotic chemical routes to polyphosphates.[17] The most common include (1) the heating of apatite (a phosphate-containing mineral); (2) the high-temperature heating (from 392 to 1,112 °F, 200 to 600 °C) of dihydrogen phosphates; and (3) the phosphates' reaction with high-energy organic compounds.

Although several plausible routes to polyphosphates exist, researchers wonder if these chemical pathways have any relevance to early Earth.[18] For example, to produce polyphosphates from apatite and dihydrogen phosphate, water must be completely driven from the system—an impossibility for phosphate minerals confined to rocks. Furthermore, the high temperatures needed to form polyphosphates would in turn destroy any organic material.

The suggested production of polyphosphates from high-energy chemicals (allegedly formed in spark-discharge reactions on early Earth) lacks chemical robustness. These reactions require unrealistically high levels of starting materials and produce low yields. Laboratory spark-discharge experiments performed under a wide range of chemical conditions failed to yield polyphosphates when phosphates were included in the reaction vessel.

Even if a means existed on primordial Earth to form polyphosphates, their availability for prebiotic reactions is unlikely because calcium ions drive polyphosphates to precipitate out of solutions. These ions would have been everywhere on early Earth.[19] Given the extreme rarity (or nonexistence) of polyphosphate minerals on Earth today, the conclusion that prebiotic polyphosphate synthesis could not have taken place on early Earth seems justifiable.

Studies on possible prebiotic production of cytosine, ribose, and polyphosphates demonstrate that even though researchers have identified chemical pathways to them, the lack of available starting materials, plus chemical interference by other environmental materials and rapid decomposition, would have precluded formation. In other words, viable chemical routes to these key life molecules have not been found.

The origin-of-life community widely acknowledges the prebiotic production of ribose, cytosine, and polyphosphates as painfully problematic. In fact, at the opening plenary lecture of ISSOL 2002, after summarizing these and other problems, distinguished origin-of-life researcher Leslie Orgel stated, "It would be a miracle if a strand of RNA ever appeared on the primitive Earth."[20] As a preface to this conclusion, Orgel remarked that he "hoped no creationists [were] in the audience." Laughter erupted throughout the room.

Orgel did not advocate a supernatural explanation for life's origin. Rather, he acknowledged the intractable problem of accounting for its emergence through natural processes. However, the problems are not limited to the prebiotic production of chemical compounds. Critical analysis of any proposed prebiotic route exposes similar problems.

For the sake of argument, however, one might ask, "What if these molecules were freely available? Can unattended chemical events account for the emergence of the cell's metabolic systems and the origin of self-replicating molecules?"

First to Function

Considerable efforts have gone into developing both a metabolism-first model and a replicator-first model. And while both approaches have shown some promise, both have also run into some major obstacles.

Metabolism first? Some origin-of-life researchers postulate that once prebiotic materials formed, these relatively small molecules self-organized to form chemical cycles and networks of reactions that, with time, gave rise to life's metabolic systems. Once encapsulated or sequestered, these complex weblike systems served as the first protocells.[21] According to this view, molecular self-replicators emerged later along with enzymes that catalyzed each step in the chemical cycles and networks. Some proponents of metabolism-first scenarios maintain that these cycles and networks closely resembled the metabolic pathways found in the cell today. Metabolism-first adherents suggest that either (1) individual chemical species involved in these cycles and networks could have catalyzed these same reactions—a type of autocatalysis; or (2) mineral surfaces catalyzed the protometabolic pathways.

Though at first glance seemingly plausible, metabolism-first models have only superficial merit because they appeal to unrealistic chemistry. Orgel has specifically identified a number of problems.[22] He points out that cycles and networks operating on early Earth would have been highly susceptible to disruption by chemical interferents and competing side reactions. Without enzymes, protometabolic reactions cannot proceed rapidly enough to sustain a protocell unless aided by some sort of chemical accelerant.[23] Mineral surfaces are the only reasonable candidates for service as prebiotic catalysts. While mineral surfaces can catalyze specific reactions, to propose that a mineral will catalyze the range of chemical reactions required for cycles or chemical networks to operate is simply unrealistic. An attempt to increase the catalytic range by invoking the availability of many different types of mineral surfaces only creates an additional problem—the need to efficiently transport "metabolites" from mineral site to mineral site. These parameters question how a chemical cycle could be maintained and evolve into a protocell's metabolic system. In Orgel's words, metabolism-first scenarios require an "appeal to magic," a "series of remarkable coincidences," or a "near miracle."[24]

Investigators Antonio Lazcano and Stanley L. Miller identify another problem with the metabolism-first scenarios, particularly for those models asserting that protometabolic systems resemble the contemporary metabolism found in cells.[25] They point out that postulated prebiotic routes for key biomolecules dramatically differ from the metabolic pathways that produce the same compounds.

Though some experimental support exists, a thorough chemical analysis of these models exposes fundamental flaws. Metabolism-first scenarios seem unlikely to explain the first life forms.[26]

Replicator first? Most origin-of-life researchers maintain that the first step to living entities took place when a self-replicating molecule emerged. Only later did this naked self-replicator become encapsulated within a primitive membrane. According to this view, after encapsulation, metabolism emerged as a means to support the production of the self-replicator, providing the necessary building-block molecules to sustain its activity.

Candidates for the first self-replicating molecule possess common chemical features. These relatively complex molecules are made up of smaller chemical subunits that link to form chainlike molecules. The side groups that extend from the self-replicator's backbone must be chemically and physically varied to provide the physiochemical information essential to the self-replication process. However, the self-replicator's backbone must consist of a repetitious structure.

To function as a self-replicator, a molecule needs a template to direct the assembly of subunit molecules into an identical copy of itself. Self-templating (and therefore self-replication) is possible only if the backbone's structure repeats with little if any interruption.[27] Therefore, the subunit molecules comprising the self-replicator all must consist of the same chemical class.

Chemists call these chainlike molecules with structurally repetitive backbones *homopolymers* (homo = same; poly = many; mer = units). DNA, RNA, proteins, and the proposed pre-RNA world self-replicators, such as peptide-nucleic acids, are all homopolymers and thus satisfy the chemical requirements to function as self-replicators.

Chemist Robert Shapiro has convincingly demonstrated that while undirected chemical processes can produce homopolymers under carefully controlled pristine laboratory conditions, such processes cannot generate these types of molecules under early Earth's conditions.[28] The chemical compounds found in the complex chemical mixture that researchers think existed on early Earth would interfere with homopolymer formation. Instead, polymers with highly heterogeneous backbone structures would be produced—molecular entities that cannot function as self-replicators. Shapiro has shown this interference to be the case specifically for proteins, RNA, and peptide nucleic acids. The likely chemical components of any prebiotic soup would not only interrupt the structural regularity of the self-replicator's backbone; they would also prematurely terminate its formation or introduce branch sites.

The homopolymer problem devastates the replicator-first hypothesis for the origin of life. For Shapiro, the only alternatives are the metabolism-first models—models that Leslie Orgel maintains cannot work.

While undirected natural processes cannot generate homopolymers under the conditions of primordial Earth, the biochemical processes of the cell can. The cell makes homopolymers with efficiency because of the high degree of specificity possessed by its biochemical machinery. This specificity overcomes the thermodynamic tendency of random chemical processes to produce polymers with a haphazard backbone composition.

RNA Assembly on Mineral Surfaces

In the mid-1990s, researchers Leslie Orgel and James Ferris stirred excitement within the scientific community by assembling lengthy RNA molecules from chemically activated RNA subunits (nucleotides). This assembly was accomplished by washing solutions of the reactants over mineral surfaces, then allowing the solutions to evaporate.[29] Commentators heralded this work as a key demonstration that prebiotic conditions could have produced self-replicators.[30]

Closer evaluation of this effort, however, prompts a different conclusion. As Shapiro points out, Orgel's and Ferris's teams conducted these experiments under selective conditions that excluded potential chemical interferents. The homopolymer problem was ignored.[31] To prove the point, Orgel's team demonstrated that even the incorporation of opposite-handed nucleotides (see chapter 9) disrupts RNA chain formation.[32] Orgel's team also showed that though mineral surfaces may promote RNA formation, they also catalyze its decomposition.[33] RNA breakdown occurs on surfaces of both lead-containing and calcium-containing minerals.

In addition, these workers discovered that the amino acids glutamate and histidine stimulate the breakdown of RNA in a solution. A Japanese team demonstrated that rare Earth elements (like cerium) present in the primordial oceans would have catalyzed the breakdown of the RNA backbone linkage.[34] Inhibition of this cleavage would require an unrealistically high level of proteins in the early oceans.

Other problems for mineral-assisted RNA formation include (1) the irreversible attachment of RNA to mineral surfaces once the molecular chain grows to a certain length and (2) researchers' use of "activated" monomers unlikely to occur under prebiotic conditions. Also, the clay catalysts must be carefully treated to remove all metal ions except sodium. If not, no catalytic reactions occur.[35] The bottom line is: Laboratory simulation experiments that synthesize RNA on mineral surfaces differ substantially from early Earth's conditions.[36] When scientists consider more realistic scenarios, they quickly discover that homopolymer assembly could not have occured in the prebiotic realm.

How Likely the RNA World?

Significant chemical challenges face the RNA-world scenario. Given the conditions of primordial Earth, researchers can find no chemical route to form RNA's building blocks (adenine, cytosine, ribose, polyphosphates, and so on). Even if these routes exist, experimental work and the theoretically demonstrated homopolymer problem show the assembly of RNA or other possible self-replicators unlikely.

What if, however, origin-of-life researchers were to overcome these problems? The next stage in the RNA-world scenario requires the self-replicating RNA to evolve into a full ensemble of RNA molecules with a wide range of catalytic activity that could sustain the life processes of the first protocells. For this idea to have merit, researchers must demonstrate (at a minimum) that RNA molecules inherently manifest adequate catalytic activity to support a comprehensive biochemical system.

Origin-of-life investigators have met with some success toward this end. A laboratory process called *in vitro* evolution has produced RNA enzymes (ribozymes) that can catalyze a number of different types of chemical reactions essential to the RNA world.[37] Beyond this success, however, little if any real progress has been made toward validating the RNA-world scenario. Though researchers have made ribozymes that can extend RNA chains, they have yet to make RNA with self-replicating capability.[38]

Meanwhile, the applicability of the *in vitro* evolutionary mechanism to early Earth and the putative RNA world is questionable. The process of *in vitro* evolution begins with a large pool of RNA molecules with random nucleotide sequences and hence random structures.[39] From this pool, through detailed experimental design and researcher intervention, RNA molecules with a prespecified set of chemical properties are selected. These selected RNA molecules are recovered and the number amplified by the enzyme reverse transcriptase and the polymerase chain reaction (PCR). PCR also employs an enzyme (a DNA polymerase). The new RNA sequence is then randomly altered to generate a new pool of RNA molecules, and the process is repeated over and over again until RNA molecules with the desired chemical properties emerge.

The "evolution" of RNA molecules in the laboratory is carefully orchestrated and extensively manipulated. Its success hinges on thoughtful experiment design, to the extent that the enzymes (protein molecules with a complex, fine-tuned structure), reverse transcriptase, and DNA polymerase—molecules that would never exist in an RNA-world scenario—must be present. It stretches the bounds of credulity to think that this process, or one like it, could ever have occurred naturalistically on early Earth. Origin-of-life researchers have fallen short of demonstrating RNA's ability to evolve.

Some origin-of-life workers have proposed that proteins (peptides) were the first self-replicators. This idea, which fell by the wayside with the advent of the RNA-world scenario, reemerged with some vigor in the late 1990s. Scientists have developed systems of short protein fragments (peptides) that self-replicate.[40] However, as with the case of the *in vitro* evolution of ribozymes, extensive preplanning, experimenter intervention, and careful fine-tuning of the peptide's structure all contribute to creation of a self-replicating system. In the words of Leslie Orgel, "It is instructive to notice how much synthetic skill is needed to develop even the simplest cycles."[41] Orgel's comment, with reference to nucleic acid systems, applies just as aptly to peptide replicators.

Putting the RTB Model to the Test

The biblical creation model does not preclude the existence of chemical routes that can spontaneously generate biologically interesting compounds. Nor does a Creator require these chemical pathways to bring life into existence. Such pathways to prebiotic materials on early Earth have no substantial bearing on RTB's origin-of-life model and are readily accommodated by it.

Evaluating the Evidence

Naturalistic origin-of-life scenarios make two key predictions based on chemical routes (see page 58):

- *Prediction #2* asserts that chemical pathways yielded complex biomolecules, self-replicators, and metabolic systems, and
- *Prediction #3* expects that those pathways operated efficiently under the conditions of primordial Earth.

Do the scientific findings bear out their speculations?

Researchers have achieved some success with respect to the first prediction. They have discovered several chemical routes capable of yielding life-essential molecules. Still, prelife pathways to other crucially important biochemical compounds have yet to be discovered and the real possibility remains that these undiscovered prebiotic pathways do not exist.

More problematic, however, is the failure of naturalistic models to fulfill the second prediction. The conditions of earlier Earth were incompatible with many key prebiotic routes advocated by the origin-of-life community. Important starting materials were either absent from early Earth or occurred at unproductive levels. Researchers' laboratory experiments have met with some success under pristine and highly controlled conditions. But these stringent conditions did not exist on early Earth. And in many cases, the reaction parameters needed for producing prebiotic compounds would have destroyed these materials if they happened to form. Other physicochemical processes on early Earth would also have frustrated origin-of-life pathways.

The hypothetical primordial soup would have undoubtedly been a complex mixture comprised of numerous chemical species. Among the materials present in this soup would have been compounds that chemically interfered with most, if not all, prebiotic pathways.

Given these chemical problems, several origin-of-life researchers have concluded that the RNA world is not viable.[42] Others suggest that any replicator-first scenario is unworkable. Still other researchers conclude that the metabolism-first models are hopelessly flawed. In other words, for fundamental chemical reasons, undirected chemical processes cannot lead to life.

Still, one could rightly argue that just because the pathways to life have not yet been identified, it doesn't mean that future discoveries won't uncover them. This assertion appeals to the future, however, and therefore is illegitimate. All origin-of-life models must be evaluated based on currently available data, and as this chapter demonstrates, the data at hand strongly argues against all naturalistic scenarios. As researchers make new discoveries, it is safe to predict that they will identify novel pathways in the laboratory that lead to biologically interesting and important compounds. Based on the fastidiousness of the chemistry typically needed to produce these compounds and the growing understanding of early Earth's conditions, however, it is also safe to predict that any newly discovered pathway will fail to successfully contribute to a naturalistic origin-of-life model.

How the models fare when scrutinizing the "handedness" of molecules is a question for the following chapter.

CHAPTER 9

LOOK! ONLY ONE HAND

S ome people are right-handed—others left. This designation signifies which hand they use for writing, eating, throwing, and so forth. Life's chemical building blocks also feature a molecular "handedness." But, rather than referring to a dominant *hand*, the three-dimensional configurations chemists refer to as right- or left-handed are mirror images. This imagery can be illustrated by placing the palms of the right and left hands together. Known as chirality, this "handedness" occurs in any molecule that has four different chemical groups attached to a central carbon atom.

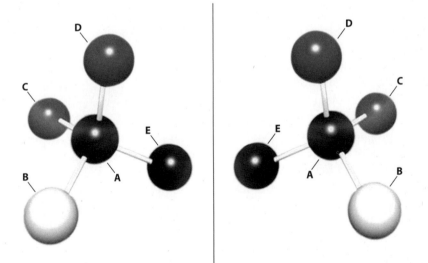

Figure 9.1: Chiral Molecules

In this example, the amino acid has two mirror-image configurations. In life molecules, the building blocks must all be of only one configuration—either all right-handed or all left-handed. (Illustration courtesy of Digital Vision)

Nineteen of the twenty biological amino acids and the two sugars (ribose and deoxyribose) that contribute to the nucleotide building blocks of RNA and DNA are chiral compounds. The amino acids in proteins have the left-handed configuration (except the simplest one, glycine, which lacks any asymmetry). The sugars in DNA and RNA all have right-handed configurations. Biochemists wonder why this homochirality (homo = same; chirality = handedness) exists. They also want to know how it developed in living systems.

Which Hand?

Nonbiological processes (labwork or nature) produce chiral molecules in equal proportion. These random mixtures, known as *racemic*, are 50 percent left-handed and 50 percent right-handed.

Laboratory experiments demonstrate that the presence of racemic mixtures of amino acids and sugars strongly inhibits the formation of amino acid and nucleotide chains.[1] For example, the synthesis of an RNA or DNA strand that consists of right-handed ribose or deoxyribose is stymied by the presence of the same sugar in the left-handed configuration (and vice versa). Also, one wrong-handed amino acid incorporated in a protein is enough to disrupt the folding of the protein, thereby blocking its capacity to function. Moreover, without homochirality, genetic material cannot copy itself.[2] Two complementary strands of DNA cannot bind with each other into the crucial double helix structure unless all the nucleotides are of the same handedness.

These requirements dictate that the origin of homochirality must precede the origin of proteins, DNA, and RNA. In other words, without pre-existing reservoirs of exclusively left-handed amino acids and exclusively right-handed sugars, the naturalistic assembly of proteins, DNA, and RNA is prohibited. (The exact reverse—reservoirs of exclusively right-handed amino acids and exclusively left-handed sugars—could also provide the building blocks for proteins, DNA, and RNA.)

Does any physical or chemical process in the context of early Earth drive a racemic mixture of amino acids or sugars into one handedness or the other? Chemically, the answer is no—unless the starting materials are enriched with one chiral form. All attempts to synthesize amino acids and sugars in laboratory simulation experiments produce racemic end products only.[3] Prebiotic synthesis of amino acids and sugars, whether on Earth or anywhere else in the universe, would be expected to produce only racemic mixtures. Therefore, hope for a natural path toward homochirality must lie in a physical mechanism.

On One Hand

To date, the only viable physical mechanism for driving racemic mixtures of amino acids and sugars into homochiral ones is an effect called magnetochiral anisotropy, which links chirality and magnetism.[4] So far, the two most probable sources of magnetochiral anisotropy are (1) photochemistry (light-induced chemistry) with circularly polarized light, and (2) parity violations in electroweak interactions (a particle physics phenomenon).

Photochemistry with circularly polarized light, if sufficiently concentrated and tuned to the appropriate wavelengths, can generate significant chirality. However, no natural circularly polarized light exists on Earth other than a tiny amount produced in the daylight sky. This amount falls far short of what would be needed to generate an excess of one configuration over its mirror image.

Parity violations in electroweak interactions have never been observed in a natural realm. This effect is only seen in particle accelerator experiments. Calculations establish that, at best, these parity violations in the context of early Earth cannot achieve an excess of one-handedness over the other any better than 10^{-17} (that is, 0.000000000000001) percent.[5] For this excess to be of any benefit, an incredibly efficient amplification mechanism would be required. No such mechanism has ever been identified or even speculated about.

Other possible Earth-based mechanisms as the source of homochirality yield even more dismal prospects. Organic chemist William Bonner offered this summation: "I spent 25 years looking for terrestrial mechanisms for homochirality and trying to investigate them and didn't find any supporting evidence. Terrestrial explanations are impotent or nonviable."[6] In a detailed review of homochirality's origin, Bonner concluded that the source must be extraterrestrial.[7]

On the Other Hand

The possibility of an astronomical mechanism believed to generate homochirality—circularly polarized ultraviolet (uv) light emanating from neutron stars and black holes—evokes enthusiasm for an extraterrestrial source. Circularly polarized uv light is the only proven means for generating significant homochirality.

However, using 100 percent circularly polarized uv light, the most successful laboratory experiments yielded only a 20 percent excess of left-handed amino acids over right-handed ones.[11] (Experiments using polarized electrons and polarized positrons [anti-electrons] yielded much more disappointing results.) However, this excess was achieved not by production but by destruction. The uv light destroyed a large fraction of the

---

Mineral Surfaces: A Source of Homochirality?

Some origin-of-life investigators suggest that mineral surfaces can generate homochirality.[8] This idea (gaining in popularity) maintains that mineral surfaces with specific spatial orientations selectively adsorbed either left-handed or right-handed amino acids and this prompted the emergence of homochirality. The chief problem with this concept, however, is that only limited chiral enrichment (about 10 percent or less) occurs on such surfaces.[9] Furthermore, opposite-handed crystal surfaces would occur with equal frequency in nature, so chiral buildup could take place only in microscopically local environments, not everywhere on Earth. These two factors prohibit the natural development of homochiral reservoirs of amino acids or sugars.[10]

---

amino acids, and depending on the direction of the rotation of the circular polarization, one configuration of the molecules suffered significantly more destruction than the other. Therefore, what remained was an excess of one particular handedness.

A recent Japanese study calls into question whether polarized light can produce more of one configuration than another anywhere near the 20 percent level.[12] Noting that the best astronomical source of circular polarized light is the synchrotron radiation emitted by neutron stars, the Japanese team used a cyclotron to simulate such radiation. They shined this radiation on samples of amino acids but could produce an excess of only 1.12 percent left-handed compared to right-handed molecules.

In reality, neutron stars do not deliver 100 percent circularly polarized light. Only a small percentage emit more than 40 percent.[13] For example, the Crab Nebula—the best-known supernova remnant and a prolific producer of ultraviolet light—emits none.[14] (All pulsars are neutron stars.) All neutron stars exhibit large fluctuations in both the degree and the intensity of their circularly polarized light.[15] These fluctuations either destroy whatever homochiral amino acids are produced, or they generate an insufficient chiral excess.

In addition to ultraviolet light, neutron stars emit copious quantities of x-rays and gamma rays. A molecular cloud close enough to a neutron star to receive adequate ultraviolet radiation to drive even a little homochirality also receives enough x- and gamma-ray radiation to destroy any resident amino acids.

At the Anglo-Australian Observatory, astronomers measured circular polarization at infrared wavelengths as high as 17 percent in small reflection nebulae near the center of the Orion Nebula complex.[16] They deduced that the circular polarization occurred when magnetically aligned nonspherical dust grains in the reflection nebulae scattered the light from a bright infrared source. However, circularly polarized infrared radiation does not pack the energy needed to destroy amino acids and therefore cannot generate a chiral excess. A more destructive radiation source is required.

The same team of astronomers also speculated that the mechanism responsible for producing the infrared circularly polarized light might also produce circularly polarized ultraviolet light at the same level of polarization, though probably limited to a smaller region. Unfortunately, astronomers cannot confirm the presence of this ultraviolet radiation because the huge quantity of dust in the Orion Nebula obscures such radiation from view. No neutron stars currently exist in the Orion Nebula. The only conceivable source of the necessary ultraviolet radiation would be super-giant stars near the nebula's core. However, the intense radiation and strong stellar winds from these super giants would prove deadly to both amino acids and to any sites where they could come together to form life-essential proteins. Putting enough dust between the super-giant stars and the amino acid formation site to shield the site from such catastrophes would block out much—if not all—of the needed flow of ultraviolet light.

While circularly polarized light destroys one configuration of amino acids more efficiently than it does the other, to some degree it destroys both configurations. This destruction is not trivial. In one laboratory experiment chemists irradiated the amino acid leucine enough to generate a 2 percent excess of left-handed molecules. In the process, they destroyed from 59 to 75 percent of the leucine.[17]

Too much ultraviolet radiation threatens the survival of amino acids. Moreover, one strong burst of ultraviolet radiation can decimate an entire molecular cloud of amino acids. Any momentary instability in either a super-giant star or a dust cloud would spell disaster.

Too little ultraviolet radiation also poses a problem. Too little amino acid destruction leads to no significant chiral excess. In laboratory experiments the intensity of the circularly polarized ultraviolet radiation must be carefully controlled to produce chiral excesses. This circumstance would unlikely be fulfilled in an interstellar molecular cloud and certainly the long-term stability would be even less likely.

The lack of any known amplification mechanism multiplies these difficulties. Astronomers see no process in operation, nor can they conceive of one, in which any chiral excess produced by circularly polarized ultraviolet light can be boosted from a low percentage to the high percentage biogenesis demands. At best, astrophysical mechanisms can generate chiral excesses of only a few percent. Such low excesses provide no benefit to assist in the origin of life.

Kuhn-Condon Rule

A further problem often overlooked or minimized by researchers is that only one "species" of the circularly polarized ultraviolet light—the mono-chromatic kind—generates a chiral excess. To be effective in driving chiral excess, the circularly polarized ultraviolet light must be a narrow band emitted at essentially one wavelength.

Werner Kuhn observed in 1930 and Edward Condon proved in 1937 from quantum mechanical principles that while one wavelength of circularly polarized light would preferentially destroy chiral molecules of, for instance, the left-handed configuration, a different wavelength of the same circularly polarized light would preferentially destroy molecules of the right-handed configuration.[18] Therefore, any broad band of circularly polarized radiation destroys the same number of left-handed molecules as right-handed ones. Thus, broadband circularly polarized light is totally impotent in its capacity to produce a chiral excess.

While astrophysical sources of monochromatic light do exist at radio wavelengths (namely, maser sources), none are known to exist at ultraviolet wavelengths. Both neutron stars and super-giant stars, for example, are broadband in their ultraviolet emissions.

In their search for a naturalistic explanation for the origin of homochirality, researchers must propose ad hoc radiation filters.[19] Either some kind of material is needed between the ultraviolet light source and the molecular cloud that in a stable fashion absorbs all but one wavelength, or else there must be some kind of exotic reflector that consistently scatters all but one. Astronomers have yet to observe any such adequately narrow-band filters or reflectors in operation.

The Kuhn-Condon rule similarly limits the production of homochirality on Earth. If there were any source of circularly polarized ultraviolet light on Earth (no significant source, either past or present, is known), it would require filtering. The only such filter ever proposed was a prebiotic pool on an east-facing slope exposed to scattered solar radiation that is limited to a few minutes at dawn.[20] However, as already noted, the percentage of scattered daylight that is circularly polarized is much too tiny to accomplish the task. What's more, Earth's atmosphere at the time of life's origin blocked ultraviolet light (especially at dawn).

Amino Acids from Beyond

The remaining naturalistic scenario for homochirality's origin involves the inexplicable spawning of a huge concentration of amino acids in an interstellar cloud. That cloud then somehow gets exposed to monochromatic circularly polarized ultraviolet light that is neither too weak nor too strong. Afterward, an unknown amplification mechanism boosts the excess of left-handed compared to right-handed amino acids from 20 percent (or less) up to 100 percent. The homochiral amino acids then get incorporated into comets and/or meteorites, which then fall to Earth. There, before the delivered homochiral amino acids can decay into a racemic mixture, they naturally assemble into proteins. These proteins are somehow protected from decay until they are incorporated, along with the necessary complement of naturally and simultaneously evolved RNA and DNA molecules (or their precursors), inside a naturally and simultaneously evolved cell membrane. All these steps must be in place for this scenario to work. Serious scientific objections block each of these steps, including the first.

Missing Sugars

Although production of homochiral sugars (such as ribose and deoxyribose) is critical for naturalistic origin-of-life scenarios, nearly all attention has focused on amino acids. However, scientists have yet to detect any of the biological five- and six-carbon sugars, such as ribose, deoxyribose, glucose, lactose, and fructose, in the nonbiological realm. The closest success was the discovery of extremely low levels of one three-carbon sugar in the Murchison and Murray (probably a piece of the Murchison) meteorites.[21] The absence of these homochiral sugars is as difficult for the naturalistic research to deal with as is the absence of homochiral amino acids.

Amino acids in space. So far, astronomers have failed to detect with certainty a single amino acid, nucleobase, or five- or six-carbon sugar in outer space. Searches of comets, interplanetary dust, and interstellar gas and dust clouds have all come up empty.

This null result comes not for lack of effort. Since astrochemistry launched as a formal discipline in the 1960s, hundreds of astronomers have competed to be the first to discover some exotic carbonaceous compound in outer space. From all over this galaxy and several others, over 120 different carbon compounds have been added by astronomers to their discovery bag.[22] But the real prize—an actual molecular building block for life—has eluded them.

The European Space Agency will soon launch the Rosetta spacecraft. During its intended orbit around the comet Wirtanen, Rosetta will attempt to land two probes to see if tiny amounts of amino acids might be hidden there. This mission and similar ones in the future are unlikely to overturn what astronomers already know. Amino acids, if they exist at all in space, do not exist in large concentrated quantities. Nor have chemists yet found any of the sugars critical for the construction of RNA or DNA.

Amino acids in meteorites. On September 28, 1969, a fireball exploded with loud bangs, hissing sounds, and smoke rings over the town of Murchison, Australia.[23] Over the next several weeks and months, more than 1,500 pounds (700 kilograms) of a carbonaceous chondrite were recovered from people's yards and city streets. The largest piece of this meteorite weighed only fifteen pounds (seven kilograms).

Within a few months, organic chemist Keith Kvenvolden made the first identification ever of nonterrestrial amino acids.[24] A whole suite of seventy-four different amino acids was found in the meteorite, several of which had never been seen before on Earth.[25] The most amino-acid-laden meteorite in existence, the Murchison meteorite contained sixty parts per million of amino acids. Of these, nearly fifteen parts per million were amino acids typically found in proteins.[26]

This meteorite is one of two meteorites in which some limited propensity toward homochirality in the amino acids has been detected. Biochemists John Cronin and Sandra Pizzarello found a small (from 1 to 9 percent) excess of left-handed molecules among six different amino acids.[27] The recent claim for a 33 percent excess in the left-handed con-figuration for alanine[28] resulted from inadequate instrumental resolution.[29] At issue, however, is the degree to which the Murchison fragments suffered contamination or chemical change during and after their journey through Earth's atmosphere and onto its surface. Another consideration is the degree to which the Murchison fragments fairly represent other car-bonaceous chondrites.

In light of conflicting claims about the excess of left-handed amino acids in the Murchison meteorite,[30] Kvenvolden performed a complete reanalysis using more sensitive techniques.[31] In particular, he compared the amino acid abundances near the exteriors of the samples with the abundances at the interiors. The exterior samples had higher concentrations of amino acids. He also noted that the exterior samples revealed higher excesses of left-handed amino acids. The one chiral nonprotein (an extraterrestrial amino acid named isovaline) for which he was able to accurately determine the ratio of left-handed to right-handed molecules proved to be racemic.[32] Considering how highly fractured the Murchison fragments were and their exposure to organic contaminants (by landing in a populated area), Kvenvolden issued a warning: "These results indicate that the outside of the meteorite had been exposed to significant terrestrial contamination and serve as a warning that samples of the Murchison meteorite can be affected to varying degrees by terrestrial influences."[33] In other words, the excesses of left-handed amino acids found in the Murchison meteorite may simply reflect the chiral excesses found in organic material in the vicinity of where it fell.

The one other meteorite in which an excess of left-handed amino acids has been measured is the Nakhla meteorite, which fell in the Nile River Delta in 1911. The Nakhla meteorite had amino acid abundances of only 20 to 330 parts per billion, and the most abundant extraterrestrial amino acids found in the Murchison meteorite were missing in the Nakhla fragments (less than one part per billion).[34] Its stones were buried in the delta sediment some four inches to twelve inches (10 to 30 centimeters) deep. In the words of the latest team to perform a chemical analysis on these fragments, "The distribution of amino acids in Nakhla, as well as their enantiomeric abundance [excess of left-handed amino acids], is very similar to what we found in a Nile Delta sediment core sample collected off the coast of Egypt, close to where Nakhla fell."[35]

The team concluded that bacterially derived amino acids present in sediment groundwater probably penetrated the meteorite's interior shortly after its fall. Given that the Nakhla meteorite is of Martian origin, the team also concluded that because contamination is "evidently a rapid process," the use of meteorites to assess whether organic compounds were present on Mars is "greatly compromised."[36] Likewise, meteorites are of little value in assessing the presence of organic compounds in any extraterrestrial source.

Even the most pristine of recovered meteorites, the Tagish Lake meteorite from northern Canada, is not free of contamination problems. Airborne amino acids can significantly contaminate an exposed meteorite left in freezing conditions for just one week.[37] As one origin-of-life researcher commented, "If we want any information from meteorites about the state of amino acids in outer space, we must capture a meteorite before it hits the ground."[38]

Steady Hands

The second law of thermodynamics—the law of entropy—guarantees that time and heat will drive any set of homochiral molecules into a racemic mixture (unless some direct repair work occurs, such as that in the molecular machinery inside a living cell). For example, a set of homochiral amino acids becomes completely racemic in one thousand years at 122 °F and in one million years at 32 °F under dry conditions.[39] The presence of water pushes the process much faster.[40] Local production of racemic amino acids dilutes homochiral mixtures, further shortening the time scales.

All amino acids, homochiral and racemic, are subject to destruction from too much radiation or heat. Ultraviolet, x-ray, and gamma-ray radiation decompose amino acids. So, too, does exposure to radioactivity, temperatures too high or too low, and pH levels too acidic or too alkaline. The challenge, then, for a naturalistic explanation of life's origin is to preserve not only homochirality but also the amino acids themselves in the face of entropy and environmental changes.

A further challenge is the transport problem. Preservation issues are critical because of the long travel times. If homochiral molecules are somehow manufactured in outer space, a means must be found to transport them in adequate quantities to Earth's surface before the homochiral molecules decay into a racemic mixture. No such transport mechanism is known to exist.

Look—No Hands!

The homochirality problem was a major theme at ISSOL 1999. It dominated discussion in several question-and-answer sessions. At the end of one such session, a researcher expressed the collective frustration of the nearly 300 assembled scientists. Recognizing that no naturalistic explanation for the homochirality that life's origin demands seems possible, he came to the microphone and asked, "Why do we need homochirality for life? Could not life originate without homochirality?"[41]

No one answered. No one doubts that homochirality is a precondition for life's origin. Nevertheless, the intractable nature of this problem has moved a few to consider the unthinkable alternatives.

Since that time, a few researchers have begun to entertain the possibility of a nonchiral origin of life. Such a hypothesis requires the introduction of additional steps to the origin-of-life scenario and an additional suite of new molecules with the capacity to store and transmit information and carry out enzymatic activities. These nonchiral molecules must evolve naturally from simple carbon compounds. Later, they must naturally evolve into chiral molecules without leaving any trace of their nonchiral origin.[42]

This nonchiral proposal for life's origin makes an extremely complex problem all the more complicated. Greater complication, and especially all the extra assembly steps, means more time and more resources. As noted in chapter 6, this additional time does not exist. And as noted in chapter 7, the additional resources do not exist.

The Peptide-Nucleic Acid Proposal

Several years ago, Stanley Miller (of spark-experiment fame) formally acknowledged the intractability of the problem of homochirality's origin. Consequently, he proposed that the first self-replicating molecules were the achiral peptide nucleic acids (PNA).[43] He was attracted to PNA molecules because they contain no sugars or phosphates and because they can form base pairs and helical structures just as DNA can.

The nucleobases of PNA are joined together through a molecule of acetic acid and a non-naturally occurring achiral amino acid, 2-aminoethyl glycine (AEG). For a PNA origin-of-life option to be viable, an abundant pre-life source of nucleobases, acetic acid, and AEG must be found. So far, a source has been identified only for the simplest of these molecules (acetic acid). AEG has not been detected in outer space sites or in the nonorganic terrestrial realm.

Stanley Miller's team has made AEG in the laboratory, but the conditions have questionable relevance for early Earth.[44] A source of PNA either on Earth or in outer space at the time of life's origin, or a naturalistic pathway for adequate PNA production, also needs to be demonstrated. Perhaps most troubling, PNA molecules, once assembled, are stable—too stable. Highly reluctant to let go of the daughter molecules they may have duplicated, the reproduction of PNA would have been extremely slow, if it occurred at all. Scientists also have yet to demonstrate that PNAs can perform the variety of enzymatic activities that would drive evolution from a PNA world to an RNA world.

Putting the RTB Model to the Test

The requirement of homochirality places no limitation on the RTB origin-of-life model. The naturalistic barriers to homochirality can be overcome by the direct supernatural intervention of the Creator.

Evaluating the Evidence

Homochirality places a demand on naturalistic origin-of-life explanations—a demand that goes beyond the production of life's building blocks and their assembly into complex molecules. And this demand goes unmet.

The next chapter explains an additional requirement for the origin-of-life models: the generation of biological information.

CHAPTER 10

THE CODES OF LIFE

"Structure and function" is the biochemist's mantra. It reflects the intimate relationship between a biomolecule's structure and its functional role in the cell. Life's complex molecules (proteins, DNA, and RNA) exhibit a wide range of molecular architectures, and these architectures determine the way they carry out their biochemical operations.

Proteins, DNA, and RNA—all chainlike molecules—form when the cell's machinery links smaller subunit molecules together in a head-to-tail manner. In all cases, the chain's backbone consists of a repeating structure. Though the backbone is structurally monotonous, the chemical groups that extend from the backbone (the side chains) differ widely. The side-chain sequence provides the chemical variability needed for proteins, RNA, and DNA to build the numerous chemical structures required by the cell to function. Just as different letter combinations form a variety of words, so different side-chain sequences form various molecular architectures.

Side-chain sequences are a type of information—chemical information—making proteins, DNA, and RNA information-rich molecules. Their origin stands as a challenge distinct from that of such processes as homochirality, metabolism, and self-replication. The question must be asked: Can undirected chemical and physical processes generate the information-rich molecules needed for life?

A close look at proteins can help answer this question. *The principles that govern the hypothetical prebiotic origin of proteins can be directly applied to all of life's information-containing molecules.* This concept is key, especially because many origin-of-life investigators don't consider proteins a significant player in life's initial stages. They think RNA makes the most likely candidate for the first information-containing molecules. However, current understanding does not permit rigorous analysis of the origin of biological information in the context of RNA systems.

Biochemists currently lack even a basic understanding of the relationship between side-group sequence in RNA, and RNA's structure and activity. They have developed this understanding to a greater extent for proteins, although it is not complete. At least for now, proteins serve as the best source of insight into how information arose in living systems.

The Workhorse Molecules

Proteins take part in essentially every cellular (and extracellular) structure and function associated with life. They catalyze chemical reactions, harvest chemical energy, and store and transport molecules. Proteins form when the cellular machinery (directed by information stored in DNA) link together smaller molecules called amino acids.[1] The cell employs twenty different genetically encoded amino acids to make proteins. These amino acids possess a range of chemical and physical properties.[2] In principle, they can link up in any possible sequence.

Each sequence gives the protein chain a specific chemical and physical profile. The amino acids interact with one another in three-dimensional space. Some attract and others repel. Therefore, the amino acid sequence and the overall chemical and physical properties along the chain cause the protein to fold into a complex and precise three-dimensional structure. This architecture determines the function a protein assumes in the cell. To say this another way, the protein's amino acid sequence determines its structure and hence its function.[3]

Not all amino acid sequences are equal. Some form useful proteins; others produce "junk" to the cell.[4] These "junk" proteins adopt three-dimensional shapes with no biochemical utility. Thus, one can't help but wonder, how likely was it for chance chemical and physical processes to build useful proteins that could have played a role in the origin of life?

Could It Happen by Chance?

In a hypothetical prebiotic soup, information-rich molecules (whether proteins, RNA, or some yet-to-be-identified RNA forerunner) could have emerged only through undirected processes. Theoretically, under prebiotic conditions, amino acids could have randomly reacted with one another to form protein chains if heated in the presence of condensing agents (see chapter 4, pages 52-53). Some researchers speculate that these conditions could have occurred when tidal waters evaporated at the shoreline of volcanic islands, leaving behind prebiotic compounds.

Laboratory simulation experiments designed to mimic these chemical reactions on early Earth show "proteins" that formed by heating amino acid solutions to dryness essentially have a random amino acid sequence,

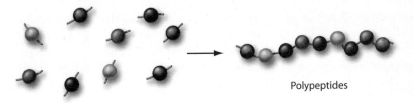

Amino Acids

Polypeptides

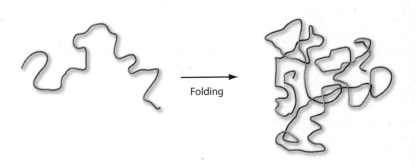

Folding

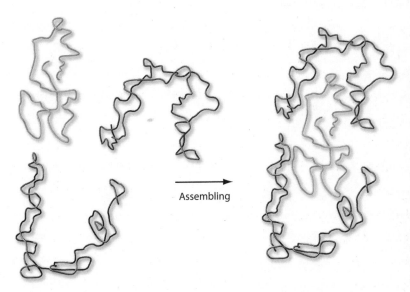

Assembling

Figure 10.1: The Different Levels of Protein Structure

Amino acids combine in a head-to-tail manner to form a polypeptide chain. The polypeptide chain folds into a precise three-dimensional structure based on its amino acid sequence and then interacts with other polypeptides to form a functional protein. (Illustration courtesy of Terry Guyer) though some selective enrichment occurs for a few amino acids.[5] This observation means that any "proteins" formed under prebiotic conditions likewise would have consisted of random sequences of amino acids. The production of biologically meaningful proteins, then, becomes a probability problem. Some of the random proteins produced by prebiotic pathways would have been "junk," while others would have been potentially useful biological properties. Therefore, the question is, what is the likelihood that the proteins needed to carry out essential life functions could form through random assembly of amino acids?

Amino acid probability. Chemists Charles Thaxton, Walter Bradley, and Roger Olsen have rigorously addressed this problem.[6] They argue that in the absence of any chemical competition with non-amino acids and nonbiologically relevant amino acids (the best-case scenario), the probability of getting the right amino acid in a specific position in a protein molecule is 1.25 percent. (There is a 50 percent chance of natural processes randomly selecting a left-handed amino acid, a 50 percent chance of joining the two amino acids in the appropriate chemical bond, and roughly a 5 percent chance of selecting the right amino acid.) The probability of undirected processes assembling a protein one hundred amino acids long, therefore, becomes roughly one chance in 10^{191}.

This probability still falls short of the real objective. Proteins in the cell typically consist of several hundred amino acids. This means that the likelihood of random chemical processess generating most proteins is far more remote.

In effect, there is no chance that even a relatively small protein made up of a specified sequence could ever form by undirected processes. In the words of Bradley and Thaxton,

> If we assume that all carbon on earth exists in the form of amino acids and that the amino acids are allowed to chemically react at the maximum possible rate of 10^{12}/s for one billion years (the greatest possible time between the cooling of the earth and the appearance of life), we must still conclude that it is incredibly improbable ($\sim 10^{-65}$) that even one functional protein would be made.[7]

Protein library probability. Biochemists working in the unrelated field of protein design run into the same problems that origin-of-life researchers face as they try to account for the emergence of bioinformation molecules like proteins. Their goal is to produce new "designer" proteins.

These designer molecules have specially tailored biological properties with potential use in biomedical applications. Because the researchers lack a full understanding of the relationship between amino acid sequence and protein structure—hence function—they face significant hurdles. This problem makes developing a designer protein from scratch extremely difficult, if not impossible. Some biochemists suggest a possible way around this obstacle. Instead of building designer proteins from the ground up, they propose the synthesis of a large number of proteins with random but varied amino acid sequences (a protein "library"). Once in place, protein libraries can be searched for a protein with the desired properties. Conceptually, this procedure closely resembles the random chemical processes that would have operated in the hypothetical prebiotic soup to produce proteins with biologically useful properties.

The use of random-sequence libraries to discover necessary proteins faces an inherent problem that affects all its practical implementation. Researchers from Brandeis University and the Swiss Federal Institute of Technology, for example, point out that to find a protein with a specified sequence one hundred amino acids in length from a fully randomized collection of proteins is impossible.[8] There are about 10^{130} potential sequences. If a library of all these random-sequence proteins were created, a library with *a mass equivalent to that of Earth's* (about 15 trillion trillion pounds) would contain only about 10^{47} of those possible proteins. A library with the mass equivalent of the entire observable universe still would be 10^{54} times too small.

This finding has dire consequences for the naturalistic paradigm. Even if the entire primordial earth were comprised of nothing but the twenty amino acids used by the cell to produce proteins, and if those amino acids reacted to produce proteins all 100 amino acids in length, there would still be only one chance in 10^{83} that the desired amino acid sequence would be formed. Physicists consider any probability smaller than one chance in 10^{50} as equivalent to impossible.

Function by Chance
Though principally sound, these two probability analyses neglect an important factor that bears on the origin-of-life question: Some proteins with different amino acid sequences actually share the same structure and activity. Some amino acid positions in a protein can be freely varied with no effect on the protein's structure and function. Others can be varied to a limited extent, and some not at all. This means that some amino acid sequences are biologically indistinguishable. This phenomenon, referred to as functional equivalency, improves the likelihood that random chemical

processes could stumble upon a biologically useful protein. But does it improve *enough* to allow natural-process origin-of-life explanations to work?

Currently, scientists are unable to determine the probability that a specific protein *function* emerged by random chemical events. They simply lack a full understanding of the relationship among amino acid sequence, protein structure, and protein function. Yet in the absence of full knowledge, biophysicist Hubert Yockey has ventured to estimate this probability for the protein cytochrome C.[9]

Involved in energy-harvesting pathways, cytochrome C contains about 110 amino acids and is found throughout the living realm. Biochemists have determined the cytochrome C amino acid sequence for numerous organisms. By aligning and comparing all known cytochrome C sequences, Yockey estimated the range of variability for each amino acid position.[10]

With some understanding of functional equivalency, Yockey determined that the probability of random chemical events stumbling upon a *functionally equivalent* cytochrome C is roughly on the order of 10^{-75}.[11] (The number of protons and neutrons in the universe is only about 10^{78}.) According to Yockey, if one assumes a chemically pristine primordial soup (containing only biologically significant amino acids) composed of 10^{44} amino acids (the largest conceivable soup possible), to have a 95 percent chance of producing a functional cytochrome C would take 10^{23} years at one chance per second.[12] With the universe's age being 14 billion years, less than one-trillionth of the time needed to produce a functional cytochrome C has transpired.

Yockey's analysis has one limitation. He may not have identified all possible cytochrome C amino acid sequences. Perhaps amino acid sequences not known to exist in nature could have yielded functional cytochrome C-like proteins. In other words, Yockey's analysis may not have fully sampled all "sequence space" for functional cytochrome C molecules. A study by biochemists from Stanford University addresses this concern.[13] Based on mathematical modeling, these researchers determined that for a given protein structure, the amino acid sequences found in nature do indeed encompass all those that are theoretically allowed. Yockey's analysis appears comprehensive.

Putting the RTB Model to the Test

From the standpoint of the RTB creation model, the enormous improbabilities that information-rich molecules could emerge randomly point to a supernatural basis for life. An all-powerful Creator God could create the codes of life fully formed.

Examining the Evidence
To repeat a key principle, the difficulty of accounting for the origin of proteins through natural processes can reasonably be assumed to apply equally to the other information-bearing molecules—DNA and RNA. The chance that any of these biomolecules could be a product of spontaneous interactions among prebiotic compounds is remote in the extreme.

For naturalistic origin-of-life accounts, this fact is a significant, if not insurmountable, hurdle. While biochemists do not yet fully understand the relationship between amino acid sequence and function, preliminary estimates demonstrate that the universe possesses insufficient time and material to produce even the simplest information-containing molecules. As work proceeds toward developing a better understanding of the determinants of protein structure, these types of probability calculations will become more robust in addressing the origin-of-life question. For now, understanding the boundaries of life through the formation of cell membranes provides another opportunity for the models to face off.

CHAPTER 11

BENEFICIAL BOUNDARIES

B orders are important. They define cities, counties, states, and nations. Sometimes natural boundaries such as rivers, mountain ranges, and coastlines determine borders. Other times they are determined by careful design.

Just as borders delineate cities, cell membranes form borders that define life's boundaries.[1] The membrane separates a cell's contents, structures, and chemical processes from the exterior environment.

Biological membranes play a critical role in the cell. Like a well-guarded border, the cell membrane keeps harmful materials from entering the cell and sequesters the beneficial compounds inside it. Proteins embedded in the cell's membrane act as border patrol agents, regulating the traffic of materials into and out of the cell. These transport proteins ensure that the cell has the necessary nutrients and can efficiently expel waste products. Membranes also serve as the site for photosynthesis and energy production.

Because the cell membrane defines life, determining whether it could have developed through natural means is important. If life's border occurred through natural processes, evolutionary models must account for its occurrence relatively early in the origin-of-life pathway.[2] The beginning of cell membranes represents one of the first steps in the emergence of protocells. However, in spite of cell membranes' importance, researchers focus sparse attention on their start. For the most part, naturalists assume that once membrane components appeared on early Earth, the components readily self-assembled to form the first cell membranes.[3] Understanding a cell membrane's structure can help assess the accuracy of that assumption.

Cell Membrane Criteria
The membranes that form a cell's boundary are only 3.5 to 4 nanometers thick.[4] (A nanometer is one-billionth of a meter.) In spite of their tiny

dimensions, cell membranes are incredibly complex. Their structure looks like a chocolate sandwich cookie in electron micrographs.

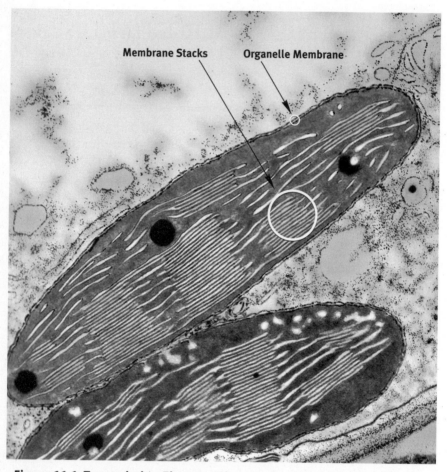

Figure 11.1: Transmission Electron Micrograph of Biological Membranes
(Illustration courtesy of Dr. Kari Lounatmaa/SPL/Photo Researchers, Inc.)

Two general classes of biomolecules—lipids and proteins—interact to form cell membranes. Lipids are a group of structurally dissimilar compounds that share water insolubility as a common and defining property. These compounds readily dissolve in organic solvents. Cholesterol, triglycerides, saturated and unsaturated fats, oils, and lecithin are some of the more widely recognized examples of lipids.

Odd-Shaped Balloons

Phospholipids are the cell membrane's major lipid component.[5] A phospholipid roughly resembles a distorted balloon with two strings attached. Biochemists divide phospholipids into two regions that possess markedly different physical properties. The head region, corresponding to the "balloon," is water soluble (hydrophilic — "water-loving"). The phospholipid tails, corresponding to the balloon's "strings" are water insoluble (hydrophobic — "water-hating").

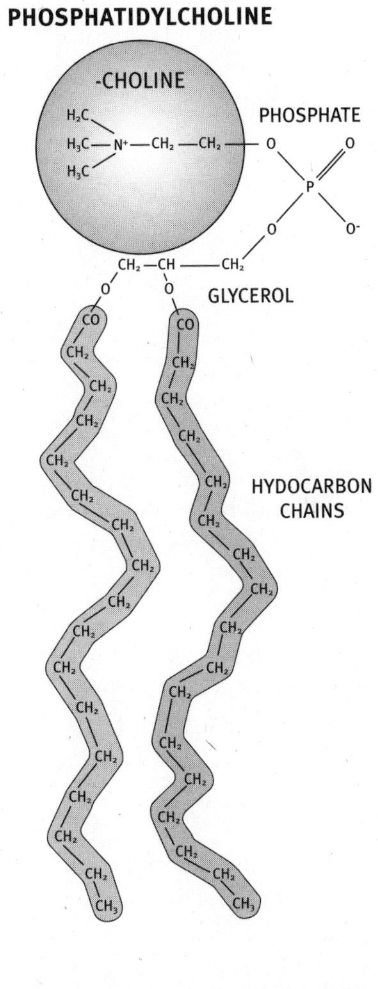

PHOSPHATIDYLCHOLINE

Figure 11.2: The Molecular Structure of a Typical Phospholipid with a Schematic Representation of Its Structure Superimposed upon It

Note the phospholipid's head group and tail regions. (Illustration courtesy of Phillip Chien)

Chemists refer to molecules, such as phospholipids, in which distinct molecular regions possess different solubility characteristics, as amphiphilic ("ambivalent in its likes"). Soaps and detergents are commonly recognized examples of amphiphilic compounds.

Phospholipids' schizoid solubility properties cause them to organize into cell membranes. When added to water, phospholipids spontaneously organize into bilayers—sheets two molecules thick. In a bilayer, phospholipid molecules align into two monolayers with the phospholipid head groups adjacent to one another and the phospholipid tails packed close together. The monolayers, in turn, collect so that the phospholipid tails of one monolayer interface with the phospholipid tails of the bilayer's other monolayer. This tail-to-tail arrangement ensures that the water-soluble head groups contact water and the water-insoluble tails stay away from water.

BILAYER

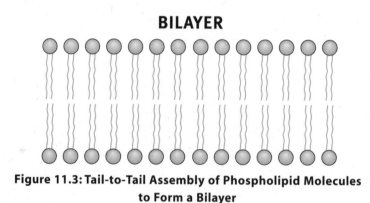

Figure 11.3: Tail-to-Tail Assembly of Phospholipid Molecules to Form a Bilayer

(Illustration courtesy of Phillip Chien)

This bilayer structure gives cell membranes their sandwich-cookie appearance. The head groups, which form the cell membrane's inner and outer surfaces, are electron dense, rendering them dark (like chocolate). The phospholipid tails are less electron-dense than the head groups and, therefore, appear light (like vanilla frosting) in electron micrographs (see figure 11.1).

Phospholipids found in cell membranes show a wide range of chemical variability (see figure 11.2). Their head groups typically consist of a phosphate group bound to a glycerol (glycerin) backbone. The phosphate group in turn binds one of a number of possible compounds that vary in their chemical and physical properties. Frequently, phospholipids are identified by their head-group structure.

Phospholipids also vary in tail length and structure. The tails are typically long, linear hydrocarbon chains linked to the glycerol backbone. These chains are commonly sixteen to eighteen carbon atoms long.

A Jack-of-All Trades

The other major biomolecular class that plays a role in cell membrane structure and function are proteins. These molecules associate with the cell membrane in a variety of ways. Peripheral proteins bind to the inner or outer membrane surfaces. Integral proteins embed into the cell membrane. Some integral proteins insert only partially into the membrane interior and still others span the entire membrane.

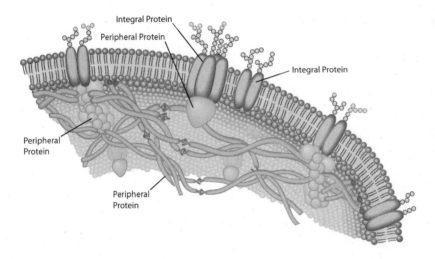

Figure 11.4: The Different Ways Proteins Interact with Phospholipid Bilayers

(Illustration courtesy of Phillip Chien)

Membrane proteins function as receptors, binding compounds that allow the cell to communicate with its external environment. They catalyze chemical reactions at the cell's interior and exterior surfaces. They shuttle molecules across the cell membrane and form pores and channels through the membrane. Some of these proteins impart structural integrity to the cell membrane.

The inner and outer monolayers of cell membranes differ in composition, structure, and function. These differences make them asymmetric. The phospholipid classes on the inner and outer membrane surfaces are unique; the membrane proteins, likewise, are specific to either the inner or outer surfaces. Proteins that span the cell membrane possess a specific orientation. Because of protein dissimilarity, the functional characteristics of the inner and outer surfaces vary.

A Liquid-Looking Glass

Since the early 1970s, the fluid mosaic model has provided the framework to understand membrane structure and function.[6] This model views the phospholipid bilayer as a two-dimensional fluid serving as both a barrier and as a solvent for integral membrane proteins. The fluid mosaic model has the membrane proteins and lipids freely diffusing laterally throughout the cell membrane structure. Beyond bilayer organization and membrane asymmetry, the fluid mosaic model fails to attribute much structural or functional organization to cell membranes.

In recent years, biochemists have revised the fluid mosaic model.[7] Instead of freely diffusing in the phospholipid bilayers, most proteins find themselves confined to domains within the membrane. Other proteins diffuse throughout the membrane, but instead of moving randomly, these proteins move in a directed fashion. Phospholipids, too, organize into domains with certain phospholipid classes laterally segregating in the bilayer. Bilayer fluidity also varies from region to region in the membrane.

In short, cell membranes are not inert barriers. These dynamically intricate biosystems display a structure critical to life. How do researchers account for cell membrane origin?

Evolutionary Explanations

To explain the beginning of cell membranes (and along with it, the emergence of the first protocell), origin-of-life investigators try to identify compounds likely present on early Earth with the potential to spontaneously assemble into the bilayer structures that form the cell membrane's inner and outer surfaces. These scientists also strive to define mechanisms by which the bilayer structures can encapsulate more complex self-replicating molecules and acquire properties and functionality that resemble those of contemporary cell membranes.

Prebiotic production. In the quest to identify bilayer-forming molecules, researchers attempt to discover chemical pathways that can form long amphiphilic hydrocarbon chains from simple compounds. These scientists also investigate chemical routes with the potential to yield more complex phospholipids.

One such route has been known since the 1930s. This process (the Fischer-Tropsch reaction) converts carbon monoxide and hydrogen into long-chain hydrocarbons in the presence of iron or nickel at high temperatures. Origin-of-life workers have identified modifications to this process (for example, the inclusion of carbonates) that yield amphiphilic compounds such as fatty acids and fatty alcohols instead of long-chain hydrocarbons.[8] Fatty acids make up the phospholipid tail region.

Some researchers question the applicability of the Fischer-Tropsch reaction to early Earth's conditions since this process requires gaseous carbon monoxide and hydrogen plus high temperatures and pressures.[9] Until recently, chemists did not think the reaction could occur in the presence of water. This notion has now been overturned. Scientists from Oregon State have produced numerous compounds containing long-chain hydrocarbons in a Fischer-Tropsch–type reaction under aqueous conditions at relatively moderate temperatures (from 302 to 482 °F or 150 to 250 °C) starting with oxalic acid.[10] These conditions are potentially relevant to early Earth because they model conditions found at deep-sea hydrothermal vents. Other researchers challenge these claims, however, because hydrogen sulfide (present at hydrothermal vents) inhibits Fischer-Tropsch reactions.[11]

Origin-of-life investigator Arthur Weber proposed a synthetic cycle to account for prebiotic fatty acid production.[12] This complex cycle starts with glycolaldehyde (a compound thought to have existed on early Earth) and proceeds through six steps that involve either loss of water or the addition of hydrogen. While each reaction of the cycle is feasible, the complexity of the cycle, the catalytic requirements for each step, and the need for the cycle to "turn" at least seven times to produce a fatty acid capable of forming membrane lipids call into question the relevance of the glycolaldehyde pathway as a meaningful source of prebiotic fatty acids.[13]

Once formed, fatty acids must react with glycerin and phosphate to form phospholipids. Origin-of-life researchers suggest that this reaction could have occurred on early Earth if these three compounds experienced moderate heating (150 °F or 65 °C) to dryness.[14] The relevance of this reaction is somewhat questionable because it requires complete dehydration; it does not occur in the presence of *any* water. In fact, water's presence breaks down phospholipids by reversing the proposed reaction. These phospholipid-forming reactions also require reactant concentrations not likely to have occurred on early Earth.

Chemists Thaxton, Bradley, and Olsen identified an additional problem that confounds natural-process phospholipid production.[15] Two key ingredients needed for phospholipid formation, fatty acids and phosphates, form water-insoluble complexes with calcium and magnesium ions. The tendency of these two compounds to physically associate with calcium and magnesium is so great that, once formed, fatty acids and phosphates would have precipitated out of any possible early Earth environment. The precipitation of the fatty acid and phosphate complexes, in effect, would have made these compounds unavailable for prebiotic formation of the phospholipids that are so vital to cell membranes.

Extraterrestrial delivery. In the face of the questions that surround prebiotic synthesis, some researchers appeal to the infall of extraterrestrial materials to early Earth as the source of bilayer-forming compounds.[16] Analysis of carbon-containing meteorites (carbonaceous chondrites like the Murchison meteorite) initially indicated the presence of compounds consisting of long hydrocarbon chains. However, subsequent analysis demonstrated that these compounds resulted from terrestrial contamination.[17]

Recent laboratory experiments seemingly rejuvenate support for an extraterrestrial source of amphiphilic materials on early Earth.[18] Scientists from NASA Ames, the SETI Institute, and the University of California, Santa Cruz, demonstrated that ultraviolet light irradiation of simulated cometary and interstellar ice (water, methanol, ammonia, and carbon monoxide) produces a complex mixture of compounds that include bilayer-forming materials. This result led to speculation that the infall of these materials might have provided the compounds needed to form the first cell membranes.

Primitive membrane emergence. Even though phospholipids comprise the dominant lipid species of contemporary cell membranes, origin-of-life researchers think that simpler lipids may have assembled to form the first ones.

Amphiphilic compounds all form aggregates when added to water. These aggregates take on a variety of forms, depending on the amphiphile's molecular structure.[19] Phospholipids with *two* long hydrocarbon chains can form bilayers. Amphiphilic compounds with a *single* long hydrocarbon chain generally form spherical structures called micelles. Several origin-of-life researchers regard micelles as having no importance in forming the first protocells because they have no internal aqueous compartment.

In spite of their tendency to form nonbilayer micelles, some amphiphilic compounds that consist of a single long hydrocarbon chain can form bilayers under highly specific solution conditions (for example, pH and temperatures) when mixed with the right materials.[20] Some origin-of-life researchers regard these results as key to explaining the first appearance of cell membranes. Their significance increases based on the observation that lipidlike materials extracted from the Murchison meteorite form bilayer structures under specific solution conditions.[21] Similar bilayer structures also form from extracts of simulated cometary and interstellar ice irradiated with ultraviolet light.[22] Origin-of-life researchers point to these compounds as possibly the first cell membrane components, and as evidence that the materials necessary to form the first protocell boundary structures were present on early Earth. They also argue that these results seem to indicate the ease with which bilayers can spontaneously form once the right components appear. However, this formation under natural conditions has never been observed.

Encapsulated and acquired. Once bilayer-forming compounds appeared on early Earth, investigators speculate, cycles of dehydration and rehydration served to encapsulate large self-replicating molecules (proteins, DNA, and RNA) and smaller subunit molecules within the bilayer's confines. Support for this claim comes from experiments that show bilayer vesicles made of phospholipids encapsulating DNA during drying and subsequent water addition.[23] These same researchers presume that once formed, bilayer vesicles containing encapsulated self-replicating molecules could carry out the chemical processes needed to sustain growth, self-replication, and acquisition of transport and energy transduction capabilities.[24]

Lipid bilayers are generally impermeable to the types of molecules needed to maintain the activity of encapsulated self-replicators. However, a few researchers have shown that if the chain length of the lipids that form the bilayers is carefully adjusted, enough of the compounds needed to sustain the self-replicator can pass through the bilayer.[25] While not the focus for most origin-of-life researchers, cell membrane studies seem to reinforce the view that cell membranes readily self-assembled on early Earth. Once formed, these primitive bilayers also seemingly acquired the functional attributes of contemporary biological membrane systems.

Not so simple. Other research designed to characterize the structure of lipid aggregates and delineate the principles governing cell membrane biophysics indicates that naturalistic models for the cell membrane's origin are oversimplified. The emerging tenets of cell membrane biophysics demand a more involved, convoluted, and intricate pathway from simple lipid molecules to bilayers that resemble those found in contemporary cell membrane systems.

Origin-of-life researchers suggest that the primitive membranes of the first protocells were composed of aromatic hydrocarbons mixed with octanoic and nonanoic acid. Extracts from the Murchison meteorite that contain these compounds form bilayer structures. But these results prove misleading.

Neither octanoic nor nonanoic acid would likely have occurred at levels significant for origin-of-life scenarios. Researchers have recovered only extremely low levels of these compounds from the Murchison meteorite.[26] Moreover, the abundance of individual amphiphilic species decreases exponentially with increasing chain length.[27] While extraterrestrial infall could potentially deliver octanoic and nonanoic acid to early Earth, the levels would be far too low to participate in primitive membrane structures. Octanoic and nonanoic acids can form bilayer structures only at relatively high concentrations.[28]

In addition to the concentration requirements, octanoic and nonanoic acids also require exacting environmental conditions. These compounds can form bilayers only at very specific pHs.[29] Octanoic and nonanoic bilayers become unstable if the solution pH deviates from near-neutral values. The solution temperature is critical for bilayer stability as well.[30] Another complication is the solution salt level—research shows that model primitive membranes fall apart in the presence of salt. These structures display stability only in pure water.[31]

Octanoic and nonanoic bilayer stability also requires just-right molecular companions. Inclusion of nonanol (a nine-carbon alcohol) extends the pH range for nonanoic bilayers.[32] The increased stability results from specific interactions between the nonanoic acid head group and nonanol. Only when nonanol is present at specific levels does bilayer stability result.

To date, no studies have been conducted on the long-term stability of octanoic and nonanoic bilayers. These acid bilayers may or may not lack long-term stability under conditions that allow them to form. Regardless, the strict requirements needed for bilayer formation make it unlikely that these compounds could ever have contributed to the formation of the first protocell's membranes. Formation of nonanoic acid bilayers (or bilayers comprised of any amphiphile with a single hydrocarbon chain) is improbable, because several just-right conditions must be met simultaneously. If a bilayer structure were to form, any environmental fluctuations or compositional deviations would destabilize them and cause them to revert to micelle structures.

The instability of primitive bilayers in salt may represent the greatest problem. Imagining any salt-free aqueous environment on early Earth is difficult. In fact, primitive bilayer stability is compromised at salt levels far less than those in today's oceans. Early Earth's oceans were from one and a half to two times saltier than modern seas.[33] This complication makes the emergence of primitive membranes even less likely. Recent work indicating that salt in early Earth's oceans would inhibit the production of RNA molecules further exacerbates this problem.[34]

The exacting requirements for primitive bilayer assembly also decrease the likelihood that these structures could encapsulate a self-replicator via dehydration-hydration cycles. Once dehydrated, unless the just-right conditions exist upon rehydration, bilayers will not re-form.

Contemporary Formation

At some point in the various naturalistic origin-of-life scenarios, cell membranes composed of phospholipids must emerge. This necessity is real whether the pathway that leads to the first contemporary cell membranes begins with primitive membranes comprised of simple amphiphiles, or whether the initial cell membranes appeared anew as phospholipid bilayers. Naturalistic scenarios that attempt to explain the formation of the first phospholipid-containing biological membranes face enormous difficulties.

Robust chemical pathways leading to phospholipids have not yet been identified. Plus, the first phospholipids likely possessed a tendency to form nonbilayer aggregates that could not perform as a barrier.

One can reasonably assume that the first phospholipid species on early Earth, and hence the first contemporary cell membranes, consisted of phosphatidylethanolamines (PEs) and phosphatidylglycerol (PGs). These two phospholipid classes have ethanolamine and glycerol as head-groups respectively (see figure 11.2). PEs and PGs are the primary phospholipid classes found in bacterial membranes, and bacteria were among the first life forms to appear on Earth.[35]

Because PEs and PGs stand as the dominant phospholipid species in bacterial membranes, origin-of-life scenarios must specifically account for the formation of biological membranes comprised of these two phospholipid types. Herein lies the problem. While phospholipids do self-assemble into bilayers, they also form nonbilayer structures. Phospholipids display rich and complex phase behavior. They tend to form specific aggregate

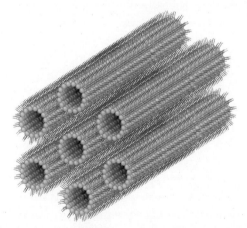

Figure 11.5: Structures of Different Phospholipid Aggregates

Note the nonbilayer structure formed by phosphatidylethanolamines.

(Illustration courtesy of Phillip Chien)

types based on the head-group structure (see figure 11.2). Head-group characteristics determine a specific phospholipid's overall molecular shape, which in turn dictates the type of aggregates it forms.

PEs tend to form nonbilayer phases, and in the presence of calcium, PGs also form nonbilayer structures.[36] Cardiolipin (a derivative of PGs also present in bacterial membranes) likewise readily forms nonbilayer states. Finally, PGs' presence in PE aggregates increases their tendency to form nonbilayer aggregates.[37]

Biochemists are uncertain of the biological significance of these nonbilayer structures, but they agree that if the nonbilayer structures do play a role in cell membrane processes, they must quickly pass in and out of existence. These nonbilayer phases compromise the cell membrane's structural integrity and also its barrier function.[38] Permanent or long-lived nonbilayer phases would rapidly lead to cell death.

In the early 1980s, Swedish researchers conducted experiments that highlighted the relationship between bilayer stability, lipid composition, and lipid shape.[39] These workers showed that the bacterium *Acholeplasma laidlawii* adjusted its membrane's lipid composition as environmental conditions changed. These changes preserved the proper lipid shape, thereby maintaining bilayer stability. If the lipid composition was not altered as environmental conditions changed, the bacteria's cell membrane adopted a nonbilayer structure that led to cell death.

With respect to the origin of life and the emergence of the first protocell, calcium's presence in early Earth's environment and the tendency of PEs and PE/PG mixtures to form nonbilayer aggregates means that these phospholipids may not have readily formed bilayers, frustrating the pathway leading to the first cell membranes. Moreover, fluctuating environmental conditions and altered bilayer composition would have given early bilayers comprised of PE and PG the potential to transition to nonbilayer phases. This transition would have inhibited the origin-of-life process.

Fine-Tuned Molecular Aggregates
Even if the first phospholipids on Earth were the ones that readily formed bilayers, they still would not have led to the spontaneous assembly of cell membrane systems. Bilayer-forming phospholipids display complex properties. Phospholipid bilayers spontaneously stack into sheets (multilamellar bilayers) or spherical structures (resembling an onion) that consist of multiple bilayer sheets.[40] These aggregates only superficially resemble the cell membrane's single bilayer structure.

Bilayer-forming phospholipids can form structures composed of a single bilayer. These particular aggregates arrange into a hollow spherical

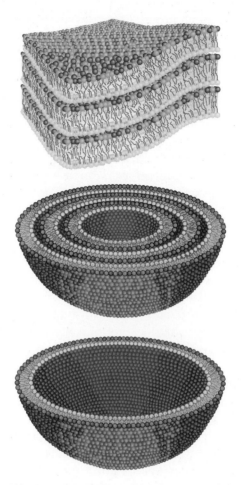

Figure 11.6: Different Bilayer Structures Formed by Phospholipids

Typically, phospholipids spontaneously assemble into stacks of bilayer sheets or spherical multilamellar bilayer vesicles. The formation of single lamellar bilayer vesicles, which directly resemble the bilayer structure of cell membranes, only form through researcher manipulation and are only temporarily stable.

(Illustration courtesy of Phillip Chien)

structure called liposomes or unilamellar vesicles. Liposomes do not form spontaneously. Rather they result *only* with laboratory manipulation.[41] They exist for a limited lifetime and are considered a metastable phase. Liposomes fuse to revert to multilamellar sheets or vesicles.[42]

How is it that bilayer-forming lipids form multiple-bilayer sheets or relatively unstable single-bilayer vesicles (liposomes) when the cell membrane is made up of a stable single bilayer phase? During the

1980s and early 1990s, National Institutes of Health (NIH) researcher Norman Gershfeld successfully addressed this question. Gershfeld's discoveries challenge any naturalistic explanation for cell membrane origins.

As it turns out, single bilayer phases, similar to those that constitute cell membranes, are stable but form only under unique conditions.[43] (Chemists refer to phenomena that occur under a unique set of conditions as *critical phenomena*.) Formation of single bilayer vesicles occurs only at a specific temperature (the critical temperature). Pure phospholipids spontaneously transform from either multiple bilayer sheets or unstable liposomes into stable single bilayers only at the critical temperature.[44] This temperature depends on the specific phospholipid or on the bilayer's phospholipid composition.[45]

Gershfeld and his team made some intriguing observations along these lines. For example, they noted that phospholipids extracted from rat and squid nervous-system tissue assemble into single bilayer structures at critical temperatures that correspond to the physiological temperatures of these two organisms.[46] Gershfeld's group also observed that for the cold-blooded sea urchin L. *pictus,* the cell membrane composition of the earliest cells in the embryo varies in response to the environment's temperature to maintain a single bilayer phase with a critical temperature matching the environmental conditions.[47] Gershfeld's team noted that the bacterium E. *coli* also adjusted its cell membrane phospholipid composition to maintain a single bilayer phase.[48]

These studies highlight the biological importance of the critical bilayer phenomena. So do other studies that indicate the deadly effects of the cell membrane's deviation from critical conditions. Gershfeld's team identified correlation between the rupture of human red blood cells and incubation at temperatures exceeding 98.6 °F (37 °C), the normal human body temperature. Transformation of the cell membrane from a single bilayer to multiple bilayer stacks accompanies the rupture of red blood cells—a loss of the cell membrane's critical state.[49] Gershfeld and his colleagues have even provided some evidence that cell membrane defects at the sites of neurodegeneration may play a role in Alzheimer's disease.[50] Presumably, collapse of the cell membrane's single bilayer into a multiple bilayer results from altered membrane phospholipid composition.

Gershfeld and his team's work indicates that cell membranes are highly fine-tuned molecular structures dependent on an exacting set of physical and chemical conditions. It is highly unlikely that chemical and physical processes operating on early Earth could have produced the precise phospholipid composition to form the stable single bilayer phase that universally defines cell membranes. Even if chance events arrived at this just-right phospholipid composition, any fluctuations in temperature would have destroyed the single bilayer structure. With the loss of this structure, the first protocells would have fallen apart.

The problem of membrane formation begins to resemble the problem of accounting for development of information-containing molecules such as proteins and DNA. Though amino acids can assemble to form protein chains, only very specific amino acid sequences make the chains functional. Likewise, although phospholipids readily aggregate, and in many cases form bilayer structures, only very specific phospholipid compositions and exacting environmental temperatures (and other conditions) lead to single bilayer structures and cell membranes.

Putting the RTB Model to the Test

The exacting conditions needed to self-assemble and maintain biological membranes reduce the likelihood that these structures could emerge by natural processes. The fine-tuning and specificity of conditions needed for cell membrane structure and function stand as indicators of supernatural design. These characteristics support prediction 6 of the RTB biblical creation model: Life's chemistry displays hallmark characteristics of design. This model predicts that the evidence for membrane design will grow stronger and become more extensive as scientists learn more about the details of membrane structure and chemistry.

Evaluating the Evidence

Within the evolutionary framework, the emergence of cell membrane systems represents a necessary stage in life's origin and the initial step toward forming the first protocells. Despite its importance to naturalistic origin-of-life scenarios, researchers in this field focus only limited attention on membrane origins. Those few experiments and observations conducted over the last two decades or so, designed to address the questions of membrane beginnings, seem — on the surface — to support the view held by a majority of origin-of-life investigators. That is, they superficially suggest that membranes of the first protocells could have readily assembled on early Earth and adopted the structure and acquired the important life functions assumed by contemporary cell membrane systems.

Viewing the same results in a broader scientific context yields different conclusions. Advances in biophysics have uncovered many of the important principles underlying membrane structure. The advances in membrane biophysics challenge natural-process explanations for cell membrane origins.

While a wide range of amphiphilic compounds that could serve as the lipid components for primitive biological membranes can self-assemble into bilayers, this self-assembling process requires just-right conditions and just-right molecular components. It is unlikely that such conditions would exist or persist for long on early Earth. And therefore both naturalistic prediction 2 (Chemical pathways must have existed that yielded complex biomolecules such as DNA, RNA, proteins, and membrane and all cell wall components.) and prediction 3 (The chemical pathways that yielded life's building blocks and complex molecular constituents must have operated in early Earth's conditions.) are contradicted by the evidence.

Additionally, the self-assembly of phospholipids—the dominant lipid component of contemporary cell membranes—also requires just-right concentrations, temperatures, and compositions. Deviation from these conditions leads to a loss of the cell membrane's structural and functional integrity and has been implicated in disease processes.

CHAPTER 12

LIFE'S MINIMUM COMPLEXITY

"Today, we are learning the language in which God created life."[1] President Clinton spoke these dramatic words on June 26, 2000, in honor of the two men who stood beside him: Craig Ventor of Celera Genomics and Francis Collins, chief of the Human Genome Project (HGP). He was lauding their completion of the human genome sequence.

Scientists, health professionals, politicians, and laypeople alike hope this new understanding of human genetic makeup will lead to cures for genetic disorders. Further, this project fuels hopes that gene sequencing may help predict the onset of future disease in individual patients and revolutionize the development of pharmaceuticals. In short, the HGP offers the real possibility of transforming health care. Still, its greatest impact may not be advances in medicine and the understanding of human biology. History is likely to view the HGP's greatest accomplishment as spawning the scientific discipline called genomics.

In the past, origin-of-life investigators used a bottom-up approach to figure out how life began and led to life today. This techinque involved research on chemical pathways, homochirality, information-bearing molecules, and cell membranes. The study of genomics, however, provides a top-down approach. This endeavor starts with life today and probes an organism's entire genetic makeup to learn about the first living entities. The general excitement about mapping the human genome gives many scientists fresh hope that this new scientific approach could provide clues as to how life emerged through natural processes.

Genomics, from the Beginning
Genomics combines genetics, biochemistry, computer science, and molecular biology to sequence and characterize an organism's entire DNA content. Scientists hope that this endeavor will give them new insight into the

biology and comparative biological relationships of all life forms (both living and extinct).

When the HGP began, techniques to sequence DNA were time and
labor intensive. For researchers to have any hope of sequencing the massive quantities of DNA found in even the simplest organisms, let alone the
human genome with its three billion genetic letters, new and automated
sequencing techniques had to be developed. Ways to handle, organize,
and analyze the vast quantities of sequence data to be generated by the
HGP also had to be found.

Focused research efforts into these areas, coupled with advances in
computer technology, remedied the problems and along the way gave
birth to genomics. As new methodologies developed, scientists became
anxious to try them out. The obvious model organisms on which to test
emerging techniques were microbes. Easy to manipulate, these organisms
possess relatively small genomes and are important for biomedical, agricultural, industrial, and environmental reasons.

In 1995, The Institute of Genomic Research (TIGR) reported a his-
toric first—they had sequenced an organism's entire genome. Using their
new "shotgun" sequencing strategy, TIGR scientists (including founder
Craig Ventor) determined the DNA sequence of the *Haemophilus influenzae* genome.[2] This bacterium has been implicated in bronchitis, meningi-
tis, and pneumonia and also plays a key role in origin-of-life research.

Since this sequencing achievement, scientific reports of fully
sequenced genomes have poured forth. A substantial database of microbial genomes now exists and is growing by one or two genomes per
month. Additionally, efforts have extended to sequencing the genomes of
complex organisms routinely used for laboratory studies—fruit flies,
nematodes, and mice.[3] Work is also underway to sequence the chimpanzee
genome.[4] Genomics has arrived as a mature discipline.

As more and more microbial genomes become available for study,
origin-of-life researchers recognize the usefulness of this data. Inherent in
the top-down method of genomics is the assumption that all life shares
common ancestry and evolved from the last universal common ancestor
(LUCA). In recognition of the value of genomics data, some researchers
have even focused their sequencing efforts exclusively on microbes
thought to be the oldest representatives of life—organisms that play a
prominent role in naturalistic origin-of-life scenarios.

Genomics data provides insight into the complexity of Earth's first
independent life forms and minimum complexity in its barest form.
Application of genomics to life's beginning provides an important opportunity to test the biblical creation and naturalistic models. These models

make opposite predictions regarding life's minimum complexity. The RTB biblical creation model predicts that, in its minimal form, life is complex (prediction 5). All naturalistic scenarios demand that, in its minimal form, life must be simple (prediction 8).

Genome Size

One way to explore the minimum complexity of independent life is to survey the microbial database for the smallest genome. Table 12.1 lists the results of this survey. The data indicate that the microbes possessing the smallest known genomes and capable of living *independently* in the environment are extremophilic archaea and eubacteria. (For more details on extremophiles, see chapter 13.)

These organisms also happen to represent what many scientists consider to be the oldest life on Earth.[5] This crude estimate seems to suggest that, to exist independently, life requires a minimum genome size of about 1,500 to 1,900 gene products. (A gene product refers to proteins and functional RNAs, such as ribosomal and transfer RNA.) The late evolutionary biologist Colin Patterson acknowledges the 1,700 genes of *Methanococcus* are "perhaps close to the minimum necessary for independent life."[6]

Organism	Domain	Approximate Genome Size (Gene Products)
Thermoplasma acidiphilum	Archaea	~1,509
Aquifex aeolicius	Bacteria	~1,512
Methanopyrus Kandleri AV19	Archaea	~1,692
Methanococcus jannaschii	Archaea	~1,738
Methanobacterium thermoautotrophicum	Archaea	~1,855
Thermotoga maritima	Bacteria	~1,877

Table 12.1: Organisms with the Smallest Genomes

Given the relatively small sample of organisms currently available for assessing life's minimum complexity, investigators may well find the minimum requirement for independent life extends below 1,500 gene products. A newly discovered hyperthermophilic microbe helps establish a lower boundary. This organism, *Nanoarchaeum equitans,* lives as a parasite attached to the surface of its independently existing hyperthermophile host.[7] Because it is a parasite, *N. equitans* exploits and depends upon its host cell's metabolism to exist. (In general, parasitic microbes have reduced genome sizes because of their reliance on host cell biochemistry.)

Researchers have yet to estimate the N. *equitans'* genome size, but based on its amount of DNA, its genome size likely falls within the range of about 450 to 500 gene products.

Even though incapable of independent existence, N. *equitans* yields insight into independent life's minimal complexity. Because this parasite thrives with a genome size of about 450 to 500 gene products, the minimum complexity for independent life must reside somewhere between about 500 and 1,500 gene products. So far, as scientists have continued their sequencing efforts, all microbial genomes that fall below 1,500 belong to parasites. Organisms capable of permanent independent existence require more gene products.

A minimum genome size (for independent life) of 1,500 to 1,900 gene products comports with what the geochemical and fossil evidence (discussed in chapter 5) reveals about the complexity of Earth's first life. Earliest life forms displayed metabolic complexity that included:

- photosynthetic and chemoautotrophic processes
- protein synthesis
- the capacity to produce amino acids, nucleotides, fatty acids, and sugars
- the machinery to reproduce

Some 1,500 different gene products would seem the bare minimum to sustain this level of metabolic activity. For instance, the *Methanococcus jannaschii* genome (the first to be sequenced for the archaea domain) possesses about 1,738 gene products. This organism contains the enzymatic machinery for energy metabolism and for the biosynthesis and processing of sugars, nucleotides, amino acids, and fatty acids.[8] In addition, the *M. jannaschii* genome can encode for repair systems, DNA replication, and the cell division apparatus. The genes for protein synthesis and secretion and the genes that specify the construction and activity of the cell membrane and envelope also belong as part of this organism's genome.

The Bare Necessity
The discovery of parasitic microbes with reduced genome sizes, like *Mycoplasma genitalium*, *Mycoplasma pneumoniae*, and *Barrelia burgdorferi* (with 470, 677, and 863 gene products, respectively), indicates that life exists, though not independently, with genome sizes made up of smaller than 1,500 genes.[9] These microbes are not good model organisms for Earth's first life forms because they cannot exist independently. But they do have some relevance to life's beginning. These parasitic microbes help

determine the barest minimal requirements for life, given that building block molecules (sugars, nucleotides, amino acids, and fatty acids as well as other nutrients) are readily available.

Scientists from NIH have used the *M. genitalium* and *H. influenzae* genomes to estimate the minimum gene set needed for independent life.[10] These researchers compared the two for genes with common function and reasoned that these constitute the minimum gene products necessary for life. This approach indicated that a set of 256 genes represents the lower limit on genome size needed for life to operate.

Using a similar approach, an international team produced a slightly lower minimum estimate of 246.[11] This group developed a universal set of proteins by comparing representatives from life's three domains—eukarya, archaea, and bacteria.

In addition to theoretical estimates, researchers have also attempted to make experimental measurements of the minimum number of genes necessary for life. These approaches involve the mutation of randomly selected genes to identify those that are indispensable. One experiment performed on the bacterium *Bacillus subtilis* estimated the minimal gene set numbers between 254 and 450.[12] A similar study with *M. genitalium* determined the minimum number of genes to fall between 265 and 350.[13] Random mutations of the *H. influenzae* genome indicate that 478 genes are required for life in its bare minimal form.[14]

The genome of the extreme parasite *Buchnera* provides another means to determine the size of the minimal gene set.[15] This parasite exists permanently inside aphid cells and has a remarkably tiny genome size. Scientists believe its gene set consists solely of those products essential for life. In contrast, *M. genitalium*'s genome includes genes essential for life *and* genes that mediate host-parasite interactions. Presumably the genes disabled by mutation eliminated those involved in its host-parasite interactions. The genome size of the *Buchnera* species varies, with the smallest estimated to contain 396 gene products.

Theoretical and experimental studies designed to discover the bare minimum number of gene products necessary for life all show significant agreement. Life seems to require between 250 and 350 different proteins to carry out its most basic operations. That this bare form of life cannot survive long without a source of sugars, nucleotides, amino acids, and fatty acids is worth noting.

The Magnitude of Life's Minimum

What does it mean for origin-of-life scenarios that independent life requires at least 1,500 gene products and that life in its bare minimal form seems to demand no less than 250 different types of proteins? These numbers define the minimum number of different proteins that must come together *all at once* to form the cell's structural features and execute the basic functions necessary to sustain life. To explain life's "ignition," both naturalistic scenarios and the biblical creation model must account for a simultaneous occurrence of all the essential gene products and for their perfectly engineered assembly.

Biophysicist Hubert Yockey's calculation for cytochrome C (discussed in chapter 9) represents the best probability estimate for a single gene product or protein to come into existence exclusively by natural means.[16] If one assumes that the value Yockey obtained for cytochrome C (approximately one chance in 10^{75}) is roughly representative of all proteins contained in the minimum gene set, then it becomes unimaginable that even 250 different proteins could come into existence simultaneously, let alone 1,500. Table 12.2 lists these probabilities.

Minimum Number of Genes	Probability of Simultaneous Occurrence
250	$10^{18,750}$
350	$10^{26,250}$
500	$10^{37,500}$
1,500	$10^{112,500}$
1,900	$10^{142,500}$

Table 12.2: Probabilities That Proteins Could Come into Existence Simultaneously

This probability analysis agrees with a calculation done by biophysicist Harold Morowitz. He conducted a thought experiment in which he broke every chemical bond in the bacterium *E. coli* and then let those bonds re-form randomly. He assumed that none of the relevant atoms escaped and no contaminant atoms interfered. Morowitz performed this calculation in an attempt to dimensionalize the magnitude of the problem researchers face as they attempt to account for life's beginning through natural means.

He determined the likelihood that *E. coli* would randomly re-form is on the order of one chance in $10^{100,000,000,000}$.[17] If all the matter in the observable universe were somehow converted to life's building blocks and were then brought to bear on *E. coli* formation—being allowed to attempt combination a million times a second for the entire duration of the universe's existence—the odds of generating this bacterium change to about one chance in $10^{99,999,999,916}$ (an imperceptible change).[18] Such a number implies that neither enough matter nor enough time in the universe exists for even the simplest bacterium to emerge by undirected chemical and physical processes.

Researchers have long considered this result to be irrelevant to the origin-of-life question. They maintain that while *E. coli* is simple, it is still a complex organism compared to the first life forms. In other words, life in its minimal form was far simpler than *E. coli,* and therefore this first life did not face such daunting probabilities as it came into existence. (Interestingly, *E. coli's* genome has been sequenced and consists of about 4,288 gene products.)[19] However, in light of the growing genomics database, the probability problem cannot be escaped. While larger than those possessed by the simplest microbes, *E. coli's* genome still falls within the same order of magnitude with respect to its size as those others (1.5×10^3 compared with 4.3×10^3). In other words, Morowitz's calculations for *E. coli* apply to these organisms and remain entirely relevant to the origin-of-life question.

The Synergy Problem

The problem for the origin of life extends beyond trying to account for the simultaneous occurrence of over 250 different proteins. It also demands the appearance of DNA, RNA, and complex carbohydrates to form the cell wall, plus the lipids to form the cell's membrane. All these molecules must come together at once and operate in an orchestrated fashion for life to be possible.

Herein lies the dilemma: The cell wall and membrane cannot be constructed without proteins, RNA, and DNA, and these molecules cannot achieve stability without the cell wall and membrane. There can be no proteins without DNA and RNA, and there can be no DNA and RNA without proteins.

Location, Location, Location

As biochemists labored to determine the minimum number of gene products necessary for life, microbiologists made discoveries that revolutionized scientists' understanding of bacteria. These discoveries show that life at its minimum complexity requires not only the simultaneous occurrence of a certain number of proteins but also includes the strategic organization of these gene products within the cell.

Prior to the mid-1990s, microbiologists viewed bacteria as simply little "vessels" that contained a jumbled assortment of life molecules randomly dispersed inside the cell. In short, microbiologists did not think that bacteria possessed any significant internal organization.

This perception of bacteria stood in sharp contrast to the remarkable internal organization displayed by the complex cells (eukaryotes) that make up the multicellular plant, fungi, and animal kingdoms as well as the single-celled protozoans. Eukaryotic cells possess a nucleus, organelles, membrane systems, a cytoskeleton, numerous internal compartments, and other components that organize their cell contents at the subcellular and even molecular level.

Microbiologists now recognize, however, that bacteria also display a remarkable degree of internal organization. Though this arrangement does not involve subcellular structures, it occurs at the molecular level, both spatially and temporally.[20] Microbiologists Lucy Shapiro (Stanford) and Richard Losick (Harvard) state their observation: "The use of immunogold electron microscopy and fluorescence microscopy to study the subcellular organization of bacterial cells has revealed a surprising extent of protein compartmentalization and localization."[21]

Shapiro and Losick point out that while not all this internal ordering of proteins is necessary for cell survival, some does involve essential activities. The following few examples highlight the remarkable internal organization displayed by bacteria.

Bacterial chromosome. Unlike eukaryotic cells, which have several linear pieces of DNA interlaced with proteins inside the cell nucleus, bacteria and archaea possess one or more small naked strands of DNA that loop to form a circle. Microbiologists long thought that bacterial chromosomes diffused freely and randomly throughout the cell and that when the cell divided, the segregation of the two duplicate DNA molecules between the daughter cells was a passive process. This view, however, turns out to be incorrect. Microbiologists now observe that the bacterial chromosome must have a specific orientation within the cell. Moreover, during cell division, a complex ensemble of proteins must not only segregate the two newly reproduced DNA circles, but must also maintain the chromosomes in the correct orientation.[22] If not, the cell dies.

Bacteria also contain extremely small extrachromosomal strands of circular DNA called plasmids. Again, plasmids were long regarded as randomly dispersed and free to migrate throughout the cell. But scientists have now determined that even plasmids cluster and localize inside the cell.[23]

DNA polymerase. DNA polymerases are enzymes that duplicate DNA molecules during cell replication. Instead of moving along the DNA double strand like a "train on a track" to produce two copies of DNA from the parent DNA molecule, these enzymes must be localized near the center of the cell.[24] In other words, instead of being randomly distributed, DNA polymerases must be located in a specific region of the cell. Microbiologists now view bacterial DNA polymerases as "replication factories" precisely anchored near midcell. During cell replication, polymerase activity appears intimately connected to the machinery that orients and segregates the bacterial chromosome.

Cell division proteins. Bacterial cell division (in which the mother cell divides near its midplane to produce two daughter cells) requires dynamic spatial and temporal localization of several proteins. A key player in this process is the FtsZ protein. Several copies of FtsZ accumulate at the center of the cell and aggregate to form a ring that extends around the inner surface of the cell wall.[25] During cell division, this ring contracts to pinch the mother cell into two daughters.

An ensemble of proteins regulates the way that FtsZ binds to the inner cell wall and ensures that the ring forms at the proper location.[26] For example, the Min C and Min D proteins keep the FtsZ proteins from binding to the wrong place in the cell wall. The Min E protein interacts with the Min C and Min D proteins to promote FtsZ binding at the cell's midplane or "waistline." Any disruption of FtsZ, Min C, Min D, or Min E functions and interactions will compromise cell replication.

The example of cell division proteins, along with the previous examples of bacterial chromoses and DNA polymerase, represent only a few of a growing number of bacterial biochemical systems that display spatial and temporal ordering. Table 12.3 lists (without explanation) bacterial biochemical systems and individual proteins that research has shown to require exacting intracellular localization and timing. This organization

---

- Bacterial Chromosome

- DNA Polymerase

- Replication and Cell Division Proteins

Fts Z	Etr A
Fts A	SMC Proteins
Min C	Spo ØJ
Min D	
Min E	

- Chemotaxis Proteins
  Chemoreceptor Proteins
  Che W
  Che A

- Sporulation Proteins
  Spo VG
  Spo//E
  Spo ØJ

- Periplasmic Space
  Maltose Binding Proteins

- Membrane Domains

- Photosynthesis and Nitrogen Fixation

Table 12.3: Bacterial Components Displaying Organization

extends beyond a handful of examples and currently represents a defining characteristic of bacteria.

A little more than a decade of research has overturned the traditional view of bacteria. Bacteria are not little grab bags of molecules but rather organisms that display an incredible degree of internal organization and possess an exquisite orchestration of biochemical activity in spatial and temporal terms.

The type of internal organization found in bacteria seems to be universal among microorganisms. Therefore, from an evolutionary perspective, internal organization must be a property possessed by the last universal common ancestor (LUCA) and likely by organisms that proceeded from it. Internal organization of biomolecules would seem a necessity for life. Bacteria-like internal organization must, then, be accounted for in origin-of-life models.

This organization feature adds another dimension to life's minimal complexity. In summary, origin-of-life researchers must account not only for the simultaneous occurrence of a relatively large number of gene products but also for their spatial and temporal organization.

Putting the RTB Model to the Test

The top-down approach to the origin of life demonstrates that life in its most minimal form, whether independent or parasitic, is complex. The science of genomics has proved that hundreds of gene products are required for even the simplest microbial life forms. Furthermore, those gene products must be organized in specific, not random, order for them to function. This intricacy validates the RTB creation model's prediction 5: Life in its most minimal form is complex. The remarkable internal organization of "simple" life hints of a Creator at work.

Evaluating the Evidence

Naturalistic models for life's origin theorize simplicity for minimal life. Prediction 8 sets an expectation for an earliest life form that is extremely basic. Yet such simplicity is not the case.

With all common bottom-up and top-down approaches exhausted, creation appears to be the most reasonable explanation for how life got its start. Yet, several loophole theories remain under investigation.

Part IV

LOOKING

FOR

LOOPHOLES

CHAPTER 13

EXTREME LIFE

Scientists probing the harshest environments on Earth have repeatedly made the same astonishing discovery—thriving life.[1] Investigators studying the Dead Sea in Israel and the Great Salt Lake in Utah have encountered single-celled organisms that thrive on high salt levels. Located 1,300 feet (400 meters) below sea level, the Dead Sea is 28 percent salt by weight. The Great Salt Lake is nearly as salty.

Microbes have also been harvested from the hot, acidic soil in zones of fading volcanic activity. The volcanically active soil (*solfatara*) literally boils with temperatures reaching as high as 212 °F (100 °C). At the same time, sulfurous gas makes this soil extremely acidic. The microbes, though, don't seem to mind the heat or the acid.

These remarkably hardy creatures are considered extremophiles (the term means extreme-loving). They can survive and even thrive in extreme environments that present severe challenges to other forms of life. With standard bottom-up and top-down approaches to the origin of life meeting frustration at every turn, some scientists are looking for loopholes—alternative ways to naturally generate life. The development of life under early Earth's extreme conditions would provide such a way. Do these strange organisms explain the mystery behind the origin of life?

Single-celled microorganisms have been recovered at thermal vents located on the ocean floor. The water pressure at such depths is nearly three hundred times the air pressure at sea level. This intense pressure keeps water from boiling until its temperature exceeds 750 °F (400 °C). These vents spew out hot water at 660 °F (350 °C).

Single-celled microbes have also been found in the 2.5-mile- (4-kilometer-) thick ice sheet above Lake Vostok, Antarctica. The ice sheet's temperature ranges between –40 and –58 °F (–40 and –50 °C).

Meet the Squad — Introducing Extremophiles

Extremophiles are a diverse bunch, inhabiting extreme environments for a variety of reasons.[2] Researchers have identified the following classes of these organisms:

Thermophiles love high temperatures, typically growing at temperatures between 120 and 160 °F (50 and 70 °C). These microbes thrive in hot springs and undersea vents.

Hyperthermophiles are extreme heat lovers. They grow at temperatures between 176 and 235 °F (80 and 113 °C) and cannot be cultivated at temperatures below 176 °F (80 °C). *Pyrolobus fumaris* holds the thermophilic record, growing at hot locations between 194 and 235 °F (90 and 113 °C).

Psychrophiles live at cold temperatures. *Polaromonas vacuolata*, recovered from the Antarctic Ocean, grow best at 39 °F (4 °C) and cannot survive at temperatures above 54 °F (12 °C).

Acidophiles are acid lovers. Found in volcanic pools and hot sea vents, these organisms thrive at pHs of less than 2. (A neutral pH is 7.) Amazingly, *Picrophilus oshimae* and *Picrophilus torridus* can survive at a pH of 0 — an extreme acidity.

Alkalophiles require extreme alkaline conditions. Recovered in alkaline lakes and deserts, these bacteria grow at a pH greater than 10.

Halophiles make their home in salt mines and lakes. These environments contain from 20 to 30 percent salt.

Barophiles need high pressures to grow. Some of these microorganisms require pressures hundreds of times greater than those found on Earth's surface. The first barophile (MT41) discovered in the Pacific Ocean's Mariana Trench (the deepest sea-floor depression in the world) grows best at 300 to 700 times sea-level air pressure.

Some extremophiles perform double duty, existing under dually harsh conditions. For example, many thermophiles are also acidophiles. *Sulfolobus acidocldaruis*, a thermoacidophile, makes its home in the hot acidic waters of thermal springs. *Natronobacterium pharaonis*, a haloalkalophile, was first discovered in the alkaline lakes near Cairo, Egypt. These lakes possess high carbonate levels as well.

Scientists have even stumbled upon thriving complex microbial communities far down in Earth's subsurface—as deep as 9,200 feet (2.8 kilometers) underground. Virtually no organic nutrients exist at such depths. The extremophiles there use chemical energy to convert molecular hydrogen (produced by weathering reaction and carbon dioxide) into the organic substances needed for life.

Most extremophiles are single-celled microbes assigned to the domain (a biological classification) called *archaea*.[3] Prior to 1977, scientists viewed bacteria as a homogeneous group. Then University of Illinois microbiologist Carl Woese published two papers demonstrating that bacteria actually divide into two groups, based on their fundamental biochemical differences.[4] Organizing bacteria into two domains, archaea and eubacteria, Woese also suggested a third domain—eukarya, which includes the protozoans, fungi, plant, and animal kingdoms.

Most bacteria are mesophiles (organisms requiring moderate conditions). Yet a few eubacteria live at temperatures between 140 and 180 °F (60 and 80 °C). These eubacteria are considered extremophiles.

An Extreme Origin

Extremophiles inhabit environments that simulate some of the extreme conditions of early Earth. This leads some researchers to learn more about them and investigate whether they could have been Earth's first life forms.

To review briefly, advances in research during the past decade challenge the notion that life emerged from nonliving systems through strictly physical and chemical means. Life appeared early in Earth's history. Geochemical evidence indicates life's presence at or slightly before 3.8 billion years ago. The oldest rocks date 3.9 billion years ago. Prior to this time Earth existed (with a few intermittent exceptions) in a molten state unsuitable for living organisms.

Life also appeared suddenly. Between 4.5 and 3.9 billion years ago, Earth experienced numerous impact events that sterilized its surface and subsurface. These impacts—frustration events to life's origin—melted rock and volatilized oceans. Then, as soon as Earth's conditions were remotely able to support life, life appeared.

The discovery of archaea (and a few eubacteria) in hostile environments suggests to some researchers that life could have arisen under the extreme conditions of early Earth prior to 3.9 billion years ago. This loophole could keep a naturalistic explanation viable.[5] According to this view, extremophiles emerged first and paved the way for mesophiles.

The extremophilic origin-of-life scenarios garner support, say proponents, from evolutionary analysis of DNA sequences. This analysis places extremophiles at the base of the evolutionary tree.[6] Extremophiles seem to be the oldest and most primitive organisms on Earth. Laboratory experiments simulating a hot, chemically harsh early Earth environment—modeled after deep-sea hydrothermal vents—indicate that peptides, amino acids, and other biologically interesting molecules might form under harsh conditions.[7] These reactions represent necessary early steps in an extremophilic origin-of-life pathway.

Many investigators consider that any life emerging on Earth's surface prior to 3.9 billion years ago would seem to have required a hot start. They hope to extend the time available for life's beginning by pushing its events beyond 3.9 billion years to a time when Earth experienced hellish conditions. A thermophilic origin of life presumably provides the additional time needed for natural processes to generate life.

Other researchers point to the extremophilic microbial communities below Earth's surface as evidence that life first arose deep in the planet's crust and later evolved to produce mesophiles (organisms requiring moderate conditions) that lived above ground. Advocates of this view suggest that by emerging from within Earth's subsurface, life escaped the sterilizing impact events and harmful solar and stellar ultraviolet and ionizing radiation that frustrated life's origin on Earth's surface.[8]

This deep microbial biosphere hypothesis suggests to some investigators that life may have begun and still exists below the surface of other astronomical bodies with hostile exteriors.[9] This idea currently fuels the quest to discover Martian life forms. Researchers look to the discovery of microorganisms in the subzero ice of Antarctica as support for the existence of life on Europa, the frozen water world orbiting Jupiter.[10] Extremophiles' capacity to flourish in Earth's extreme environments seems to suggest the possibility for life to survive the adverse conditions of other planets and moons.

The circumstantial evidence favoring any of these extremophilic origin-of-life scenarios may appear impressive at first glance. However, the discovery of extremophiles does not automatically translate into mounting evidence for a naturalistic start to life. Just because life exists in extreme environments doesn't mean it originated there.

Scientific Challenges

Origin-of-life explanations involving extremophiles face most of the same challenges as those describing life's start in more moderate surroundings. The harsh chemical and physical conditions of radical environments further complicate the already significant chemical problems (see chapters 7 through 9) and information issues (see chapter 10) facing any naturalistic model.

As with mesophilic origin-of-life explanations, a source of prebiotic molecules must be established. While researchers performing laboratory experiments simulating deep-sea hydrothermal vents have produced biologically important molecules, these compounds represent only the first step in a thermophilic beginning to life. As discussed in chapter 7, prebiotic molecules that form at high temperatures or under highly acidic or highly alkaline conditions face a dramatically increased likelihood of rapid chemical destruction.

The biochemical modifications needed to stabilize proteins and RNA structures in extreme environments exacerbate the already enormous problems of producing these information-rich molecules via natural mechanisms. Scientists studying thermophile biochemistry are making progress toward understanding the molecular alterations needed to stabilize proteins at high temperatures.[11] They have learned that thermophile proteins possess amino acid compositions, three-dimensional structures, and chemical mechanisms similar to those of mesophile proteins.

Thermophiles achieve high-temperature stability for their proteins by distributing key amino acids throughout the protein's amino acid sequence. Upon folding, these vital residues interact in three-dimensional space to stabilize the protein. Mesophilic proteins do not require these stabilizing interactions. Thus, amino acids can vary much more freely at these positions in mesophilic proteins than they can in thermophilic proteins. In other words, the amino acid sequences of thermophilic proteins prove more restrictive rather than less. This fact reduces the likelihood that an amino acid sequence will translate into a functional thermophilic protein.

If extremophiles were the first life, at some point within the evolutionary paradigm they must have given rise to mesophiles. Envisioning this transition is difficult. The fossil and geochemical record indicates that surface mesophiles appeared as soon as Earth could possibly support life. This timing leaves only a few million years for subsurface or surface extremophiles, employing chemoautotrophic pathways (pathways that extract chemical energy from inorganic materials in the environment) to evolve into mesophilic photoautotrophs (organisms that rely on photosynthesis).

Biochemical changes to support this transition would have had to occur all at once in practically every protein, transfer RNA, and ribosomal RNA molecule. But biochemical alterations stabilizing extremophilic biomolecules typically make them unsuitable for mesophilic environments. For example, for many thermophilic proteins, the stabilizing alterations make the protein rigid at mesophilic temperatures.[12] Proteins need a certain level of molecular flexibility to function. At high temperatures, thermophilic proteins possess the necessary freedom of motion to function. At low temperatures the necessary stabilizing interactions reduce molecular mobility and, hence, function. An extremophile in a mesophilic environment will struggle to survive because its proteins experience diminished, and sometimes even a complete loss of, function.

Microbiology further highlights the difficulty of an extremophile-to-mesophile transformation. Though extremophiles thrive under conditions inhospitable for most life, they are still fastidious. Typically, researchers experience great difficulty in isolating extremophiles from their natural surroundings and finding conditions that permit their cultivation in the laboratory.[13]

Extremophiles simply do not tolerate mesophilic conditions very well. While they can survive nonextreme conditions in a dormant state, they do not grow under mesophilic conditions. For instance, *Pyrolobus fumarii* cannot grow below 194 °F (90 °C).[14] The need for wholesale biochemical changes, coupled with extremophiles' inability to grow and flourish (and therefore to produce population numbers necessary to evolve) upon migration into mesophilic environments, raises questions as to the likelihood of mesophiles' rapid emergence from extremophiles.

In addition to these general problems for extremophilic origin-of-life models, recent scientific discoveries expose some specific challenges to the thermophilic and psychrophilic origin-of-life explanations.

Some Like It Hot

Of the three basic extremophile scenarios for the origin of life, the thermophilic scenario is perhaps the most popular. Early Earth was a hot place. It seems reasonable to think that the first life forms might have been heat-loving extremophiles.

Nevertheless, researchers have raised some important questions to consider about this scenario.

Was there enough time? Scientists from Stanford University and the NASA Ames Research Center explored the likelihood that life originated under hot surface conditions prior to 3.9 billion years ago. They estimated the time frame in which Earth's temperature resided in the vicinity of 212 °F (100 °C)—within the temperature range required by hyperthermophiles.[15]

A collision between Earth (soon after its formation) and an object roughly the size of Mars was the most significant event during Earth's Hadean era.[16] Upon impact both bodies' cores fused, spewing the impactor's lighter elements into Earth's orbit, where they quickly coalesced to form the Moon.[17] Earth's surface heated enough to vaporize silica (sand). As the surface cooled, the temperature would have persisted within a thermophilic window for at least 100,000 years but for no more than 10 million years—a time period far shorter for life than that on which natural process life-origin models depend.

The window determined by the Stanford University and NASA Ames scientists likely overestimates the available time for a high-temperature origin of life. The Moon-forming impactor stands as only one of many large objects striking Earth between 4.5 and 3.9 billion years ago.[18] Each impactor would have reset the molten rock clock on Earth's surface and subsurface, elevating the temperature well above thermophiles' maximum survivable range. (See "The Greatest Frustration Event," page 87.) The Stanford and NASA Ames scientists conclude that early Earth's history simply does not allow sufficient time for a thermophilic beginning to life.

Were thermophiles first? Just as natural history calls into question a hot origin of life, so the constraints imposed by thermophilic biochemistry also show a high-temperature beginning for life unlikely.

Prompted by a number of genetic comparisons, a team of French scientists questioned the traditional evolutionary tree and the placement of thermophiles at the tree's base.[19] These scientists (working within the evolutionary paradigm) compared DNA sequences from a large collection of organisms in an attempt to define the deepest branches of the tree of life. Using improved methods, their analysis indicates that mesophiles, not thermophiles, root the tree. While evolutionary biologists initially viewed these results as controversial, two follow-up studies confirm the work of the French scientists.[20] Extremophiles have been uprooted from their position as life's first organisms.

Further corroborative evidence comes from another team of French researchers. They exploited the correlation between ribosomal RNA's (rRNA's) guanine (G) and cytosine (C) content and its growth temperature to estimate the environmental temperature of the last universal common ancestor (LUCA).[21] Assuming that all life evolved from LUCA, the team compared rRNA sequences for representatives from life's major lineages. This approach allowed an estimation of LUCA's G and C content. Though these scientists' work has not yet gained universal acceptance by the origin-of-life community, their results indicate that LUCA's G and C content would have been too low to support a thermophilic lifestyle.[22] In other words, within the evolutionary paradigm, LUCA must have been a mesophile, not a thermophile.

Could thermophiles come from an RNA-world? Scientists from New Zealand examined the likelihood of a thermophilic origin by characterizing the stability of RNA three-dimensional structures at high temperatures.[23] These researchers chose to focus attention on RNA molecules because the RNA-world hypothesis for the origin of life is so widely accepted.

The New Zealand investigators showed that at thermophilic temperatures RNA molecules isolated from the specialized proteins inside the cell that maintain and repair RNA unfold and lose their three-dimensional structure and functional capacity. Those RNA molecules capable of retaining some folded character at high temperatures lost structural specificity, rapidly transitioning among a variety of three-dimensional shapes. Although magnesium ions can physically stabilize the RNA three-dimensional structure, rather than preserving the likelihood of a thermophilic RNA-world origin of life, this ion's presence creates additional problems. Biochemists have known for some time that magnesium ions promote the chemical breakdown of RNA.[24]

Without the ability to produce RNA or other essential codes under conditions of extreme heat, thermophiles could not have been Earth's first life. This line of investigation dims the hope raised by a thermophilic scenario for life's origin. But what about the scenario at the other end of the thermometer?

Baby, It's Cold Outside

Psychrophilic scenarios for the origin of life are typically connected with ideas about life emerging not on Earth but elsewhere—someplace like Europa, the Jovian moon. However, a few scientists think that such a low-temperature concept for life's start may apply to Earth. If life could originate and persist in cold environments, its habitable zone greatly expands.

Researchers Jeffrey Bada and Antonio Lazcano are leading proponents of pyschrophilic pathways to life's origin on Earth.[25] They have several reasons for advancing such a hypothesis. Bada and Lazcano acknowledge, for example, the long-term instability of biomolecules at both high and more moderate temperatures. They also note the fact that some of life's building blocks cannot be made in the laboratory unless the reaction temperature is near 32 °F (0 °C).

Regardless of where life started, the greatest biochemical challenge to a low-temperature beginning comes from water, which all life requires. Existing at subzero temperatures, life uses a variety of methods to hold on to liquid water.[26] For example, some psychrophiles produce an abundance of small molecules in their cytoplasm as well as in the environment outside the cell to lower water's freezing point to below 32 °F (0 °C). Other psychrophiles produce antifreeze proteins that halt the formation of an extensive ice lattice. Depending on location, antifreeze proteins keep internal and external water from freezing.

For life to begin under cold conditions, either antifreeze proteins or an abundance of small molecules must form in the environment early in the chemical evolutionary pathway. The necessity of this sequential step adds to the already daunting requirements for natural-process scenarios.

Both temperature extremes—high and low—pose problems. At high temperatures the complex structure of proteins and RNA unfolds. This occurs because high temperatures disrupt the interactions that stabilize the biomolecules' three-dimensional architecture. Ironically, temperatures approaching 32 °F (0 °C, water's freezing point) also threaten protein and RNA structure.

In large part, the three-dimensional structure of cellular membranes and proteins, as well as DNA's double helix, all form as a consequence of the "hydrophobic effect"—the aggregation of water-insoluble, oil-like materials in aqueous systems.[27] This effect occurs, not because of attraction among the aggregates, but because of repulsion between water and the oil-like materials. Aggregation segregates the oil-like compounds from the water molecules. These processes maintain water molecules in a disordered state, keeping the system's entropy at a relatively high level. If aggregation and segregation do not occur, water forms a more ordered, icelike structure as it interacts with the oil-like materials. This formulation decreases the water's entropy and therefore is thermodynamically unfavorable. Proteins, RNA, DNA, and cell membrane components possess oil-like regions as part of their molecular makeup. To maintain water in the maximum disordered state, these oil-like regions aggregate, thereby sequestering themselves from contact with water.

At cold temperatures, as water begins to develop a more orderly icelike structure (below 39 °F or 4 °C), membrane aggregation and the folding of protein, RNA, and DNA molecules become less likely because water already possesses a high degree of order. The hydrophobic effect ceases to operate at cold temperatures. Aggregation and segregation cannot produce disordered water because the reduced temperature has already forced water into an ordered state. Biochemists refer to the loss of biomolecular structure that occurs below 39 °F (4 °C) as cold denaturation.[28]

This phenomenon has important implications for a cold origin of life. The three-dimensional structures of proteins, RNA, and DNA—critical to their function—cannot be maintained (without all the protective features of living cells already in place) at temperatures near or below 39 °F (4 °C). Here again, the naturalistic emergence of life meets frustration. As confirmation, biochemists recently demonstrated the cold denaturation of an RNA enzyme (the hammerhead ribozyme).[29] This finding means that cold denaturation thwarts any low temperature origin-of-life scenario that proceeds through an RNA world.

Deep-Down Life

Much of the enthusiasm for the deep-biosphere model stems from the perception that Earth's crust teems with life, perhaps as far down as 3.7 miles (6 kilometers). In the opinion of many researchers, this possibility makes the deep biosphere an imperative on Earth and on other solar-system bodies, such as Mars. Moreover, proponents maintain that the ecology of today's deep biosphere resembles the environment of early Earth as well as the ecology below the surface of Mars and other solar system bodies. They hypothesize that deep-biosphere communities make their living by feeding off carbon dioxide in Earth's crust and hydrogen gas generated by reactions that take place between water and the rock's surface.

Continued exploration and characterization of life in Earth's crust, however, increasingly contradict the idea of a robust, deep biosphere that feeds off rock.[30] Instead of finding abundant microbial ecosystems nourished by inorganic geochemicals, microbiologists exploring Earth's crust more routinely find trace life that survives on the organic remains of photosynthetic activity trickled down from above. Furthermore, the microbes in Earth's crust exist for the most part in a near-dormant state, displaying incredibly slow metabolic rates.[31]

Even the relatively rare underground microbial ecologies based on hydrogen metabolism cannot salvage the deep-biosphere origin-of-life model.[32] Though these ecosystems function in isolation from surface life, they depend on unusual and just-right chemical conditions as well as tectonic activity unique to Earth. Hydrogen gas used by subsurface microbes forms when water reacts with the iron(2) in basalt. But this reaction doesn't occur under normal conditions. Rather, the reaction takes place only because the iron(2) produced by it precipitates in the specific environment of Earth's crust and pulls the reaction along.[33] Moreover, this reaction requires unusual pH conditions and quickly ceases once the iron(2) on the basalt surface has been consumed.[34]

If not for fine-tuned tectonic activity that periodically exposes fresh rock surfaces at exactly the right rate, hydrogen production would not continue, nor would it likely be significant over geological time frames. This tectonic requirement means that subsurface life based on a hydrogen gas ecology is not very likely for Mars because that planet lacks the necessary tectonic activity. The stringent geochemical requirements also reduce the likelihood that the deep biosphere explanation could account for life's start on Earth.

One final point deserves consideration. Earth's hydrogen-based ecosystems reside in crustal regions devoid of all organic materials except those generated by methanogenic microbes. Without organic materials, life cannot emerge by naturalistic processes alone. As new discoveries accumulate, the deep biosphere explanation for life's beginning becomes less plausible.

Putting the RTB Model to the Test

Though not explicitly listed as a prediction in chapter 3, the RTB origin-of-life model foresees that any appeal to extremophilic naturalistic origin-of-life scenarios will fail. The RTB Model, however, does require the early appearance of extremophiles on Earth. Chapter 17 explains the reasons why.

Evaluating the Evidence

Extremophiles are remarkable organisms that challenge the traditional view of what constitutes a habitable environment. Origin-of-life researchers understandably exploit these expanded domains of habitability in an attempt to find naturalistic explanations for life's start. As work continues along these lines, however, the extremophile option loses credibility. But, perhaps another loophole theory—the origin of life on Mars—can help solve the problems connected with a naturalistic beginning for life.

CHAPTER 14

LIFE ON MARS?

M ore than thirty years ago, Carl Sagan declared that discovery of life on Mars would prove life originated naturally and with relative ease.[1] Such a find would transform the statistics dramatically. No longer the unique treasure of one planet in a billion trillion, life would be the offspring of two planets out of nine in a single planetary system. Such a revelation would magnify the idea that life is abundant throughout the universe.

Sagan's opinion proved contagious. Hoping to establish naturalism, many scientists and laypeople alike see Mars as a nursery for life—the place of its origin and incubation. This loophole hypothesis makes them eager to discover whether Mars supports, or has ever supported, any form of life. Later, they believe, meteorites transported life to Earth.

A Rock Celebrity

Announcements on national television riveted public attention on the idea that early Martian life seeded Earth. On August 7, 1996, people watching the evening news heard President Bill Clinton and a team of NASA researchers celebrate the discovery of a four-pound rock from Mars—a meteorite that reportedly contained fossils and chemical signatures of life.

Overnight, it seemed, the meteorite (ALH84001) became a sensation. But in fact, it had been found in the Allan Hills region of Antarctica and sat for nine years in a vault before geologists and chemists performed their analysis and released the results. When at last released, those results convinced many people that the meteorite had drastically and forever changed beliefs on Earth's first life and humanity. UCLA astronomer David Paige described the findings on this meteorite as "the most spectacular scientific discoveries since humans first gazed skyward."[2] Planetary astronomer Tobias Owen announced, "It will change the way that we think about life in the universe."[3]

Figure 14.1: Martian Meteorite ALH84001

(Photo courtesy of NASA, Jet Propulsion Laboratory, and Caltech)

What about this hunk of rock held such promise?

Tiny air pockets inside the rock matched the composition of the Martian atmosphere. The iron oxides, iron sulfides, and oxygen isotope ratios matched those found in eleven other known Martian meteorites.[4] These details gave the NASA team confidence that ALH84001 came from Mars. However, it was the great age of ALH84001 that singled this rock out for special attention.

Potassium-argon dating placed the meteorite's origin at 4.56 ± 0.13 billion years ago.[5] Rubidium-strontium dating established that it suffered at least a partial melt 4.0 billion years ago.[6] These dates made ALH84001 the oldest known rock from *any* planet. This meteorite is the oldest from Mars by a factor of three. (The next was only 1.3 billion years old.)

Recognition that ALH84001 provided a sample from when the planet was still relatively warm and wet generated even more excitement. (Mars' atmosphere became thin and its surface dry and cold 3.8 billion years ago.) The warm, wet past of ALH84001 and the presence of carbonate globules along its fracture line motivated a NASA research team to examine it closely for signs of life.

A few days after the initial television announcements, a team headed by NASA geologist David McKay published its initial findings.[7] Four indicators signified past Martian life. Mars meteorite ALH84001 contained:

(1) carbonate globules similar to the carbonate deposits produced by Earth life
(2) polycyclic aromatic hydrocarbons (PAHs), which organisms often produce when they die and decay
(3) magnetic mineral crystals of the size and type used by bacteria to help them navigate
(4) elongated ovoids resembling the microfossils of extremely tiny bacteria

The team acknowledged that by themselves none of these evidences qualified as proof that life once existed in the rock or on Mars. In their opinion, however, the sum of evidence made a compelling case.

Only the strength of the media attention and popular enthusiasm for this case can explain the lack of fanfare given the research findings of the succeeding five years. This data calls into question all four evidences.

A Fall from Fame
Astronomers cast the first doubts, noting that ALH84001 was far from a pristine sample. Radioactive nuclei found inside the meteorite established its exposure to deep-space radiation for 16 million years. That's how long the rock wandered in interplanetary space.[8] Other evidence showed that the meteorite was buried under Antarctic ice for another 13,000 years before being discovered—an extended opportunity for contamination.[9]

A melted meteorite. Nine months after NASA's and Clinton's televised celebration, three geophysicists in Hawaii published their conclusion that the carbonate globules in ALH84001, said to have arisen from biological processes, most likely crystallized from shock-melted inorganic materials.[10] This shock melting could have occurred either as the meteorite was exposed to intense radiation in interplanetary space or when it passed through Earth's atmosphere. Biologically produced carbonates require temperatures to stay below 235 °F (113 °C).[11] The shock melting evident in ALH84001 suggests that these carbonates formed at temperatures above 930 °F (500 °C).

A different research team cast some uncertainty on the Hawaiian team's conclusion when they found that ALH84001's ancient magnetization apparently had not been disturbed.[12] That apparent lack of disturbance indicated that at least some of the rock had stayed cooler than 570 °F (300 °C) and possibly as cool as 235 °F (113 °C). Because inorganic carbonate formation can occur at both low and high temperatures, the source of this meteorite's carbonate globules could not yet be nailed down.

More recent research on the carbonate formation question supports a nonbiological origin. Geologists from the Johnson Space Center, Lockheed, the University of Texas, and the University of New Mexico determined that the carbonates in ALH84001 range from 3.90 ± 0.04 billion years old (by the rubidium-strontium dating method) to 4.04 ± 0.10 billion years old (by the lead-lead dating method).[13] These dates place carbonate formation time squarely in the era of the solar system's heavy asteroid bombardment and of Mars' relatively abundant surface water. An impact could have resulted in a high-temperature origin of the carbonates and/or a low-temperature origin—if it shocked the rock and melted ice in its vicinity, thereby leading to carbonate precipitation.[14]

The carbonates might even be primordial, based on the findings of an international team of astronomers. They recently detected carbonates in the dust shells around ancient stars nearing the end of their burning cycles and about to eject large quantities of gas and dust into interstellar space.[15] These carbonates could not have formed in the presence of liquid water but rather must have developed on the surface of dust and ice grains. This research indicates that at least some carbonates in the solar system existed before the large solar system bodies formed and before liquid water or life.

A sticky substance. Relatively simple and common molecules, PAHs can be the residue of decaying organisms. They also can be the product of high-temperature hydrocarbon reactions.The sticky tars that accumulate on barbecue grills are examples of PAHs.

PAHs are abundant in both Earth's solar system and galaxy. They exist in interstellar molecular clouds, comets, interplanetary and interstellar dust, and in carbonaceous meteorites. Anywhere carbon compounds meet the right temperatures (900 to 2,000 °F or 500 to 1,100 °C), PAHs form.[16]

How did the PAHs in meteorite ALH84001 form?

The same shock melting that led to the formation of most of the carbonates in ALH84001 would also have produced most, if not all, of its PAHs. Given the plentiful supply of nonbiological PAHs in both the solar system and galaxy, the Martian surface must also be littered with them. Contamination by any of the meteorite's organically produced PAHs most likely came from its terrestrial organics once the meteorite had arrived on Earth.

The considerable quantity of carbon-14 in ALH84001's carbonaceous material lends credence to this conclusion.[17] With a half-life of just 5,730 years, any carbon-14 from Mars would have vanished during the meteorite's 16-million-year journey through interplanetary space.

Questionable crystals. The initial identification of the magnetic mineral crystals' origin seemed reasonable. A few bacterial species (magnetotactic bacteria) manufacture miniature magnets for use as compasses. A small fraction make magnetic crystals, either magnetite (an iron oxide) or greigite (an iron sulfide). McKay's NASA team identified magnetite and pyrrhotite (similar to greigite) crystals in ALH84001. These crystals measured 40 to 50 nanometers (one nanometer = one-billionth of a meter) in diameter, roughly the size and shape of those in magnetotactic bacteria. However, the crystals lacked the uniformity in appearance characteristic of organic magnetites.

In its most recent analysis, the team compared ALH84001's magnetites with inorganically produced terrestrial magnetites and magnetite crystals produced by the bacterial strain MV-1.[18] Three-fourths of the meteorite's magnetites resembled the inorganic magnetites; one-fourth resembled those found in MV-1.

Despite this partial resemblance to bacterial crystals, a British team determined that all the magnetites in ALH84001 are "entirely consistent with in situ [natural or original] growth by solid-state diffusion as a result of carbonate decomposition during impact heating."[19] They concluded that a biological origin "should not be invoked for any magnetites" in ALH84001.[20]

A biological origin for the pyrrhotite crystals has also been put in doubt. Eleven astronomers from western Europe and the United States discovered pyrrhotite grains in abundance in both interplanetary dust and in the circumstellar dust disks of young stellar objects.[21]

Even among die-hard enthusiasts for a biological origin of the crystals, hope has faded. The ultrasimplicity of magnetic crystals in ALH84001 and the existence of terrestrial analogues for all of them point to terrestrial contamination as the source. Magnetotactic bacteria are found only in pools of water—the only place a magnet would be of any use to a bacterium. Years of lying upon Antarctic ice frequently exposed the meteorite to water from melting snow. Indeed, the amino acids found in ALH84001—glycine, serine, and alanine—are also the most common amino acids in Antarctic meltwater.[22] Moreover, their relative abundance makes an identical match with that of amino acids found in the meltwater.

The most conclusive evidence against a Martian source for the supposed organics in ALH84001 also comes from biochemistry. All the amino acids in ALH84001 are left-handed.[23] Life chemistry demands they either be all left- or all right-handed. However, once an organism dies, its amino acids gradually decay into a random mixture of left- and right-handed configurations (see chapter 9). After a million years at freezing temperatures, roughly half the amino acids from decaying life will be left-handed and the other half right-handed. Since ALH84001 was last in contact with Mars 16 million years ago, its amino acids must not be from Mars. Most likely they are Earth-life contaminants.

Notorious nanobacteria. The claimed microfossils found in ALH84001 have received perhaps the greatest media attention. Yet few news reports have included significant details. Most people remain unaware, for example, that these egg-shaped, tubelike structures are just 20 nanometers (0.8 millionths of an inch) in diameter.

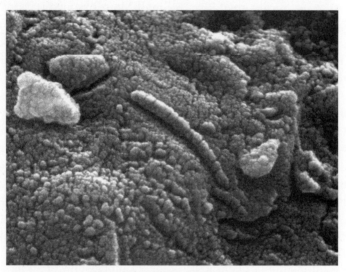

Figure 14.2: Tiny Martians?

Some people believed these structures to be the fossils of extremely tiny bacteria from Mars. (Photo courtesy of NASA)

The microfossils found in ALH84001 were inside carbonate globules only fifty micrometers (two-thousandths of an inch) across. These numbers raise the question, how small can life be? A survey of the smallest forms of life on Earth gives an idea.

A microfossil twenty nanometers in diameter accommodates just one ribosome—only one of the thousands of complex molecular structures essential to internal cell functions. Yet the most familiar of cells, the eukaryotes (cells with a nucleus containing genetic material, a cytoskeleton, and cytoplasmic organelles) range from 10,000 to 100,000 nanometers in diameter.[24] The simplest cells, the prokaryotes, have diameters that range from 1,000 to 10,000 nanometers in diameter.[25] The smallest cells ever found measure 250 nanometers by 1,200 nanometers.[26] These organisms, though self-replicating, are not self-sustaining. As parasites, they require the molecular machinery of other organisms to sustain their life functions. Yet they are still more than five times the size of the supposed microfossils on the Mars meteorite.

In letters to the journal *Science*, three different researchers explained why the "microfossils" in ALH84001 were much too small to be fossils of organisms.[27] Explanations also came from other widely recognized sources. The National Academy of Sciences hosted a 1998 workshop for physicists, biochemists, ecologists, and microbiologists on the subject "Size Limits of Very Small Microorganisms." Workshop participants concluded that self-replicating cells smaller than two hundred nanometers in diameter are theoretically impossible.[28] Cells need room for the minimum number of DNA molecules, ribosomes, and proteins, or their molecular equivalent. These theoretical limits were generous, calculated for parasitic cells with molecular machinery borrowed from other more complex cells. At twenty nanometers in diameter, ALH84001's "microfossils" are much too small to be fossils of organisms.

This conclusion was temporarily shaken by the findings of two Finnish scientists. They rekindled the hope that the tiny oval structures in ALH84001 might well be bacteria when they claimed to have discovered bacteria (called nanobacteria) one-tenth the size of a typical bacterium.[29] Even though these ultratiny microbes defied the theoretical lower limit for life, the case for nanobacteria seemed airtight at first. The Finnish scientists reportedly cultivated these bacteria, prepared subcultures, and even isolated and sequenced DNA attributed to the nanomicrobes.

Recently, scientists from the National Institutes of Health (NIH) exploded this "nanobacteria" bubble. They showed that experimental artifacts and contamination accounted for it.[30] The DNA sequenced by the Finnish scientists came from an environmental bacterium (*Phyllobacterium mysinaceareum*) that frequently contaminates DNA amplification and sequencing experiments.

So what *are* the "microfossils" in ALH84001? One independent research team demonstrated that the wormlike structures are simply "the jutting edges of mineral crystals reshaped by a coating used to prepare the sample for the scanning electron microscope."[31] In general, the problem at the nanometer scale is that inorganic deposition can easily take on various lifelike shapes. Therefore, shape alone proves nothing, and neither do mineral deposits.

Five years and many millions of research dollars have strengthened understanding of meteors and organisms but weakened all four evidences for life in ALH84001. Though McKay's team still holds out hope, the rest of the scientific community has abandoned the conclusion that

Martian life rode to Earth on ALH84001. One geologist commented, "I never bought the reasoning that the compounding of inclusive arguments is conclusive."[32]

Other Martian Immigrants
ALH84001 is not the only Martian meteorite to find its way to Earth, nor the biggest. At last count, twenty other Martian rocks are known to have arrived. The largest is the Nakhla meteorite, weighing in at 90 pounds.[33]

Nakhla is the only Martian meteorite (besides ALH84001) stirring speculation about past biological activity on Mars. Researchers have found amino acids, PAHs, as well as the structures that resemble microfossils.[34] However, as with ALH84001, the amino acids clearly result from terrestrial contamination (see chapter 9, pages 130-131), the PAHs are fully accounted for by Nakhla's past chemical environments, and non-organic chemical pathways explain the "microfossils."

Most ejecta from Mars is dust, but no scientist has yet isolated any for analysis. The motivation to do so has been low since Scripps scientists demonstrated that no amino acids or any other biological building blocks in interplanetary or interstellar dust could survive the heat of entry into Earth's atmosphere.[35]

A Martian Mantra
Researchers looking to Mars for a solution to the life-origin mystery on Earth have coined a mantra: "Follow the water."[36] This phrase acknowledges that all physical life needs water for its birth, survival, and reproduction. For life to originate on Mars and later seed Earth, a large quantity of liquid water must have been on or near Mars' surface during its youth. Because a wet, youthful Mars would have left a residual trace of water in the recent history of the planet, the feverish search for its evidence continues.

Yet for the past 4 billion years, Mars has been very dry. If all the water in the Martian atmosphere rained down at once, the depth of water on the planet's surface would be only one-millionth of a meter deep—shallower than the thickness of a single sheet of tissue paper.[37] But that water will not get the chance to precipitate. Mars' air pressure is so low that ice never melts and water vapor never liquefies. The past and present climate of Mars has dehydrated its crust to a depth of about a thousand feet (300 meters).[38] Because the atmosphere is so thin, any ground ice that might have arrived on board comets is unstable (proceeds to evaporate) whenever the surface temperature rises above $-105\ °F$ ($-76\ °C$).[39]

Air Pressure and Liquid Water

Low air pressure is one reason Mars is so dry. The lower the atmospheric pressure, the lower the boiling point of water. This effect can be noticed when one boils water at high altitudes. On top of Pikes Peak in Colorado the air pressure is only half that at sea level. Consequently, water boils at 175 °F (80 °C). As air pressure drops further, water boils at its freezing point and liquid water can no longer exist in its liquid state. With an air pressure of just a tiny fraction (0.006) of Earth's, Mars cannot hold liquid water on its surface.

Besides some deep crustal ice, surface water has only been positively identified at Mars' north pole, where temperatures never get warm enough for frozen water to sublime (evaporate without passing through the liquid state). There, water ice becomes exposed when the top cap of frozen carbon dioxide evaporates in Mars' summer.

A June 22, 2000, press conference, however, raised enthusiasm that water may have been more common on Mars not long ago, geologically speaking. NASA astronomers announced their discovery of relatively recent water flows on Mars.[40] They deduced from the lack of cratering and significant dust erosion in Martian channels that some of these channels must be young. Otherwise, meteorites would have pocked these channels with craters and/or Martian dust storms would have filled them in or worn them down. On this basis, astronomers calculated the channels' age as younger than a few million years.[41]

These channels were found only at high southern latitudes. This location made sense, because only at high latitudes does the possibility of a water channel exist in recent Martian history. The NASA team suggested that a small amount of water (either from 4 billion years ago or from the recent arrival of comets) might have seeped underground into an aquifer. A recent crustal episode—for example, a volcanic or geothermal event—could have forced the underground water to the surface, where it instantly froze, forming a dam and blocking the liquid water behind it from reaching the surface. Eventually, the buildup of pressure would have caused the dam to break, unleashing a torrent of liquid water upon the Martian surface. If the dam developed high enough on a steep slope, the unleashed water could have cut a channel before it all evaporated or froze.[42] The observation seemed to fit this hypothesis.

More than a year after the press conference, however, a geologist from the Lunar and Planetary Institute announced a more probable scenario involving no water. Allan Treiman demonstrated that "the gully flows are the remnants of massive dust avalanches, comparable to large climax snow avalanches seen on Earth."[43] Dust is everywhere on Mars and (as frequently observed dust storms attest) is easily moved by wind. For a large avalanche, the dust particles must first stick together. Such stickiness could come from the shapes of the particles or from cementation like that observed at the Viking landing sites. The preference for high southern latitudes may be explained by (1) the dusts' abundance in the southern highlands and (2) the consistency with which giant dust storms originate at those high southern latitudes.

Evidence that Mars has been dry for at least the past 3 to 4 billion years comes from the chemistry of the Martian meteorites. All manifest an extremely low content of hydrates and other stored water indicating the home planet was dry when they left.[44]

Hints of earlier liquid water appeared in the late 1960s and early 1970s when the Mariner spacecraft photographed Mars' entire surface. These photos revealed some sinuous channels that resemble dry riverbeds on Earth. The Viking orbiters confirmed the ancient water channels and the Mars Global Surveyor images later provided even more detail.

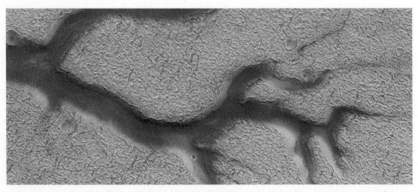

Figure 14.3: Outflow Channels and Valley Networks on Mars' Surface
The planet was wet early in its history but has been dry for 3.8 billion years.
(Photo courtesy of NASA, Jet Propulsion Laboratory, and Caltech)

Measured erosion rates indicate that any liquid water ever existing on Mars dates back to the time of the heavy asteroidal bombardment. The rate of erosion since the end of this time, at 3.8 billion years ago, measures no more than a hundredth of a micrometer (0.000003 inches) per year.[45] Craters that formed after the heavy bombardment are perfectly preserved. Until the end of this bombardment, erosion rates were a thousand times greater or more. Craters that survived this era are heavily degraded. Given that even a tiny quantity of liquid water on Mars would have increased erosion rates to *much* more than a hundredth of a micrometer per year, most astronomers agree that Mars must have been dry for the past 3.8 billion years.

Mars also shows no conclusive evidence of oceans or seas at any time in its history. Some indicators of ancient lakes can be seen, though possible outflow channels seem relatively few in number.

This limited water supply matches the predictions of the best solar system models. Given its weak surface gravity (only 40 percent as strong as Earth's), Mars would never have been able to retain water for long. But until 3.8 billion years ago, collisions by comets and planetesimals (bodies smaller than planets but larger than comets or asteroids) brought large quantities of water to Mars. Ancient gases around the planet set up a greenhouse effect and trapped more of the Sun's heat than does the current thin atmosphere, thereby permitting some water retention. These factors suggest Mars could have possessed liquid water in various locations early in its history.

Direct evidence that water was never plentiful on Mars comes from ALH84001. This rock remained on the planet for 4.5 billion years before being flung to Earth. It experienced all of Martian history. Thus, its very low water and hydrate content implies that the meteorite saw little or no water thoughout that time.

The likelihood of water on Mars prior to 3.8 billion years ago also can be discerned from indirect evidence. As the young channels seen in the southern highlands could have been cut by water or by dust avalanches, so too could have been the ancient channels. Just how much water actually flowed across the Martian surface during the heavy bombardment cannot be known for certain until more Martian meteorites the age of ALH84001 have been recovered and analyzed.

Yet another line of reasoning suggests to astronomers that liquid water could have remained no more than a brief time on Mars. Given the planet's distance from the Sun and the Sun's faint luminosity during Mars' youth (see "A Brighter Young Sun," page 218), Mars would have needed an enormous carbon-dioxide mantle to trap sufficient solar heat for the frozen water to melt. However, liquid water reacts with carbon dioxide to form carbonic acid. This carbonic acid falling upon Mars' surface rocks would have produced carbonates. Carbon dioxide would then be rapidly depleted from the atmosphere, lowering Mars' capacity to trap the Sun's heat and thus swiftly transforming Mars into a frozen, dry wasteland—not a hospitable place for life.[46]

Bigger Challenges to Life on Mars

For some, Mars' proximity makes it an attractive possibility as the site for the "seeds" of Earth life. However, in their zeal to find such a nearby source, many researchers have overlooked the mounting evidence that Mars presents even harsher conditions for life's origins than does Earth. In addition to being much drier than Earth, Mars has always been colder. Thus, chemical reactions would run slower there. The lack of a carbonate-silicate cycle would leave Mars with no means to handle the continual increase in the Sun's heat and light. (See "Racing the Solar Clock," page 216 for an explanation as to why the Sun continually brightens.) Any possible conditions for life's origins would, therefore, be fleeting at best.

In addition, the Martian atmosphere has always been thinner than Earth's, thus exposing its surface to more ultraviolet radiation and hastening the departure of water. A thinner atmosphere would imply fewer resources for emerging life to exploit. Ultraviolet radiation would impair, if not shut down, prebiotic chemical pathways.

The Martian crust offers a less hospitable, dangerously corrosive chemical environment. Specifically, the soil is more oxidizing.[47] Prebiotic chemical pathways, if they did develop, would therefore be destroyed even more surely than on Earth.

Mars' obliquity (the tilt of its rotation axis) varies chaotically. Astronomers calculate that Mars' axis sometimes tilts by sixty degrees relative to perpendicular in the solar system plane. At other times the tilt is zero degrees.[48] Such severe changes lead to radical climatic disturbances, putting more stringent limits on the time windows for life's origins and limiting the habitat for incubation of life chemistry.

Moving the locale of life's origin from Earth to Mars hurts the naturalistic model more than it helps. All the strikes against a naturalistic origin of life on Earth apply to Mars, including the deadly ultraviolet-oxygen paradox (see chapter 7). Oxygen (whether present or absent) guarantees the shutdown of prebiotic chemistry in both places.

The late heavy bombardment 3.85 billion years ago affected Mars with sterilizing events to nearly the same extent as it did Earth. Then, as astronomer Michael Carr showed, carbonate formation during Mars' early and relatively warm-wet era rapidly plummeted Mars' surface temperatures below freezing.[49] By 3.80 billion years ago, Mars had become as cold and dry as it is today. Thus to suggest Earth's first life came from Mars means virtually no time elapsed between the bombardment, life's origin, and life's transport to Earth.

Like Earth, Mars fails to deliver a chemical environment in which the natural assembly of sugars, lipids, amino acids, and nucleotides could occur. Nor does Mars provide an environment that would assist their assembly into membranes, DNA, RNA, proteins, or their equivalents. Mars offers no mechanism to solve the homochirality problem.

Some researchers who acknowledge the chemical and physical limitations presented to naturalistic life-origins scenarios hypothesize that Mars served merely as a steppingstone. They propose that another heavenly body seeded Mars with life and then Mars, in turn, seeded Earth. Such a proposal, however, only further complicates an already complex problem. It also forces upon the first life forms the challenge of additional complex, fine-tuned features to enable survival for millions of years in interplanetary space, through not one but two trips.

Putting the RTB Model to the Test

The RTB Model foresees that the search for life (or life's remains) on Mars will inevitably prove successful. It must, given the proximity of Mars to Earth. In the same manner as nearly twenty Martian rocks traveled to this planet, numerous Earth rocks have landed on Mars. This exchange of rocks resulting from impact events proceeded throughout the two planets' history. Given the abundance of life on (and in) Earth throughout the past 3.8 billion years, several million pounds, perhaps even tons, of Earth's organic material have been deposited by now on Mars' surface.

The immediate question that arises when one considers how much Earth-life material has been transported to Mars is whether any possibility exists for finding viable (still surviving) Earth life on Mars. The answer is that while it is not probable, it is possible. Evidence to that effect comes from laboratory experiments in which scientists kept several different species of microorganisms at a temperature of −321 °F (colder than the coldest temperatures on Mars) for more than six months. Those organisms maintained their capacity to germinate.[50] Several other microorganism species were kept in the vacuum conditions of outer space for five days without losing their viability.[51] Other microbes remained viable after absorbing 600 kilorads of x-rays.[52] These experiments show that if certain very hardy microorganisms deep within a rock expelled from Earth reach the Martian surface quickly, they would have a chance of germinating. However, that chance is vanishingly small for two reasons.

First, quick trips are highly improbable. Journeys of millions and tens of millions of years are orders of magnitude more probable than trips of thousands or hundreds of years. Second, for the past 3.8 billion years conditions on the Martian surface have rarely been conducive to germination. Under ideal Martian conditions, a drop of water evaporates in less than one second. The atmosphere affords little protection from solar ultraviolet radiation. Lacking a magnetic field and therefore a deflecting magnetic shield, solar x-ray radiation arrives unimpeded. While temperatures at certain locations occasionally rise above water's freezing point, they do so for only minutes or a few hours at a time.

A greater likelihood exists for discovering fossils of Earth life or of its biochemical remains. Though certainly not an easy task, in light of how thinly Earth-life material has been distributed over the Martian surface, NASA does have the technology today to achieve such a discovery. If Mars exploration remains a high priority, in a matter of time, probably only decades, evidence for life will be found. Considering the entrenched presumption of a nonsupernatural explanation for life's origins, many people will be tempted to interpret such a finding as evidence for indigenous Martian life rather than for life transported from Earth.

To prove with some certainty that these remains of life really are remains of Earth life will be difficult. While the recovery of Earth-life biochemical signatures—for example, similar sequences of nucleotides and amino acids—may help, two problems arise: (1) not all the biochemical signatures of past Earth life are available, and (2) such biochemical signatures rapidly decay under the harsh Martian environment.

Evaluating the Evidence

With Mars proving too dry, cold, windy, radiation saturated, and chemically hostile, naturalists must reach farther for a viable origin-of-life scenario. In response to the mantra "Follow the water," many researchers are shifting their focus to Europa and beyond.

CHAPTER 15

EUROPA AND BEYOND

Disappointed with the findings on Earth, scientists gaze into the heavens looking for a more likely cradle of life. They hope to find a place where organisms, or at least complex life components spontaneously assembled, then traveled to Earth. First, they look to other planets and moons in the solar system. These bodies are easiest to observe. Plus, life on them would have the shortest trip. Yet some scientists are bold enough to speculate that life may have come from more distant locales—from other planetary systems in the Milky Way galaxy. The vastness of the universe appears to hold an immense potential for life. But does it?

Besides pointing to Mars, the clues also seem to implicate one of Jupiter's four large moons as a candidate—Europa.

A Water World

The possibility of an ocean locked inside a ball of crustal ice makes Europa a focal point of NASA's quest to find life's extraterrestrial origin. The way Europa's gravity affects spacecraft trajectory, together with spectral mapping measurements indicates it has a rocky core surrounded by a water shell ninety miles (150 kilometers) deep—nearly seventeen times as deep as Mt. Everest is high![1] In fact, water constitutes about 15 percent of Europa's mass. By comparison, Earth is only 0.02 percent water, comets are about 75 percent water, and Ganymede and Callisto (two of Jupiter's other large moons) may be as much as 65 percent water. However, Europa likely is the richest in liquid water of all Jupiter's moons because its relatively close orbit around Jupiter (at only 417,000 miles/671,000 kilometers) means tidal heating may be adequate to melt much of Europa's interior ice.

The unmanned Galileo spacecraft measured and imaged Europa, determining its surface temperature to be a frigid –275 °F (–170 °C).[2] Galileo also documented the cracks on Europa's surface, reminiscent of those seen at the edges of Earth's arctic ice cap.[3] Members of Galileo's research team hypothesized that pieces of Europa's crust "cracked apart, moved slightly, and then [were] frozen together again."[4] If that did happen, some kind of plastic or fluid medium must exist below the surface—either ductile ice (ice so soft and pliable it can easily move) or liquid water.[5]

Figure 15.1: Galileo Spacecraft Image of Europa's Surface
Giant ice floes above an interior ocean may shift, causing jagged cracks.
(Photo courtesy of NASA, Jet Propulsion Laboratory, and Caltech)

The decay of radiometric isotopes in Europa's rocky interior provides negligible heat.[6] Only friction from Jupiter's enormous tidal forces could possibly provide enough heat to melt Europa's interior water. Whether or not this tidal heating is adequate to melt ice depends on the nature of the tidal dissipation within Europa.

The greater Europa's orbital eccentricity (departure from a perfect circular shape), the greater the tidal heating. Europa's eccentricity varies. Jupiter's tidal forces reduce the eccentricity, while Europa's gravitational relationship with two other sizable moons (Io and Ganymede) increases the eccentricity.[7] While Europa's current eccentricity is observable, how much that eccentricity changes and its maximum and minimum values remain unknown. Until a future mission provides the data, astronomers are left to wonder whether Europa's interior is liquid water or ductile ice.[8]

On Thin Ice

The possibility that Europa contains an ocean beneath its ice surface has propelled researchers' hope that they will soon solve the riddle of Earth-life's birthplace. In the flush of anticipation, however, some may be tempted to overlook the fact that the presence of liquid water is only one of more than 150 different fine-tuned requirements necessary for the survival of life.[9]

Additional necessities for life's origin include the availability of C-H-O-N molecules (molecules containing carbon, hydrogen, oxygen, and nitrogen) and a source of energy to drive metabolism, growth, repair, and reproduction. Calculations by astrobiologists Christopher Chyba and Cynthia Phillips suggest that Europa's rocky interior may provide at least some of the necessary C-H-O-N molecules.[10] But a suitable energy source remains missing because solar radiation cannot fill the role. The meteorite and comet craters that pockmark Europa's surface indicate the ice crust is thick enough to block these colliders' breakthrough and thus also to block sunlight. No sunlight means no photosynthesis.

Recognizing the unavailability of this important energy source, some researchers have proposed a geothermal equivalent. However, Europa is too small and too distant from Jupiter to maintain significant geothermal activity. (Jupiter's tidal heating of Europa is only one-sixteenth of its heating of Io.)

A more serious problem for the Europa-life scenario is this: the energy-sustaining life at Earth's deep-sea vents does not come from the vents. It comes from oxidants (which come from the oxygen produced by phytoplankton) dissolved and transported from the surface down to the vents. Thus, for life to be possible on Europa, a sustained flow of oxidants from the surface down to the possible deep-sea vents at the floor of Europa's possible liquid ocean would be required. However, even in the unlikely event that all these conditions were met, Europa's prospects as a life site face a more fundamental barrier. As explained in chapter 7, a naturalistic origin of life is highly unlikely to occur at or near a deep hydrothermal vent.

Christopher Chyba and an independent team of fourteen astronomers and geologists suggested a mechanism for generating the necessary oxidants on Europa's surface.[11] They hypothesized that charged particles energized by Jupiter's magnetosphere (the volume around Jupiter that is strongly influenced by its magnetic field) collide with the surface ice to produce hydrogen peroxide and oxygen. Recent spectrographs provided by the Galileo spacecraft prove their hypothesis correct. The oxidants magnesium sulfate, sulfuric acid, hydrogen peroxide, and oxygen all have been discovered on Europa's surface.[12] Chyba further hypothesized a surface ice layer thin enough for tidal cracking and breakthrough melting, thus for delivery of the oxidants to the ocean below.

All these speculations reach a dead end, however, if the ice on Europa is in fact not thin but deep.

The Ice Thickens

A recent study by the Lunar and Planetary Laboratory (LPL) challenges the notion of thin ice on Europa. LPL astronomers calculated the ice thickness needed to sustain crater formation from impact events.[13] When comets and meteorites collide with Europa, some surface ice melts and vaporizes. If the ice is thin, its melt-through erases evidence of the collision event. If the ice is thick, the impacts leave craters.

The research team modeled impact events to determine a lower boundary on Europa's surface ice thickness. They concluded that the ice must be at least two miles thick (three to four kilometers).

The images taken by Galileo revealed a 16-mile-wide (26 kilometers) crater recently named Pwyll.[14] The crater's size and shape show the collidor neither punched through nor cracked Europa's surface. Thus the ice in that area must be more than 6 miles (10 kilometers) thick. Two craters even larger than Pwyll—Callanish and Tyre—measure 20 and 25 miles (33 and 41 kilometers) across, respectively.[15] Their dimensions speak of a surface ice thickness substantially greater than 6 miles (10 kilometers).

Paul Schenk of the Lunar and Planetary Institute went on to determine just how much thicker than 6 miles (10 kilometers) Europa's ice crust must be. By analyzing crater size, depth, and shape, as well as diameter, Schenk concluded that the outer ice shell must be at least 12 miles (19 kilometers) thick.[16] Similar analyses for craters on Jupiter's other two water-rich moons, Ganymede and Callisto, showed that their outer ice crusts must be at least two to four times thicker than Europa's.

Little doubt remains that Europa's outer ice shell is too thick to allow contact between its surface and any possible liquid water below. Without a flux of oxidants, no life can survive even *if* an ocean does exist.

Oxidants Paradox

Indeed, the issue of oxidants frames another origin-of-life paradox. Even more surely than the oxygen-ultraviolet paradox interferes with life's origin (see chapter 7), the presence of oxidants such as hydrogen peroxide and sulfuric acid guarantees its shutdown. These oxidants prevent the prebiotic chemical reactions that could produce life-essential molecules. Therefore, the presence of oxidants renders origin-of-life chemistry impossible. But without oxidants, no organism isolated from the surface environment could function.

When taken together, the two paradoxes—the oxygen-ultraviolet paradox and the no-oxidants-versus-oxidants paradox—leave materialists from the origin-of-life research camp without a viable Europan model. The first paradox argues against a naturalistic explanation for the origin of surface life, while the second argues against a naturalistic explanation for even the existence of, much less the origin of, deep interior life.

With Europa a no-show for life, might another site be viable?

Saturn's Dry Moon

The atmosphere around Titan (Saturn's largest moon) makes Titan the last remaining solar-system candidate for the production of prebiotics in large quantities. Its low temperature (−292 °F, −180 °C) prevents Titan from being considered a candidate for life sustenance. However, it is the only solar system body with a large quantity of hydrocarbons in its atmosphere and the only solar system body besides Earth with a large quantity of atmospheric nitrogen. An abundance of both hydrocarbons and nitrogen is necessary for the production of prebiotics.

The hydrocarbons on Titan temporarily reside at whichever pole is currently experiencing winter. During that seven-and-a-half-year season, no sunlight shines on the pole. The lack of sunlight means photolytic breakdown of hydrocarbons does not occur. Once sunlight reappears, the hydrocarbons disappear. Thus the hydrocarbons produced in Titan's upper atmosphere lack the locale, longevity, temperature, and abundance essential to foster the production of life molecules or even the building blocks of life molecules. This conclusion finds corroboration in new evidence that contradicts previous claims for an ocean of hydrocarbons on Titan.[17]

Though nitrogen rich, Titan is ammonia poor. In fact, ammonia has not been detected there at all. By itself, molecular nitrogen cannot generate prebiotic molecules.

Titan's lack of oxygen products poses an equally serious problem for prebiotic chemistry. Water is found only in the moon's upper atmosphere.

At 250 miles (400 kilometers) above Titan's surface, water is scarce.[18] Comets could account for this tiny amount. No indigenous water appears to exist there. As for other oxygen compounds, only traces of carbon monoxide and carbon dioxide exist on Titan. Delivery of these minuscule amounts could also be expected from comets. With so little oxygen compounds on Titan or in its atmosphere, prebiotic chemistry cannot work.

Astrobiologists have identified no other solar system candidates beyond Earth, Mars, Europa, and Titan as possible sites for life's origins. The harsher conditions on other sites make the chances for life on them even more remote. At best, comets or meteorites may be locales where some, but not all, of the simpler carbon compounds needed for life can be synthesized.

Still, the question remains: Where did Earth life originate? Interstellar panspermia is the currently popular answer.

Spores from Outer Space

Nobel Prize–winning Swedish chemist Svante Arrhenius was the first to develop the idea of panspermia as a serious scientific proposal in 1907. This theory suggests that one or more distant heavenly bodies expelled microorganisms into the interstellar medium and that some of them eventually fell upon Earth. The context for Arrhenius's proposal was his assumption that the universe is infinitely old and large and that Earth is only a few billion years old. He reasoned that Earth is far too young for the ensemble of complex molecules inside the cell to arise by chance chemical interactions. In an infinitely old universe, however, Arrhenius saw at least a possibility for life's origin. He presumed, therefore, that spores somehow escaped from an extraterrestrial life site. Interstellar radiation pressure then wafted the spores throughout the universe and eventually they germinated on Earth.

Scientists now know that Arrhenius was wrong about the age of the universe. The different methods for measuring its age all yield results converging on 14 billion years.[19] This age is only about three times greater than Earth's age and thus does not significantly enhance the probability for life's origin.

Arrhenius was also wrong about the availability of extraterrestrial incubators for life. Today scientists know enough about the universe, solar system, and extrasolar planets to recognize that the possibility of a naturalistic origin of life is even more remote for some other heavenly body than it is for Earth. Even if the observable universe were to contain as many as 10 billion trillion planets, the probability that one of them, besides Earth, would happen to possess all the conditions necessary for

Export of Earth Life

In one sense, astrobiologists are too pessimistic about finding evidence of life someplace besides Earth. The remains of once living organisms should be found on all solar system bodies except the Sun. Just as millions of pounds (or more) of Earth's life organic material has been deposited on Mars through meteoritic transport, collision events on Earth have hurtled rocks containing Earth life all over the solar system.

Using a computer model analysis of solar system dynamics presented at the Twentieth Lunar and Planetary Science Conference (Houston, TX, 1989), planetary astronomers demonstrated that of 1,000 rocks launched from Earth by collision events powerful enough to propel them past Earth's gravitational pull, 291 would land on Venus, 20 on Mercury, 17 on Mars, 14 on Jupiter and its satellites, and 1 would go all the way to Saturn. The remaining 657 rocks would either be consumed by the Sun, land on the Moon, or return to Earth. Uranus, Neptune, Pluto, and the asteroids combined would receive less than one-tenth as much Earth debris as does Saturn and its satellites.

The degradation of Earth-life material on these other solar system bodies depends on three factors: (1) how long the Earth rock or dust particle spent in transit, (2) how long the Earth rock or dust particle has remained on that solar system body, and (3) how harsh the conditions on the solar system body.

Taking into account all three factors, the upper atmosphere of Venus and the surface of Mars offer the best hope for the discovery of the remains of Earth's emigrant life. Such a discovery is within the capability of current technology. Therefore, a future discovery of life or life's remains on a solar system body should not be taken as evidence for life originating on that body.

the support of physical life, much less its origin, is less than one in 10^{172}. In other words, the possibility is unimaginably remote.[20]

Arrhenius was also incorrect about stellar radiation pressure. All stars manifest radiation pressure—light intense enough to push tiny particles (microbes) through interstellar space. But light this powerful includes enough ultraviolet radiation to kill such organisms in just a few days. Indeed, in a recent experiment on board the Russian orbiting FOTON satellite, unprotected spores of the highly radiation-resistant bacterium known as *Bacillus subtilis* were wiped out in just fifteen days.[21] Spores protected by a thin layer of clay fared no better. Microscopic cracks in the clay shield let in enough ultraviolet radiation to kill all the spores.[22]

There is a second reason the proposal that microbial spores arrived here from space encased in small dust grains does not work.[23] Moving a dust grain massive enough to contain a spore requires a certain intensity of starlight. The ultraviolet and x-ray radiation in such starlight would penetrate the dust grain and destroy the spore. Furthermore, the only light source strong enough to move a spore-carrying dust grain is a supergiant star. For physics reasons alone, life cannot arise or survive anywhere in the vicinity of a supergiant star.[24]

The only remaining possibility for the natural transport mechanism essential to the panspermia hypothesis, then, is for the seeds of life to hitch a ride on meteors.[25] This method presumes the spores of extraterrestrial microorganisms lie deep within relatively large rocks hurled throughout interstellar space as a consequence of collision events on a distant life-supporting heavenly body. But this last remaining possibility is also a remote one.

At the 32nd Annual Lunar and Planetary Science Conference held in 2001, Jay Melosh from the LPL and the University of Arizona reported on the feasibility of Earth's capturing an interstellar wandering rock.[26] According to Melosh's studies, this probability is about 3×10^{-16} per year. In other words, there exists only one chance in ten thousand for Earth to receive just one interstellar sample over the entire history of the solar system. The transport of significant pieces of interstellar rock, let alone life, to Earth would seem virtually impossible.

Putting the RTB Model to the Test
This scenario is consistent with the RTB Model. The inability of Europa and Titan to originate and sustain life supports the RTB Model—as does the failure of interstellar panspermia.

Evaluating the Evidence
Panspermia thus represents the end of the line for naturalists within the origin-of-life research camp. Recognizing the intractable problems for a naturalistic explanation for life's origin on Earth, many researchers turned their attention to Mars, Europa, Titan, and other possible solar system sites. Disappointed by discoveries at those sites, some have looked to the stars, specifically to interstellar grains, dust, dirt, and rocks. The determination that interstellar material cannot transport life, or even life molecules, to Earth has led to sheer frustration. At least a few scientists are beginning to consider a nonnatural explanation for life's origins on Earth. This option raises intriguing possibilities as the investigation continues.

Chapter 16

LIFE, SEEDED ON PURPOSE

I n the beginning—or so the story goes—nearly four billion years ago, an alien intelligence purposefully planted the seeds of life on planet Earth. Who that intelligence was, how he delivered those seeds, and why remain open questions. At ISSOL 1999, one scientist speaking from the response microphone, obviously frustrated by the lack of viable naturalistic explanations, proposed this idea of directed panspermia as the explanation for life's start.[1]

This concept is not new. Nobel laureate Francis Crick and origin-of-life researcher Leslie Orgel first proposed the concept of directed panspermia in 1973.[2] Later, Crick expanded upon the hypothesis in his book *Life Itself*.[3] Specifically, he suggested that a highly advanced alien species sent one or more spacecrafts to Earth with the intent of peppering it with the necessary life forms (or components of life) to generate a zoo of diverse species.

According to origin-of-life researcher Robert Shapiro, Crick made his proposal somewhat tongue-in-cheek in order to highlight the implausibility of current naturalistic explanations.[4] While this motive may explain the paper he authored with Orgel, Crick in his full-length book seems far too serious and detailed to be joking. Nor does a mere desire to expose problems seem his sole purpose. The book's tone suggests that the evidence leaves no alternative but to consider directed panspermia as an explanation for life on Earth.

Mounting Frustration

Thirty years have passed since the publication of Crick and Orgel's paper. Although the naturalistic explanations offered for life's origins have grown in both number and creativity—the credibility of these explanations has waned. At the same time additional challenges to naturalism have risen.

The sudden and simultaneous appearance of more than seventy complex animal phyla (groups of animals with the same basic body plan) 543 million years ago (the Cambrian explosion) defies a naturalistic explanation, especially considering that only thirty of those phyla exist today and none of the thirty are new.[5] With more than forty such phyla disappearing and zero new ones appearing over the past half billion years, evolution's going the wrong way. Likewise, the rapid introduction of hundreds of thousands of radically different species after each mass extinction event defies naturalistic explanations.[6] These additional challenges have prompted many scientists to consider repeat directed panspermia—the hypothesis that an intelligent alien species made several space trips to Earth over the past 4 billion years first to place life here, then again periodically to restore and upgrade it.

But whether directed panspermia makes more sense than any other naturalistic theory is another matter.

Who? How?

Directed panspermia acknowledges the implausibility that seeds of life arrived here by natural means whether from Earth's solar system, from somewhere else in the Milky Way, or from another galaxy "far, far away." Further, it admits that the origin of life requires a powerful, intelligent personal agency.

However, directed panspermia avoids the most fundamental origin issues. It fails to address where the highly advanced aliens came from or how they got to Earth.

Explaining the origin of an intelligent species on some distant planet presents a challenge as big as (if not bigger than) the explanation for life's origin here on Earth. As noted in chapter 14, even if the observable universe contained as many as 10 billion trillion planets, the probability that even one of them would possess all the conditions necessary to support physical life, much less to explain its origin, is less than one in 10^{172}.

Appealing exotic conditions or physics in some distant corner of the galaxy or the cosmos will not work. The universe is homogeneous and uniform, almost perfectly so. Physical life would be impossible otherwise. If homogeneity and uniformity were either increased or decreased, none of the stars, planets, and moons necessary for any conceivable physical life would ever have formed.[7]

Directed panspermia also ignores such practical problems as transportation. No species subject to the laws of physics and the dimensions of the universe—however intelligent, technologically advanced, and well funded—can traverse significant interstellar distances and deposit working sets of complex life molecules or viable life forms on planet Earth. Two lines of research show that the travel problems are far beyond trivial.

First, the distance (hence time) such life would have to travel lies beyond all practical limits. Nearby starting points for the journey are non-existent. While nearby Earth-sized planets may exist, stars and star-planet systems within fifty light-years are ruled out by their mass, by their age, or by life-eliminating features (such as companion stars and planets large or close enough to disrupt the orbit of the "life" planet, or the lack of a "shield" planet like Jupiter to absorb or deflect dangerous impactors).[8] The SETI (search for extraterrestrial intelligent life) efforts stretch the minimum travel distance even farther.

In 1996 a SETI research group scanned all 202 of the solar-type stars within 155 light-years, listening for intelligent electromagnetic signals. They found none.[9] The source of ETI must lie beyond that distance.

A second line of research addresses the conditions of space that would be destructive to travelers. The traveling life, or life products, would have to steer around nova and supernova remnants, giant stars, young stars, galactic arms, and radiation from the galactic bulge. A straight-line travel path is not possible. Given the zigzagging required, the minimum travel distance would likely exceed 250 light-years. The latest SETI search effort places the minimum travel distance much farther away again.[10]

Distance and other dangers pose a daunting dilemma. Any reasonably large spacecraft transporting physical life cannot travel at speeds greater than about 1 percent of the velocity of light (and even that's not a safe speed). The risk of damage to any conceivable physical craft—damage from cosmic rays, space dust, debris, and mechanical wear and tear—increases with the square of the velocity.

Yet the longer the trip, the higher the risk from all other sources. A spacecraft traveling at 1 percent the velocity of light (nearly 7 million miles per hour) would require 25,000 years to traverse 250 light-years. And this makes for a quick trip. The odds of the travelers surviving so long in radiation and sustaining the journey's supplies—not to mention psychological isolation—seem utterly remote. Maintaining motivation for the mission presents yet another problem. (Extinction time for a small-population species confined in a spacecraft exposed to radiation is relatively brief.)

Evaluating the Evidence

The origin of the alien intelligent species and the difficulty of traversing interstellar distances are only two challenges facing the directed panspermia hypothesis. Many more exist.[11] But even these two obstacles make a single act of directed panspermia inconceivable. Repeated trips are even more unthinkable.

Putting the RTB Model to the Test

An appeal to *supernaturally* directed panspermia overcomes the problems connected with directed panspermia. A personal, all-powerful, all-knowing God who transcends the laws of physics and the space-time dimensions of the universe is capable of preparing a just-right environment for life, creating all the molecular machinery necessary for life, simultaneously putting all that machinery together in the required manner, and finally imparting to all that assembled machinery the property of life (that is, turning on the ignition switch that sets the machinery in motion).

Two Kinds of Miracles

Supernatural interventions, according to the Bible, are not always transcendent miracles (those only explained by a God acting independent or outside of matter, energy, space, and time). Examples of transcendent miracles are Jesus of Nazareth walking on water[12] and the creation of the universe.

Far more frequent are the miracles God performs within His chosen physical laws. One example would be the perfectly fine-tuned collision Earth received from a Mars-sized planet that enabled Earth to support both primitive and advanced life. The story of Sennacherib is another. The night after he boasted that his military would destroy Jerusalem and that Jerusalem's God would be powerless to stop them, a mysterious illness killed 185,000 of Sennacherib's fighting men, thwarting his battle plans.[13]

This brief proposal is, in essence, the RTB biblical creation model for life's origin. This origin-of-life model and its predictions began with ancient biblical texts. Still, the scientific data that come from more than fifty years of scientific research affirms the reasonableness of this scenario. The data indicate a supernatural origin of life and validate the key assumptions undergirding the model—including the involvement of a transcendent Creator. Such a Being has the capability to create more and more advanced species of life. Chapter 17 explores some of the reasons why He may have done so.

Part V

A

MODEL

FOR LIFE

CHAPTER 17

SOLVING THE MYSTERY

Figuring out the "why" often solves a mystery. Establishing motive sometimes clinches a case. One of the biggest unresolved dilemmas behind the enigma of life's origin is, why were the seeds of life planted so early? The beginning of life (relative to cosmic history) under hellacious conditions poses initial problems for creationists and evolutionists alike.

From a biblical perspective, why would the all-powerful, all-knowing, all-loving God of the Bible create microorganisms 3.8 billion years prior to creating human beings? If humanity represents God's goal in creating Earth, why bother with nearly 4 billion years of preexisting life? And why only microorganisms or colonies of microorganisms for the first 3.3 billion years of life history? From a naturalistic perspective, how does one explain why life appeared at the earliest possible moment physics allowed? And why, given the natural assembly time for even the simplest organism, was life's introduction on Earth so sudden?

For primitive life to exist as early as it did on Earth, many remarkably fine-tuned events had to occur in the just-right timing, order, and location. These amazing actions prepared the planet for early life, which in turn protected future life from poisonous elements and provided advanced life with rich biodeposits.

Prepared for Life
The number of just-right qualities required for life to survive on Earth may be in the hundreds. Examing a few major characteristics reveals the necessary attention to detail required for life to survive.

Putting a planet together. Given the laws of physics and the characteristics of the cosmos (in particular its expansion rate), the cosmic conundrum for life's origin is that the universe took a long time (several billion years) to become adequately enriched with all the elements necessary for life. The universe began with one element: hydrogen. Between three and three and a half minutes after the big-bang creation event, as the cosmos cooled through nuclear fusion temperatures (a few tens of billions degrees), nearly 25 percent of the hydrogen, by mass, converted into helium plus trace amounts of lithium and deuterium (heavy hydrogen).[1] The cooling continued, and after two hundred million years nuclear furnaces originally ignited in the cores of the first stars.[2] These stars then began to manufacture all the remaining elements.[3]

At least two generations of stars had to form, burn, and explode their nuclear ashes into interstellar space to provide the elements and compounds necessary for rocky planets to form and for life chemistry to be possible. Earth's star (the Sun) had to form in a just-right locale—adjacent to a recently exploded Type I supernova *and* to a recently exploded Type II supernova—to obtain enough ashes to mold a planet like Earth so early in cosmic history.[4] (A supernova is a supergiant star that has undergone or is undergoing a catacylsmic explosion. Type II supernovae typically are larger than Type I.) Each of these supernovae made a different suite of life-essential heavy elements. The two had to explode near enough to enrich the solar nebula with heavy elements, yet sufficiently distant to keep from blasting that nebula apart.

The timing of the two supernovae eruptions also was critical. If they exploded too early or too late, too few heavy elements would have been incorporated into the solar nebula or the nebula would have dispersed.

The accumulating evidence for these two supernovae eruptions at just the right time and place in the solar system's formation confirms the fine-tuning in the explosions—a fine-tuning too extreme to chalk up to sheer coincidence.[5] It fits well, however, with the intent of a supernatural Creator to work within His chosen laws of physics to create life—and in particular, advanced life—as quickly as those laws allowed.

The heavy element enrichment the solar nebula received from the two supernovae eruptions was still not quite enough to sustain an abundance of diverse life for 4 billion years. Nor could it fuel life-essential rates of tectonics and volcanism for as long as life needed them. As chapter 6 explains, an exceptionally fine-tuned collision event (just-right collider mass, just-right collision location, just-right collision time, and so forth) salted Earth with enough extra uranium, thorium, iron, molybdenum, copper, silver, zinc, chromium, and other elements to enable Earth eventually to sustain advanced life.

Stabilizing the Sun. The gravitational collapse of a gas cloud gave birth to Earth's Sun. During the collapse phase, the Sun at times acquired

---

Why These Laws of Physics?

Some scientists, like origin-of-life researcher and Nobel laureate Christian de Duve, question why a Creator would choose the physical laws that govern the universe.[6] In fact, de Duve's failure to see any divine purpose in the laws of physics is one of his reasons for rejecting a biblical creation model.[7] However, the Bible addresses four specific reasons for God's choice of the physical laws:[8]

(1) To provide a home for humanity and the means for humanity to develop civilization, technology, and affluence

(2) To provide a viewing platform for humans to witness God's glory, power, righteousness, care, and love

(3) To facilitate a relatively rapid and efficient conquest of evil

(4) To provide instruction for the angels

---

gas and dust and at other times lost gas and dust. All the while, different nuclear reactions turned on and off. At this infant period, which lasted 50 million years, the Sun's luminosity was highly unstable.[9] For the following 500 million years, solar ionizing radiation, especially x-rays, poured forth at a level fifty times higher than today's.[10] The infant Sun's unstable luminosity and the juvenile Sun's intense ionizing radiation were two of several reasons why life most likely could not have survived on Earth until 3.9 billion years ago.

When life first appeared on Earth 3.8 billion years ago, the Sun was 25 percent dimmer than it is today, assuming that the Sun did not lose any mass during its youth. (See box, "A Brighter Young Sun," page 218, for a new solar model that better explains Earth's early chemical and life histories.) This lesser luminosity poses a problem, for if the Sun today were brighter or dimmer by just a percent or two, the oceans would either boil away or freeze up, killing all life in the process.[11] How, then, did life survive on Earth in great abundance and diversity for such a long time with so much less sunlight? Scientists call this question the "faint Sun paradox."

About 50 million years after the solar nebula's initial collapse, the Sun's core temperature rose to nearly 31 billion °F (17 billion °C). At this temperature, nuclear fusion of hydrogen into helium began. For the first time in the Sun's history, energy released from nuclear reactions in the interior fully compensated for energy losses due to radiation from the Sun's surface (or photosphere). Thus, the Sun entered a long period of stable nuclear burning.

Ignition of nuclear burning of hydrogen into helium took place at the

Climatic Runaways

Earth's biosphere remains poised between a runaway freeze-up and runaway evaporation. If the mean temperature of Earth's surface cools by even a few degrees, more snow and ice than normal will form. Snow and ice reflect solar energy much more efficiently than do other surface materials. This greater reflection translates into a lower surface temperature, which in turn causes more snow and ice to form and subsequently lowers temperatures further.

If the mean temperature of Earth's surface warms just a few degrees, more water vapor and carbon dioxide collect in the atmosphere. This extra water vapor and carbon dioxide create a better greenhouse effect in the atmosphere. This effect in turn causes the surface temperature to rise again, which releases even more water vapor and carbon dioxide into the atmosphere, resulting in still higher surface temperatures.

Earth's surface temperature 3.8 billion years ago was not much different from today. Though the Sun was 25 percent fainter (15 percent fainter in the case of early solar mass loss), Earth's atmosphere was more effective in its capacity to trap heat. Carbon dioxide, water vapor, and methane are greenhouse gases. The existence of abundant biodeposits (coal, oil, limestone, marble, kerogen, natural gas, and so on), carbonates, and sand in Earth's crust establishes that billions of years ago Earth's atmosphere did have higher quantities of these gases than it does now. Though the Sun was fainter, the temperature at Earth's surface was similar to today's because Earth's early atmosphere trapped more of the Sun's heat.

If, at any time, the quantity of greenhouse gases had risen even a little higher, too much heat would have been trapped and the oceans would have boiled away. Likewise, at any time, if the quantity had dropped even a little too low, too little heat would have been captured and the oceans would have frozen. The quantity of greenhouse gases in early Earth's atmosphere is only one of many fine-tunings manifested in the faint Sun paradox.

Sun's center. The gradual increase in the Sun's luminosity (the consequence of this nuclear fusion) arose from the increase in the amount of helium relative to hydrogen at the solar core. More helium meant a higher core density that produced a higher core temperature that in turn increased the rate of nuclear fusion of hydrogen into helium.

This extra fusion gradually made the Sun brighter, and this brightening will continue until nuclear fusion converts all the hydrogen into helium in the inner 10 percent of the Sun's mass.[12] How long can stable hydrogen fusion last for a star as massive as the Sun? The answer is 9 billion years.[13] Astronomers calculate that the Sun is now about halfway through its stable hydrogen fusion phase. Therefore, it will continue to brighten gradually over the next 4.5 billion years.

To maintain the necessary physical conditions for life, the greenhouse gases from Earth's atmosphere must be removed in direct proportion to the increase in the Sun's luminosity. The erosion of silicates and the burial of organic carbon are the only known physical mechanisms for maintaining proportionality. The water in rain, streams, and mist acts as a catalyst so that exposed silicates chemically react with carbon dioxide in the atmosphere to form carbonates and silicon dioxide (sand). To get the necessary amount of exposed silicates, efficient plate tectonics must rapidly build islands and continents. The rate of silicate erosion depends on multiple factors, including the quantity and type of plant species on the landmasses.

Organisms—in particular, photosynthetic plants, bacteria, and methanogens (methane-consuming bacteria)—also help take greenhouse gases such as carbon dioxide, water, and methane out of the atmosphere and chemically transform them into fats, sugars, starches, proteins, and carbonates. As these are buried via wind and water erosion, volcanism, and plate tectonics, physical and chemical processes operating in the crust convert them into biodeposits.

Though proportions differed in the past, today about 80 percent of the greenhouse gas removal takes place through silicate erosion into carbonates and sand; the remaining 20 percent takes place through burial of organisms and organic material. To remove greenhouse gases so as to compensate for the increase in solar luminosity, all the factors that govern silicate erosion plus all the factors governing the quantity, diversity, growth, total mass, decay, and burial of organisms must be fine-tuned.

Constructing the continents. Perhaps the factor most taken for granted in the perfectly timed gradual removal of greenhouse gases from Earth's atmosphere is the presence of exposed silicates. That adequate exposed silicates even exist on Earth, however, is nothing short of a miracle.

Continents are composed of light silicate rocks, whereas the crust lying below ocean floors is made up of heavier basaltic rocks. Being lighter, the continents float higher above the mantle than do the basaltic rocks under the oceans. Plate tectonics separates Earth's primordial crust into silicates and basalts. Without plate tectonics, Earth never would have formed significant silicates or continental landmasses.

For plate tectonics to occur on Earth, three things must exist: (1) an abundant supply of liquid surface water, (2) a powerful source of interior

Racing the Solar Clock

Environmental scientists report that before long carbon dioxide and water vapor removal from Earth's atmosphere will be inadequate to compensate for the Sun's increasing luminosity. Removing even a little more water vapor from Earth's atmosphere will significantly diminish rainfall levels. Removing even a little more carbon dioxide from Earth's atmosphere will significantly reduce plant productivity. In less than 30 million years, either all the green plants on Earth will be scorched by the Sun's heat or they will all starve from a lack of rainfall and a lack of carbon dioxide in the atmosphere.

Thirty million years from now, researchers say, Earth will be completely sterilized. Land life will disappear before marine life. Advanced life will disappear before primitive life. Creatures with large body sizes will be the first to go extinct.

The Sun's increasing luminosity means there was no time to waste in preparing Earth for humans and for their civilization. From a creation perspective, this time limit explains why the origin of life occurred so early in Earth's history and with such diversity and abundance, and why life remained abundant and diverse on Earth.

Optimized diversity, abundance, and timing are consistent with the RTB creation model. Natural mechanisms would not be expected to show the foresight and planning for optimization that life's record on Earth manifests.

radioactive decay, and (3) a highly fine-tuned core dynamo. The stability and efficiency of Earth's dynamo depends on the fine-tuning of still more factors, each of which also must fall within a certain narrow range.[14]

Any hope of removing enough greenhouse gases from the atmosphere to keep up with the Sun's increasing luminosity springs from the buildup of continental landmasses through plate tectonics. This buildup must exceed and later at least keep pace with the reduction of continental landmasses through erosion.[15] The difficulty here is that the energy release from radioactive decay declines over time. The level of plate tectonic activity today is only a fifth of what it was when life first appeared on Earth. However, the collision that helped enrich Earth with radioactive elements also gave Earth a gigantic moon. The Moon acts as a tidal brake on Earth, gradually slowing its rotation rate. A slower rotation rate means less erosion.

So many factors must be fined-tuned to sustain both large oceans and large silicate continents that the provision of them qualifies as a miracle.

Even nontheistic scientists acknowledge how amazing is their simultaneous existence. They also admit that Earth may well be the only planet in the universe to have them.[16]

For powerful plate tectonics and volcanism to be sustained for several billion years, Earth had to be endowed with a huge quantity of long-lived radioactive elements. The physical processes that salted Earth with these elements also salted Earth with large quantities of all the other heavy elements. Almost all of them required careful redistribution by specialized microbial life to make Earth a safe environment for advanced life.

Protected Life

Among the oldest life forms, sulfate-reducing bacteria made a significant contribution to preparing Earth's environment for humanity. These bacteria were dominant in the geologic record from 3.8 to 2.9 billion years ago—an era of relatively low oxygen levels in Earth's atmosphere. Researchers discovered not long ago that sulfate-reducing bacteria played a critical role not only in Earth's life-essential sulfur and carbon cycles but also in redistributing heavy elements for the protection of advanced life.[18] The primordial salting of Earth with heavy elements formed global concentrations of them. In concentrated soluble form, these elements—arsenic, boron, chlorine, chromium, cobalt, copper, fluorine, iodine, iron, manganese, molybdenum, nickel, phosphorous, potassium, selenium, sulfur, tin, vanadium, and zinc—poison advanced life.[19] Yet human life requires a certain minimum quantity of each of these otherwise deadly elements. Certain bacteria provided for these poisons' safe redistribution.[20]

Researchers now recognize that sulfate-reducing bacteria engineered much, if not all, of various ores' concentrated deposits. Iron, magnesium, zinc, and lead, as well as the ores of trace metals such as silver, arsenic, and selenium owe their concentrations (and accessibility for mining) to sulfate-reducing bacteria.

From a biblical creation perspective, the dominance of sulfate-reducing bacteria for nearly a billion years of life's history makes sense. These bacteria reduced soluble (thus poisonous) concentrations of certain elements in Earth's environment from a level where they were poisonous to advanced life to the level where they provided nutrients for advanced life. From 2.9 billion years ago to the present, the abundance and diversity of sulfate-reducing bacteria have remained at maximally beneficial levels. This fine-tuning ensures that neither too much of the insoluble forms of these elements return (through erosion) to water-soluble forms nor too much of the soluble forms convert to insoluble forms (no longer available to meet minimum nutrient requirements).

A Brighter Young Sun

The faint Sun paradox presumes that the Sun has maintained the same mass throughout its history. Astronomers observe, however, that solar-sized stars throughout the Milky Way galaxy lose significant mass during their infancy and youth. They also note that old lunar rocks and old grains from meteorites show evidence for a much more intense solar wind (the mechanism for solar mass loss) 3 to 4 billion years ago. Therefore, a more reasonable model for the Sun recently produced by astrophysicists Juliana Sackmann and Arnold Boothroyd is one where the Sun starts off with between 4 and 7 percent more mass than it has today.[17] That extra mass translates into a brighter Sun. (The Sun's luminosity increases with the fourth power of its mass.)

Specifically, from the time when the Sun was 40 million years old to when it was about 1.0 to 1.5 billion years old, it gradually grew dimmer as it lost mass. At 1.0 to 1.5 billion years old, the Sun stopped shedding significant mass. Thus, from 1.0 to 1.5 billion years old onward the Sun gradually got brighter and brighter.

In Sackmann and Boothroyd's model the Sun at the time hydrogen fusion burning was first ignited (4.52 billion years ago) would have been between 90 and 105 percent of its current brightness (cf 71 percent for no solar mass loss). At the time of life's origin on Earth (3.8 billion years ago) the Sun would have been between 84 and 86 percent of its current brightness (cf 75 percent for no solar mass loss). From 3.0 billion years ago to the present, there would be no difference in the Sun's luminosity between Sackmann and Boothroyd's model and a solar model with no mass loss.

Compared to no mass loss, the Sun losing mass in its youth would not demand the quantity of powerful greenhouse gases such as methane and ammonia in Earth's early atmosphere at the time of life's origin. In fact, it may not have required any methane or ammonia at all. This lack of dependence on ammonia and methane could be critical for life's stability, abundance, and diversity on the early Earth because both ammonia and methane are not only very difficult to produce in Earth's atmosphere but also extremely unstable. Lessening the dependence on greenhouse gases to sustain adequate temperatures for life permits much greater temperature variation over Earth's surface. (The greater the quantity of greenhouse gases, the less temperature variation that is possible in Earth's atmosphere.) A greater temperature variation allows for a much higher diversity of bacteria at the time of life's origin. Increasing the diversity, abundance, and stability of life on Earth previous to 3 billion years ago shortens the time window needed to prepare Earth for humans and human civilization.

Provided for Life

Advanced land life requires specially conditioned soils and an oxygen-rich atmosphere. Both the soil conditioning and the oxygen enrichment happen only if specialized life forms exist for a long time. For a technologically advanced civilization to become possible, enormous and varied biodeposits had to be laid in the crust of the Earth.

Enriched soil. Tyler Volk (New York University) and David Schwartzman (Howard University) analyzed cryptogamic crusts to uncover many details of life's history on Earth's landmasses. These soils are comprised of cyanobacteria (photosynthetic or oxygen-producing bacteria), fungi, mosses, sand, and clay all existing symbiotically. Volk and Schwartzman's findings led them to conclude that such microbial soils may have dramatically transformed both the temperature and the chemistry of Earth's early landmasses, thus preparing the way for the introduction of more advanced vegetation.[21] These findings could solve one of biologists' long-held puzzles—the lack of evidence for advanced land vegetation until about a half billion years ago.

Volk and Schwartzman found evidence that Earth's early landmasses were relatively hot and soil deficient. They demonstrated, however, that cryptogamic colonies could withstand these harsh conditions. Even more, these colonies provided an effective means to limit erosion. At the same time, they enhanced chemical conditioning of the soil, cooled the environment, and oxygenated the atmosphere. In other words, these microbial colonies probably took hold on the few pockets of loose rock that existed on barren continental masses and transformed them over 2 or 3 billion years into deep layers of stable, nutrient-rich soil, which later made possible the introduction of vascular plants. This provision explains why God would have waited 3.3 billion years between creating the first life forms and creating the first advanced life forms. This history also harmonizes beautifully with the events of the first five creation days, as described in Genesis 1 and amplified in Psalm 104.[22]

Enriched atmosphere. Although cryptogamic colonies played a vital role in oxygenating Earth's atmosphere, their role was minor compared to that of cyanobacteria in the oceans. Today, oxygen-producing cyanobacteria account for nearly 70 percent of the total biomass on Earth. As chapter 5 explains, cyanobacteria were present on Earth at least as far back as 3.5 billion years ago. Why did it take 3 billion years for photosynthetic life to push atmospheric oxygen concentrations to their current levels?

In the absence of oxygen-consuming animals, cyanobacteria could have transformed Earth's atmosphere from 1 or 2 percent oxygen to about

20 percent oxygen in no more than a few million years except for the presence of enormous, highly efficient phosphate and oxygen "sinks."

One type of sink, banded iron deposits (BIDs) in Earth's crust, hindered atmospheric oxygen enrichment in two ways. BIDs absorbed so much phosphate as to dramatically reduce its concentration in seawater.[23] This low concentration inhibited the growth of cyanobacteria.

BIDs also directly absorbed enormous amounts of oxygen. Whenever erosion washed unoxidized iron and sulfur into the ocean, the oxygen produced there by photosynthesis reacted with these elements to form oxide deposits. It took several global cycles of erosion, deposition, and tectonic uplift for unoxidized iron and sulfur to become fully oxidized.

Earth's mantle, the soft layer between Earth's crust and core, was an even larger sink of oxygen-grabbing material. Again, several global cycles of erosion, deposition, tectonic activity, and volcanic eruptions were necessary to plug that sink (via full oxidation of mantle minerals).

How long did nature take to fill all the oxygen and phosphate sinks? Geochemical analysis of preserved deep-water marine sediments indicates that the oceans did not become fully aerobic (oxygenated) until roughly a half billion years ago.[24] From a creation perspective, the timing of this process explains the timing of the Cambrian explosion—the sudden, widespread, and extremely diverse appearance of more than seventy phyla of complex animals—543 million years ago.

Enriched supplies. Without abundant life on Earth, greenhouse gases would not be pulled from the atmosphere and converted into biodeposits. Without abundant life on island and continental landmasses, the conversion of silicates and carbon dioxide into carbonates and sand would be inadequate to help absorb greenhouse gases and prevent overheating of the planet.

Certain life forms (for example, vascular plants) are much more effective than other organisms in stimulating silicate erosion.[25] To properly compensate for the increase in solar luminosity in the context of Earth's declining plate tectonic activity *and* declining rotation rate, the just-right species of life had to be present at the just-right locations at the just-right times and in the just-right quantities. Moreover, for all these to be maintained, the just-right ecological balances had to support the necessary life forms. That is, the key species for reducing the quantities of atmospheric greenhouse gases needed the existence of many other diverse species of life at the just-right population levels in their environment in order to keep their own populations in the just-right locations, at the just-right levels of health, and at the just-right numbers of individuals.

The need to balance step by step the increase in the Sun's luminosity with commensurate reduction in the levels of greenhouse gases in Earth's atmosphere may explain why the history of life looks the way it does. Rather than reflecting naturalistic evolution, life's step-by-step origins, the fossil record, and Earth's biodeposits testify to the Creator's carefully timed and well-designed introductions, and later removals, of the just-right species at the just-right locations at the just-right population levels (see Psalm 104:27-30).

Human beings reap the benefit of nearly 4 billion years' worth of biodeposits. Without easy-to-mine deposits of tin, zinc, lead, copper, iron, silver, magnesium, and so forth, humanity could never have risen beyond stone-age technology. Construction of cities and all the transportation arteries that link them depends on materials such as concrete, steel, sand, copper, limestone, marble, bricks, mortar, and asphalt. These materials depend on raw resources that come from biodeposits. Nearly all the energy that drives civilization also comes from biodeposits—coal, oil, wood, natural gas, and kerogen, to name just a few. Nearly all the fertilizers that support agricultural production come from biodeposits—phosphates, nitrates, and so forth.

Answers to the Questions

The RTB biblical creation model continues to accurately predict future scientific discoveries.[26] It also offers explanations and answers that the naturalistic models do not. For example:

- How life appeared early and rapidly
- How life originated even without a prebiotic soup
- How life found apparently nonexistent chemical pathways
- How the homochirality problem was overcome
- How the information problem was solved
- How life's essential boundaries formed
- How life achieved minimum complexity
- How life filled even the harshest niches of Earth's ecosystem
- Why life was so abundant and diverse for the past 3.8 billion years
- Why life from elsewhere within the cosmos makes no sense
- Why directed panspermia—supernaturally directed panspermia—does make sense

Understanding the "why" helps solve the mystery behind the origins of life.

The faint Sun paradox by itself offers overwhelming evidence for the divine design of Earth and a solar system deliberately prepared for human

life. But it is not alone. A total of more than two hundred known characteristics of the Milky Way galaxy, the solar system, and Earth required
fine-tuning to prepare the planet for the arrival and survival of life—and
ultimately human life.[27] The infinitesimal probability of all these factors
coming together goes beyond coincidence. Add the odds against their
occurrence to the indicators for care involved in an origin-of-life process
that protects and provides for humanity, and the answers to the origins
questions become evident.

EPILOGUE

by Fazale Rana

Stradivarius violins usually carry a label with the Latin inscription, "*Antonius Stradivarius Cremonensis Faciebat Anno* [date]." This label alone, however, does not guarantee that the instrument is genuine, because thousands of copies bear that same identification. A violin is only authenticated by a thorough examination of its design, wood characteristics, and varnish. The specific features contribute to the weight of evidence for the identity of the maker.

If life's beginning has a supernatural cause, then much like an original Stradivarius, the cell's biochemical systems will display certain hallmark characteristics—individual features that indicate design.

Over the last forty years, biochemists have made progress toward understanding life's chemistry. The cell's major biochemical systems have been identified and characterized, and thanks to advances in measurement technology, biomolecular structure and function can now be determined in a detail that takes us down to the individual atom. These advances have exposed numerous features that build to a preponderance of evidence for the design and craftsmanship of a Creator.

Irreducible complexity: This term describes a system comprised of numerous components, all of which must be present and must interact precisely for the system to function. Many man-made systems are irreducibly complex. The cell's biochemical systems appear to be irreducibly complex.[1]

Chicken-and-egg systems: Many biochemical systems are called chicken-and-egg systems (after the old conundrum, "Which came first: the chicken or the egg?") because they consist of components that require each other for the components to be produced. For example, ribosomes make proteins, yet they in turn consist of proteins. Proteins can't be formed without ribosomes (proteins), and ribosomes (proteins) can't be made without proteins.[2]

Fine-tuning and high precision: Long recognized as design features, fine-tuning and high precision traditionally signify a device's superior engineering and craftsmanship. Many biochemical structures and activities depend on precise location and orientation of chemical groups in three-dimensional space, just-right chemical composition, and exacting chemical rates. Molecular fine-tuning is a defining property of life's chemical systems.

Compositional fine-tuning and complexity of cell membranes: These structures form the cell's external and internal boundaries and require precise chemical compositions to assemble. Cell membranes possess vast complexity. Both reflect design.

Molecular motors: These protein complexes are found inside the cell and are literal machines. Many possess an eerie resemblance to man-made machines. Those molecular machines revitalize the watchmaker argument for a Creator's existence.[3]

Biochemical information systems: Experience teaches that intelligible messages come from intelligent sources. The cell's biochemical machinery (proteins, DNA, RNA, and oligosaccharides) is information-based and therefore must come from an intelligent source.[4]

Genetic code: Encoded information indicates intelligence beyond the mere presence of information. An intelligent being must develop and employ the code. The cell's information exists in a coded format that defines the cell's information systems.[5]

Genetic code fine-tuning: The rules that comprise the genetic code are better designed than any conceivable alternative code to resist error caused by mutations.[6] This fine-tuning powerfully indicates that a superior intelligence developed the cell's information systems.

Preplanning: Planning ahead indicates purpose and reflects design. Many biochemical processes consist of a sequence of molecular events and chemical reactions. Often the initial steps of these pathways elegantly anticipate the final steps.

Quality control: Designed processes incorporate quality-control procedures to ensure efficient and reproducible manufacture of quality product. Many biochemical operations employ sophisticated quality-control processes.[7]

Molecular convergence: Several biochemical systems and/or biomolecules found in different organisms are structurally, functionally, and mechanistically identical. Yet they appear to have independent origins. Given the complexity of these systems, it is not rational to conclude that blind, random, natural processes independently produced them. Molecular convergence reflects the mark of a Creator.[8]

Man can't do it better: Humans' attempts to duplicate the cell's complex and elegant chemical processes in the laboratory frequently fail. When scientists can mimic these systems, their best efforts are crude, cumbersome, and inefficient. How can blind, random events account for the elegance of life's chemistry when the world's best researchers fail?[9]

Describing each of these design features in suitable detail is beyond this book's scope. For now, the point can be made that each of these characteristics comports with the notion that a Creator brought life into existence. The collective weight of evidence further compels design.

These hallmark characteristics of design, together with the mounting evidence recorded throughout this book, give me strong factual reasons to believe in God. The scientific harmony between the Bible and nature's record reinforces my conviction.

As Hugh Ross and I have demonstrated, the last two decades of research have moved the scientific community no closer to understanding—at least in naturalistic terms—life's origin. With an ironic twist, the research meant to explain life's origins by natural means repeatedly reveals a Creator's touch. The record of nature shows how He brought life into existence in a way that matches the expectations set up by the biblical account (see Genesis 1:2 and Deuteronomy 32:9-12).

The scientific data also indicate that the origin of life was only a small part of a grander plan. Scripture shows how God began with an amazing vision nearly 4 billion years ago when He spawned first life. He then hovered over early Earth like a mother eagle brooding over her young to preserve this life under hellish conditions. Thus began a process that connects the origins of early life to mankind's beginning in a deeply meaningful way, as a progression of miracles making Earth suitable for human beings.

God's plan and purpose for humanity can be glimpsed from the scientific evidence. The pages of the Bible unfold this plan and bring the purpose into fuller view.

A pastor once challenged me to read the Bible with an objective mind open to the truth. In its pages I encountered not only the Creator but also a Savior, and to this day I continue to discover the rewards of knowing Him. My hope and desire is for every reader to do the same.

APPENDIX A

Biblical Creation References

Reference	Theme
Genesis 1	primarily physical events
Genesis 2	primarily spiritual events
Genesis 3–5	sin's impact
Genesis 6–9	creation's renewal
Genesis 10–11	humanity's dispersion
Job 9	God's power
Job 34–41	creation's complexity
Psalm 65	optimal care
Psalm 104	Genesis 1 amplification
Psalm 139	creation of humans
Psalms 147–148	creation's praises
Proverbs 8	God's eternality
Ecclesiastes 1–3,8–12	laws of physics
Isaiah 40–51	cosmic creation
Romans 1–8	creation's purpose
1 Corinthians 15	creation, death, and resurrection
2 Corinthians 4	glory in creation's "weakness"
Hebrews 1	angels in creation
2 Peter 3	creation's end
Revelation 20–22	the new creation

For a more comprehensive list of Scripture passages addressing creation issues, visit Reasons To Believe's website at www.reasons.org and type "Scriptures Related to Creation" in the search window.

APPENDIX B

Carbon-12 Enrichment in Photosynthesis

The photosynthetic metabolic process uses solar energy to convert carbon dioxide (CO_2) and water (H_2O) into the sugar glucose (H_2O + CO_2 + sunlight $\rightarrow$ $C_6H_{12}O_6$).

The enzyme, ribulose-1,5-bisphosphate carboxylase (rubisco) catalyzes or assists the first step in the carbon fixation pathway of photosynthesis.[1] This enzyme adds CO_2 to the 5-carbon sugar, ribulose-1,5-bisphosphate to produce a 6-carbon sugar that decomposes into two molecules of the 3-carbon sugar called 3-phosphoglycerate. This 3-carbon sugar then enters into a series of reactions that transform them into glucose using energy harvested from sunlight.

The rubisco-catalyzed reaction utilizes more carbon-12 CO_2 ($^{12}CO_2$) than carbon-13 CO_2 ($^{13}CO_2$) as it converts the 5-carbon sugar into two 3-carbon sugars.[2] There are two reasons for this. First, $^{12}CO_2$, being lighter in mass, moves more rapidly than $^{13}CO_2$. This causes more $^{12}CO_2$ to encounter and bind to rubisco. Once bound, rubisco more rapidly incorporates $^{12}CO_2$ into ribulose-1,5-bisphosphate than it does $^{13}CO_2$. This again occurs because of $^{12}CO_2$'s lighter mass relative to $^{13}CO_2$. Because rubisco adds $^{12}CO_2$ more rapidly than $^{13}CO_2$ to ribulose-1,5-bisphosphate in a given period of time, more $^{12}CO_2$ becomes incorporated into the photosynthetic organism's biomass than $^{13}CO_2$.

NOTES

Introduction: In Pursuit of My Passion

1. See Michael Behe, *Darwin's Black Box: The Biochemical Challenge to Evolution* (New York: Free Press, 1996); Fazale R. Rana, "What Is Irreducible Complexity?" *Facts for Faith* 3 (Q3 2000), pp. 37-41.
2. Joe Aguirre, "Biochemistry and the Bible: Collaborators in Design," *Facts for Faith* 3 (Q3 2000), pp. 34-41.
3. Naively, at the time, I failed to recognize the significant differences that exist among all religions. See Kenneth Richard Samples, "Thinking Biblically About the World's Religions," *Facts for Faith* 10 (Q3 2002), pp. 54-61; Kenneth Richard Samples, "Do All Religions Lead to God?" *Facts for Faith* 8 (Q1 2002), pp. 52-58.
4. As a youth, Hugh Ross reasoned that a creator must exist if the universe had a beginning as espoused by all forms of the big bang theory. A thorough survey of the holy books of the world's religions convinced him that the Creator had communicated this message to humanity through the Bible. Dr. Ross discovered after eighteen months of study that the Bible did not contain any provable errors, and it had remarkable support from a litany of historical and scientific evidence. This study compelled him to trust the Bible's message and acknowledge Jesus Christ as his Savior. Hugh Ross's complete conversion experience can be heard on *Can Science Prove There's a God?*, an audiotape produced by Life Story Foundation, 1997. Available from www.reasons.org.

Chapter 1: Questions, Questions — Always Questions

1. One of the best scholarly treatments on the history and philosophy of origin-of-life research is Iris Fry, *The Emergence of Life on Earth: A Historical and Scientific Overview* (New Brunswick, N.J.: Rutgers University Press, 2000), pp. 54-88.
2. Fry, pp. 54-57.
3. For a detailed account of Haeckel and Huxley's studies on monera see Stephen Jay Gould, "Bathybius and Eozoon," *The Panda's Thumb: More Reflections in Natural History* (New York: Norton, 1980), pp. 236-244.
4. Fry, pp. 57-59.
5. Gould, pp. 236-244.
6. Fry, pp. 59-62.
7. Fry, pp. 62-64.

8. Stanley L. Miller, J. William Schopf, and Antonio Lazcano, "Oparin's 'Origin of Life': Sixty Years Later," *Journal of Molecular Evolution* 44 (1997), pp. 351-353.

9. Stanley L. Miller, "A Production of Amino Acids Under Possible Primitive Earth Conditions," *Science* 117 (1953), pp. 528-559; Stanley L. Miller, "Production of Some Organic Compounds Under Possible Primitive Earth Conditions," *Journal of the American Chemical Society* 77 (1955), pp. 2351-2361.

10. Fry, pp. 79-83.

11. John Horgan, *The End of Science: Facing the Limits of Knowledge in the Twilight of the Scientific Age* (New York: Broadway, 1997), pp. 138-142.

12. Fry, pp. 83-88.

13. Paul Davies, *The Fifth Miracle: The Search for the Origin and Meaning of Life* (New York: Simon & Schuster, 1999), pp. 17-18.

14. Davies, pp. 17-18.

15. For an inside report on the 12th International Conference on the Origin of Life and the 9th Meeting of the International Society for the Study of the Origin of Life (ISSOL 1999), July 11-16, 1999, San Diego, California, see Fazale R. Rana and Hugh Ross, "Life From the Heavens? Not This Way . . . ," *Facts for Faith* 1 (Q1 2000), pp. 11-15.

16. Fazale R. Rana, "Origin-of-Life Predictions Face Off: Evolution vs. Biblical Creation," *Facts for Faith* 6 (Q2 2001), pp. 41-47.

17. Francis Crick and Leslie E. Orgel, "Directed Panspermia," *Icarus* 19 (1973), pp. 341-346.

18. See Davies; See Robert Shapiro, *Planetary Dreams: The Quest to Discover Life Beyond Earth* (New York: Wiley, 1999).

Chapter 2: Are There Any Answers?

1. John Horgan, *The End of Science: Facing the Limits of Knowledge in the Twilight of the Scientific Age* (New York: Broadway, 1996), pp. 138-142.

2. Paul Davies, *The Fifth Miracle: The Search for the Origin and Meaning of Life* (New York: Simon & Schuster, 1999), pp. 81-82.

3. Francis Crick, *Life Itself: Its Origin and Nature* (New York: Simon & Schuster, 1981), p. 88.

4. Iris Fry, *The Emergence of Life on Earth: A Historical and Scientific Overview* (New Brunswick, N.J.: Rutgers University Press, 2000), p. 132.

5. In this work, Eldredge fails to convincingly demonstrate evolution's triumph and only demonstrates the failure of young-Earth creationism. See a book review by Fazale R. Rana in *Facts for Faith* 3 (Q3 2000), pp. 60-61.

6. Niles Eldredge, *The Triumph of Evolution and the Failure of Creationism* (New York: Freeman, 2000), p. 13.

7. Eldredge, pp. 20-21.

8. Eldredge, p. 91.

9. Eldredge, pp. 146-147.

10. For example, see Job 12:7-9; Psalm 8:1-3; Psalm 19:1-6; Psalm 36:5-6; Psalm 50:6; Psalm 97:6; Romans 1:20.

11. A commonly recognized observational method in science, this involves the human sensory capacity.

12. Stephen C. Meyer, "The Methodological Equivalence of Design and Descent: Can There Be a Scientific 'Theory of Creation'?" in *The Creation Hypothesis: Scientific*

Evidence for an Intelligent Designer, ed. J. P. Moreland (Downers Grove, Ill.: InterVarsity, 1994), pp. 67-112.

13. Francis Crick and Leslie E. Orgel, "Directed Panspermia," *Icarus* 19 (1973), pp. 341-346.

Chapter 3: Putting Creation to the Test

1. Hugh Ross, "Can Science Test a 'God-Created-It' Origins Model? Yes!" *Facts for Faith* 2 (Q2 2000), pp. 40-47, 55-58; Hugh Ross, "Putting Creation to the Test," lecture presented at Reasons To Believe Conference, June 22-24, 2000, Cypress, California; Hugh Ross, "Beyond Genesis 1," lecture presented at Reasons To Believe Conference, June 28-30, 2001, Cypress, California.

2. See Gordon D. Fee and Douglas Stuart, *How to Read the Bible for All Its Worth*, 2d ed. (Grand Rapids, Mich.: Zondervan, 1993); See Robert H. Stein, *A Basic Guide to Interpreting the Bible: Playing by the Rules* (Grand Rapids, Mich.: Barbor Books, 1994); See Grant R. Osbourne, *The Hermeneutical Spiral: A Comprehensive Introduction to Biblical Interpretation* (Downers Grove, Ill.: InterVarsity, 1991); See William W. Klein, Craig L. Blomberg, and Robert L. Hubbard, Jr., *Introduction to Biblical Interpretation* (Dallas: Word, 1993).

3. Paul Davies, *The Fifth Miracle: The Search for the Origin and Meaning of Life* (New York: Simon & Schuster, 1999), p. 22.

4. While there are other interpretive views as to the frame of reference, this view is preferred by the authors.

5. Hugh Ross, *The Genesis Question: Scientific Advances and the Accuracy of Genesis*, 2d expanded ed. (Colorado Springs, Colo.: NavPress, 2001), pp. 19-21; Kenneth A. Matthews, *The New American Commentary: Genesis 1:11-26*, vol. 1A (Nashville: Broadman and Holman, 1996), p. 130.

6. Victor P. Hamilton, *The New International Commentary on the Old Testament: The Book of Genesis Chapters 1-17* (Grand Rapids, Mich.: Eerdmans, 1990), pp. 108-109; Matthews, pp. 130-136.

7. Henry H. Halley, *Halley's Bible Handbook: An Abbreviated Bible Commentary*, 20th ed., rev. (Chicago: Halley, 1955), p. 60.

8. For references and an overview of the original scientific studies on solar system formation, see Ross, pp. 24-25.

9. Derek Kidner, *Tyndale Old Testament Commentaries: Psalms 73-150*, vol. 146 (Downers Grove, Ill.: InterVarsity, 1973), pp. 367-373; A. A. Anderson, *The New Century Bible Commentary, The Book of Psalms: Psalms 73-150*, vol. II (Grand Rapids, Mich.: Eerdmans, 1972), pp. 717-725; Leslie C. Allen, *Word Biblical Commentary: Psalms 101-150*, vol. 21 (Waco, Tex.: Word, 1983), pp. 23-25.

10. These authors consider the psalmist to be David, but authorship for Psalm 104 is debated by biblical scholars.

11. Peter D. Ward and Donald Brownlee, *Rare Earth: Why Complex Life Is Uncommon in the Universe* (New York: Springer-Verlag, 2000), p. 202.

12. Ward and Brownlee, pp. 44-48.

13. In establishing a creation model that tests a supernatural origin of life, correct rendering of the phrase *rûah 'ĕlōhîm* (translated here as "the Spirit of God") becomes important. Some commentators suggest that *rûah 'ĕlōhîm* should translate as "mighty wind," not "the Spirit of God." While this translation seems conceivable, it finds limited support among Bible scholars. After all, Genesis 1:1 says, "In the beginning God

['ĕlōhîm] created the heavens and the earth." Rûah 'ĕlōhîm in Genesis 1:2 would seem to refer to this same Creator. 'Ĕlōhîm also recurs throughout Genesis 1 specifically in reference to God. (See Matthews, pp. 134-136.) Further, nowhere else in the Old Testament does the phrase rûah 'ĕlōhîm denote a mighty wind. (See Hamilton, pp. 111-114.) Rûah 'ĕlōhîm most likely means "the Spirit of God."

14. John Rea, Charisma's Bible Handbook on the Holy Spirit (Orlando: Creation House, 1998), pp. 23-27; George A. F. Knight, The Song of Moses: A Theological Quarry (Grand Rapids, Mich.: Eerdmans, 1995), pp. 45-53.

15. Rea, p. 25, emphasis added; citing J. Rodman Williams, Renewal Theology: God, the World and Redemption, vol. 1 (Grand Rapids, Mich.: Academie Books, Zondervan, 1988), p. 345.

16. Ross, pp. 35-62.

17. It is important to note that the RTB Model represents only one of several possible biblically-derived models for life's origin. We think that the RTB Model reflects an accurate interpretation of the biblical texts; however we understand that others may disagree. Thoughtful challenges are desirable, and we encourage those who disagree to advance their own interpretations and models. We also acknowledge that some may dispute our predictions or even offer additional predictions. We encourage this effort as well.

Chapter 4: The Naturalistic Approach

1. I. S. Shklovskii and Carl Sagan, Intelligent Life in the Universe (San Francisco: Holden-Day, 1966), pp. 203-245.

2. For representative presentations of the "textbook" description for the origin of life that span the last fifteen years, see Karen Arms and Pamela S. Camp, Biology, 3d ed. (Philadelphia: Saunders College, 1987), pp. 412-428; Sylvia S. Mader, Inquiry into Life, 6th ed. (Dubuque, Iowa: Brown, 1991), pp. 552-562; Richard Cowen, History of Life, 3d ed. (Malden, Mass.: Blackwell Science, 2000), pp. 1-18.

3. Arms and Camp, pp. 412-428; Mader, pp. 552-562; Cowen, pp. 1-18.

4. Stanley L. Miller, J. William Schopf, and Antonio Lazcano, "Oparin's 'Origin of Life': Sixty Years Later," Journal of Molecular Evolution 44 (1997), pp. 351-353.

5. The concept for Table 2 was taken and expanded from C. P. McKay, "Life in Comets," in Comets and the Origin and Evolution of Life, ed. Paul J. Thomas, Christopher F. Chyba, and Christopher P. McKay (New York: Springer-Verlag, 1997), p. 275; T. Fenchell, G. M. King, and T. H. Blackburn, Bacterial Biogeochemistry: The Ecophysiology of Mineral Cycling, 2d ed. (San Diego: Academic Press, 1998), p. 255.

6. Paul Davies, The Fifth Miracle: The Search for the Origin and Meaning of Life (New York: Simon & Schuster, 1999), pp. 187-243.

7. Francis Crick and Leslie E. Orgel, "Directed Panspermia," Icarus 19 (1973), pp. 341-346; See Francis Crick, Life Itself: Its Origin and Nature (New York: Touchstone, 1981).

8. David Darling, The Extraterrestrial Encyclopedia: An Alphabetical Reference to All Life in the Universe (New York: Three Rivers, 2000), pp. 291, 311.

9. The funding for NASA's exobiology program has quadrupled during the past five years.

10. James F. Kasting and Lisa L. Brown, "The Early Atmosphere as a Source of Biogenic Compounds," in The Molecular Origins of Life: Assembling Pieces of the Puzzle, ed. André Brack (Cambridge: Cambridge University Press, 1998), pp. 35-36.

11. Rafael Navarro-Gonzalez, Mario J. Molina, and Luisa T. Molina, "Production of Reactive Nitrogen in Explosive Volcanic Clouds," *Book of Abstracts,* 12th International Conference on the Origin of Life and the 9th Meeting of the International Society for the Study of the Origin of Life (ISSOL 1999), July 11-16, 1999, San Diego, California, p. 34.

12. Christopher Wills and Jeffrey Bada, *The Spark of Life: Darwin and the Primeval Soup* (Cambridge: Perseus, 2000), pp. 97-101; Leslie E. Orgel, "The Origin of Life—A Review of Facts and Speculations," *Trends in Biochemical Sciences* 23 (1998), pp. 491-495.

13. Karl O. Stetter, "Hyperthermophiles and their Possible Role as Ancestors of Modern Life," in *The Molecular Origins of Life: Assembling Pieces of the Puzzle,* ed. André Brack (Cambridge: Cambridge University Press, 1998), pp. 315-335.

14. Michael Hagmann, "Between a Rock and a Hard Place," *Science* 295 (2002), pp. 2006-2007; Noam Lahav, *Biogenesis: Theories of Life's Origin* (New York: Oxford University Press, 1999), pp. 266-281; Orgel, *Origin of Life*, pp. 491-495.

15. Lahav, pp. 169-171.

16. J. Oró and A. Lazcano, "Comets and the Origin and Evolution of Life," pp. 3-27, and C. F. Chyba and C. Sagan, "Comets as a Source of Prebiotic Organic Molecules for the Early Earth," pp. 147-173, in *Comets and the Origin and Evolution of Life,* ed. Paul J. Thomas, Christopher F. Chyba, and Christopher P. McKay (New York: Springer-Verlag, 1997).

17. James P. Ferris and David A. Usher, "Origins of Life," in *Biochemistry*, Geoffrey Zubay, coordinating author (Reading, Pa.: Addison-Wesley, 1984), pp. 1191-1241.

18. Wills and Bada, pp. 101-103.

19. Lahav, pp. 168-169; James P. Ferris, "Catalyzed RNA Synthesis for the RNA World," in *The Molecular Origins of Life: Assembling Pieces of the Puzzle*, ed. Andrè Brack (Cambridge: Cambridge University Press, 1998), pp. 255-268.

20. Christian de Duve, "Clues from Present-Day Biology: The Thioester World," in *The Molecular Origins of Life: Assembling Pieces of the Puzzle*, ed. Andrè Brack (Cambridge: Cambridge University Press, 1998), pp. 219-236.

21. See Harold J. Morowitz, *Beginnings of Cellular Life: Metabolism Recapitulates Biogenesis* (New Haven, Conn.: Yale University Press, 1992).

22. Iris Fry, *The Emergence of Life on Earth: A Historical and Scientific Overview* (New Brunswick, N.J.: Rutgers University Press, 2000), pp. 100-102.

23. Antonio Lazcano, "The RNA World, Its Predecessors, and Its Descendents," in *Early Life on Earth: Nobel Symposium No. 84,* ed. Stefan Bengtson (New York: Columbia University Press, 1994), pp. 70-80.

24. Fry, pp. 135-137.

25. Arthur J. Zaug and Thomas R. Cech, "The Intervening Sequence of RNA of *Tetrahymena* Is an Enzyme," *Science* 231 (1986), pp. 470-475; Thomas R. Cech, "A Model for the RNA-Catalyzed Replication of RNA," *Proceedings of the National Academy of Sciences, USA* 83 (1986), pp. 4360-4363.

26. Kenneth D. James and Andrew D. Ellington, "Catalysis in the RNA World," in *The Molecular Origin of Life: Assembling Pieces of the Puzzle*, ed. Andrè Brack (Cambridge: Cambridge University Press, 1998), pp. 269-294.

27. Elizabeth Finkle, "DNA Cuts Its Teeth—As an Enzyme," *Science* 286 (1999), pp. 2441-2442; Stephen W. Santoro and Gerald Joyce, "A General Purpose RNA-Cleaving DNA Enzyme," *Proceedings of the National Academy of Sciences, USA* 94

(1997), pp. 4262-4266; Terry L. Sheppard et al., "A DNA Enzyme with N-Glycosylase Activity," *Proceedings of the National Academy of Sciences, USA* 97 (2000), pp. 7802-7807; Stuart Kauffman, "Self-Replication: Even Peptides Do It," *Nature* 382 (1996), pp. 496-497; D. H. Lee et al., "A Self-Replicating Peptide," *Nature* 382 (1996), pp. 525-528.

28. Alan W. Schwartz, "Origins of the RNA World," in *The Molecular Origin of Life: Assembling Pieces of the Puzzle*, ed. Andrè Brack (Cambridge: Cambridge University Press, 1998), pp. 237-254.

29. D. W. Deamer, "Membrane Compartments in Prebiotic Evolution," in *The Molecular Origin of Life: Assembling Pieces of the Puzzle*, ed. Andrè Brack (Cambridge: Cambridge University Press, 1998), pp. 189-205; David W. Deamer et al., "Self-Assembly and Function of Primitive Membrane Structures," in *Early Life on Earth: Nobel Symposium No. 84*, ed. Stefan Bengtson (New York: Columbia University Press, 1994), pp. 107-123.

30. Deamer, "Membrane Compartments," pp. 189-205; Deamer et al., "Self-Assembly," pp. 107-123.

31. Carl Woese, "The Universal Ancestor," *Proceedings of the National Academy of Sciences, USA* 95 (1998), pp. 6854-6859; Carl R. Woese, "On the Evolution of Cells," *Proceedings of the National Academy of Sciences, USA* 99 (2002), pp. 8742-8747.

32. Carl Woese, "Interpreting the Universal Phylogenetic Tree," *Proceedings of the National Academy of Sciences, USA* 97 (2000), pp. 8392-8396; W. Ford Doolittle, "Phylogenetic Classification and the Universal Tree," *Science* 284 (1999), pp. 2124-2128.

33. For a detailed discussion of the different approaches that constitute the origin-of-life research program, see Lahav, *Biogenesis*.

Chapter 5: An Early or Late Appearance?

1. *World Book Millennium 2000* s.v. "Greenland," CD-ROM.

2. Available from www.greenland-guide.dk/nuuktour/info.htm; Internet; accessed September 16, 2002.

3. Peter D. Ward and Donald Brownlee, *Rare Earth: Why Complex Life Is Uncommon in the Universe* (New York: Springer-Verlag, 2000), pp. 35-60.

4. J. William Schopf, *Cradle of Life: The Discovery of Earth's Earliest Fossils* (Princeton, N.J.: Princeton University Press, 1999), pp. 79-81; J. William Schopf, "The Oldest Known Records of Life: Early Archaean Stromatolites, Microfossils, and Organic Matter," in *Early Life on Earth, Nobel Symposium No. 84*, ed. Stefan Bengtson (New York: Columbia University Press, 1994), pp. 193-206.

5. Schopf, *Cradle of Life*, pp. 73-75.

6. Schopf, *Cradle of Life*, pp. 80-81.

7. For a readable description of stromatolites see Schopf, *Cradle of Life*, pp. 183-208; Richard Cowen, *History of Life*, 3d ed. (Malden, Mass.: Blackwell Science, 2000), pp. 28-29; R. P. Reid et al., "The Role of Microbes in Accretion, Lamination and Early Lithification of Modern Marine Stromatolites," *Nature* 406 (2000), pp. 989-992; David J. Des Marais, "Microbial Mats and the Early Evolution of Life," *Trends in Ecology and Evolution* 5 (1990), pp. 140-144.

8. Malcolm R. Walter, "Stromatolites: The Main Geological Source of Information on the Evolution of the Early Benthos," in *Early Life on Earth: Nobel Symposium No. 84*, ed. Stefan Bengtson (New York: Columbia University Press, 1994), pp. 270-286;

Roger Buick, "The Antiquity of Oxygenic Photosynthesis: Evidence from Stromatolites in Sulphate-Deficient Archaean Lakes," *Science* 255 (1992), pp. 74-77.

9. Walter, "Main Geological Source," pp. 270-286.

10. Walter, "Main Geological Source," pp. 270-286.

11. Donald R. Lowe, "Stromatolites 3,400 Myr Old from the Archaean of Western Australia," *Nature* 284 (1980), pp. 441-443; M. R. Walter et al., "Stromatolites 3,400-3,500 Myr Old from the North Pole Area, Western Australia," *Nature* 284 (1980), pp. 443-445; Gary R. Byerly et al., "Stromatolites from the 3,300-3,500 Myr Swaziland Supergroup, Barberton Mountain Land, South Africa," *Nature* 319 (1986), pp. 489-491; J. L. Orpen and J. F. Wilson, "Stromatolites at ~3,500 Myr and a Greenstone-Granite Unconformity in the Zimbabwean Archaean," *Nature* 291 (1981), pp. 218-220.

12. Donald R. Lowe, "Abiological Origin of Described Stromatolites Older than 3.2 Ga," *Geology* 22 (1994), pp. 387-390; Malcolm Walter, "Old Fossils Could Be Fractal Frauds," *Nature* 383 (1996), pp. 385-386; John P. Grotzinger and Daniel H. Rothman, "An Abiotic Model for Stromatolite Morphogenesis," *Nature* 383 (1996), pp. 423-425; John P. Grotzinger and Andrew H. Knoll, "Stromatolites in Precambrian Carbonates: Evolutionary Mileposts or Environmental Dipsticks?" *Annual Review of Earth and Planetary Science* 27 (1999), pp. 313-358.

13. Roger Buick et al., "Abiological Origin of Described Stromatolites Older than 3.2 Ga: Comment and Reply," *Geology* 23 (1995), p. 191; Stanley M. Awramik, "The Oldest Record of Photosynthesis," *Photosynthesis Research* 33 (1992), pp. 75-89; Schopf, *Cradle of Life*, pp. 196-197.

14. Walter, "Main Geological Source," pp. 270-286.

15. Schopf, "Oldest Known Records," pp. 191-206.

16. Schopf, *Cradle of Life*, pp. 81-83; Cowen, *History of Life*, p. 30.

17. Schopf, "Oldest Known Records," pp. 191-206; Andrew H. Knoll and Elso S. Barghoorn, "Archaean Microfossils Showing Cell Division from the Swaziland System of South Africa," *Science* 198 (1977), pp. 396-398; Maud M. Walsh, "Microfossils and Possible Microfossils from the Early Archaean Onverwacht Group, Barberton Mountain Land, South Africa," *Precambrian Research* 54 (1992), pp. 271-293.

18. Knoll and Barghoon, pp. 396-398.

19. Frances Westall et al., "Early Archaean Fossil Bacteria and Biofilms in Hydrothermally-Influenced Sediments from the Barkerton Greenstone Belt, South Africa," *Precambrian Research* 106 (2001), pp. 93-116; Frances Westall, "On the Diversity and Distribution of Early Archaea Life," lecture presented at the 13th International Conference on the Origin of Life and the 10th Meeting of the International Society for the Study of the Origin of Life (ISSOL 2002), June 30-July 5, 2002, Oaxaca, Mexico.

20. Schopf, "Oldest Known Records," pp. 191-206; S. M. Awramik et al., "Filamentous Fossil Bacteria from the Archaean of Western Australia," *Precambrian Research* 20 (1983), pp. 357-374; S. M. Awramik et al., "Carbonaceous Filaments from North Pole, Western Australia: Are They Fossil Bacteria in Archaean Stromatolites? A Discussion," *Precambrian Research* 39 (1988), pp. 303-309; J. William Schopf and Bonnie M. Packer, "Early Archaean (3.3-Billion to 3.5-Billion-Year-Old) Microfossils from Warrawoona Group, Australia," *Science* 237 (1987), pp. 70-73; J. William Schopf, "Microfossils of the Early Archaean Apex Chert: New Evidence of the Antiquity of Life," *Science* 260 (1993), pp. 640-646.

21. Richard A. Kerr, "Earliest Signs of Life Just Oddly Shaped Crud," *Science* 295 (2002), pp. 1812-1813; Martin D. Brasier et al., "Questioning the Evidence for Earth's Oldest Fossils," *Nature* 416 (2002), pp. 76-81; Rex Dalton, "Squaring Up Over Ancient Life," *Nature* 417 (2002), pp. 782-783.

22. Brasier et al., pp. 76-81; Christopher H. House et al., "Carbon Isotopic Composition of Individual Precambrian Microfossils," *Geology* 28 (2000), pp. 707-710.

23. Anatoliy B. Kudryartser et al., "*In-Site* Laser-Raman Imagery of Precambrian Microscopic Fossils," *Proceedings of the National Academy of Sciences, USA* 98 (2001), pp. 823-826; J. William Schopf et al., "Laser-Raman Imagery of Earth's Earliest Fossils," *Nature* 416 (2002), pp. 73-76.

24. Martin D. Brasier et al., "Questioning the Evidence for Earth's Oldest Fossils," lecture presented at ISSOL 2002; J. William Schopf, "The Oldest Evidences for Life," lecture, ISSOL 2002.

25. André Kempe et al., "Atomic Force Microscopy of Precambrian Microscopic Fossils," *Proceedings of the National Academy of Sciences, USA* 99 (2002), pp. 9117-9120.

26. Jozef Kaxmierczak and Barbara Kremer, "Thermal Alteration of the Earth's Oldest Fossils," *Nature* 420 (2002), pp. 477-478.

27. Westall, "On the Diversity"; Yuichiro Veno et al., "Early Archaea (ca. 3.5 Ga) Microfossils and ^{13}C-Depleted Carbonaceous Matter in the North Pole Area, Western Australia: Field Occurrence and Geochemistry," in *Geochemistry and the Origin of Life*, ed. S. Nakashima, S. Maruyama, A. Brack, and B. F. Windley (Tokyo: Universal Academy Press, 2001), pp. 203-236.

28. Schopf, *Cradle of Life*, pp. 174-177; Manfred Schidlowski, "A 3,800-Million-Year Isotopic Record of Life from Carbon in Sedimentary Rocks," *Nature* 333 (1988), pp. 313-318; Manfred Schidlowski, "Carbon Isotopes as Biogeochemical Recorders of Life over 3.8 Ga of Earth History: Evolution of a Concept" *Precambrian Research* 106 (2001), pp. 117-134.

29. Carbon-13 depletion is measured in units called parts per mil ($\delta^{13}C$ ‰) compared to an inorganic standard (Pee Dee Belemnite). For example, photosynthetic microbes generate biomass with a carbon-12 enrichment (or a carbon-13 depletion) measured as $\delta^{13}C$ of about –10 to –35‰. Methanogenic microbes—organisms that convert hydrogen (H_2) and either carbon dioxide (CO_2) or carbon monoxide (CO) into methane (CH_4) as a means to extract energy from the environment—also cause a carbon-12 enrichment ($\delta^{13}C$) of about –10 to –35‰. However, the methane produced by methanogenesis has a carbon-12 enrichment of about –30 to –90‰. Organisms that consume this methane, called methanotrophic bacteria, produce a biomass that is much more enriched in carbon-12 than that produced by photosynthesis or methanogenesis. See Schopf, *Cradle of Life*, pp. 174-181; Schidlowski, "Carbon Isotopes," pp. 117-134.

30. See details in the preceding note.

31. This carbon-12 enrichment clusters on average near –25 to –30‰. See Schopf in *Early Life on Earth*, pp. 191-206; Westall et al., *Precambrian Research*, pp. 93-116.

32. The carbon-12 enrichment of the bulk kerogen, the most ancient rocks of western Greenland, is not as extensive as that for kerogen and graphite residues that undeniably represent biological activity recovered from other geological formations. (The carbon-12 enrichment of the bulk kerogen is -10 to –17‰.) Researchers suggest the reduced carbon-12 content reflects isotope exchange of carbon-12 of biological residue for carbon-13 from inorganic materials during geological metamorphosis.

(See Schidlowski, "Isotopic Record," pp. 313-318; Schidlowski, "Carbon Isotopes," pp. 117-134.) Because kerogens decompose under the temperature and pressure extremes caused by geological activity, the carbon-carbon bonds of kerogen preferentially break to release carbon dioxide or methane enriched in carbon-12. (See Schopf, in *Early Life on Earth*, pp. 193-206.) This chemical breakdown causes kerogen to become progressively enriched in the heavier carbon isotope. If this is the case, then the kerogen remains in the oldest rocks provide evidence for life on Earth 3.8 billion years ago. Within this framework, the kerogen deposits started out with a carbon-12 enrichment well within a range that reflects a biological origin. They lost carbon-12 through isotope exchange and possibly chemical decomposition. Recent isotopic analysis provides corroboration that isotope exchange enriched the Greenland kerogen in carbon-13. (See Yuichiro Ueno et al., "Ion Microprobe Analysis of Graphite from Ca. 3.8 Ga Metasediments, Isua Supracrustal Belt, West Greenland: Relationship Between Metamorphism and Carbon Isotopic Composition," *Geochimica et Cosmochimica Acta* 66 (2002), pp. 1257-1268.) Scientists are unaware of any inorganic process that can cause isotopic enrichment within the observed and corrected range; therefore, they take the carbon-12 enrichment as life's signature.

33. John M. Hayes, "The Earliest Memories of Life on Earth," *Nature* 384 (1996), pp. 21-22; S. J. Mojzsis et al., "Evidence for Life on Earth before 3,800 Million Years Ago," *Nature* 384 (1996), pp. 55-59; Heinrich D. Holland, "Evidence for Life on Earth More than 3850 Million Years Ago," *Science* 275 (1997), pp. 38-39.

34. Schopf, *Cradle of Life*, pp. 180-181.

35. S. J. Mojzsis et al., pp. 55-59.

36. Christopher M. Fedo, "Setting and Origin for Problematic Rocks from the >3.7 Ga Isua Greenstone Belt, Southern West Greenland: Earth's Oldest Coarse Clastic Sediments," *Precambrian Research* 101 (2000), pp. 69-78.

37. Yuji Sano et al., "Origin of Life from Apatite Dating?" *Nature* 400 (1999), p. 127; John S. Meyers and James L. Crowley, "Vestiges of Life in the Oldest Greenland Rocks? A Review of Early Archaean Geology in the Godthabsfjord Region, and Reappraisal of Field Evidence for >3850 Ma Life on Akilia," *Precambrian Research* 103 (2000), pp. 101-124.

38. Craig E. Manning et al., "Geology and Age of Supracrustal Rocks, Akilia Island, Greenland: New Evidence for a >3.83 Ga Origin of Life," *Astrobiology* 1 (2001), pp. 402-403.

39. Christopher M. Fedo and Martin J. Whitehouse, "Metasomatic Origin of Quartz-Pyroxine Rock, Akilia, Greenland, and Implications for Earth's Earliest Life," *Science* 296 (2002), pp. 1448-1452; Richard A Kerr, "Reversals Reveal Pitfalls in Spotting Ancient and E.T. Life," *Science* 296 (2002), pp. 1384-1385.

40. Mark A. Van Zuilen et al., "Reassessing the Evidence for the Earliest Traces of Life," *Nature* 418 (2002), pp. 627-630; Mark A. Van Zuilen et al., "Tracing Life in the Early Archaea: The 3.8 Ga Isua Supracrustal Belt, Southern West Greenland," lecture, ISSOL 2002.

41. Minik T. Rosing, "^{13}C-Depleted Carbon Microparticles in >3700-Ma Sea-Floor Sedimentary Rocks from West Greenland," *Science* 283 (1999), pp. 674-676.

42. Ueno et al., "Ion Microprobe Analysis," pp. 1257-1268.

43. V. Beaumont and F. Robert, "Nitrogen Isotope Ratios of Kerogens in Precambrian Cherts: A Record of the Evolution of Atmosphere Chemistry?" *Precambrian Research* 96 (1999), pp. 63-82.

44. δ ^{15}N value of +6‰.

45. Kerogen remains derived from organisms that live in an anoxic environment typically display a nitrogen-14 excess (δ ^{15}N values that range from about –3 to –10‰).

46. Beaumont and Robert, pp. 63-82; Daniele L. Pinti et al., "Nitrogen and Argon Signatures in 3.8 to 2.8 Ga Metasediments: Clues on the Chemical State of the Archaean Ocean and Deep Biosphere," Geochimica et Cosmochimica Acta 65 (2001), pp. 2301-2315.

47. Pinti et al., pp. 2301-2315.

48. Schopf, Cradle of Life, pp. 177-179.

49. Yanan Shen et al., "Isotopic Evidence for Microbial Sulphate Reduction in the Early Archaean Era," Nature 410 (2001), pp. 77-81.

50. Cowen, History of Life, pp. 31-32.

51. Schopf, Cradle of Life, pp. 171-172; Cowen, History of Life, pp. 31-32.

52. Cowen, History of Life, pp. 31-32.

53. Schopf, Cradle of Life, pp. 171-172; Heinrich D. Holland, "Early Proterozoic Atmospheric Change," in Early Life on Earth: Nobel Symposium No. 84, ed. Stefan Bentson (New York: Columbia University Press, 1994), pp. 237-244; Kenneth M. Towe, "Earth's Early Atmosphere: Constraints and Opportunities for Early Evolution," in Early Life on Earth: Nobel Symposium No. 84, ed. Stefan Bengtson (New York: Columbia University Press, 1994), pp. 36-47.

54. Peter W. Uitterdijk Appel, "On the Early Archaean Isua Iron-Formation, West Greenland," Precambrian Research 11 (1980), pp. 73-87.

55. Schopf, Cradle of Life, pp. 209-235; J. William Schopf, "Disparate Rates, Differing Fates: Tempo and Mode of Evolution Changed from the Precambrian to the Phanerozoic," Proceedings of the National Academy of Sciences, USA 91 (1994), pp. 6735-6742.

56. Stanley M. Awramik, "The Oldest Record of Photosynthesis," Photosynthesis Research 33 (1992), pp. 75-89.

57. Stryer, pp. 517-543.

58. Jin Xiong et al., "Molecular Evidence for the Early Evolution of Photosynthesis," Science 289 (2000), pp. 1724-1730; G. C. Dismukes et al., "The Origin of Atmospheric Oxygen on Earth: The Innovation of Oxygenic Photosynthesis," Proceedings of the National Academy of Sciences, USA 98 (2001), pp. 2170-2175.

59. David J. Des Marais, "When Did Photosynthesis Emerge on Earth?" Science 289 (2000), pp. 1703-1705.

60. Shen et al., pp. 77-81.

61. Schopf, Cradle of Life, p. 3.

62. Schopf, Cradle of Life, p. 98.

Chapter 6: A Slow or Sudden Arrival?

1. I. S. Shklovskii and Carl Sagan, Intelligent Life in the Universe (San Francisco: Holden-Day, 1966), p. 237.

2. C. J. Allègre, G. Manhès, and C. Göpel, "The Age of the Earth," Geochemica et Cosmochemica Acta 59 (1995), pp. 1445-1456.

3. J. William Schopf, "The Oldest Known Records of Life: Early Archean Stromatolites, Microfossils, and Organic Matter," in Early Life on Earth, Nobel Symposium No. 84, ed. Stefan Bengtson (New York: Columbia University Press, 1994), pp. 193-206; J. William Schopf and Malcolm R. Walter, "Archean Microfossils: New Evidence of

Ancient Microbes," in *Earth's Earliest Biosphere: Its Original Evolution,* ed. J. William Schopf (Princeton, N.J.: Princeton University Press, 1983), pp. 214-239.

4. R. Kippenhahn and A. Weigert, *Stellar Structure and Evolution,* study ed. (Berlin: Springer-Verlag, 1994), p. 269.

5. Icko Iben, Jr., "Stellar Evolution. I. The Approach to the Main Sequence," *Astrophysical Journal* 141 (1965), pp. 993-1018, especially p. 1000; G. Wuchteri and Ralf S. Klessen, "The First Million Years of the Sun: A Calculation of the Formation and Early Evolution of a Solar Mass Star," *Astrophysical Journal Letters* 560 (2001), pp. L185-L188.

6. Frederick M. Walter and Don C. Barry, "Pre- and Main-Sequence Evolution of Solar Activity," in *The Sun in Time,* ed. C. P. Sonett, M. S. Giampapa, and M. C. Matthews (Tucson: University of Arizona Press, 1991), pp. 633-657 (note Table IV on page 653); David R. Soderblom, Burton F. Jones, and Debra Fischer, "Rotational Studies of Late-Type Stars. VII. M34 (NGC 1039) and the Evolution of Angular Momentum and Activity in Young Solar-Type Stars," *Astrophysical Journal* 563 (2001), pp. 334-340.

7. Katherine L. Rhode, William Herbst, and Robert D. Mathieu, "Rotational Velocities and Radii of Pre-Main-Sequence Stars in the Orion Nebula," *Astronomical Journal* 122 (2001), pp. 3258-3279; Silvia H. P. Alencar, Christopher M. Johns-Krull, and Gibor Basri, "The Spectral Variability of the Classical T Tauri Star DR Tauri," *Astronomical Journal* 122 (2001), pp. 3335-3360.

8. Kevin A. Maher and David J. Stevenson, "Impact Frustration of the Origin of Life," *Nature* 331 (1988), pp. 612-614; Verne R. Oberbeck and Guy Fogleman, "Impacts and the Origin of Life," *Nature* 339 (1989), p. 434; Norman H. Sleep et al., "Annihilation of Ecosystems by Large Asteroid Impacts on the Early Earth," *Nature* 342 (1989), pp. 139-142.

9. Llyd E. Wells, John C. Armstrong, and Guillermo Gonzalez, "Reseeding of Early Earth by Impacts of Returning Ejecta During the Late Heavy Bombardment," *Icarus* 162 (2003), pp. 38-46.

10. Stephen J. Mojzsis, "Lithosphere-Hydrosphere Interactions on the Hadean (>4.0 Ga) Earth," *Astrobiology* 1 (2001), pp. 382-383; Christopher Wills and Jeffrey Bada, *The Spark of Life: Darwin and the Primeval Soup* (Cambridge: Perseus, 2000), pp. 71-74.

11. Craig E. Manning et al., "Geology and Age of Supracrustal Rocks, Akilia Island, Greenland: New Evidence for a >3.83 Ga Origin of Life," *Astrobiology* 1 (2001), pp. 402-403.

12. Richard A. Kerr, "Beating Up on a Young Earth, and Possibly Life," *Science* 290 (2000), p. 1677; B. A. Cohen, T. D. Swindle, and D. A. Kring, "Support for the Lunar Cataclysm Hypothesis from Lunar Meteorite Impact Melt Ages," *Science* 290 (2000), pp. 1754-1756.

13. Ronny Schoenberg et al., "Tungsten Isotope Evidence from ~ 3.8-Gyr Metamorphased Sediments for Early Meteorite Bombardment of the Earth," *Nature* 418 (2002), p. 403.

14. A. D. Anbar et al., "Extraterrestrial Iridium, Sediment Accumulation and the Habitability of the Early Earth's Surface," *Journal of Geophysical Research* 106 (2001), pp. 3219-3236; Schoenberg et al., p. 403.

15. Schoenberg et al., pp. 403-405.

16. Hugh Ross, "The Faint-Sun Paradox," *Facts for Faith* 8 (Q2 2002), pp. 26-33.

17. Ross, pp. 26-33.

18. Stephen J. Mojzsis, p. 383; See Stephen J. Mojzsis and Graham Ryder, "Accretion to

Earth and Moon ~3.85 Ga," in *Accretion of Extraterrestrial Matter Throughout Earth's History,* ed. B. Peuckner-Ehrinbrink and B. Schmitz (New York: Kluwer Academic/Plenum Publishers, 2001); Stephen J. Mojzsis and T. Mark Harrison, "Establishment of a 3.83-Ga Magmatic Age for the Akilia Tonalite (Southern West Greenland)," *Earth and Planetary Science Letters* 202 (2002), pp. 563-576.

19. Wells, Armstrong, and Gonzalez, pp. 38-46.

20. For example: Smadar Levin-Zaidman et al., "Ringlike Structure of *Deinococcus radio-durans* Genome: A Key to Radioresistance?" *Science* 299 (2003), pp. 254-256.

21. Christopher Wills and Jeffrey Bada, *The Spark of Life: Darwin and the Primeval Soup* (Cambridge: Perseus, 2000), p. 83.

22. James K. W. Lee, Ian S. Williams, and David J. Ellis, "Pb, U, and Th Diffusion in Natural Zircon," *Nature* 390 (1997), pp. 159-161.

23. Yuri Amelin, Der-Chuen Lee, Alex N. Halliday, and Robert T. Pidgeon, "Nature of the Earth's Earliest Crust from Hafnium Isotopes in Single Detrital Zircons," *Nature* 399 (1999), pp. 252-255.

24. Stephen J. Mojzsis, T. Mark Harrison, and Robert T. Pidgeon, "Oxygen-Isotope Evidence from Ancient Zircons for Liquid Water at the Earth's Surface 4,300 Myr Ago," *Nature* 409 (2001), pp. 178-181.

25. Simon A. Wilde et al., "Evidence from Detrital Zircons for the Existence of Continental Crust and Oceans on the Earth 4.4 Gyr Ago," *Nature* 409 (2001), pp. 175-178.

26. G. Brent Dalrymple, *The Age of the Earth* (Stanford, Calif.: Stanford University Press, 1991), pp. 203-256.

27. Dalrymple, pp. 203-256.

28. Neil F. Comins, *What If the Moon Didn't Exist? Voyages to Earths That Might Have Been* (New York: HarperCollins, 1993), pp. 62, 64-65.

29. Comins, pp. 4-5, 53-65, 68; W. R. Kuhn, J. C. G. Walker, and H. G. Marshall, "The Effect on Earth's Surface Temperature from Variations in Rotation Rate, Continent Formation, Solar Luminosity, and Carbon Dioxide," *Journal of Geophysical Research* 94 (1989), pp. 11, 129-131, 136.

30. Jay Melosh, "A New Model Moon," *Nature* 412 (2001), pp. 694-695; Robin M. Canup and Erik Asphaug, "Origin of the Moon in a Giant Impact Near the End of the Earth's Formation," *Nature* 412 (2001), pp. 708-712; Sigeru Ida, Robin M. Canup, and Glen R. Stewart, "Lunar Accretion from an Impact-Generated Disk," *Nature* 389 (1997), pp. 353-357; Hugh Ross, *The Genesis Question: Scientific Advances and the Accuracy of Genesis,* 2d ed. (Colorado Springs, Colo.: NavPress, 2001), pp. 29-31.

31. Louis A. Codispoti, "The Limits to Growth," *Nature* 387 (1987), p. 237; Kenneth H. Coale, "A Massive PhytoPlankton Bloom Induced by an Ecosystem-Scale Iron Fertilization Experiment in the Equatorial Pacific Ocean," *Nature* 383 (1996), pp. 495-499.

32. Earth preferentially absorbed heavy elements from the collider, whereas Earth and the collider preferentially ejected light elements. P. Jonathan Patchett, "Scum of the Earth After All," *Nature* 382 (1996), p. 758.

33. William R. Ward, "Comments on the Long-Term Stability of the Earth's Obliquity," *Icarus* 50 (1982), pp. 444-448; Carl D. Murray, "Seasoned Travelers," *Nature* 361 (1993), pp. 586-587; Jacques Laskar and P. Robutel, "The Chaotic Obliquity of the Planets," *Nature* 361 (1993), pp. 608-612; Jacques Laskar, F. Joutel, and P. Robutel,

"Stabilization of the Earth's Obliquity by the Moon," *Nature* 361 (1993), pp. 615-617.

34. Antonio Lazcano and Stanley Miller, "How Long Did it Take for Life to Begin and Evolve to Cyanobacteria?" *Journal of Molecular Evolution* 39 (1994), pp. 546-554.

35. Robert Irion, "Ocean Scientists Find Life, Warmth in the Seas," *Science* 279 (1998), pp. 1302-1303.

36. Irion, p. 1303; Matthew Levy and Stanley L. Miller, "The Stability of the RNA Bases: Implications for the Origin of Life," *Proceedings of the National Academy of Sciences, USA* 95 (1988), pp. 7933-7938.

37. Irion, p. 1303; Levy and Miller, pp. 7933-7938.

38. Donald Goldsmith, *The Hunt for Life on Mars* (New York: Dutton, Penguin Books, 1997), p. 143.

39. John M. Hayes, "The Earliest Memories of Life on Earth," *Nature* 384 (1996), p. 21.

40. Peter D. Ward and Donald Brownlee, *Rare Earth: Why Complex Life Is Uncommon in the Universe* (New York: Copernicus, Spinger-Verlag, 2000), pp. 61, 66.

41. Niles Eldredge, *The Triumph of Evolution and the Failure of Creationism* (New York: Freeman, 2000), p. 36.

42. Stuart Kauffman, *Investigations* (New York: Oxford University Press, 2000), pp. 35, 43, 46.

43. Kauffman, p. 151.

44. See, for example, L. H. Ford and Thomas A. Roman, "Classical Scalar Fields and the Generalized Second Law," *Physical Review D* 64 (2001), pp. 4023-4034. In this paper Ford and Roman reject an entire class of proposed models for the origin of the universe because these models permit violations of the second law of thermodynamics. Because the possible violation of the second thermodynamic law places much, if not most, of particle physics, black hole physics, and quantum mechanics in jeopardy, such models for the universe's origin, in the opinion of the authors, must be judged unreasonable.

45. Hubert P. Yockey, *Information Theory and Molecular Biology* (New York: Cambridge University Press, 1992), p. 290.

46. Yockey, p. 291.

47. Yockey, p. 289.

48. Yockey, p. 289; Niels Bohr, "Light and Life," *Nature* 131 (1933), pp. 421-423, 457-459.

Chapter 7: Where's the Soup?

1. John Emsley, *The Elements,* 3d ed. (Oxford: Clarendon, 1998), p. 153.

2. Emsley, p. 153.

3. Emsley, p. 153.

4. T. Graham Solomons, *Organic Chemistry*, 2d ed. (New York: Wiley, 1980), pp. 48-49.

5. F. Albert Cotton and Geoffrey Wilkinson, *Advanced Inorganic Chemistry*, 5th ed. (New York: Wiley, 1988), pp. 234-304; F. Albert Cotton and Geoffrey Wilkinson, *Basic Inorganic Chemistry*, 2d ed. (New York: Wiley, 1987), pp. 322-341.

6. Stanley L. Miller, "The Endogenous Synthesis of Organic Compounds," in *The Molecular Origins of Life: Assembling Pieces of the Puzzle*, ed. André Brack (Cambridge: Cambridge University Press, 1998), pp. 59-85.

7. Michael P. Robertson and Stanley L. Miller, "An Efficient Prebiotic Synthesis of Cytosine and Uracil," *Nature* 375 (1995), pp. 772-774.

8. J. L. Bada, C. Bigham, and S. L. Miller, "Impact Melting of Frozen Oceans on the Early Earth: Implications for the Origin of Life," *Proceedings of the National Academy of Sciences, USA* 91 (February 1994), pp. 1248-1250; Robert Irion, "Ocean Scientists Find Life, Warmth in the Seas," *Science* 279 (1998), pp. 1302-1303.

9. For some relevant quotes from leading researchers and the press see Robert Shapiro, *Origins: A Skeptic's Guide to the Creation of Life on Earth* (New York: Summit, 1986), pp. 98-99; Peter D. Ward and Donald Brownlee, *Rare Earth: Why Complex Life Is Uncommon in the Universe* (New York: Copernicus, 2000), pp. 63-66.

10. Miller, p. 79; David W. Deamer, Elizabeth Harang Mahon, and Giovanni Bosco, "Self-Assembly and Function of Primitive Membrane Structures," in *Early Life on Earth: Nobel Symposiom No. 84*, ed. Stafan Bengtson (New York: Columbia University Press, 1994), pp. 119-120.

11. J. R. Cronin, "Origin of Organic Compounds in Carbonaceous Chondrites," *Advances in Space Research* 9 (1989), pp. 54-64; M. H. Engel and S. A. Macko, "Isotopic Evidence for Extraterrestrial Non-Racemic Amino Acids in the Murchison Meteorite," *Nature* 389 (1997), pp. 265-268; Keith A. Kvenvolden, "Chirality of Amino Acids in the Murchison Meteorite—A Historical Perspective," *Book of Abstracts,* 12th International Conference on the Origin of Life and the 9th Meeting of the International Society for the Study of the Origin of Life (ISSOL 1999), July 11-16, 1999, San Diego, California, p. 41.

12. G. Kminch et al., "Amino Acids in the Tagish Lake Meteorite," *Meteorites and Planetary Science* 37 (2002), pp. 697-701; Sandra Pizzarello et al., "The Organic Content of the Tagish Lake Meteorite," *Science* 293 (2001), pp. 2236-2239; Everett L. Shock, "Seeds of Life," *Nature* 416 (2002), p. 380.

13. Pizzarello et al., endnotes #15, 28, p. 2239.

14. Christopher Chyba and Carl Sagan, "Endogenous Production, Exogenous Delivery and Impact-Shock Synthesis of Organic Molecules: An Inventory for the Origins of Life," *Nature* 355 (1992), pp. 125-132.

15. Juan Oró, "Early Chemical Stages in Origin of Life," in *Early Life on Earth: Nobel Symposium No. 84,* ed. Stefan Bengtson (New York: Columbia University Press, 1994), pp. 49-50.

16. Miller, p. 79.

17. Chyba and Sagan, p. 127.

18. James B. Kaler, *Cosmic Clouds: Birth, Death, and Recycling in the Galaxy* (New York: Scientific American Library, 1997), pp. 111-119; the latest figure of 120 different molecules were given in a lecture by Pascale Ehrenfreund, "Formation and Evolution of Organics in Space," presented at the 13th International Conference on the Origin of Life and the 10th Meeting of the International Society for the Study of the Origin of Life (ISSOL 2002), June 30-July 5, 2002, Oaxaca, Mexico.

19. Max P. Bernstein et al., "Racemic Amino Acids from the Ultraviolet Photolysis of Interstellar Ice Analogues," *Nature* 416 (2002), pp. 401-403.

20. G. M. Munoz Caro et al., "Amino Acids from Ultraviolet Irradiation of Interstellar Ice Analogues," *Nature* 416 (2002), pp. 403-406.

21. P. Ehrenfreund et al., "The Photostability of Amino Acids in Space," *Astrophysical Journal Letters* 550 (2001), pp. L95-L99.

22. Ehrenfreund et al., p. L98.

23. Ehrenfreund et al., p. L98.

24. Curt Mileikowsky et al., "Natural Transfer of Viable Microbes in Space. 1. From Mars

to Earth and Earth to Mars," *Icarus* 145 (2000), pp. 391-427; C. Mileikowsky et al., "Risks Threatening Viable Transfer of Microbes Between Bodies in Our Solar System," *Planetary and Space Science* 48 (2000), pp. 1107-1115.

25. Daniel P. Glavin and Jeffrey L. Bada, "Survival of Amino Acids in Micrometeorites During Atmospheric Entry," *Astrobiology* 1 (2001), pp. 259-269.

26. Chyba and Sagan, pp. 125-128.

27. Keith A. Kvenvolden, "Chirality of Amino Acids in the Murchison Meteorite—A Historical Perspective," *Book of Abstracts*, ISSOL 1999, p. 41 (Kvenvolden gave the latest abundance assessments in his talk); Sandra Pizzarello et al., "The Organic Content of the Tagish Lake Meteorite," *Science* 293 (2001), p. 2237.

28. Jeffrey L. Bada and Gerhard Kminek, "Radiolytic Decomposition of Amino Acids in Carbonaceous Chondrites," *Book of Abstracts,* ISSOL 2002, p. 71. The figures for the upward adjustment were given during Bada's lecture at the conference.

29. The damaging radiation comes from two sources: (1) radiometric decay of uranium, thorium, and potassium-40 trapped inside the meteorites; and (2) galactic and intra-galactic cosmic radiation. Over the course of the past 3.8 billion years, Bada estimated, 17% of the amino acids inside meteorites would be destroyed. In the presence of water or ice (as would be the case for meteorites arising from the breakup of comets), up to 50% of the amino acids would be destroyed.

30. S. Pizzarello and J. R. Cronin, "Alanine Enantiomers in the Murchison Meteorite," *Nature* 394 (1998), p. 236; Jeffrey L. Bada, "Origins of Homochirality," *Nature* 374 (1995), pp. 594-595; Pizzarello et al., pp. 2236-2239; Kvenvolden, p. 41.

31. Sherwood Chang, "The Planetary Setting of Prebiotic Evolution," in *Early Life on Earth: Nobel Symposium No. 84*, ed. Stefan Bengtson (New York: Columbia University Press, 1994), pp. 10-23; Donald R. Lowe, "Early Environments: Constraints and Opportunities for Early Evolution," in *Early Life on Earth: Nobel Symposium No. 84,* ed. Stefan Bengtson (New York: Columbia University Press, 1994), pp. 24-35; Kenneth M. Towe, "Earth's Early Atmosphere: Constraints and Opportunities for Early Evolution," in *Early Life on Earth: Nobel Symposium No. 84,* ed. Stefan Bengtson (New York: Columbia University Press, 1994), pp. 36-47.

32. Francios Raulin, "Atmospheric Prebiotic Synthesis," lecture presented at the 12th International Conference on the Origin of Life and the 9th International Society for the Study of the Origin of Life (ISSOL 1999), July 11-16, 1999, San Diego, California.

33. Gordon Schlesinger and Stanley L. Miller, "Prebiotic Synthesis in Atmospheres containing CH_4, CO and CO_2. I. Amino Acids," *Journal of Molecular Evolution* 19 (1983), pp. 376-382; Gordon Schlesinger and Stanley L. Miller, "Prebiotic Synthesis in Atmospheres Containing CH_4, CO and CO_2. II. Hydrogen Cyanide, Formaldehyde, and Ammonia," *Journal of Molecular Evolution* 19 (1983), pp. 383-390.

34. Stanley L. Miller, "The Endogenous Synthesis of Organic Compounds," in *The Molecular Origins of Life: Assembling Pieces of the Puzzle*, ed. André Brack (Cambridge: Cambridge University Press, 1998), pp. 59-85.

35. Shin Miyakawa et al., "Prebiotic Synthesis from Carbon Monoxide Atmospheres: Implications for the Origin of Life," *Proceedings of the National Academy of Sciences, USA* 99 (2002), pp. 14628-14631.

36. S. Fox and K. Dose, *Molecular Evolution and the Origin of Life* (San Francisco: Freeman, 1972), pp. 44-45; I. S. Shklovskii and Carl Sagan, *Intelligent Life in the Universe* (San Francisco: Holden-Day, 1966), p. 231.

37. Ivan G. Draganic, "Oxygen and Oxidizing Free-Radicals in the Hydrosphere of Early Earth," *Book of Abstracts*, ISSOL 1999, p. 34; I. G. Draganic, Negron-Mendoza, and S. I. Vujosevis, "Reduction Chemistry of Water in Chemical Evolution Emploration," *Book of Abstracts*, ISSOL 2002, p. 139.

38. Uwe H. Wiechert, "Earth's Early Atmosphere," *Science* 298 (2002), pp. 2341-2342; J. Farquhar et al., "Mass-Independent Sulfur of Inclusions in Diamond and Sulfur Recycling on Early Earth," *Science* 298 (2002), pp. 2369-2372.

39. Rafael Navarro-Gonzáles et al., "Production of Reactive Nitrogen in Explosive Volcanic Clouds," lecture, ISSOL 1999; Christopher Wills and Jeffrey Bada, *The Spark of Life: Darwin and the Primeval Soup* (Cambridge: Perseus, 2000), pp. 74-76.

40. John W. Delano, "Cr Oxygen Barometry: Oxidation State of Mantle-Derived Volatiles Through Time," lecture, ISSOL 1999; John W. Delano, "Redox History of the Earth's Interior Since ~3900 Ma: Implications for Prebiotic Molecules," *Origins of Life and Evolution of the Biosphere* 31 (2001), pp. 311-341.

41. For example, J. P. Amend and E. L. Shock, "Energetics of Amino Acid Synthesis in Hydrothermal Ecosystems," *Science* 281 (1998), pp. 1659-1662; Sarah Simpson, "Life's First Scalding Steps," *Science News* 155 (1999), pp. 24-26; Ei-ichi Imai et al., "Elongation of Oligopeptides in a Simulated Submarine Hydrothermal System," *Science* 283 (1999), pp. 831-833; George Cody et al., "Primordial Carbonylated Iron-Sulfur Compounds and The Synthesis of Pyruvate," *Science* 289 (2000), pp. 1337-1340.

42. Stanley L. Miller and Jeffrey L. Bada, "Submarine Hot Springs and the Origin of Life," *Nature* 334 (1988), pp. 609-611; Matthew Levy and Stanley L. Miller, "The Stability of the RNA Bases: Implications for the Origin of Life," *Proceedings of the National Academy of Sciences, USA* 95 (1998), pp. 7933-7938.

43. Martin A. A. Schoonen and Yong Xu, "Nitrogen Reduction Under Hydrothermal Vent Conditions: Implications for the Prebiotic Synthesis of C-H-O-N Compounds," *Astrobiology* 1 (2001), pp. 133-142.

44. Minik T. Rosing, "^{13}C-Depleted Carbon Microparticles in >3700-Ma Sea Floor Sedimentary Rocks from West Greenland," *Science* 283 (1999), pp. 674-676; S. J. Mojzsis et al., "Evidence for Life on Earth Before 3,800 Million Years Ago, *Nature* 384 (1996), pp. 55-59; John M. Hayes, "The Earliest Memories of Life on Earth," *Nature* 384 (1996), pp. 21-22; Manfred Schidlowski, "A 3,800-Million-Year Isotopic Record of Life from Carbon in Sedimentary Rocks," *Nature* 333 (1988), pp. 313-318.

45. S. J. Mojzsis et al., p. 56.

46. Hubert P. Yockey, "Comments on 'Let There Be Life: Thermodynamic Reflections on Biogenesis and Evolution' by Avshalom C. Elitzur," *Journal of Theoretical Biology* 176 (1995), p. 351.

47. Daniele L. Pinti, Ko Hashizume, and Jun-Ichi Matsuda, "Nitrogen and Argon Signatures in 3.8 to 2.8 Ga Metasediments: Clues on the Chemical State of the Archean Ocean and the Deep Biosphere," *Geochemica et Cosmochimica Acta* 65 (2001), p. 2309.

48. V. Beaumont and F. Robert, "Nitrogen Isotope Ratios of Kerogens in Precambrian Cherts: A Record of the Evolution of Atmosphere Chemistry?" *Precambrian Research* 96 (1999), pp. 63-82; Jay A. Brandes et al., "Abiotic Nitrogen Reduction on the Early Earth," *Nature* 395 (1998), pp. 365-367.

Chapter 8: The Search for Chemical Pathways

1. Christopher Wills and Jeffrey Bada, *The Spark of Life: Darwin and the Primeval Soup* (Cambridge: Perseus, 2000), pp. 40-49.

2. See Stanley L. Miller and Leslie E. Orgel, *The Origins of Life on Earth* (Englewood Cliffs, N.J.: Prentice-Hall, 1974).

3. J. Oró et al., "The Origin and Early Evolution of Life on Earth," *Annual Review of Earth and Planetary Science* 18 (1990), pp. 317-356; Leslie E. Orgel, "The Origin of Life—A Review of Facts and Speculations," *Trends in Biochemical Sciences* 23 (1998), pp. 491-495; See Geoffrey Zubay, *Origins of Life on the Earth and in the Cosmos*, 2d ed. (San Diego: Academic Press, 2000).

4. Charles B. Thaxton, Walter L. Bradley, and Roger L. Olson, *The Mystery of Life's Origin: Reassessing Current Theories* (Dallas: Lewis and Stanley, 1984), pp. 99-112.

5. For a more comprehensive discussion on the chemical problems for naturalistic origin-of-life scenarios, see *The Mystery of Life's Origin* by Thaxton, Bradley, and Olsen. Though somewhat dated, this work still contains accurate and relevant information and complements our discussion here.

6. R. A. Sanchez et al., "Cyanoacetylene in Prebiotic Synthesis," *Science* 154 (1966), pp. 784-785; Michael P. Robertson and Stanley L. Miller, "An Efficient Prebiotic Synthesis of Cytosine and Uracil," *Nature* 375 (1995), pp. 772-774; Michael P. Robertson and Stanley L. Miller, "Corrections: An Efficient Prebiotic Synthesis of Cytosine and Uracil," *Nature* 377 (1995), p. 257; Stanley L. Miller, "The Endogenous Synthesis of Organic Compounds," in *The Molecular Origins of Life: Assembling Pieces of the Puzzle*, ed. André Brack (Cambridge: Cambridge University Press, 1998), pp. 59-85.

7. Robert Shapiro, "Prebiotic Cytosine Synthesis: A Critical Analysis and Implications for the Origin of Life," *Proceedings of the National Academy of Sciences, USA* 96 (1999), pp. 4396-4401.

8. Matthew Levy and Stanley L. Miller, "The Stability of the RNA Bases: Implications for the Origin of Life," *Proceedings of the National Academy of Sciences, USA* 95 (1998), pp. 7933-7938.

9. Shapiro, "Prebiotic Cytosine Synthesis," pp. 4396-4401.

10. Robert Shapiro, "The Prebiotic Role of Adenine: A Critical Analysis," *Origin of Life and Evolution of the Biosphere* 25 (1995), pp. 83-98.

11. H. James Cleves II and Stanley C. Miller, "The Prebiotic Synthesis of Nucleoside Analogues from Mixed Formose Reactions: Implications for the First Genetic Material," poster presented at the 13th International Conference on the Origin of Life and the 10th Meeting of the International Society for the Study of the Origin of Life (ISSOL 2002), June 30-July 5, 2002, Oaxaca, Mexico.

12. Norman W. Gabel and Cyril Ponnamperuma, "Model for Origin of Monosaccharides," *Nature* 216 (1967), pp. 453-455; A. G. Cairns-Smith et al., "Formose Production by Minerals: Possible Relevance to the Origin of Life," *Journal of Theoretical Biology* 35 (1972), pp. 601-604; Alan W. Schwartz and R. M. de Graaf, "The Prebiotic Synthesis of Carbohydrates: A Reassessment," *Journal of Molecular Evolution* 36 (1993), pp. 101-106; Miller, pp. 59-85.

13. Schwartz and de Graaf, pp. 101-106; Miller, pp. 59-85.

14. A. Seetharama Acharya and James M. Manning, "Reaction of Glycolaldehyde with Proteins: Latent Crosslinking Potential of (αHydroxyaldehydes," *Proceedings of the National Academy of Sciences, USA* 80 (1983), pp. 3590-3594; Miller, pp. 59-85.

15. Rosa Larralde et al., "Rates of Decomposition of Ribose and Other Sugars: Implications for Chemical Evolution," *Proceedings of the National Academy of Sciences, USA* 92 (1995), pp. 8158-8160.

16. R. Cowen, "Did Space Rocks Deliver Sugar?" *Science News* 160 (2001), p. 388; Mark A. Sephton, "Life's Sweet Beginnings," *Nature* 414 (2001), pp. 857-858; George Cooper et al., "Carbonaceous Meteorites as a Source of Sugar-Related Organic Compounds for the Early Earth," *Nature* 414 (2001), pp. 879-883.

17. Anthony D. Keefe and Stanley L. Miller, "Are Polyphosphates or Phosphate Esters Prebiotic Reagents?" *Journal of Molecular Evolution* 41 (1995), pp. 693-702.

18. Keefe and Miller, pp. 693-702; Ramanarayanan Krishnamurthy, "Challenges in 'Prebiotic' Chemistry," lecture, ISSOL 2002.

19. Keefe and Miller, pp. 693-702; Thaxton, Bradley, and Olsen, p. 56.

20. Leslie Orgel, "The RNA World and the Origin of Life," lecture, ISSOL 2002.

21. See Harold J. Morowitz, *Beginnings of Cellular Life: Metabolism Recapitulates Biogenesis* (New Haven, Conn.: Yale University Press, 1992); Robert Shapiro, "Monomer World," lecture, ISSOL 2002.

22. Leslie E. Orgel, "Self-Organizing Biochemical Cycles," *Proceedings of the National Academy of Sciences, USA* 97 (2000), pp. 12503-12507.

23. Richard Wolfenden and Mark J. Snider, "The Depth of Chemical Time and the Power of Enzymes as Catalysts," *Accounts of Chemical Research* 34 (2001), pp. 938-945.

24. Orgel, "Self-Organizing Biochemical Cycles," pp. 12503-12507.

25. Antonio Lazcano and Stanley L. Miller, "On the Origin of Metabolic Pathways," *Journal of Molecular Evolution* 49 (1999), pp. 424-431.

26. See Morowitz; Shapiro, "Monomer World," lecture, ISSOL 2002.

27. Robert Shapiro, "A Replicator Was Not Involved in the Origin of Life," *IUBMB Life* 49 (2000), 173-176; Robert Shapiro, "The Homopolymer Problem in the Origin of Life," lecture presented at the 12th International Conference on the Origin of Life and the 9th Meeting of the International Society for the Study of the Origin of Life (ISSOL 1999), July 11-16, 1999, San Diego, California.

28. Shapiro, "A Replicator Was Not Involved," pp. 173-176; Shapiro, "Monomer World," ISSOL 2002.

29. Gözen Ertem and James P. Ferris, "Synthesis of RNA Oligomers on Heterogeneous Templates," *Nature* 379 (1996), pp. 238-240; James P. Ferris et al., "Synthesis of Long Prebiotic Oligomers on Mineral Surfaces," *Nature* 381 (1996), pp. 59-61.

30. R. Lipkin, "Early Life: In the Soup or on the Rocks?" *Science News* 149 (1996), p. 278.

31. Shapiro, "A Replicator Was Not Involved," pp. 173-176.

32. Gerald F. Joyce et al., "The Case for An Ancestral Genetic System Involving Simple Analogues of the Nucleotides," *Proceedings of the National Academy of Sciences, USA* 84 (1987), pp. 4398-4402; Igor A. Koslov et al., "Oligomerization of Activated D- and L-Guanosine Mononucleotides on Templates Containing D- and L-Deoxycytidylate Residues," *Proceedings of the National Academy of Sciences, USA* 95 (1998), pp. 13448-13452.

33. Leslie E. Orgel, "NSCORT 2000 Progress Report," available from http://exobio.ucsd.edu/00Orgel.htm; Internet; accessed 08/07/01.

34. Mitsuhiko Akaboshi et al., "Dephosphorylating Activity of Rare Earth Elements and Its Implication in the Chemical Evolution," poster, ISSOL 1999; M. Akaboshi et al., "Inhibition of Rare Earth Catalytic Activity by Proteins," *Origin of Life and Evolution of the Biosphere* 30 (2000), pp. 25-32.

35. James Ferris, "Prebiotic Chemistry Catalysis and RNA Synthesis," lecture, ISSOL 2002; Gözen Ertem, "Montmorillonite, Oligonucleotides, RNA and Origin of Life," lecture, ISSOL 2002.

36. Wills and Bada, pp. 101-103.
37. Some examples: Laura F. Landweber and Irina D. Pokrovskaya, "Emergence of a Dual-Catalytic RNA with Metal-Specific Cleavage and Ligase Activities: The Spandrels of RNA Evolution," *Proceedings of the National Academy of Sciences, USA* 96 (1999), pp. 173-178; Peter J. Unrau and David P. Bartel, "RNA-Catalyzed Nucleotide Synthesis," *Nature* 395 (1998), pp. 260-263; Charles Wilson and Jack W. Szostak, "*In Vitro* Evolution of a Self-Alkylating Ribozyme," *Nature* 374 (1995), pp. 777-782; Theodore M. Tarasow et al., "RNA-Catalyzed Carbon-Carbon Bond Formation," *Nature* 389 (1997), pp. 54-57; Jeff Rodgers and Gerald F. Joyce, "A Ribozyme That Lacks Cytidine," *Nature* 402 (1999), pp. 323-325; Jon R. Lorsch and Jack W. Szostak, "*In Vitro* Evolution of New Ribozymes with Polynucleotide Kinase Activity," *Nature* 371 (1994), pp. 31-36.
38. Wendy K. Johnston et al., "RNA-Catalyzed RNA Polymerization: Accurate and General RNA-Templated Primer Extension," *Science* 292 (2001), pp. 1319-1325; Michael S. Lawrence and David P. Bartel, "Processivity of Ribozyme-Catalyzed RNA Polymerization," lecture, ISSOL 2002.
39. Laura F. Landweber, "Experimental RNA Evolution," *Trends in Evolution and Ecology* 14 (1999), pp. 353-358; David P. Bartel and Peter J. Unrau, "Constructing an RNA World," *Trends in Cell Biology* 9 (1999), pp. M9-M13; Martin C. Wright and Gerald F. Joyce, "Continuous *In Vitro* Evolution of Catalytic Function," *Science* 276 (1997), pp. 614-617; David P. Bartel and Jack W. Szostak, "Isolation of New Ribozymes from a Large Pool of Random Sequences," *Science* 261 (1993), pp. 1411-1418.
40. David H. Lee et al., "A Self-Replicating Peptide," *Nature* 382 (1996), pp. 525-528; Stuart A. Kauffman, "Self-Replication: Even Peptides Do It," *Nature* 382 (1996), pp. 496-497; Shao Yao, "Selective Amplification by Auto- and Cross-Catalysis in a Replicating Peptide System," *Nature* 396 (1998), pp. 447-449.
41. Leslie Orgel, "Self-Organizing Biochemical Cycles," *Proceedings of the National Academy of Sciences, USA* 97 (2000), pp. 12503-12507.
42. Gerald F. Joyce, "RNA Evolution and the Origins of Life," *Nature* 338 (1989), pp. 217-224.

Chapter 9: Look! Only One Hand

1. G. F. Joyce et al., "Chiral Selection in Poly(C)-Directed Synthesis of Oligo(G)," *Nature* 310 (1984), pp. 602-604; G. F. Joyce et al., "The Case for an Ancestral Genetic System Involving Simple Analogues of the Nucleotides," *Proceedings of the National Academy of Sciences, USA* 84 (1987), pp. 4398-4402; G. F. Joyce, "RNA Evolution and the Origins of Life," *Nature* 338 (1989), pp. 217-224; Eörs Szathmáry, "The First Two Billion Years," *Nature* 387 (1997), pp. 662-663.
2. Jon Cohen, "Getting All Turned Around Over the Origins of Life on Earth," *Science* 267 (1995), p. 1265.
3. Jeffrey L. Bada, "Origins of Homochirality," *Nature* 374 (1995), p. 594; Jeffrey L. Bada, "Extraterrestrial Handedness?" *Science* 275 (1997), p. 942.
4. G. L. J. A. Rikken and E. Raupach, "Enantioselective Magnetochiral Photochemistry," *Nature* 405 (2000), pp. 932-935.
5. Rikken and Raupach, p. 934.
6. Quoted in Cohen, p. 1265. Bonner made this comment at "Physical Origin of Homochirality in Life," a conference held in Santa Monica, California, February 1995.

7. William A. Bonner, "The Origin and Amplification of Biomolecular Chirality," *Origin of Life and Evolution of the Biosphere* 21 (1991), pp. 59-111.

8. Robert M. Hazen, "Life's Rocky Start," *Scientific American* (April 2001), pp. 77-85.

9. Robert M. Hazen, Timothy R. Filley, and Glenn A. Goodfriend, "Selective Adsorption of L- and D-Amino Acids on Calcite: Implications for Biochemical Homochirality," *Proceedings of the National Academy of Sciences, USA* 98 (2001), pp. 5487-5490.

10. Hazen, pp. 77-85.

11. Jeremy Bailey et al., "Circular Polarization in Star-Formation Regions: Implications for Biomolecular Homochirality," *Science* 281 (1998), p. 672 (see also endnote #8 on p. 674); G. Balavoine, A. Monadpour, and H. B. Kagan, "Preparation of Chiral Compounds with High Optical Purity by Irradiation with Circularly Polarized Light, a Model Reaction for the Prebiotic Generation of Optical Activity," *Journal of the American Chemical Society* 96 (1974), pp. 5152-5158.

12. Yoshinori Takano et al., "Asymmetric Photolysis of (DL)–Isovaline by Synchrotron Radiation," *Book of Abstracts*, 13th International Conference on the Origin of Life and the 10th Meeting of the International Society for the Study of the Origin of Life (ISSOL 2002), June 30-July 5, 2002, Oaxaca, Mexico, pp. 92-93. The figure, 1.12%, was presented in a poster paper.

13. Mark M. McKinnon, "Statistical Modeling of the Circular Polarization in Pulsar Radio Emission and Detection Statistics of Radio Polarimetry," *Astrophysical Journal* 568 (2002), pp. 302-311.

14. W. J. Cocke, G. W. Muncaster, and T. Gehrels, "Upper Limit to Circular Polarization of Optical Pulsar NP 0532," *Astrophysical Journal Letters* 169 (1971), pp. L119-L121.

15. McKinnon, p. 302.

16. Bailey et al., pp. 672-674.

17. Josc J. Flores, William A. Bonner, and Gail A. Massey, "Asymetric Photolysis of (RS)-Leucine with Circularly Polarized Ultraviolet Light," *Journal of the American Chemical Society* 99 (1977), pp. 3622-3625.

18. Werner Kuhn, "The Physical Significance of Optical Rotary Power," *Transactions of the Faraday Society* 26 (1930), pp. 293-308; E. U. Condon, "Theories of Optical Rotary Power," *Reviews of Modern Physics* 9 (1937), pp. 432-457.

19. Stephen F. Mason, "Extraterrestrial Handedness," *Nature* 389 (1997), p. 804.

20. Mason, p. 804; Stephen F. Mason, "Biomolecular Homochirality," *Chemical Society Reviews* 17 (1988), p. 347-359.

21. George Cooper et al., "Carbonaceous Meteorites as a Source of Sugar-Related Organic Compounds for the Early Earth," *Nature* 414 (2001), pp. 879-883; Mark A. Sephton, "Life's Sweet Beginnings?" *Nature* 414 (2001), pp. 857-858.

22. James B. Kaler, *Cosmic Clouds: Birth, Death, and Recycling in the Galaxy* (New York: Scientific American Library, 1997), pp. 111-119; Pascale Ehrenfreund, "Formation and Evolution of Organics in Space," *Book of Abstracts*, ISSOL 2002, p. 39. The figure of 120 different carbon atoms was an update presented in a lecture by Ehrenfreund.

23. Mike D. Reynolds, *Falling Stars: A Guide to Meteors and Meteorites* (Mechanicsburg, Pa.: Stackpole, 2001), p. 141.

24. Keith A. Kvenvolden, James G. Lawless, and Cyril Ponnamperuma, "Nonprotein Amino Acids in the Murchison Meteorite," *Proceedings of the National Academy of Sciences, USA* 68 (1971), pp. 486-490.

25. J. R. Cronin, S. Pizzarello, and D. P. Cruikshank, "Organic Matter in Carbonaceous Chondrites, Planetary Satellites, Asteroids, and Comets," in *Meteorites and the Early*

Solar System, ed. J. F. Kerridge and M. S. Matthews (Tucson: University of Arizona Press, 1988), pp. 819-857.

26. Cronin, Pizzarello, and Cruikshank, pp. 819-857.

27. John R. Cronin and Sandra Pizzarello, "Enantiomeric Excesses in Meteoritic Amino Acids," *Science* 275 (1997), pp. 951-955; S. Pizzarello and J. R. Cronin, "Alanine Enantiomers in the Murchison Meteorite," *Nature* 394 (1998), p. 236; John Cronin and Sandra Pizzarello, "Meteorite Amino Acids and the Origin of Homochirality," *Book of Abstracts*, 12th International Conference on the Origin of Life and the 9th Meeting of the International Society for the Study of the Origin of Life (ISSOL 1999), July 11-16, 1999, San Diego, California, p. 41.

28. M. H. Engel and S. A. Macko, "Isotopic Evidence for Extraterrestrial Non-Racemic Amino Acids in the Murchison Meteorite," *Nature* 389 (1997), pp. 265-268.

29. Pizzarello and Cronin, p. 236.

30. Sandra Pizzarello and Mike Zolensky, "Chirality and Mineral Association of Isovaline in the Murchison Meterorite," *Book of Abstracts*, ISSOL 2002, p. 56. Pizzarello claimed to have found chiral excesses for isovaline ranging from 0 to 12% in four different samples from the Murchison meteorite and an additional sample from the Murray meteorite (probably from the same parent body as the Murchison).

31. Keith A. Kvenvolden, "Chirality of Amino Acids in the Murchison Meteorite—A Historical Perspective," *Book of Abstracts*, ISSOL 1999, p. 41.

32. Kvenvolden, p. 41.

33. Kvenvolden, p. 41.

34. Daniel P. Glavin et al., "Amino Acids in Martian Meteorite Nakhla, " *Book of Abstracts*, ISSOL 1999, p. 62.

35. Glavin et al., p. 62.

36. Glavin et al., p. 62.

37. Sandra Pizzarello et al., "The Organic Content of the Tagish Lake Meteorite," *Science* 293 (2001), p. 2239, endnotes #15 and #28.

38. This is a statement made at the question and comment microphone by one of the participants at ISSOL 1999, on the last day of the conference.

39. Jeffrey L. Bada, "Origins of Homochirality," *Nature* 374 (1995), p. 594.

40. Robert Irion, "Did Twisty Starlight Set Stage for Life?" *Science* 281 (1998), p. 627.

41. These questions were asked after the presentation of paper c2.6 on July 13 by Gyula Palyi et al., "Enantioselection Through Chiral Conformations," ISSOL 1999, p. 42.

42. Christof Böhler, Peter E. Nielsen, and Leslie E. Orgel, "Template Switching Between PNA and RNA Oligonucleotides," *Nature* 376 (1995), pp. 578-581.

43. Jeffrey L. Bada, "Origins of Homochirality," *Nature* 374 (1995), p. 594. Report on "Physical Origin of Homochirality in Life," a conference held in Santa Monica, California, February 1995. For Miller's latest work on PNA as the first genetic material, see Kevin E. Nelson, Matthew Levy, and Stanley L. Miller, "The Prebiotic Synthesis of the Components of Peptide Nucleic Acid, A Possible First Genetic Material," *Book of Abstracts*, ISSOL 1999, p. 55.

44. Kevin E. Nelson, Matthew Levy, and Stanley Miller, "Peptide Nucleic Acids Rather than RNA May Have Been the First Genetic Molecule," *Proceedings of the National Academy of Sciences*, USA 97 (2000), pp. 3868-3871.

Chapter 10: The Codes of Life

1. Harvey Lodish et al., *Molecular Cell Biology*, 4th ed. (New York: Freeman, 2000), pp. 51-54.
2. Lodish et al., p. 52.
3. Lodish et al., pp. 54-60.
4. Lodish et al., p. 257.
5. Geoffrey Zubay, *Origins of Life on the Earth and in the Cosmos*, 2d ed. (San Diego: Academic Press, 2000), pp. 320-321.
6. Charles B. Thaxton, Walter L. Bradley, and Roger L. Olsen, *The Mystery of Life's Origin: Reassessing Current Theories* (Dallas: Lewis and Stanley), pp. 113-166.
7. Walter L. Bradley and Charles B. Thaxton, "Information and the Origin of Life," in *The Creation Hypothesis: Scientific Evidence for an Intelligent Designer*, ed. J. P. Moreland (Downers Grove, Ill.: InterVarsity, 1994), p. 190.
8. Sean V. Taylor et al., "Searching Sequence Space for Protein Catalysts," *Proceedings of the National Academy of Sciences, USA* 98 (2001), pp. 10596-10601.
9. Hubert P. Yockey, *Information Theory and Molecular Biology* (Cambridge: Cambridge University Press, 1992), pp. 246-257.
10. Yockey, pp. 131-172.
11. Yockey, pp. 254-255.
12. Yockey, p. 255.
13. Patrice Koehl and Michael Levitt, "Protein Topology and Stability Define the Space of Allowed Sequences," *Proceedings of the National Academy of Sciences, USA* 99 (2002), pp. 1280-1285.

Chapter 11: Beneficial Boundaries

1. Robert C. Bohinski, *Modern Concepts in Biochemistry*, 4th ed. (Boston: Allyn and Bacon, 1983), pp. 8-28.
2. Geoffrey Zubay, *Origins of Life on the Earth and in the Cosmos*, 2d ed. (San Diego: Academic Press, 2000), p. 371.
3. Zubay, pp. 371-376.
4. Much of the material in this section is based on Bohinksi, pp. 243-253; Lubert Stryer, *Biochemistry*, 3d ed. (New York: Freeman, 1988), pp. 283-312; Gary R. Jacobson and Milton H. Saier, Jr., "Biological Membranes: Structure and Assembly," in *Biochemistry*, ed. Geoffrey Zubay (Reading, Pa.: Addison-Wesley, 1983), pp. 573-619.
5. Some biological membranes also contain cholesterol and another class of lipids known as glycolipids. Glycolipids possess a sugar headgroup (that sometimes can be quite large) instead of a phosphate headgroup.
6. S. J. Singer and G. L. Nicolson, "The Fluid Mosaic Model of the Structure of Cell Membranes," *Science* 175 (1972), pp. 720-731.
7. Ken Jacobson et al., "Revisiting the Fluid Mosaic Model of Membranes," *Science* 268 (1995), pp. 1441-1442.
8. Zubay, p. 347.
9. Zubay, p. 347; Stanley L. Miller and Jeffrey I. Bada, "Submarine Hot Springs and the Origin of Life," *Nature* 334 (1998), pp. 609-611; Nils G. Holm and Eva M. Andersson, "Hydrothermal Systems," in *The Molecular Origins of Life: Assembling Pieces of the Puzzle*, ed. André Brack (Cambridge: Cambridge University Press, 1998), pp. 86-99.
10. Ahmed I. Rushdi and Bernd R. T. Simoneit, "Lipid Formation by Aqueous Fischer-Tropsch Type Synthesis Over a Temperature Range of 100 to 400°C," *Origin of Life*

and Evolution of the Biosphere 31 (2001), pp. 103-118.

11. Miller and Bada, pp. 609-611.

12. Zubay, pp. 348-350; Arthur L. Weber, "Origin of Fatty Acid Synthesis: Thermodynamics and Kinetics of Reaction Pathways," *Journal of Molecular Evolution* 32 (1991), pp. 93-100.

13. Leslie E. Orgel, "Self-Organizing Biochemical Cycles," *Proceedings of the National Academy of Sciences, USA* 97 (2000), pp. 12503-12507.

14. Zubay, p. 350; W. R. Hargreaves, S. Mulvihill, and D. W. Deamer, "Synthesis of Phospholipids and Membranes in Prebiotic Conditions," *Nature* 266 (1977), pp. 78-80; J. Eichberg et al., "Cyanamide Mediated Syntheses Under Plausible Primitive Earth Conditions. IV. The Synthesis of Acylglycerols," *Journal of Molecular Evolution* 10 (1977), pp. 221-230; D. E. Epps et al., "Cyanamide Mediated Syntheses Under Plausible Primitive Earth Conditions. V. The Synthesis of Phosphatidic Acid," *Journal of Molecular Evolution* 11 (1978), pp. 279-292; D. E. Epps et al., "Cyanamide Mediated Syntheses Under Plausible Primitive Earth Conditions. VI. The Synthesis of Glycerol and Glycerolphosphates," *Journal of Molecular Evolution* 14 (1979), pp. 235-241; M. Rao et al., "Synthesis of Phosphatidylcholine Under Possible Primitive Earth Conditions," *Journal of Molecular Evolution* 18 (1982), pp. 196-202; M. Rao et al., "Synthesis of Phosphatidylethanolamine Under Possible Primitive Earth Conditions," *Journal of Molecular Evolution* 25 (1987), pp. 1-6.

15. Charles B. Thaxton, Walter L. Bradley, and Roger L. Olsen, *The Mystery of Life's Origin: Reassessing Current Theories* (Dallas: Lewis and Stanley, 1984), pp. 56, 177-178.

16. David W. Deamer, Elizabeth Harany Mahon, and Giovanni Bosco, "Self-Assembling and Function of Primitive Membrane Structures," in *Early Life on Earth: Nobel Symposium No. 84,* ed. Stefan Bengtson (New York: Columbia University Press, 1994), pp. 107-123; D. W. Deamer, "Membrane Compartments in Prebiotic Evolution," in *The Molecular Origins of Life: Assembling The Pieces of the Puzzle,* ed. André Brack (Cambridge: Cambridge University Press, 1998), pp. 189-205.

17. John R. Cronin, "Clues from the Origin of the Solar System: Meteorites," in *The Molecular Origin of Life: Assembling Pieces of the Puzzle,* ed. André Brack (Cambridge: Cambridge University Press, 1998), pp. 119-146.

18. Jason P. Dworkin et al., "Self-Assembling Amphiphilic Molecules: Synthesis in Simulated Interstellar/Precometary Ices," *Proceedings of the National Academy of Sciences, USA* 98 (2001), pp. 815-819; R. Cowen, "Life's Housing May Come from Space," *Science News* 159 (2001), p. 68.

19. J. N. Israelachvili et al., "Physical Principles of Membrane Organization," *Quarterly Review of Biophysics* 13 (1980), pp. 121-200.

20. William R. Hargreaves and David W. Deamer, "Liposomes from Ionic, Single-Chain Amphiphiles," *Biochemistry* 17 (1978), pp. 3759-3768.

21. Deamer, Mahon, and Bosco, pp. 107-123; D. W. Deamer, pp. 189-205; D. W. Deamer and R. M. Pashley, "Amphiphilic Components of the Murchinson Carbonaceous Chondrite: Surface Properties and Membrane Formation," *Origins of Life and Evolution of the Biosphere* 19 (1989), pp. 21-38; David W. Deamer, "Boundary Structures Are Formed by Organic Components of the Murchinson Carbonaceous Chondrite," *Nature* 317 (1985), pp. 792-794.

22. Dworkin, pp. 815-819.

23. Deamer, Mahon, and Bosco, pp. 107-123; David W. Deamer and Gail L. Barchfield,

"Encapsulation of Macromolecules by Lipid Vesicles Under Simulated Prebiotic Conditions," *Journal of Molecular Evolution* 18 (1982), pp. 203-206; David W. Deamer, "The First Living Systems: A Bioenergetic Perspective," *Microbiology and Molecular Biology Reviews* 61 (1997), pp. 239-261.

24. Deamer, Mahon, and Bosco, pp. 107-123; Deamer, "Membrane Compartments," pp. 189-205.

25. Deamer, "Membrane Compartments," pp. 189-205.

26. Deamer, Mahon, and Bosco, pp. 107-123; Deamer, "Membrane Compartments," pp. 189-205.

27. J. G. Lawless and G. U. Yuen, "Quantitation of Monocarboxylic Acids in the Murchinson Carbonaceous Meteorite," *Nature* 282 (1979), pp. 396-398.

28. Deamer, Mahon, and Bosco, pp. 107-123; Deamer, "Membrane Compartments," pp. 189-205.

29. David W. Deamer, "Boundary Structures are Formed by Organic Components of the Murchinson Carbonaceous Chondrite," *Nature* 317 (1985), pp. 792-794.

30. William R. Hargreaves and David W. Deamer, "Liposomes From Ionic, Single-Chain Amphiphiles," *Biochemistry* 17 (1978), pp. 3759-3768.

31. Matt Kaplan, "A Fresh Start: Life May Have Begun Not in the Sea but in Some Warm Little Freshwater Pond," *New Scientist* (11 May 2002), p. 7.

32. Charles L. Apel et al., "Self-Assembled Vesicles of Monocarboxylic Acids and Alcohols: Conditions for Stability and for the Encapsulation of Biopolymers," *Biochimica et Biophysica Acta* 1559 (2002), pp. 1-9.

33. Kaplan, p. 7.

34. Pierre-Alain Monnard et al., "Influence of Ionic Inorganic Solutes on Self-Assembly and Polymerization Processes Related to Early Forms of Life: Implications for a Prebiotic Aqueous Medium," *Astrobiology* 2 (2002), pp. 139-152.

35. Shlomo Rottem, "Transbilayer Distribution of Lipids in Microbial Membranes," in *Membrane Lipids of Prokaryotes*, ed. S. Razin and R. Ralter, Current Topics in Membranes and Transport, no. 17 (New York: Academic Press, 1982), pp. 235-261.

36. John M. Seddon, "Structure of the Inverted Hexagonal (H_{11}) Phase, and Non-Lamellar Phase Transitions of Lipids," *Biochimica et Biophysica Acta* 1031 (1990), pp. 1-69; Göran Lindblom and Leif Rilfors, "Cubic Phases and Isotropic Structures Formed by Membrane Lipids—Possible Biological Relevance," *Biochimica et Biophysica Acta* 988 (1989), pp. 221-256.

37. Fazale R. Rana, "Structure and Function of Outer Membranes and LPS from Wild-Type and LPS-Mutant Strains of *Salmonella typhimurium* and Their Interaction with Magainins and Polymyxin B.," Ph.D. Dissertation, Ohio University, 1990; also see references therein.

38. Seddon, pp. 1-69.

39. Ake Wieslander et al., "Lipid Bilayer Stability in Membranes. Regulation of Lipid Composition in *Acholeplasma laidlawii* as Governed by Molecular Shape," *Biochemistry* 19 (1980), pp. 3650-3655.

40. Danilo D. Lasic, "The Mechanism of Vesicle Formation," *Biochemical Journal* 256 (1988), pp. 1-11.

41. Lasic, pp. 1-11.

42. For example, see Barry L. Lentz et al., "Spontaneous Fusion of Phosphatidylcholine Small Unilamellar Vesicles in the Fluid Phase," *Biochemistry* 26 (1987), pp. 5389-5397.

43. N. L. Gershfeld, "The Critical Unilamellar Lipid State: A Perspective for Membrane Bilayer Assembly," *Biochimica et Biosphysica Acta* 988 (1989), pp. 335-350.

44. For example, see Norman L. Gershfeld et al., "Critical Temperature for Unilamellar Vesicle Formation in Dimyristoyl Phosphatidylcholine Dispersions from Specific Heat Measurements," *Biophysical Journal* 65 (1993), pp. 1174-1179.

45. N. L. Gershfeld, "Spontaneous Assembly of a Phospholipid Bilayer as a Critical Phenomenon: Influence of Temperature, Composition, and Physical State," *Journal of Physical Chemistry* 93 (1989), pp. 5256-5264.

46. Lionel Ginsberg et al., "Membrane Bilayer Assembly in Neural Tissue of Rat and Squid as a Critical Phenomena: Influence of Temperature and Membrane Proteins," *Journal of Membrane Biology* 119 (1991), pp. 65-73.

47. K. E. Tremper and N. L. Gershfeld, "Temperature Dependence of Membrane Lipid Composition in Early Blastula Embryos of *Lytechinus pictus*: Selective Sorting of Phospholipids into Nascent Plasma Membranes," *Journal of Membrane Biology* 171 (1999), pp. 47-53.

48. A. J. Jin et al., "A Singular State of Membrane Lipids at Cell Growth Temperatures," *Biochemistry* 38 (1999), pp. 13275-13278.

49. N. L. Gershfeld and M. Murayama, "Thermal Instability of Red Blood Cell Membrane Bilayers: Temperature Dependence of Hemolysis," *Journal of Membrane Biology* 101 (1988), pp. 67-72.

50. Lionel Ginsberg et al., "Membrane Instability, Plasmalogen Content and Alzheimer's Disease," *Journal of Neurochemistry* 70 (1998), pp. 2533-2538.

Chapter 12: Life's Minimum Complexity

1. Kevin Davies, *Cracking the Genome: Inside the Race to Unlock Human DNA* (New York: Simon & Schuster, 2001), p. 6.

2. Davies, pp. 103-108; Robert D. Fleischmann et al., "Whole-Genome Random Sequencing and Assembly of *Haemophilus influenzae* Rd" *Science* 269 (1995), pp. 496-512; Rachel Nowak, "Bacterial Genome Sequence Bagged," *Science* 269 (1995), pp. 468-470.

3. Mark D. Adams et al., "The Genome Sequence of *Drosophila Melanogaster*," *Science* 287 (2000), pp. 2185-2195; Jonathan Hodgkin et al., "The Nematode *Caenorhabditis elegans* and Its Genome," *Science* 270 (1995), pp. 410-414; The *C. elegans* Sequencing Consortium, "Genome Sequence of the Nematode *C. elegans*: A Platform for Investigating Biology," *Science* 282 (1998), pp. 2012-2018; Eriak Check, "Draft Mouse Genome Makes Public Debut," *Nature* 417 (2002), p. 106.

4. Dennis Normile, "Genomics: Chimp Sequencing Crawls Forward," *Science* 291 (2001), p. 2297.

5. Don Cowan, "Use Your Neighbor's Genes," *Nature* 407 (2000), pp. 466-467; Andreas Ruepp et al., "The Genome Sequence of the Thermoacidophilic Scavenger *Thermoplasma acidophilum*," *Nature* 407 (2000), pp. 508-513; Gerard Deckert et al., "The Complete Genome of the Hyperthermophilic Bacterium *Aquifex aeolicus*," *Nature* 392 (1998), pp. 353-358; Alexei I. Slesarev et al., "The Complete Genome of Hyperthermophile *Methanopyrus* kandleri AV19 and Monophyly of Archael Methanogens," *Proceedings of the National Academy of Sciences, USA* 99 (2002), pp. 4644-4649; Virginia Morell, "Life's Last Domain," *Science* 273 (1996), pp. 1043-1045; Carol J. Bult et al., "Complete Genome Sequence of the Methanogenic Archaeon, *Methanococcus jannaschii*," *Science* 273 (1996), pp. 1058-1073; Elizabeth

Pennisi, "Microbial Genomes Come Tumbling In," *Science* 277 (1997), p. 1433; Karen E. Nelson et al., "Evidence for Lateral Gene Transfer Between Archaea and Bacteria from Genome Sequence of *Thermotoga maritima*," *Nature* 399 (1999), pp. 323-329.

6. Colin Patterson, *Evolution*, 2d ed. (Ithaca: Comstock, 1999), p. 23.

7. J. Travis, "Small Wonder: Microbial Hitchhiker Has Few Genes," *Science News* 161 (2002), p. 275; Harald Huber et al., "A New Phylum of Archaea Represented by a Nanosized Hyperthermophilic Symbiont," *Nature* 417 (2002), pp. 63-67; Yan Boucher and W. Ford Doolittle, "Something New Under the Sea," *Nature* 417 (2002), pp. 27-28.

8. Bult et al., pp. 1058-1073.

9. Pennisi, p. 1433; André Goffeau, "Life with 482 Genes," *Science* 270 (1995), pp. 445-446; Claire M. Fraser et al., "The Minimal Gene Complement of *Mycoplasma genitalium*," *Science* 270 (1995), pp. 397-403.

10. Arcady R. Mushegian and Eugene V. Koonin, "A Minimal Gene Set for Cellular Life Derived by Comparison of Complete Bacterial Genomes," *Proceedings of the National Academy of Sciences, USA* 93 (1996), pp. 10268-10273; Hugh Ross, "Simplest Bacterium Not So Simple," *Facts & Faith*, vol. 10, no. 4 (1996), p. 5.

11. Nikos Kyrpides et al., "Universal Protein Families and the Functional Content of the Last Universal Common Ancestor," *Journal of Molecular Evolution* 49 (1999), pp. 413-423.

12. Jack Maniloff, "The Minimal Cell Genome: 'On Being the Right Size'," *Proceedings of the National Academy of Sciences, USA* 93 (1996), pp. 10004-10006; Mitsuhiro Itaya, "An Estimation of Minimal Genome Size Required for Life," *FEBS Letters* 362 (1995), pp. 257-260.

13. Clyde A. Hutchinson III et al., "Global Transposon Mutagenesis and a Minimal Mycoplasma Genome," *Science* 286 (1999), pp. 2165-2169.

14. Brian J. Akerley et al., "A Genome-Scale Analysis for Identification of Genes Required for Growth or Survival of *Haemophilus influenzae*," *Proceedings of the National Academy of Sciences, USA* 99 (2002), pp. 966-971.

15. Rosario Gil et al., "Extreme Genome Reduction in *Buchnera* spp.: Toward the Minimal Genome Needed for Symbiotic Life," *Proceedings of the National Academy of Sciences, USA* 99 (2002), pp. 4454-4458.

16. Hubert P. Yockey, *Information Theory and Molecular Biology* (Cambridge: Cambridge University Press, 1992), pp. 246-257.

17. Robert Shapiro, *Origins: A Skeptic's Guide to Creation of Life on Earth* (New York: Bantam Books, 1986), p. 128.

18. Hugh Ross, *The Creator and the Cosmos: How the Greatest Scientific Discoveries of the Century Reveal God*, 3d ed. (Colorado Springs, Colo.: NavPress, 2001), pp. 204-205.

19. Frederick R. Blattner et al., "The Complete Genome Sequence of *Escherichia coli* K-12," *Science* 277 (1997), pp. 1453-1462.

20. Lucy Shapiro and Richard Losick, "Protein Localization and Cell Fate in Bacteria," *Science* 276 (1997), pp. 712-718; Richard Losick and Lucy Shapiro, "Changing Views on the Nature of the Bacterial Cell: From Biochemistry to Cytology," *Journal of Bacteriology* 181 (1999), pp. 4143-4145; Lucy Shapiro and Richard Losick, "Dynamic Spatial Regulation in the Bacterial Cell," *Cell* 100 (2000), pp. 89-98.

21. Shapiro and Losick, "Protein Localization," pp. 712-718.

22. Michaela E. Sharpe and Jeff Errington, "Upheaval in the Bacterial Nucleoid," *Trends*

in *Genetics* 15 (1999), pp. 70-74; Gideon Scott Gordon and Andrew Wright, "DNA Segregation in Bacteria," *Annual Review of Microbiology* 54 (2000), pp. 681-708.

23. Joe Pogliano et al., "Multicopy Plasmids are Clustered and Localized in *Escherichia coli*," *Proceedings of the National Academy of Sciences, USA* 98 (2001), pp. 4486-4491.

24. Katherine P. Lemon and Alan D. Grossman, "Localization of Bacterial DNA Polymerase: Evidence for a Factory Model of Replication," *Science* 282 (1998), pp. 1516-1519; Richard Losick and Lucy Shapiro, "Bringing the Mountain to Mohammed," *Science* 282 (1998), pp. 1430-1431.

25. Ken Begg, "Ring of Bright Metal," *Nature* 354 (1991), pp. 109-110; Erfei Bi and Joe Lutkenhaus, "FtsZ Ring Structure Associated with Division in *Escherichia coli*," *Nature* 354 (1991), pp. 161-164.

26. Petra Anne Levin et al., "Identification and Characterization of a Negative Regulator of FtsZ Ring Formation in *Bacillus subtilis*," *Proceedings of the National Academy of Sciences, USA* 96 (1999), pp. 9642-9647; Christine Jacobs and Lucy Shapiro, "Bacterial Cell Division: A Moveable Feast," *Proceedings of the National Academy of Sciences, USA* 96 (1999), pp. 5891-5893; Xuan-Chuan Yu and William Margolin, "Fts Z Ring Clusters in *min* and Partition Mutants: Role of Both the Min System and the Nucleoid in Regulating FtsZ Ring Localization," *Molecular Microbiology* 32 (1999), pp. 315-326; David M. Raskin and Piet A. J. de Boer, "Rapid Pole-to-Pole Oscillation of a Protein Required for Directing Division to the Middle of *Escherichia coli*," *Proceedings of the National Academy of Sciences, USA* 96 (1999), pp. 4971-4976; Debabrata RayChaudhuri et al., "Protein Acrobatics and Bacterial Cell Polarity," *Proceedings of the National Academy of Sciences, USA* 98 (2001), pp. 1332-1334; Xiaoli Fu et al., "The MinE Ring Required for Proper Placement of the Division Site Is a Mobile Structure That Changes Its Cellular Location During the *Escherichia coli* Division Cycle," *Proceedings of the National Academy of Sciences, USA* 98 (2001), pp. 980-985.

Chapter 13: Extreme Life

1. Michael Gross, *Life on the Edge: Amazing Creatures Thriving in Extreme Environments* (Reading, Pa.: Perseus, 1996), pp. 15-59.

2. Peter Gwynne, "Extremozymes: Proteins at Life's Extremes," *Chemistry* (October, 1998), pp. 15-19; See Howland; See Gross.

3. John Howland, *The Surprising Archaea: Discovering Another Domain of Life* (New York: Oxford University Press, 2000), pp. 19-48.

4. Howland, pp. 19-48.

5. Karl O. Stetter, "The Lesson of Archaebacteria," in *Early Life on Earth: Nobel Symposium No. 84*, ed. Stefan Bengtson (New York: Columbia University Press, 1994), pp. 143-151.

6. Otto Kandler, "The Early Diversification of Life," in *Early Life on Earth: Nobel Symposium No. 84*, ed. Stefan Bengtson (New York: Columbia University Press, 1994), pp. 152-160.

7. See Claudia Huber and Günter Wächtershäuser, "Activated Acetic Acid by Carbon Fixation on (Fe,Ni)S Under Primordial Conditions," *Science* 276 (1997), pp. 245-247; Claudia Huber and Günter Wächtershäuser, "Peptides by Activation of Amino Acids with CO on (Ni,Fe)S Surfaces: Implications for the Origin of Life," *Science* 281 (1998), pp. 670-672; J. P. Amend and E. L. Shock, "Energetics of Amino Acid Synthesis in Hydrothermal Ecosystems," *Science* 281 (1998), pp. 1659-1662; Sarah

Simpson, "Life's First Scalding Steps," *Science News* 155 (1999), pp. 24-26; Ei-ichi Imai et al., "Elongation of Oligopeptides in a Simulated Submarine Hydrothermal System," *Science* 283 (1999), pp. 831-833; George Cody et al., "Primordial Carbonylated Iron-Sulfur Compounds and the Synthesis of Pyruvate," *Science* 289 (2000), pp. 1337-1340.

8. Thomas Gold, *The Deep Hot Biosphere* (New York: Springer-Verlag, 1999), pp. 165-184.

9. James K. Fredrickson and Tullis C. Onstott, "Microbes Deep Inside the Earth," *Scientific American* (October 1996), pp. 68-73.

10. J. Jouzel et al., "More Than 200 Meters of Lake Ice Above Subglacial Lake Vostok, Antarctica," *Science* 286 (1999), pp. 2138-2141; John C. Priscu et al., "Geomicrobiology of Subglacial Ice Above Lake Vostok, Antarctica," *Science* 286 (1999), pp. 2141-2143; D. M. Karl et al., "Microorganisms in the Accreted Ice of Lake Vostok, Antarctica," *Science* 286 (1999), pp. 2144-2147; Christopher F. Chyba and Cynthia B. Phillips, "Possible Ecosystems and the Search for Life on Europa," *Proceedings of the National Academy of Seiences, USA* 98 (2001), pp. 801-804.

11. Claire Vieille and Gregory J. Zeikus, "Hyperthermophilic Enzymes: Sources, Uses, and Molecular Mechanisms for Thermostability," *Microbiology and Molecular Biology Reviews* 65 (2001), pp. 1-43.

12. Vieille and Zeikus, pp. 1-43.

13. Howland, pp. 49-66.

14. Karl O. Stetter, "Hyperthermophiles and Their Possible Role as Ancestors of Modern Life," in *The Molecular Origins of Life: Assembling the Pieces of the Puzzle*, ed. André Brack (Cambridge: Cambridge University Press, 1999), pp. 315-335.

15. N. H. Sleep et al., "Initiation of Clement Surface Conditions on the Earliest Earth," *Proceedings of the National Academy of Sciences, USA* 98 (2001), pp. 3666-3672.

16. R. M. Canup and E. Asphaug, "Origin of the Moon in a Giant Impact Near the End of the Earth's Formation," *Nature* 412 (2001), pp. 708-712; U. Wiechert et al., "Oxygen Isotopes and the Moon-Forming Giant Impact," *Science* 294 (2001), pp. 345-348.

17. Peter D. Ward and Donald Brownlee, *Rare Earth: Why Complex Life Is Uncommon in the Universe* (New York: Springer-Verlag, 2000), pp. 229-234.

18. Ward and Brownlee, pp. 48-50.

19. Philippe Lopez et al., "The Root of the Tree of Life in the Light of The Covarion Model," *Journal of Molecular Evolution* 49 (1999), pp. 496-506; Hervé Philippe and Patrick Forterre, "The Rooting of the Universal Tree of Life Is Not Reliable," *Journal of Molecular Evolution* 49 (1999), pp. 509-523; Henner Brinkmann and Hervé Philippe, "Archaea Sister Group of Bacteria? Indications from Tree Reconstruction Artifacts in Ancient Phylogenies," *Molecular Biology and Evolution* 16 (1999), pp. 817-825.

20. Céline Brochier and Hervé Philippe, "A Non-Hyperthermophilic Ancestor for Bacteria," *Nature* 417 (2002), p. 244; Gustavo Caetano-Anollés, "Evolved RNA Secondary Structure and the Rooting of the Universal Tree of Life," *Journal of Molecular Evolution* 54 (2002), pp. 333-345.

21. Nicolas Galtier et al., "A Nonhyperthermophilic Common Ancestor to Extant Life Forms," *Science* 283 (1999), pp. 220-221; Gretchen Vogel, "RNA Study Suggests Cool Cradle of Life," *Science* 283 (1999), pp. 155-156.

22. G. Arrhenius et al., "Origin and Ancestor: Separate Environments," *Science* 283

(1999), p. 792; Massimo Di Giulio, "The Universal Ancestor Lived in a Thermophilic or Hyperthermophilic Environment," *Journal of Theoretical Biology* 203 (2000), pp. 203-213.

23. Vincent Moulton et al., "RNA Folding Argues Against a Hot-Start Origin of Life," *Journal of Molecular Evolution* 51 (2000), pp. 416-421.

24. Thomas Lindahl, "Irreversible Heat Inactivation of Transfer Ribonucleic Acid," *The Journal of Biological Chemistry* 242 (1967), pp. 1970-1973.

25. Jeffrey L. Bada and Antonio Lazcano, "Some Like It Hot, But Not the First Biomolecules," *Science* 296 (2002), pp. 1982-1983.

26. Gross, pp. 69-75.

27. Charles Tanford, *The Hydrophobic Effect: Formation of Micelles and Biological Membranes* (New York: John Wiley and Sons, 1973); Charles Tanford, "The Hydrophobic Effect and The Organization of Living Matter," *Science* 200 (1978), pp. 1012-1018.

28. Peter L. Privalov, "Cold Denaturation of Proteins," *Critical Reviews in Biochemistry and Molecular Biology* 25 (1990), pp. 281-305; Chung-Jung Tsai et al., "The Hydrophobic Effect: A New Insight from Cold Denaturation and a Two-State Water Structure," *Critical Reviews in Biochemistry and Molecular Biology* 37 (2002), pp. 55-69; Peter J. Mikulecky and Andrew L. Feig, "Cold Denaturation of Hammerhead Ribozyme," *Journal of the American Chemical Society* 124 (2002), pp. 890-891.

29. Mikulecky and Feig, pp. 890-891.

30. Richard A. Kerr, "Deep Life in the Slow, Slow Lane," *Science* 296 (2002), pp. 1056-1058.

31. Kerr, pp. 1056-58; Steven D' Hondt et al., "Metabolic Activity of Subsurface Life in Deep-Sea Sediments," *Science* 295 (2002), pp. 2067-2070.

32. Francis H. Chapelle et al., "A Hydrogen-Based Subsurface Microbial Community Dominated by Methanogens," *Nature* 415 (2002), pp. 312-315.

33. Gross, pp. 43-48.

34. Kerr, pp. 1056-1058; Robert T. Anderson et al., "Evidence Against Hydrogen-Based Microbial Ecosystems in Basalt Aquifers," *Science* 281 (1998), pp. 976-977.

Chapter 14: Life on Mars?

1. Carl Sagan developed this deduction during a lecture he gave as part of his June Institute course taught in 1969 to the faculty and graduate students of the department of astronomy at the University of Toronto.

2. K. C. Cole, "Could There Be Life There? Rock May Bear Signs of Ancient Life on Mars," *Los Angeles Times,* 7 August 1996, p. A1.

3. Donald Goldsmith, *The Hunt for Life on Mars* (New York: Dutton, Penguin Group, 1997), pp. ix, 26.

4. Goldsmith, pp. 49-50.

5. E. Jagoutz et al., "ALH 84001: Alien or Progenitor of the SNC Family?" *Meteoritics* 29 (1994), pp. 478-479; L. E. Nyquist et al., "'Martians' Young and Old: Zagami and ALH 84001," *Abstracts of the Lunar and Planetary Science Conference* 26 (1995), p. 1065.

6. R. D. Ash, S. F. Knott, and G. Turner, "A 4-Gyr Shock Age for a Martian Meteorite and Implications for the Cratering History of Mars," *Nature* 380 (1996), pp. 57-59.

7. David S. McKay et al., "Search for Past Life on Mars: Possible Relic Biogenic Activity in Martian Meteorite ALH84001," *Science* 273 (1996), pp. 924-930.

8. D. D. Bogard, "Exposure-Age-Initiating Events for Martian Meteorites: Three or Four?" *Abstracts of the Lunar and Planetary Science Conference* 26 (1995), p. 143.

9. A. J. T. Jull et al., "Isotopic Composition of Carbonates in the SNC Meteorites Allan Hills 84001 and Nakhla," *Meteoritics* 30 (1995), p. 311.
10. Edward R. D. Scott, Akira Yamaguchi, and Alexander N. Krot, "Petrological Evidence for Shock Melting of Carbonates in the Martian Meteorite ALH84001," *Nature* 387 (1997), pp. 377-379.
11. Richard A. Kerr, "Martian 'Microbes' Cover Their Tracks," *Science* 276 (4 April 1997), pp. 30-31.
12. Richard A. Kerr, "Requiem for Life on Mars? Support for Microbes Fades," *Science* 282 (1998), p. 1400.
13. Lars E. Borg et al., "The Age of the Carbonates in Martian Meteorite ALH84001," *Science* 286 (1999), pp. 90-94.
14. Borg, p. 93.
15. F. Kemper et al., "Detection of Carbonates in Dust Shells Around Evolved Stars," *Nature* 415 (2002), pp. 295-297.
16. Akira Kouchi et al., "Rapid Growth of Asteroids Owing to Very Sticky Interstellar Organic Grains," *Astrophysical Journal Letters* 566 (2002), pp. L121-L124.
17. A. J. T. Jull et al., "Isotopic Evidence for a Terrestrial Source of Organic Compounds Found in Martian Meteorites Allan Hills 84001 and Elephant Moraine 79001," *Science* 279 (1998), pp. 366-369; Kerr, p. 1400.
18. Kathie L. Thomas-Keprta et al., "Magnetofossils in Terrestrial Samples and Martian Meteorite ALH84001," in Abstracts from the General Meeting of the NASA Astrobiology Institute, Washington, D.C., April 10-12, 2001, *Astrobiology* 1 (2001), pp. 354-356.
19. David J. Barber and Edward R. D. Scott, "Origin of Supposedly Biogenic Magnetite in the Martian Meteorite Allan Hills 84001," *Proceedings of the National Academy of Sciences, USA* 99 (2002), p. 6556.
20. Barber and Scott, p. 6556.
21. L. P. Keller et al., "Identification of Iron Sulphide Grains in Protoplanetary Disks," *Nature* 417 (2002), pp. 148-150.
22. Jeffrey L. Bada et al., "A Search for Endogenous Amino Acids in Martian Meteorite ALH84001," *Science* 279 (1998), pp. 362-365.
23. Bada et al., p. 364.
24. Geoffrey M. Cooper, *The Cell: A Molecular Approach* (Washington, D.C.: American Society for Microbiology Press, 1997), p. 4.
25. Cooper, pp. 4, 8.
26. William K. Purves et al., *Life: The Science of Biology*, 6th ed. (Sunderland, Mass.: Sinauer Associates, 2001), p. 58.
27. Three letters of correspondence under the heading, "Nanobacteria: Size Limits and Evidence" were published in *Science* 276 (1997): J. Maniloff, p. 1776; K. H. Nealson, p. 1776; R. Psenner and M. Loferer, pp. 1776-1777.
28. Gretchen Vogel, "Finding Life's Limits," *Science* 282 (1998), p. 1399.
29. E. Olavi Kajander and Neva Çiftçioglu, "Nanobacteria: An Alternative Mechanism for Pathogenic Intra- and Extracellular Calcification and Stone Formation," *Proceedings of the National Academy of Sciences, USA* 95 (1998), pp. 8274-8279; Dennis A. Carson, "An Infectious Origin of Extraskeletal Calcification," *Proceedings of the National Academy of Sciences, USA* 95 (1998), pp. 7846-7847.
30. John O. Cisar et al., "An Alternative Interpretation of Nanobacteria-Induced Biomineralization," *Proceedings of the National Academy of Sciences, USA* 97 (2000), pp. 11511-11515.

31. Kerr, "Requiem for Life on Mars?" p. 1399; Richard A. Kerr, "Putative Martian Microbes Called Microscopy Artifacts," *Science* 278 (1997), pp. 1706-1707.

32. Kerr, "Requiem for Life on Mars?" p. 1400.

33. Goldsmith, p. 57.

34. Daniel P. Glavin et al., "Amino Acids in Martian Meteorite Nakhla," *Book of Abstracts,* 12th International Conference on the Origin of Life and the 9th Meeting of the International Society for the Study of the Origin of Life (ISSOL 1999), July 11-16, 1999, San Diego, California, p. 62; I. P. Wright et al., "The Carbon Isotopic Composition of PAHs, Hydrocarbons, and Other Organic Compounds in Nakhla," 29th Annual Lunar and Planetary Science Conference, Houston, TX (1998), abstract # 1583; David S. McKay et al., "Possible Biologic Features in Martian Meteorite Nakhla," in Abstracts from the General Meeting of the NASA Astrobiology Institute, Washington, D.C., April 10-12, 2001, *Astrobiology* 1 (2001), pp. 369-371.

35. Daniel P. Glavin and Jeffrey L. Bada, "Survival of Amino Acids in Micrometeorites During Atmospheric Entry," *Astrobiology* 1 (2001), pp. 259-269.

36. See for example L. Paul Knauth and Donald M. Burt, "Follow the Water, Beware the Brine: Astrobiological Implications of Aqueous Seeps on Mars," and Allan H. Treiman, "Dry Mars: Parched Rocks and Fallen Dust," in Abstracts from the General Meeting of the NASA Astrobiology Institute, Washington, D.C., April 10-12, 2001, *Astrobiology* 1 (2001), pp. 365, 375.

37. Michael H. Carr, *Water on Mars* (New York: Oxford University Press, 1996), p. 30.

38. Carr, p. 197.

39. Carr, p. 197.

40. Maggie Fox, "NASA Photographs Show Signs of Water on Mars," *Reuters/Yahoo! News,* 22 June 2000, available from http://daily news.yahoo.com/b/nm/20000622/ts/space_mars_dc.html, accessed July 2000; Sharon Begley and Erika Check, "NASA: Mars Is All Wet," *Newsweek,* 3 July 2000, pp. 48-50.

41. M. C. Malin and K. S. Edgett, "Evidence for Recent Groundwater Seepage and Surface Runoff on Mars," *Science* 288 (2000), pp. 2330-2335.

42. F. Costard et al., "Formation of Recent Martian Debris Flows by Melting of Near-Surface Ground Ice at High Obliquity," *Science* 295 (2002), pp. 110-113.

43. Treiman, "Dry Mars", p. 375.

44. M. H. Carr and H. Wänke, "Earth and Mars: Water Inventories as Clues to Accretional Histories," *Icarus* 98 (1992), pp. 61-71.

45. Carr, p. 133.

46. Earth avoided this carbonate disaster for two reasons: (1) being much closer to the Sun, Earth did not need as much atmospheric carbon dioxide to warm up its surface, and (2) much greater and longer lasting plate tectonic activity effectively pushed carbonates below the crust where they decomposed and volcanic activity sent the carbon dioxide back up to the surface.

47. Carr, p. 202.

48. William R. Ward, "Comments on the Long-Term Stability of the Earth's Obliquity," *Icarus* 50 (1982), pp. 444-448; Jacques Laskar and P. Robutel, "The Chaotic Obliquity of the Planets," *Nature* 361 (1993), pp. 608-612; Jacques Laskar, F. Joutel, and P. Robutel, "Stabilization of the Earth's Obliquity by the Moon," *Nature* 361 (1993), pp. 615-617.

49. Michael H. Carr, "The Habitability of Early Mars," *Book of Abstracts*, ISSOL 1999, p. 61. Michael Carr presented these dates during his lecture.

50. I. S. Shklovskii and Carl Sagan, *Intelligent Life in the Universe* (San Francisco: Holden-Day, 1966), p. 209; Sir Fred Hoyle and N. C. Wickramasinghe, *Evolution From Space* (New York: Simon & Schuster, 1981), pp. 39-40.

51. D. M. Portner et al., "Effect of Ultrahigh Vacuum on Viability of Microorganisms," *Science* 134 (1961), p. 2047.

52. Ann D. Burrell, P. Feldschreiber, and C. J. Dean, "DNA-Membrane Association and the Repair of Double Breaks in X-Irradiated *Micrococcus Radiodurans*," *Biochimica et Biophysica Acta* 247 (1971), pp. 38-53; Sir Fred Hoyle and N. C. Wickramasinghe, pp. 42-46.

Chapter 15: Europa and Beyond

1. J. D. Anderson et al., "Europa's Differential Internal Structure: Inferences From Two Galileo Encounters," *Science* 276 (1997), pp. 1236-1239; R. Carlson et al., "Near-Infrared Spectroscopy and Spectral Mapping of Jupiter and the Galilean Satellites: Results from Galileo's Initial Orbit," *Science* 274 (1996), pp. 385-388; Michael H. Carr et al., "Evidence for a Subsurface Ocean on Europa," *Nature* 391 (1998), pp. 363-365.

2. Richard A. Kerr, "Putting a Lid on Life on Europa," *Science* 294 (2001), p. 1258.

3. M. J. S. Belton et al., "Galileo's First Images of Jupiter and the Galilean Satellites," *Science* 274 (1996), pp. 377-385; William B. McKinnon, "Sighting the Seas of Europa," *Nature* 386 (1997), pp. 765-767; Michael H. Carr et al., pp. 363-365; R. T. Pappalardo et al., "Geological Evidence for Solid-State Convection in Europa's Ice Shell," *Nature* 391 (1998), pp. 365-368.

4. Gretchen Vogel, "Galileo Gazes at Jupiter and Its Moons," *Science* 273 (1996), p. 1048.

5. Robert Sullivan et al., "Episodic Plate Separation and Fracture Infill on the Surface of Europa," *Nature* 391 (1998), pp. 371-373; Pappalardo et al., pp. 365-368.

6. William B. Moore, "Europa: Crunchy or Chewy Inside?" in Abstracts from the General Meeting of the NASA Astrobiology Institute, Washington, D.C., April 10-12, 2001, *Astrobiology* 1 (2001), p. 354.

7. William B. McKinnon, "Galileo at Jupiter—Meetings with Remarkable Moons," *Nature* 390 (1997), p. 24.

8. Moore, p. 354.

9. Hugh Ross, Kenneth Samples, and Mark Clark, *Lights in the Sky and Little Green Men: A Rational Christian Look at UFOs and Extraterrestrials* (Colorado Springs, Colo.: NavPress, 2002), pp. 171-189, 220-233.

10. Christopher Chyba and Cynthia B. Phillips, "Possible Ecosystems and the Search for Life on Europa," *Proceedings of the National Academy of Sciences, USA* 98 (2001), pp. 801-804.

11. Christopher F. Chyba, "Energy for Microbial Life in Europa," *Nature* 403 (2000), pp. 381-382; R. W. Carlson et al., "Hydrogen Peroxide on the Surface of Europa," *Science* 283 (1999), pp. 2062-2064.

12. R. W. Carlson, R. E. Johnson, and M. S. Anderson, "Sulfuric Acid on Europa and the Radiolytic Sulfur Cycle," *Science* 286 (1999), pp. 97-99; J. F. Cooper et al., "Energetic Ion and Electron Irradiation of the Icy Galilean Satellites," *Icarus* 149 (2001), pp. 133-159; John F. Cooper, "Radiolytic Chemistry at Europa's Doorstep—The First Meter," in Abstracts from the General Meeting of the NASA Astrobiology Institute, Washington, D.C., April 10-12, 2001, *Astrobiology* 1 (2001), p. 352.

13. E. P. Turtle and E. Pierazzo, "Thickness of a Europan Ice Shell from Impact Crater Simulations," *Science* 294 (2001), pp. 1326-1328; Kerr, pp. 1258-1259.
14. McKinnon, "Sighting the Seas of Europa," p. 767.
15. Paul M. Schenk, "Thickness Constraints on the Icy Shells of the Galilean Satellites from a Comparison of Crater Shapes," *Nature* 417 (2002), p. 419.
16. Schenk, pp. 419-421.
17. Athena Coustenis, "Titan's Exobiotical Atmosphere: Recent Revelations," *Book of Abstracts*, 13th International Conference on the Origin of Life and the 10th Meeting of the International Society for the Study of the Origin of Life (ISSOL 2002), June 30-July 5, 2002, Oaxaca, Mexico, p. 43. The comment about the lack of hydrocarbon oceans on Titan was specifically addressed during her lecture.
18. Athena Coustenis, "Titan's Exobiotical Atmosphere: Recent Revelations." The water abundance figure of 8×10^{-9} mole fraction was given during her lecture.
19. The latest and best measurement from cosmic background fluctuation measurements for the age of the universe is 13.7 ± 0.2 billion years: C. L. Bennett, et al., "First Year Wilkinson Microwave Anisotropy Probe (WMAP) Observations: Preliminary Maps and Basic Results" *Astrophysical Journal* (2003), in press (astro-ph/0302207). For a summary of results from the different cosmic age-dating methods see Hugh Ross, *The Creator and the Cosmos: The Greatest Scientific Discoveries of the Century Reveal God*, 3d ed. (Colorado Springs, Colo.: NavPress, 2001), pp. 54-62.
20. Ross, Samples, and Clark, pp. 185-189, 220-233; Ross, pp. 175-199. For the latest update of this calculation see *Fine-Tuning of Physical Life Support Body* and *Probability for a Life Support Body* both by Hugh Ross (Pasadena, Calif.: Reasons To Believe, 2002). These papers are posted at www.reasons.org. The number of characteristics that must be fine-tuned now stands at 200 and the probability that one planet in the observable universe will possess the characteristics necessary for life, without miraculous intervention, is less than one in 10^{215}.
21. Gerda Horneck et al., "Protection of Bacterial Spores in Space, a Contribution to the Discussion of Panspermia," *Origins of Life and Evolution of the Biosphere* 31 (2001), pp. 527-547.
22. Horneck et al., p. 540.
23. Paul Parsons, "Dusting Off Panspermia," *Nature* 383 (1996), pp. 221-222.
24. Ross, pp. 178-180, 188-198.
25. Interstellar meteoritic transport is known as lithopanspermia.
26. H. J. Melosh, in session 51, abstract no. 2022, "Exchange of Meteoritic Material Between Stellar Systems," Thursday morning, 8:30 A.M., "Astrobiology I: Thinking Big to the Nitty Gritty," *Lunar and Planetary Science Conference at Houston, Texas*, March 12-16, 2001; H. J. Melosh, "Exchange of Meteorites Between Stellar Systems," *Meteoritics and Planetary Science* 36, Supplement (2001), p. A130.

Chapter 16: Life, Seeded on Purpose

1. This comment was made at the question and answer microphone by one of the participants, on the last day of the 12th International Conference on the Origin of Life and the 9th Meeting of the International Society for the Study of the Origin of Life (ISSOL 1999), July 11-16, 1999, San Diego, California.
2. F. H.C. Crick and Leslie E. Orgel, "Directed Panspermia," *Icarus* 19 (1973), pp. 341-346.

3. See Francis Crick, *Life Itself: Its Origin and Nature* (New York: Simon & Schuster, 1981).

4. Robert Shapiro, *Origins: A Skeptic's Guide to the Creation of Life on Earth* (New York: Summit Books, 1986), pp. 227-228.

5. Peter D. Ward and Donald Brownlee, *Rare Earth: Why Complex Life Is Uncommon in the Universe* (New York: Copernicus, Springer-Verlag, 2000), pp. 125-156; Fazale Rana and Hugh Ross, "'Exploding' With Life!" *Facts for Faith* 2 (Q2 2000), pp. 12-17.

6. P. E. Olsen et al., "Ascent of Dinosaurs Linked to an Iridium Anomaly at the Triassic-Jurassic Boundary," *Science* 296 (2002), pp. 1305-1307; Richard A. Kerr, "Did an Impact Trigger the Dinosaurs' Rise?" *Science* 296 (2002), pp. 1215-1216; Mark K. Reichow, "^{40}Ar/^{39}Ar Dates from the West Siberian Basin: Siberian Flood Basalt Province Doubled," *Science* 296 (2002), pp. 1846-1849; Paul R. Renne, "Flood Basalts—Bigger and Badder," *Science* 296 (2002), pp. 1812-1813; Hugh Ross, "Darwinism's Fine Feathered Friends—A Matter of Interpretation," *Facts & Faith,* vol. 12, no. 3 (1998), pp. 1-3; Hugh Ross, "Creation on the 'Firing Line,'" *Facts & Faith,* vol. 12, no. 1 (1998), pp. 6-7; Hugh Ross, "Fungus Paints Darker Picture of Permian Catastrophe," *Facts & Faith,* vol. 10, no. 2 (1996), p. 3.

7. The universe is highly uniform and homogenous. If it were less uniform, then only black holes and neutron stars would form. If it were more uniform, no stars at all would form. If the universe were any more or less homogeneous, Earth would possess the wrong mix of elements for life.

8. NASA catalog of the 2,613 known stars within eighty-one light-years of Earth, available from Internet, http://nstars.arc.nasa.gov/, accessed January 30, 2003; Jean Schneider, Extra Solar Planets Catalog, a frequently updated website catalog available from Internet, http://www.obspm.fr/encycl/catalog.html, accessed January 30, 2003.

9. Christopher F. Chyba, "Life Beyond Mars," *Nature* 382 (1996), p. 577.

10. T. Joseph W. Lazio, Jill Tarter, and Peter R. Bakus, "Megachannel Extraterrestrial Assay Candidates: No Transmissions from Intrinsically Steady Sources," *Astronomical Journal* 124 (2002), pp. 560-564.

11. Hugh Ross, Kenneth Samples, and Mark Clark, *Lights in the Sky and Little Green Men: A Rational Christian Look at UFOs and Extraterrestrials* (Colorado Springs, Colo.: NavPress, 2002), pp. 55-64; Hugh Ross, "Anthropic Principle: A Precise Plan for Humanity," *Facts for Faith* 8 (Q1 2002), pp. 26-28.

12. See Matthew 14:25-27.

13. See 2 Kings 19:9-36; 2 Chronicles 32:1-23; Isaiah 36:1–37:38.

Chapter 17: Solving the Mystery

1. Bernard E. J. Pagel, *Nucleosynthesis and Chemical Evolution of Galaxies* (New York: Cambridge University Press, 1997), pp. 103-130; Hugh Ross, *The Creator and the Cosmos: How the Greatest Scientific Discoveries of the Century Reveal God,* 3d ed. (Colorado Springs, Colo.: NavPress, 2001), pp. 57-63.

2. NASA Goddard Space Flight Center, "Top Story: New Image of Infant Universe Reveals Era of First Stars, Age of Cosmos, and More," February 11, 2003, available from Internet, www.gsfc.nasa.gov/topstory/2003/0206mapresults.html, accessed March 31, 2003; Sean Carroll, "Filling in the Background," *Nature* 422 (2003), pp. 26-27; Geoff Brumfiel, "Cosmology Gets Real," *Nature* 422 (2003), pp. 108-110.

3. Pagel, pp. 198-320.

4. The universe was only about 9.5 billion years old when the solar system formed. S. Sahijpal et al., "A Stellar Origin for the Short-Lived Nuclides in the Early Solar

System," *Nature* 391 (1998), pp. 559-561; Peter Hoppe et al., "Type II Supernova Matter in a Silicon Carbide Grain from the Murchison Meteorite," *Science* 272 (1996), pp. 1314-1316; G. J. Wasserburg, R. Gallino, and M. Busso, "A Test of the Supernova Trigger Hypothesis with ^{60}Fe and ^{26}Al," *Astrophysical Journal Letters* 500 (1998), pp. L189-L193; Theodore P. Snow and Adolf N. Witt, "The Interstellar Carbon Budget and the Role of Carbon in Dust and Large Molecules," *Science* 270 (1995), pp. 1455-1460; Hugh Ross, "Our Solar System, the Heavyweight Champion," *Facts & Faith,* vol. 10, no. 2 (1996), p. 6.

5. Hoppe et al., pp. 1314-1316; Wasserburg, Gallino, and Busso, pp. L189-L193; Ross, "Our Solar System," p. 6; S. Sahijpal et al., pp. 559-561.

6. Christian de Duve, *Life Evolving: Molecules, Mind, and Meaning* (New York: Oxford University Press, 2002), pp. 53-54.

7. de Duve, pp. 284-307.

8. Hugh Ross, "The Physics of Sin," *Facts for Faith* (Q1, 2002), pp. 46-51; Hugh Ross, "Anthropic Principle," *Facts for Faith* (Q1, 2002), pp. 24-31; Hugh Ross, *Beyond the Cosmos: What Recent Discoveries in Astrophysics Reveal About the Glory and Love of God,* 2d ed. (Colorado Springs, Colo.: NavPress, 1999), pp. 195-228.

9. Icko Iben Jr., "Stellar Evolution. I. The Approach to the Main Sequence," *Astrophysical Journal* 142 (1965), pp. 993-1018.

10. Frederick M. Walter and Don C. Barry, "Pre- and Main-Sequence Evolution of Solar Activity," in *The Sun in Time,* ed. C. P. Sonett, M. S. Giampapa, and M. C. Matthews (Tuscon: University of Arizona Press, 1991), pp. 633-657 (note Table IV on page 653).

11. Hugh Ross, *The Creator and the Cosmos: How the Greatest Scientific Discoveries of the Century Reveal God,* 3d ed. (Colorado Springs, Colo.: NavPress, 2001), pp. 180-181.

12. M. Schonberg and S. Chandrasekhar, "On the Evolution of the Main Sequence Stars," *Astrophysical Journal* 96 (1942), pp. 161-173.

13. David S. P. Dearborn, "Standard Solar Models," in *The Sun in Time,* ed. C. P. Sonett, M. S. Giampapa, and M. C. Matthews (Tuscon: University of Arizona Press, 1991), p. 173.

14. Jihad Touma and Jack Wisdom, "Nonlinear Core-Mantle Coupling," *Astronomical Journal* 122 (2001), pp. 1030-1050; Gerald Schubert and Keke Zhang, "Effects of an Electrically Conducting Inner Core on Planetary and Stellar Dynamos," *Astrophysical Journal* 557 (2001), pp. 930-942; M. H. Acuña et al., "Magnetic Field and Plasma Observations at Mars: Initial Results of the Mars Global Surveyor Mission," *Science* 279 (1998), pp. 1676-1680; Peter Olson, "Probing Earth's Dynamo," *Nature* 389 (1997), p. 337; Weijia Kuang and Jeremy Bloxham, "An Earth-Like Numerical Dynamo Model," *Nature* 389 (1997), pp. 371-374; Xiaodong Song and Paul G. Richards, "Seismological Evidence for Differential Rotation of the Earth's Inner Core," *Nature* 382 (1997), pp. 221-224; Wei-jia Su, Adam M. Dziewonski, and Raymond Jeanloz, "Planet Within a Planet: Rotation of the Inner Core of the Earth," *Science* 274 (1996), pp. 1883-1887; Hugh Ross, "The Faint Sun Paradox," *Facts for Faith* 9 (Q2 2002), pp. 26-33.

15. Stephen H. Kirby, "Taking the Temperature of Slabs," *Nature* 403 (2000), pp. 31-34.

16. Peter D. Ward and Donald Brownlee, *Rare Earth: Why Complex Life Is Uncommon in the Universe* (New York: Copernicus, 2000), pp. 191-234.

17. I. Juliana Sackmann and Arnold I. Boothroyd, "Our Sun. V. A Bright Young Sun Consistent with Helioseismology and Warm Temperatures on Ancient Earth and Mars," *Astrophysical Journal* 583 (2003), pp. 1024-1039.

18. Crisogono Vasconcelos and Judith A. McKenzie, "Sulfate Reducers—Dominant Players in a Low-Oxygen World?" *Science* 290 (2000), pp. 1711-1712.

19. John Emsley, *The Elements,* 3d ed. (Oxford: Clarendon Press, 1998), pp. 24, 40, 56, 58, 60, 62, 78, 102, 106, 122, 130, 138, 152, 160, 188, 198, 214, 222, 230.

20. Specific sulfate-reducing bacteria stripped waters with a low but still deadly concentration of a particular vital poison element. For example, certain species of bacteria consumed water-soluble zinc and used it to produce precipitates of pure sphalerite. This sphalerite is insoluble and, therefore, safe for advanced life. Moreover, when the bacteria formed very large concentrated populations, they produced highly economic sphalerite ore deposits.

21. Tyler Volk and David Schwartzman, "Biotic Enhancement of Weathering and the Habitability of Earth," *Nature* 340 (1989), pp. 457-460; Richard Monastersky, "Supersoil," *Science News* 136 (1989), pp. 376-377.

22. See Hugh Ross, *The Genesis Question: Scientific Advances and the Accuracy of Genesis,* 2d ed. (Colorado Springs, Colo.: NavPress, 2001).

23. Christian J. Bjerrum and Donald E. Canfield, "Ocean Productivity Before About 1.9 Gyr Ago Limited by Phosphorus Adsorption onto Iron Oxides," *Nature* 417 (2002), pp. 159-162; John M. Hayes, "A Lowdown on Oxygen," *Nature* 417 (2002), pp. 127-128.

24. Donald E. Canfield and Andreas Teske, "Late Proterozoic Rise in Atmospheric Oxygen Concentration Inferred from Phylogenetic and Sulfur-Isotope Studies," *Nature* 382 (1996), pp. 127-132; Donald E. Canfield, "A New Model for Proterozoic Ocean Chemistry," *Nature* 396 (1998), pp. 450-453; John M. Hayes, "A Lowdown on Oxygen," *Nature* 417 (2002), p. 127.

25. Katherine L. Moulton and Robert A. Berner, "Quantification of the Effect of Plants on Weathering: Studies in Iceland," *Geology* 26 (October 1998), pp. 895-898.

26. Reasons To Believe sponsors a weekly two-hour webcast. This show reviews the theological significance of the latest scientific discoveries. Documentation for how well the RTB creation model predictions perform is posted in the *Creation Update* show notes at www.reasons.org.

27. Hugh Ross, "Probability for a Life Support Body" (Pasadena, Calif.: Reasons To Believe, 2002), available from Internet, www.reasons.org, accessed March 31, 2003.

Epilogue

1. Michael Behe, *Darwin's Black Box: The Biochemical Challenge to Evolution* (New York: Free Press, 1996), p. 39; Michael Polanyi, "Life Transcending Physics and Chemistry," *Chemical and Engineering News* 21 August 1967, pp. 54-66; Michael Polanyi, "Life's Irreducible Structure," *Science* 160 (1968), pp. 1308-1312.

2. Lubert Stryer, *Biochemistry,* 3d ed. (New York: W. H. Freeman, 1988), pp. 70-90, 649-686, 703-732; Styer, pp. 15-42, 733-766.

3. Steven M. Block, "Real Engines of Creation," *Nature* 386 (1997), p. 217; Fazale Rana and Micah Lott, "Hume vs. Paley: These 'Motors' Settle the Debate," *Facts for Faith* (Q2 2000), pp. 34-39; Fazale R. Rana, "Protein Structures Reveal Even More Evidence for Design," *Facts for Faith* (Q4 2000), pp. 4-5; Steven Block, "Fifty Ways to Love Your Lever," *Cell* 87 (1996), pp. 151-157; William Paley, *Natural Theology: Evidences of the Existence and Attributes of the Deity Collected from the Appearances of Nature* (reprint, Houston: Thomas Press, 1972), p. 1802.

4. See Hubert P. Yockey, *Information Theory and Molecular Biology* (Cambridge: Cambridge University Press, 1992); Charles B. Thaxton, Walter L. Bradley, and Roger

L. Olsen, *The Mystery of Life's Origin: Reassessing Current Theories* (Dallas: Lewis and Stanley, 1984), pp. 127-143; See Bernd-Olaf Küppers, *Information and the Origin of Life* (Cambridge: The MIT Press, 1990).

5. Stryer, pp. 106-109.

6. David Haig and Lawrence D. Hurst, "A Quantitative Measure of Error Minimization in the Genetic Code," *Journal of Molecular Evolution* 33 (1991), pp. 412-417; Stephen J. Freeland and Lawrence D. Hurst, "The Genetic Code is One in a Million," *Journal of Molecular Evolution* 47 (1998), pp. 238-248; Stephen J. Freeland et al., "Early Fixation of an Optimal Genetic Code," *Molecular Biology and Evolution* 17 (2000), pp. 511-518.

7. Tomas Lindahl and Richard D. Wood, "Quality Control by DNA Repair," *Science* 286 (1999), pp. 1897-1905; Michael Ibba and Dieter Söll, "Quality Control Mechanisms During Translation," *Science* 286 (1999), pp. 1893-1896; Sue Wickner et al., "Posttranslational Quality Control: Folding, Refolding, and Degrading Proteins," *Science* 286 (1999), pp. 1888-1893; Lars Ellgaard et al., "Setting the Standards: Quality Control in the Secretory Pathway," *Science* 286 (1999), pp. 1882-1888.

8. Russell F. Doolittle, "Convergent Evolution: The Need to Be Specific," *Trends in Biochemical Sciences* 19 (1994), pp. 15-18; Harold H. Zakon, "Convergent Evolution on the Molecular Level," *Brain, Behavior, and Evolution* 59 (2002), pp. 250-261.

9. Joe Alper, "Chemists Look to Follow Biology Lead," *Science* 295 (2002), pp. 2396-2397; Nadrian C. Seeman and Angela M. Belcher, "Emulating Biology: Building Nanostructures from the Bottom Up," *Proceedings of the National Academy of Sciences, USA* 99 (2002), pp. 6451-6455; J. Fraser Stoddart and Hsian-Rong Tseng, "Chemical Synthesis Gets a Fillip from Molecular Recognition and Self-Assembly Processes," *Proceedings of the National Academy of Sciences, USA* 99 (2002), pp. 4797-4800; George J. Whitesides, "The Once and Future Nanomachine," *Scientific American* (September 2001), pp. 78-83; Robert F. Service, "Borrowing from Biology to Power the Petite," *Science* 283 (1999), pp. 27-28; Ricky K. Soong et al., "Powering an Inorganic Nanodevice with a Biomolecular Motor," *Science* 290 (2000), pp. 1555-1558.

Appendix B

1. Lubert Stryer, *Biochemistry*, 3d ed. (New York: W. H. Freeman, 1988), pp. 534-535.

2. J. William Schopf, *Cradle of Life: The Discovery of Earth's Earliest Fossils* (Princeton, N.J.: Princeton University Press, 2001), pp. 174-177; Manfred Schidlowski, "A 3,800-Million-Year Isotopic Record of Life from Carbon in Sedimentary Rocks," *Nature* 333 (1988), pp. 313-318; Manfred Schidlowski, "Carbon Isotopes as Biogeochemical Recorders of Life over 3.8 Ga of Earth History: Evolution of a Concept," *Precambrian Research* 106 (2001), pp. 117-134.

GLOSSARY OF TERMS

Abiogenesis: Life from non-life. This scientific idea posits that life's origin resulted strictly through natural mechanisms from non-living matter.

Acetonitrile: A compound with the formula CH_3CN. Origin-of-life researchers think that this chemical existed on early Earth as a result of chemical reactions that occurred in the prebiotic soup.

Acidophile: A class of extremophilic microorganisms that thrive under highly acidic conditions.

Adenine: A key molecule needed for life. This compound, formally known as 6-aminopurine, is a component of DNA and RNA.

Adenosine Triphosphate: An important life molecule that plays a role in energy storage and use in the cell. The energy liberated when food stuff is broken down by the cell is used to form adenosine triphosphate. The breakdown of adenosine triphosphate provides energy to drive cell activities.

Aerobe: Any organism that requires oxygen to live.

Alanine: One of the twenty amino acids used by the cell to make proteins.

Aldehyde: A class of chemical compounds that possesses the CHO group. Origin-of-life researchers think that aldehydes played a key role in the production of amino acids and sugars on early Earth.

Alkalophile: A class of extremophilic microorganisms that thrive under highly alkaline conditions.

Amine: A class of nitrogen-containing chemical compounds derived from ammonia. Amines played an important role in early Earth's chemistry.

Amino Acids: Organic compounds that have both amino (NH_2) and carboxyl (COOH) groups. Amino acids join together in a chainlike fashion to form proteins. The formation of amino acids under prebiotic conditions is of chief interest to origin-of-life researchers.

Amphiphilic: Describes chemical compounds in which part of their molecular structure is water-soluble and part is water-insoluble. Cell membranes consist of amphiphilic materials.

Apatite: A class of phosphate minerals that typically contains calcium, chloride, fluoride, and hydroxide constituents.

Archaea: One of life's three domains. Bacteria-like microorganisms comprise archaea. While these microbes superficially resemble bacteria, they are genetically and biochemically distinct. Some origin-of-life researchers think that archaea were the first organisms to emerge on Earth.

Arginine: One of the twenty amino acids used by the cell to make proteins.

Autotroph: A class of organisms that can make organic nutrients directly from inorganic materials.

Barophile: A class of extremophilic microorganisms that thrive under high pressure conditions.

Basalt: A crystalline rock with volcanic origin.

Biogenicity: Describes something that has a biological origin.

Biomolecule: A molecule that is found in living organisms or plays an important role in life processes.

Cardiolipin: An amphiphilic compound found in cell membranes.

Chert: A hard rock composed primarily of quartz.

Chirality: The property of molecular handedness. Carbon-containing compounds with four different chemical substituents bound to a central carbon atom exist in two forms that are mirror images of one another.

Chondrite: A class of meteorite. Chondrites with a relatively high carbon content play an important role in origin-of-life research. The chemical compounds found in these meteorites serve as an indicator of the type of chemistry that occurred on early Earth.

Chordate: A member of the animal phylum chordate. Vertebrates (fish, amphibians, reptiles, birds, and mammals) are chordates.

Cyanamide: A chemical compound with the formula NHCNH. Origin-of-life researchers think that cyanamide was formed in prebiotic reactions on early Earth and played a role as a condensing agent.

Cyanate: The salt form of cyanic acid (HCNO). Origin-of-life researchers think that cyanogen was formed in prebiotic reactions on early Earth and played a role as a condensing agent. Cyanate also serves as a potential starting material for cytosine production.

Cyanoacetaldehyde: Origin-of-life researchers think cyanoacetaldehyde formed in prebiotic reactions on early Earth and served as a potential starting material for cytosine production.

Cyanoacetylene: Origin-of-life researchers think that cyanoacetylene was formed in prebiotic reactions on early Earth and served as a potential starting material for cytosine production.

Cyanobacteria: A group of bacteria with the capacity for photosynthesis. Cyanobacteria are also called blue-green algae.

Cyanoformamide: Origin-of-life researchers think that cyanoformamide was formed in prebiotic reactions on early Earth and played a role as a condensing agent.

Cyanogen: A chemical compound with the formula C_2N_2. Origin-of-life researchers think that cyanogen was formed in prebiotic reactions on early

Earth and played a role as a condensing agent.

Cyclotron: A particle accelerator in which charged particles are successively accelerated by a constant frequency alternating electric field.

Cytochrome C: A relatively small protein involved in energy production in the cell and found nearly ubiquitously in nature. Origin-of-life researchers have used cytochrome C to estimate the probability that random processes could generate biologically useful proteins.

Cytoplasm: The liquid/gel matrix found inside the cell and externally to the nucleus.

Cytosine: A key molecule needed for life. This compound, known as pyrimidine, is a component of DNA and RNA.

Cytoskeleton: A fibrous network of proteins that form the cell's internal structural framework.

Deoxyribose: A five-carbon sugar that helps form DNA's backbone structure.

Diaminomaleonitrile: An organic compound with the formula $C_4H_4N_4$. Diaminomaleonitrile forms from four molecules of HCN. Origin-of-life researchers think that diaminomaleonitrile served as an intermediate in the chemical route that produced adenine and guanine on early Earth.

Dihydroxyacetone: A three-carbon sugar. This compound was recently discovered at low levels in the Murchison meteorite.

Electroweak: The unification of the electromagnetic and weak nuclear forces that occurs at very high temperatures.

Eubacteria: One of life's three domains. These organisms are single-celled and lack internal structures such as a nucleus.

Eukarya: The domain of life comprised of organisms that possess a nucleus as part of their cellular makeup. Eukarya includes one-celled protists and fungi, plants, and animals.

Extremophile: A class of microbes that tolerates, and in some cases even requires, extremely harsh conditions.

Fischer-Tropsch Reaction: A chemical process that generates long-chain hydrocarbons, alcohols, and fatty acids from carbon monoxide and hydrogen. Origin-of-life researchers think that this process occurred during Earth's early history to produce molecules that contributed to the formation of cell membranes.

Formaldehyde: An organic compound with the formula CH_2O. Origin-of-life researchers think that formaldehyde formed on early Earth. This compound presumably served as an important starting material in the prebiotic production of amino acids and sugars.

Gamma Ray: Highly energetic light particles with energies that are comparable to those associated with nuclear reactions.

Genome: An organism's total genetic makeup.

Glutamate: One of the twenty amino acids used by the cell to make proteins.

Glycerin: Also called glycerol. Glycerin is a three-carbon compound that is a component of phospholipids.

Glycerol: Also called glycerin.

Glycine: One of the twenty amino acids used by the cell to make proteins.

Glycolaldehyde: An organic compound with the formula $C_2H_4O_2$. Glycolaldehyde forms when two molecules of formaldehyde combine. Origin-of-life researchers think that glycolaldehyde served as an important intermediate in the prebiotic production of sugars.

Graphite: A mineral that consists exclusively of carbon. Graphite can form when organic materials decompose under the influence of geological processes.

Greigite: An iron sulfide.

Guanine: A key molecule needed for life. This compound, known as purine, is a component of DNA and RNA.

Haloalkalophile: A class of extremophilic microorganisms that thrive under high salt and alkaline conditions.

Halophile: A class of extremophilic microorganisms that thrive under high salt conditions.

Hematite: An iron mineral crystal, Fe_2O_3.

Heterotroph: A class of organisms that lacks the capacity to produce organic nutrients from inorganic compounds. Heterotrophs must aquire organic nutrients by directly ingesting them.

Histidine: One of the twenty amino acids used by the cell to make proteins.

Homopolymer: A polymer composed of identical subunits, or subunits of the same chemical class. Homopolymers have a repetitive backbone structure.

Hydrophilic: "Water-loving"; hydrophilic compounds dissolve readily in water.

In vitro **evolution:** A laboratory procedure used by origin-of-life researchers to generate RNA molecules (ribozymes) with catalytic activity.

Ion: An atom or molecule that possesses either a positive or negative charge.

Isotope: Atoms of the same chemical element that differ in mass. Isotopes have nearly identical chemical properties.

Isovaline: An amino acid. Isovaline forms via prebiotic chemical routes, but does not occur naturally inside the cell.

Kaolinite: A type of clay mineral.

Kerogen: Insoluble decomposition products of organic materials. Kerogens in Earth's oldest rocks provide clues about the first life.

Ketone: A class of chemical compounds that possesses the CO group. The ketone group occurs in some sugars.

Kuhn-Condon Rule: While one wavelength of circularly polarized light preferentially destroys chiral molecules of, for instance, the left-handed configuration, a different wavelength of the same circularly polarized light preferentially destroys molecules of the right-handed configuration.

Lecithin: A common name used for phospholipids.

Leucine: One of the twenty amino acids used by the cell to make proteins.

Lipid: A class of chemical compounds that shares the combined properties of water-insolubility and solubility in organic solvents.

Liposome: A hollow, spherical aggregate composed of phospholipids.

Lysine: One of the twenty amino acids used by the cell to make proteins.

Magnetosphere: Region around a heavenly body in which its magnetic field plays a dominant role in controlling the physical processes that operate there.

Maser: Coherent amplification of microwave radiation (Microwave Amplification by Stimulated Emission of Radiation).

Mesophile: An organism that requires moderate environmental conditions to live.

Metabolite: Any compound involved in the chemical reactions that occur inside a cell.

Methanogenesis: The biochemical processes that generate methane.

Methanotrophic: Describes microbes that use methane as a carbon source.

Micelle: An aggregate composed of amphiphilic molecules. Typically, micelles are solid spherical structures.

Monera: The term Ernst Haeckel gave to the hypothetical organisms that reside between nonlife and life.

Monomer: A chemical compound that can be linked with other chemical compounds to form a larger, more complex molecule. Monomers are also referred to as subunits.

Montmorillonite: A type of clay mineral.

Neovitalism: The re-emergence in the early 1900s of the view that life possesses a special force distinct from the physical forces that operate in the universe.

Neutron Star: A small, compact stellar object that is left over after the evolution and destruction of a massive star.

Nucleic Acid: The class of chemical compounds that includes DNA and RNA.

Nucleoside: A class of chemical compounds that consists of either ribose or deoxyribose linked to a nucleobase (uracil, thymine, cytosine, guanine, or adenine). The addition of a phosphate to a nucleoside yields a nucleotide.

Nucleotides: The basic building blocks linked together to form DNA and RNA. A nucleotide consists of a phosphate, a sugar (either ribose or deoxyribose), and a nucleobase (uracil, thymine, cytosine, guanine, or adenine).

Organelles: Structures found inside cells, typically surrounded by membranes, that carry out specialized functions.

Oxalic Acid: A chemical compound with the formula $C_2O_4H_2$. Some origin-of-life researchers think that oxalic acid played a role in the production of primitive cell membrane components on early Earth.

Oxidation: A chemical process that involves the loss of either electrons or hydrogen atoms or the addition of oxygen atoms to the reactant(s) in question.

Parity Violation: The violation of certain symmetry properties of particle physics interactions.

Peptide: A polymer formed by linking together amino acids.

Peptide Nucleic Acid: A man-made polymer with a proteinlike backbone and side-groups like those found in DNA and RNA. Some origin-of-life researchers think that peptide nucleic acids were the first class of biomolecules in the pre-RNA world.

Periplasmic Space: The space or region between the inner and outer cell membranes of gram negative bacteria.

Phosphatidylethanolamine: A phospholipid with an ethanolamine head-group.

Phosphatidylglycerol: A phospholipid with a gylcerol head-group.

Phospholipid: An amphiphilic compound formed from phosphate, glycerin, fatty acids, and amino alcohol. Phospholipids are one of the major components of cell membranes.

Photochemistry: Chemical events or reactions that involve the interaction of electromagnetic radiation with chemical compounds.

Phototroph: An organism that uses light energy to power cellular processes.

Planetesimals: Relatively small celestial objects that combine during a solar system's early era via gravitational attraction to form planets.

Plasmids: Small pieces of circular DNA found in bacteria. Plasmids exist independent of the bacteria's primary chromosome.

Polymer: A large chainlike molecule that consists of smaller subunits linked together.

Polymerase: A class of enzymes that catalyzes the formation of DNA and RNA molecules.

Polypeptide: A synonym for peptide.

Polysaccharide: A carbohydrate polymer formed by linking together carbohydrate monomers.

Prokaryotes: Single-celled organisms that lack internal structures, specifically a nucleus. Bacteria and archaea are both prokaryotes.

Proteinoid: A proteinlike molecule formed from amino acid mixtures in prebiotic simulation experiments.

Protoplasm: Another name for cytoplasm.

Protozoan: A single-celled microbe that contains a nucleus and internal cell structures.

Psychrophile: A class of extremophilic microorganisms that thrive under cold conditions.

Pulsar: A spinning neutron star with an extremely strong magnetic field. Pulsars emit pulses of radiation of short, well-defined duration.

Purine: A class of nitrogenous compounds that consists of fused five-membered and six-membered rings. Purines are found in DNA and RNA. Adenine and guanine are two examples of a purine.

Pyrimidine: A class of nitrogenous compounds that consists of a single six-membered ring. Pyrimidines are found in DNA and RNA. Thymine, cytosine, and uracil are three examples of a pyrimidine.

Pyrite: A mineral, also called iron sulfide, with the base formula FeS^2.

Pyrophosphate: A high-energy compound that forms by linking together phosphates through the removal of water molecules. Pyrophosphates are chemical groups that the cell uses to store chemical energy.

Quantum Mechanics: A theory of physics that describes the behavior of subatomic particles. In quantum mechanics the energy possessed by subatomic particles is discrete, not continuous, and subatomic particles display wave-like properties.

Radioisotope: An unstable isotope that decays via the disintegration of its nucleus. As a result, alpha or beta particles are liberated and a new atom forms.

Reverse Transcriptase: An enzyme that produces DNA by using RNA as a template. These enzymes are used in *in vitro* evolution protocols to generate ribozymes.

Ribose: A five-carbon sugar that forms part of RNA's molecular structure.

Ribosome: Complex particles inside the cell that carry out protein production.

Ribozyme: An RNA molecule that assists (catalyzes) chemical reactions in the cell. Ribozymes play a central role in the RNA World scenario for life's origin. In this capacity ribozymes would have carried out life's chemical activities.

Serine: One of the twenty amino acids used by the cell to make proteins.

Silicate: A silicon- and oxygen-containing mineral. Sand is an example of a silicate.

Stromatolite: A complex microbial community rooted upon the activity of cyanobacteria. Stromatolites are large macroscopic structures that consist of layered bacterial mats with interspersed layers of inorganic sediments.

Synchrotron Radiation: Electromagnetic radiation generated by the acceleration of charged relativistic particles.

Thermophile: A class of extremophilic microorganisms that thrive under high-temperature conditions.

Thioesters: Compounds formed by combining carboxylic acids with thiols. Thioesters possess the chemical group, COSH. Thioesters are high-energy compounds used by the cell to store chemical energy. Some origin-of-life researchers think that thioesters played a key role in the formation of complex biomolecules.

Thiol: A class of chemical compounds that contains the SH chemical group.

Triglyceride: An organic compound formed from glycerin and fatty acids.

Trimetaphosphate: A phosphate derivative. Origin-of-life researchers think that trimetaphosphate served as a condensing agent on early Earth.

Troposphere: The portion of the atmosphere where clouds form. The troposphere is roughly seven to ten miles above the earth's surface.

Uracil: A key molecule needed for life. This compound, known as pyrimidine, is a component of DNA and RNA.

Urea: An organic compound with the formula CON_2H_4. Origin-of-life researchers think that urea was present on early Earth and played a role in the production of cytosine.

INDEX

2-aminoethyl glycine (AEG), 133
32nd Annual Lunar and Planetary
    Science Conference, 203-204

abiogenesis, 21-24, 27, 81
acetaldehyde, 112
acetonitrile, 112
Achiral peptide nucleic acids (PNA),
    133
Acholeplasma laidlawii, 154
acidophiles, 172
activated monomers, 118
activated nucleotides, 53
adenine, 95, 112-113, 118
advanced life, 87, 208, 211-212, 216-
    217, 219
aerobes, 66
aggregates, 13, 24, 150-151, 153-154,
    157, 167, 179
aggregation, 47-48, 179
airborne contaminates, 96
alanine, 97, 110, 130, 187
alcohols, 97, 113-114, 149
aldehydes, 97
aliens, 18, 28, 30, 33, 51, 94, 205-207
alkaline lakes, 172
alkalophiles, 172
Allan Hills, 183
alumina clays, 113
Alzheimer's disease, 156
ambient interplanetary dust, 82

amines, 112-113
amino acid, 17, 24-26, 48, 52-54, 58,
    78, 93-100, 102-104, 109-110,
    113, 118, 123-127, 129-133, 136-
    141, 157, 162-163, 174-175, 187-
    188, 190, 194-196, 245
amino acid sequence, 136-137, 139-
    141, 157, 175
ammonia, 22, 24, 48, 97, 100, 103-
    104, 110, 112-113, 150, 201, 218
amphiphiles, 146, 150, 152-153
amphiphilic compounds, 146, 149-
    150, 158
amphiphilic hydrocarbon chains, 148
anaerobic heterotrophs, 77
ancient stromatolites, 67
Anglo-Australian Observatory, 126
anoxic environment, 74, 240
anoxygenic photosynthesis, 74, 76-77
anoxygenic photosynthetic purple
    bacteria, 75
Antarctic Ocean, 172
anthropologists, 33
apatite, 71-73, 114, 239
apatite-encased graphite, 71-73
apex fossils, 79
Apollo lunar rock samples, 83, 87
aquifer, 191
archaea, 49-50, 58, 64, 66, 79, 161-
    163, 166, 173
archaeabacteria, 49

archaeologists, 33
arctic ice cap, 198
arginine, 95
aromatic hydrocarbons, 151, 185
Arrhenius, Svante, 23, 27, 202-203
asteroid, 38, 82-84, 97, 186, 192-193, 203
astrobiologists, 199, 202-203
Astrobiology Institute at NASA, 51
astrochemists, 96
astronomers, 39-40, 72, 82-83, 86, 90, 97, 126-130, 183, 185-187, 191, 193-194, 199-200, 203, 215, 218
astrophysicists, 27, 218
atmospheric chemistry, 99, 102
atmospheric oxygen, 48, 74, 219-220
atmospheric reactions, 51
atmospheric synthesis of prebiotics, 99
atomic force microscopy, 69
ATP (adenosine triphosphate), 71, 114
Australia, 24, 63-65, 67-68, 69-70, 74, 75, 76, 77, 130
autocatalysis, 91, 116
autotrophs, 57

Bacillus subtilis, 86, 163, 203
bacterial cell division, 167
bacterial chromosomes, 166-167
bacterial DNA polymerases, 167
bacterial groups, 77
bacterial naked strands of DNA, 166
bacterial spores, 23
Bada, Jeffrey, 85, 97-98, 178
banded iron deposits (BIDs), 220
banded iron formations (BIFs), 73, 75-76
Barberton Mountain Land, 63
barophiles, 172
Barrelia burgdorferi, 162
basaltic crustal rocks, 82
basaltic rocks, 215
basalts, 84, 180, 215

Bible, 15-16, 32, 35-38, 41, 78, 105, 208, 211, 213, 225, 231
Bible study, 36
big bang theory, 231
big bang cosmology, 27
biochemical complexity, 76, 78
biochemical information systems, 224
biochemical pathways, 78
biochemical systems, 13-14, 43, 58, 119, 167, 223-224
biodeposits, 211, 214-215, 219-221
biofilms, 68
biogenesis, 30
biogenicity, 67, 69, 127-128
bioinformation molecules, 138
biological complexity, 27
biological organization, 23
biomass, 70, 74, 219, 229
biomoleculars, 147, 179, 223
biosphere, 50, 174, 180-181, 214
biotic compounds, 49
bipedal primate fossil record, 33
Bitter Springs Formation in Australia, 69, 155
Bohr, Niels, 92
bombardments, 72-73, 83-85, 87-88, 91, 186, 192-194
Bonner, William, 125
Boothroyd, Arnold, 218
boron, 94, 217
bottom-up approach, 17-18, 159, 168, 171
Bradley, Walter L., 11, 17, 138, 149
branch sites, 117
Brandeis University, 139
Brasier, Martin, 68-69
Brownlee, Donald, 91
Buchnera, 163
building blocks, 17, 25, 47-49, 54-56, 58-59, 78, 89-90, 93, 95, 97, 102, 105, 109-110, 116, 118, 123-124, 129, 133, 158, 163-164, 178, 190, 201

bulk kerogen, 70-71, 238
Butlerow reaction (formose reaction),
    113

Cairo, Egypt, 172
calcium hydroxide, 113
calcium ions, 114
calcium oxide, 113
Callanish (crater), 200
Callisto, 197, 200
Cambrian explosion, 206, 220
Canada, 69, 72, 96, 131
carbon compounds, 22, 96, 98, 129,
    132, 186, 202
carbon deposits, 68-69
carbon dioxide, 48, 84, 90, 96-97,
    100, 102, 173, 180, 191, 193, 202,
    214-216, 220, 239, 261
carbon monoxide, 48, 52, 96-97,
    100-101, 148-150, 202, 238
carbon ratio, 104
carbon-12, 69-71, 73-74, 76-77, 104,
    239
carbon-12 enriched kerogen and
    graphite globules, 77
carbon-12 enriched kerogen, 76
carbon-12 enrichment, 69-71, 73-74,
    76-77, 229, 238
carbon-12 isotopic excess, 70
carbon-12/carbon-13 isotope
    fractionation, 70
carbon-13, 70, 238-239
carbon-13 to carbon-12 ratio, 104
carbon-14, 70, 186
carbonaceous chondrite meteorites,
    40
carbonaceous chondrite, 95-96, 98-
    99, 130, 150
carbonaceous deposits,70, 104
carbonaceous substances, 104
carbonate deposits, 65, 104, 185
carbonate globules, 184-185, 188
carbonate infusion, 73
carbonates, 73, 75, 84, 149, 185-186,

193, 214-215, 220
carbonate-silicate cycle, 84, 87, 194
carbon-dioxide mantle, 193
carbon-fixing metabolic processes, 70
cardiolipin, 154
Carr, Michael, 194
catalysis, 91
Catholic Church, 14
Celera Genomics, 159
cell activity (autotrophism), 77-78
cell division, 65, 68, 162, 166-167
cell membrane, 18, 54, 56, 78, 114,
    129, 141, 143-148, 150, 153-
    159, 162, 165, 179, 224
  biophysics, 151
  origin, 57, 151, 156, 158
cells
  replication machinery, 78
  replication, 78, 166-167
  separation, 65
  wall components, 54, 58, 78, 158
cellular evolution, 57
cellular machinery, 136
cerium, 118
chemical accelerant, 116
chemical bond, 54, 100-101, 138,
    164
chemical building blocks, 78, 123
chemical pathways, 13, 25-26, 54,
    58-59, 77, 104, 109-111, 114-115,
    120, 148, 153, 158, 159, 190, 194,
    221
chemical reactions, 23-25, 51, 53-54,
    56, 91, 97, 109-112, 116, 119,
    136, 147, 194, 201, 224
chemical signature, 75, 183
chemical signatures of life, 183
chemical soup, 48
chemoautotroph, 50, 57
chemoautotrophic microbes, 74, 78
chemoautotrophic pathways, 57-58,
    175
chert layers, 75
cherts, 68-69

chicken-and-egg systems, 55, 223
chimpanzee genome, 160
chiral excess, 126-128, 131, 251
chiral molecules, 123-124, 128, 132
chiral nonprotein, 130
chirality, 123-125
cholesterol, 144, 252
C-H-O-N molecules, 199
chondritic (rocky, carbon-rich)
    meteorites, 84
Christians, 14-15, 17, 32-33
chromium minerals, 102
chromium, 84, 212, 217
Chyba, Christopher, 98, 199, 200
circularly polarized light, 125-128
circularly polarized UV light, 125,
    127-129
civilization, 213, 216, 218-219, 221
clay catalysts, 118
Cleaves, James, 112
climatic extremes, 87
climatic runaways, 214
codes of life, 140
cold denaturation, 179-180
cold spots, 90
collapse phase, 82, 212-213
collider, 82, 212, 242
Collins, Francis, 159
collision event, 82-83, 87-88, 200,
    203-204, 212
colony(ies), 65, 211, 219
Colorado, 191
cometary delivery, 100
comets, 49-50, 52, 83-84, 95-98, 100,
    129-130, 186, 190-191, 193, 197,
    200, 202, 245
complex biochemical pathways, 77
complex microbial communities, 77,
    173
complex microbial ecosystems, 76
complex multicellular invertebrates,
    66
complex photosynthetic processes,
    69

complexity, 14, 23, 25, 27, 35, 43, 45,
    49, 57, 59, 78, 91, 94, 149, 160-
    168, 221-224
condensation reactions, 48, 50, 52-
    53, 56
condensing agents, 50, 53, 136
Condon, Edward, 128
contemporary cell membranes, 57,
    148, 150-151, 153, 157-158
continent building, 40
continental crust, 88
continental land growth, 40
continental landmasses, 67, 215-216,
    220
continents, 40, 215-216
core dynamo, 216
cosmic background fluctuation, 263
cosmic radiation, 97, 99, 245
cosmic rays, 48, 97, 100, 207
cosmologists, 23
Crab Nebula, The, 126
cratering intensity, 83
craters, 82, 191-193, 199-200
creation, 9, 15, 21, 29-31, 35-37, 39-
    45, 78, 95, 119-120, 168, 208,
    212-213, 216-217, 219-221
creation days, 37, 40, 44, 78, 219
creation of life, 44
creation psalm, 39-40, 219
creation science, 16, 31
creation-day events, 40
creationism, 30-32
Creator, the, 14-15, 30, 33, 40, 43-44,
    78, 90, 105, 120, 133, 140, 168,
    208, 212-213, 221, 223-225, 231,
    234
Crick, Sir Francis, 28, 30, 33, 56, 205
critical biomolecules, 26
critical phenomena, 156
Cronin, John, 130
crust
    Earth, 40, 63, 85-88, 94, 100,
        102, 174, 180, 214-215, 219-220
    Europa, 198-200

Mars, 190, 194
crustal ice, 191, 197
cryptogamic colonies, 219
cryptogamic crusts, 219
crystals, 13, 71-73, 85-86, 126, 185-187, 189
cyanamide, 53
cyanate, 53, 112
cyanoacetalydehyde, 112
cyanoacetylene, 112
cyanobacteria consumers, 66
cyanobacteria, 64-72, 75-77, 89, 219-220
cyanobacterial mats, 66
cyanoformamide, 53
cyanogens, 53
cyclotron, 126
cytochrome c, 140, 164
cytoplasmic organelles, 188
cytosine, 90, 95, 111-113, 115, 118, 177
cytoskeleton, 166, 188

Darwin, Charles, 22
Darwinism, 22
Darwinists, 22, 27
Davies, Paul, 25-26, 30, 37
de Duve, Christian, 53-54, 213
Dead Sea, 171
decomposition, 70, 100, 102, 113, 115, 118, 187, 239
deep microbial biosphere hypothesis, 174
deep-biosphere communities, 180
deep-sea hydrothermal vent communities, 77
deep-sea hydrothermal vent, 51-52, 70, 77, 102-103, 149, 174-175, 199
deep-sea vents, 199
deflecting magnetic shield, 196
dehydrating conditions, 53
dehydration-hydration cycles, 57, 152
Deinococcus radiodurans, 86

Denmark, 63
deoxyribose, 113, 124, 129
design, 43, 45, 90, 95, 111, 119, 138, 143, 157, 221-225
designer proteins, 138-139
diaminomaleonitrite, 53
diamonds, 85, 101
diglycine, 52
dihydrogen phosphates, 114
dihydroxyacetone, 113
divergence, 89
DNA circles, 166
DNA polymerase, 119, 166-167
DNA repair mechanisms, 86
DNA, 48, 50, 52-56, 58-59, 71, 78, 86, 89, 93-94, 102, 111-114, 117, 119, 124, 129-130, 133, 135-136, 141, 151, 157-160, 162, 165-167, 174, 177, 179, 184, 195, 224
DNA's double helix, 179
DNA-protein world, 50, 56, 89, 114
double helix, 124, 179
Draganic, Ivan, 101
Driesch, Hans, 24
ductile ice, 198-199
dust grain, 27, 127, 204
dynamo, 216

E. coli, 156, 164-165
eagle, 41, 225
Earth's
    antiquity, 42
    first life, 27, 37, 43-44, 50-51, 59, 64, 76, 78, 162-163, 173, 178, 183, 194
    initial conditions, 37-40
    mantle, 102, 220
ecology, 68, 77, 180-181
Edgeworth-Kuiper belt, 72
Egypt, 131, 172
Eldredge, Niles, 30-32, 91
electroweak interactions, 125
enantiomeric abundance, 131, 251
entropy, 91, 131-132, 179

environmental bacterium, 189
environmental scientists, 216
enzyme cofactors, 95
enzymes, 23, 78, 81, 95, 115-116,
   119, 166-167, 180, 229
erosion
   Earth, 40, 64, 84-85, 215-217,
      219-220
   Mars, 191-193
ethanolamine, 153
eubacteria, 49-50, 58, 79, 161, 173
eukarya, 49-50, 64, 79, 163, 173
eukaryotes, 166, 188
Europa, 18, 50-51, 174, 178, 196-204
evolution, 9, 13, 17, 21, 28, 35, 47-
   49, 57-58, 77, 79, 81, 91, 95, 109,
   119, 133, 157, 168, 174, 179, 206,
   221, 232
evolutionary origin of life, 13, 16-18,
   22-28, 30, 46, 48-60, 76-77, 90,
   92, 99, 111, 129, 141, 176-177,
   201-202
evolutionary paradigm, 14, 175, 177-
   178
evolutionary theory(ies), 21, 58, 79
evolutionary tree, 49, 58, 77, 174, 177
exotic physics, 206
exotic reflector, 128
extinction, 206-207
extraterrestrial amino acids, 130-131
extraterrestrial carbon material, 96
extraterrestrial delivery, 50, 52, 57,
   98-99, 150
extremophiles, 18, 50, 161, 171-177,
   181
extremophilic archaea, 161

facultative anaerobes, 66
faint Sun paradox, 213-214, 218,
   221-222
faith, 14-15, 21, 31-32
fatty acids, 48, 54, 58, 78, 93, 149,
   162-163
Ferris, James, 117-118

fertilizers, 221
fifth creation day, 44
fifth miracle, 37
Fifth Miracle, The, 25, 30, 37
filaments, 65, 68
fine-tuned events, 211, 263
fine-tuning, 36, 119, 157, 212, 214-
   217, 222, 224
first life, 16-18, 22-24, 27, 37, 43-44,
   51, 59, 63-64, 76, 78-79, 91-93,
   116, 153, 162, 165, 173, 175-178,
   183, 194-195, 219, 225
Fischer-Tropsch reaction, 148-149
formaldehyde, 48, 96, 112-113
formate, 96, 112
formose chemistry, 113
fossils, 43, 64, 67-71, 83, 183, 188-
   189, 196
   chronology, 76
   record, 25-26, 33, 44, 63, 66, 76,
      78-79, 81, 175, 221
fossilized, 64, 68
FOTON satellite, 203
fourth law of thermodynamics, 91-92
Fox, Sidney, 25
frame of reference, 37, 233
fructose, 129
fruit flies, 160
Fry, Iris, 30
FtsZ proteins, 167
fuel molecules, 54
functional equivalency, 139-140
fungi, 49-50, 64, 166, 173, 219

galactic arms, 207
galactic bulge, 207
Galaxy, 39, 129, 186, 197, 206, 218,
   222
Galileo spacecraft, 197-200
Ganymede, 197-198, 200
Garbenschiefer Formation, 73
gas cloud, 82, 129, 212
gas molecules, 109
gelatinous lumps, 22

gene duplication, 89

gene products, 161-165, 168

general relativity, 23

Genesis 1 creation account, 15, 37-41, 43-44, 78, 90, 219, 225

genetic code fine-tuning, 224

genetic code, 81, 224

genetic material, 58, 124, 188

genomes, 45, 159-163, 165

genomics, 18, 159-160, 165, 168

geochemical marker, 74

geochemical record, 25-26, 44, 63, 74, 76-79, 175

geochemists, 70, 103

geochronometers, 85-86

geologic(al) record, 17, 43, 70-72, 75-78, 85, 217

geological column, 43, 59

geological moment, 85

geophysicists, 85-86, 185

George Washington University, 73

germination, 195

Gershfeld, Norman, 156

Glavin, Daniel, 97-98

glucose, 129, 229

glycerol (glycerin) backbone, 146-147

glycerol, 147, 153

glycine molecules, 52

glycine, 52, 96-98, 110, 124, 133, 187

glycoaldehyde pathway, 149

glycoaldehyde, 149

glycolipids, 252

God, 14-16, 30, 32, 35, 37-44, 90, 105, 140, 159, 208, 211, 213, 219, 225, 227

God's fingerprints, 32

god-of-the-gaps pseudoexplanations, 26

Goldsmith, Donald, 90

Gould, Stephen Jay, 91

graphite, 70-74, 77

graphite grains, 71

graphite granules, 72-74

gravitational collapse, 82

gravitational perturbation, 72

gravity, 87, 193, 197

Great Salt Lake, 171

Great Sandy Desert, 64

green sulfur, 66

greenhouse effect, 193, 214

greenhouse gases, 84, 90, 214-216, 218, 220-221

Greenland, 63, 71-74, 76-77, 84, 90-91, 104

greigite, 186-187

guanine, 95, 112-113, 177

Gunflint Formation in Canada, 69

Hadean Era, The, 38-39, 82, 85, 88, 90-91, 177

Hades, 38, 83

Haeckel, Ernst, 22

Haemophilus influenzae genome, 160

Haldane, J. B. S., 24

half-life, 86, 102, 112-113, 186

Halley, Henry H., 38

haloalkalophile (*Natronobacterium pharaonis*), 172

halophiles, 172

Hamilton, Victor P., 38

hammerhead ribosome, 180

hardness measure, 85

Harvard University, 166

Hayes, John, 91

heavy asteroid bombardment, 186, 192

heavy element enrichment, 212

Hebrew, 37-38, 41, 44

hematite, 75

hermeneutical principles, 36

heterotrophs, 50, 57, 77

high-energy protons, 100

high-energy thioester bond, 54

high-resolution imaging, 82

high-temperature stability, 175

histidine, 95, 118

historical-grammatical method, 37

history of life, 17, 44, 221

homochiral amino acids, 26, 126, 129, 131

homochirality, 18, 26, 124-126, 128-130, 132-133, 135, 159, 195, 221

homopolymer formation, 117

homopolymers, 117-118

Hooggenoeg Formation, 68

Horgan, John, 29

hot sea vents, See hydrothermal vents

Hoyle, Fred, 27

Hubble, Edwin, 23

Human Genome Project (HGP), 159-160

human genome sequence, 159

humanity, 14-15, 21, 35, 183, 211, 213, 217, 221-222, 225, 227

Huxley, T. H., 22-23

hydrocarbons, 147-152, 185-186, 201, 263

hydrogen cyanide, 48, 96-97, 112

hydrogen gas, 24, 52, 93-94, 99-100, 102, 110, 148-149, 173, 180-181, 199, 212-215, 218, 238

hydrogen peroxide, 101, 200-201

hydrogen sulfide, 52, 74, 103, 149

hydrogen-sulfide-mediated route, 103

hydrophobic effect, 179

hydrothermal conditions, 68

hydrothermal vents, 50-52, 54, 69-70, 77, 102-103, 110, 149, 174-175, 199

hydroxyl free radicals, 101

hypersaline conditions, 64

hyperthermophile host, 161

hyperthermophiles (Pyrolobus fumaris), 172

hyperthermophilic microbe, 161

ice cap, 52, 198

ice sheet, 171

impact event, 38, 85, 87, 173-174, 195, 200

impact melt, 83

impact reseeding, 86

impact sites, 99

impactors, 39, 82, 86, 177, 207

in vitro evolution, 119

incubators, 202

India, 14

infinite life, 27

infinite matter, 27

information theory, 25, 92

information-bearing molecules, 18, 159

information-containing molecules, 135, 141, 157

information-rich molecules, 109, 135-136, 140-141, 175

inorganic magnetites, 187

inorganic mechanisms, 67

intelligence, 30-33, 205, 224

International Conference on the Origin of Life and the International Society for the Study of the Origin of Life (ISSOL), 26, 69, 115, 132, 205

interplanetary space, 39, 86, 97, 185-186, 195

interstellar and interplanetary grains, 95, 97-98

interstellar clouds, 96-97, 129

interstellar dust, 27, 52, 96, 186, 190

interstellar radiation, 202

interstellar wandering rock, 204

invertebrates, 44, 66

Io, 198-199

ion microprobe analysis, 71

ionizing radiation, 48, 82, 174, 213

iron carbonate, 75

iron formations, 72-73, 75-76

iron ore deposits, 75

iron oxide, 75, 184, 187

iron sulfides, 184, 187

iron(2) sulfide, 52, 103

iron(2), 73, 180

iron, 74-75, 84, 87, 148, 212, 217, 220-221

irreducible complexity, 14, 223

Islam, 14

isotopes, 76, 83-84, 86, 101, 104, 184, 198
  analysis, 69
  exchange, 71, 238-239
  fractionation, 70, 74
  ratio measurements, 82
isotopic analysis, 70-71, 239
isotopic profile, 71
isotopic signature, 74
isovaline, 130, 251
Israel, 40-42, 171
ISSOL 1999, 26, 132, 205
ISSOL 2002, 26, 69, 83, 115
Isua rocks, 91, 104
Isua, Greenland, 91, 104

Jacob's seed, 42
Japan, 72
Jesus Christ, 15, 41, 208
Johnson Space Center, 186
junk proteins, 136, 138
Jupiter, 18, 51, 174, 197-200, 203, 207

kaolinite, 53
Kauffman, Stuart, 91
kerogens, 68, 70-71, 74, 76-77, 104, 214, 221, 238-240
Kromberg Formation, 68
Kuhn, Werner, 128
Kuhn-Condon rule, 128
Kvenvolden, Keith, 130-131

L. pictus, 156
Labrador, 84
lactose, 129
Lake Vostok, Antarctica, 171
land formation, 40
landmasses, 39-40, 67, 88, 215-216, 219-220
laser Raman microscopic analysis, 69
laser reflectors, 87
Last Universal Common Ancestor (LUCA), 48-50, 57-58, 160, 168, 177-178

late heavy bombardment, 72-73, 83-85, 87, 194
laws of logic, 92
Lazcano, Antonio, 89, 116, 178
lead, 86, 118, 186, 217, 221
lead-lead dating method, 186
lecithin, 144
Leiden Observatory, 97
leucine, 127
Levy, Matthew, 90
life force, 24
Life Itself, 30, 205
life molecule synthesis, 103
life principle, 28
Life, 109
life's "seeds", 23, 42
life
  beginning, 14, 16, 21, 24-29, 42, 45, 47, 49, 58, 60, 160, 162, 164, 174, 181, 223
  building blocks, 47, 49, 58-59, 110, 133, 158, 164, 178
  building-block molecules, 58
  early appearance, 42, 44, 63, 69, 74, 77
  first emergence, 43
  molecules, 49, 51, 59, 94, 103-104, 109-110, 115, 123, 166, 201, 204, 206
  remains, 43, 71, 74, 195, 203
  signature, 70-71, 74
life-origin debate, 35, 54-55
light volatiles, 40
lightning, 48, 51
lipid aggregates, 151
lipid bilayers, 151
lipids, 93, 144-145, 148-151, 154-155, 158, 165, 194, 252
liposomes, 155-156
liquid water, 83-84, 88, 178, 186, 190-193, 197-200
literal machines, 224
localized evaporation, 53
Lockheed, 186

loophole, 168, 171, 173, 181, 183
Lord Kelvin, 23
Losick, Richard, 166
luminosity, 82, 84, 193, 213-216,
    218, 220
Lunar and Planetary Institute, 191, 200
Lunar and Planetary Laboratory
    (LPL), 200
lunar rock, 83, 87, 218
lysine, 95

macroscopic mats, 65
macroscopic stromatolites, 64
magnesium ion, 149, 178
magnesium sulfate, 200
magnetic field, 196, 200
magnetic mineral crystals, 185-187
magnetism, 125
magnetite, 75, 187
magnetochiral anistropy, 125
magnetosphere, 200
magnetotactic bacteria, 187
major creation accounts, 37
mantle, 40, 64, 102, 193, 215, 220
marine biologist, 91
Mariner spacecraft, 192
Mars Global Surveyor, 192
Mars, 18, 27, 50-51, 82-83, 86-88, 131,
    177, 180-181, 183-197, 202-204
Martian atmosphere, 184, 190, 194
Martian life, 174, 183-184, 189-190,
    196
Martian meteorites, 184, 190, 192-
    193
Martian rocks, 190, 195
maser sources, 128
mass extinction event, 206
materialism, 13
mathematics, 92
McKay, David, 184, 187, 189
mean temperature, 214
Melosh, Jay, 204
melting point, 85
membrane, 18, 54, 56, 58, 89, 114,

116, 129, 143-147, 149-150,
    152-155, 165-167, 179, 195, 224
biophysics, 151, 157-158
origins, 50, 57, 148, 151, 156-158
Mercury, 82-83, 203
mesophiles, 173-178
mesophilic origin-of-life explana-
    tions, 175
mesophilic photoautotrophs, 175
metabolic intermediates, 71
metabolic pathways, 52, 54, 70, 78,
    115-116
metabolic properties, 44, 76
metabolism, 47, 50, 54, 93, 109, 115-
    116, 135, 161-162, 180, 199
metabolism-first scenarios, 54, 115-
    116
metabolites, 116
metal ions, 52, 118
metamorphic event, 72-73
metamorphic heat, 72
metamorphosis, 64, 68, 73, 238
metastable phase, 155
meteorite, 23-25, 40, 49-50, 52, 82-
    84, 95-99, 112-114, 129-131, 150-
    151, 183-187, 189, 193, 199-200,
    202, 218, 245
meteors, 96, 189, 204
methane, 24, 48, 90, 99-100, 110,
    214-215, 218, 238-239
methanococcus jannaschii genome,
    161-162
methanococcus, 161
methanogenesis, 77, 238
methanogenic microbes, 181, 238
methanogens, 215
methanotrophic (methane-using)
    organisms, 71
Meyer, Stephen C., 33
mice, 160
micelle structures, 152
micelles, 150, 152
microbial
    communities, 77, 173-174

ecologies, 68, 77, 180
fossils, 67, 69
genomes, 160, 162
microbiologists, 76, 165-167, 173, 180, 189
microcrystalline silica, 68
microfossil cell walls, 69
microfossils, 67-71, 76-77, 188-190
micrometeorites, 50, 52
microscopic cellular remnants, 64
microscopy method, 69
microspheres, 25
Mileikowksy, Curt, 97
Milky Way galaxy, 39, 197, 206, 218, 222
Miller, Stanley, 24-25, 89, 96, 100-103, 109-110, 112, 116, 133
Min C, 167
Min D proteins, 167
mineral surfaces, 53-54, 115-116, 118, 126
minimal complexity, 25, 43, 45, 59-60, 78, 160-168
minimal life, 168
miracle, 30, 37, 40, 115-116, 208, 215-216, 225
models, 21, 23, 48-49, 55, 82, 89, 92, 109, 141, 149, 152, 162, 177, 193, 201, 218
    biblical creation, 43-46
    chemoautotroph-first, 58
    computer, 203
    creation, 17, 35-37, 42-46, 78, 120, 140, 157, 161, 164, 168, 208, 213, 216, 221, 233
    deep-biosphere, 180
    evolutionary, 17, 32, 45, 58, 143
    extraterrestrial origin-of-life, 51
    extremophilic origin-of-life, 173-176
    fluid mosaic, 148
    for life's beginning, 42, 45, 60, 63
    heterotroph-first, 57
    iron-sulfur world, 52
    metabolism-first, 54, 115-117, 120-121
    naturalistic, 18, 30, 46-47, 105, 120, 151, 160, 168, 175, 194, 221
    naturalistic origin-of-life, 60, 121
    origin-of-life, 43-45, 47, 51, 58-59, 105, 111-113, 120-121, 133, 176, 180-181, 208
    replicator-first, 54, 115
    RNA-world and pre-RNA-world origin-of- life, 111-112
    RTB creation, 16-18, 36, 42-46, 72, 78-79, 90, 105, 120, 133, 140, 157, 161, 168, 181, 195, 204, 208, 216, 221, 234
    RTB testable creation, 42
    scientific, 24, 29, 42, 44
    scientific creation, 36
    terrestrial, 51
    testable creation, 17, 37, 42
    testable supernatural, 33
    textbook, 58, 234
    thioester world, 53-54
molecular "handedness", 123
molecular
    aggregates, 13, 154
    building blocks, 25, 129
    cloud, 97, 126-128, 186
    convergence, 224
    events, 224
    fine-tuning, 224
    machinery, 131, 188-189, 208
    motors, 224
    oxygen, 100-101
molten rock clock, 177
molten state, 173
monera, 22-23
monochromatic circularly polarized ultraviolet light, 129
monochromatic light, 128
monolayers of cell membranes, 147
monolayers, 146-147
montmorillonite, 53

Moon rock, 83
Moon, the, 82-83, 87-88, 177, 203, 216
Morowitz, Harold, 164-165
mosses, 219
MT41, 172
mucilage, 65
Murchison meteorite, 24-25, 95-96, 98-99, 129-131, 150-151
Murchison, Australia, 24, 130
Murray meteorite, 129, 251
Muslim, 14
mutations, 163, 224
Mycoplasma genitalim, 162
Mycoplasma pneumoniae, 162
mystery of life's origin, 13, 25
Mystery of Life's Origin, The, 17

naked bacterial spores, 23
naked replicator, 55
Nakhla meteorite, 131, 190
Nanoarchaeum equitans, 161
nanobacteria, 188-189
nanometers, 143, 187-189
nanomicrobes, 189
NASA (National Aeronautics and Space Administration), 51, 82, 183-185, 187, 191, 196, 197
NASA Ames Research Center, 97, 150, 176-177
National Academy of Sciences, 189
National Institutes of Health (NIH), 156, 163, 189
natural mechanism, 22, 49, 175, 216
natural selection, 22, 49, 57
natural-history approach, 17
naturalism, 21, 29, 47, 79, 89, 183, 205
naturalists' paradigm, 91
naturalistic cold origin-of-life possibilities, 90
naturalistic framework, 29
naturalistic life origin, 89, 94, 195
naturalistic origin-of-life scenarios, 49, 51, 54, 72, 77, 89, 103, 109, 120, 129, 153, 157, 160, 174, 181, 194, 247
naturalistic paradigm, 27, 29, 33, 45, 139
naturalistic predictions, 58-60, 79, 92, 110, 120, 159-160
naturalistic process, 16, 181
naturalistic scenarios, 26, 45, 63, 121, 129, 153, 161, 164
naturalistic scientists, 17, 217
natural-process explanations, 158
near miracle, 116
nematodes, 160
neopanspermists, 27
neovitalism, 23-24
neovitalists, 28
Neptune, 203
neurodegeneration, 156
new creation, 41, 227
New Testament, 41
New York Herald Tribune, 109
New York Times, 109
New York University, 219
New Zealand, 178
Newsweek, 109
Newton's laws of motion, 82
nickel, 84, 148, 217
nitrogen, 22, 48, 74, 93-94, 100, 103-104, 112, 199, 201, 221
    isotope fractionation, 74
    isotope ratios, 104
    isotope, 74
    isotopic analysis, 74
    isotopic life signature, 74
    ratio, 104
nitrogen-14, 70, 74, 76, 240
nitrogen-14 enriched kerogen and graphite globules, 77
nitrogen-14 enrichment, 74
nitrogen-14 isotope enrichment, 70
nitrogen-15 excess, 74
nitrogen-15 to nitrogen-14 ratio, 104
nitrogen-15, 74

Nobel laureate, 23-24, 28, 30, 53-54, 110, 202, 205, 213
nonanol, 152
nonchiral origin of life, 132
no-oxidants-versus-oxidants paradox 201
north pole (Mars), 191
Norway, 73
nuclear reactions, 82, 213
nucleic acids, 50, 52-53, 93, 111-112, 117, 119, 133
nucleobases, 96, 98-99, 102, 112-113, 129, 133
nucleoside, 94, 99
nucleotide bases, 52-53, 95
nucleotide building blocks, 89-90, 124
nucleus, 49, 64, 166, 188
Nuuk, 63

Oaxaca, Mexico, 26, 83
obliquity, 194
observer, 38-39
ocean, 24, 38-40, 42, 48, 63, 66-67, 75, 86-87, 90, 94, 99, 101, 103, 118, 152, 171-173, 193, 197-201, 213-216, 219-220
oceanic or subterranean water, 101
octanoic and nonanoic acid, 151-152
Ohio University, 13, 15
oligosaccharides, 224
Olson, Roger L., 17, 138, 149
Oparin, Alexander I., 24
Oparin-Haldane hypothesis, 24, 47, 49, 51, 109
opposite-handed nucleotides, 118
orbital eccentricity, 198
Oregon State (University), 149
organic
    kerogen, 68
    magnetites, 187
    molecules, 53, 101
    phosphates, 71
    remnants, 70
    tars, 68

Orgel, Leslie, 28, 30, 33, 56, 115-119, 205
origin-of-life paradox, 201
Origins Program, 51
Orion Nebula, 127
outer ice shell, 200
Owen, Tobias, 183
oxalic acid, 149
oxidants paradox, 201
oxidation, 94, 113, 220
oxide deposits, 220
oxygen, 24, 48, 66, 74-77, 93-94, 100-102, 184, 194, 199-202, 217, 219-220
oxygen enrichment, 219-220
oxygen isotope ratios, 184
oxygenic photosynthesis, 76-77
oxygen-ultraviolet paradox, 101, 110, 201

Pacific Ocean's Mariana Trench, 172
Paige, David, 183
paleontologist, 30, 66-70, 90
panspermia, 23-24, 27-28, 30, 33, 49-52, 202, 204-208, 221
    directed, 28, 30, 33, 50-51, 205-208, 221
    nondirected, 49-50
    repeat directed, 206
panspermists, 27
paradigm, 27, 29, 33, 44-45, 91, 139, 175, 177-178
parasite, 161-163, 168, 188-189
parasitic microbes, 161-163
parity violations, 125
particle accelerator experiments, 125
particle physics, 243
pathways
    biochemical, 77-78
    chemical, 13, 25-26, 54, 58, 104, 109-110, 114, 120, 148-149, 153-154, 158-159, 179, 190, 194, 221
    chemoautotrophic, 57-58, 175

evolutionary, 13
metabolic, 52, 54, 70, 78, 115-116
naturalistic, 133
origin-of-life, 56, 143, 174
prebiotic, 138, 194
protometabolic, 57, 116
psychrophilic, 178
Patterson, Colin, 161
Penn State, 103
peptide bonds, 102
peptide, 53, 102, 119, 174
peptide-nucleic acids (PNA), 50, 56, 117, 133
periodic nutrient upswells, 75
Perth, 64
Pflüger, Edward, 22-23
pH levels, 132
pharmaceuticals, 159
Phillips, Cynthia, 199
phosphate and oxygen "sinks", 220
phosphate group, 114
phosphate, 22, 71, 93-94, 111, 113-114, 133, 149-150, 220-221, 252
phosphatidylethanolamines (PEs), 153
phosphatidylglycerol (PGs), 153
phospholipid bilayer, 147-148, 153-154
phospholipid tails, 145-146, 149
phospholipids, 114, 145-151, 153-158
phosphorus problem, 94
phosphorus, 94, 217
photoautotrophs, 50, 57, 175
photochemistry, 125
photolysis, 97
photosphere, 213
photosynthesis, 66, 74-78, 143, 167, 175, 199, 220, 229, 238
photosynthetic bacteria, 75-76
photosynthetic cyanobacteria, 71
photosynthetic microbes, 71, 76-78, 238
phyla, 206, 220
phytoplankton, 199

Pikes Peak, 191
Pilbara Supergroup, 64, 68-70
Pizzarello, Sandra, 130
planetary science, 17
planetesimals, 82, 193
plasmids, 166
plate tectonics, 64, 84, 215-217, 220, 261
Pluto, 203
polarization, 126-127
Polish Academy of Sciences, 69
polycyclic aromatic hydrocarbons (PAHs), 185-186, 190
polymerase activity, 167
polypeptide chain, 137
polypeptides, 102, 137
polyphosphate minerals, 114-115
polyphosphates, 114-115, 118
polysaccharides, 93
postbiotic decay, 104
potassium-40, 101, 245
prebiotic
    catalysts, 116
    chemical pathways, 104, 194
    chemistry, 101, 194, 201-202
    compounds, 51-54, 56-57, 59, 89, 95, 99-103, 105, 110-111, 120, 136, 141
    formation, 51, 103, 149-150
    mixture, 21
    molecular synthesis, 100
    molecule production, 51, 101-102
    molecule, 24, 26, 47-49, 51-53, 83, 93, 99-103, 110, 175, 201
    origin, 104, 135
    polyphosphate synthesis, 114-115
    reactions, 111, 114
    soup, 26, 48-49, 52-53, 57, 59, 88, 93-96, 99, 101, 103-105, 109-110, 112, 117, 136, 139, 221
    synthesis, 51, 95, 103, 124, 150
precursor molecules, 55
predators, 66
predictions, 17, 31-33, 35-36, 42-48,

58-59, 78-79, 90, 92, 110, 120,
    157-158, 160-161, 168, 181, 193,
    208, 234
prelife forms, 57
preorganic compounds, 95
preplanning, 119, 224
pre-RNA-world interpretations, 56
President Clinton, 159, 183, 185
primitive cell membranes, 57
primitive cellular system, 56
primitive membrane emergence, 150
primordial
    atmosphere, 100
    crust, 215
    Earth, 24, 26, 37-39, 41, 44, 48,
        78, 90, 111-112, 114, 117-118,
        120, 139
    Earth's surface, 37-39
    soup, 24, 52, 100, 104-105, 120,
        140
    state, 37, 43, 78
primordial-soup hypothesis, 104
prokaryote diversity, 77
prokaryotes, 49, 58, 64, 78-79, 188
prokaryotic microorganisms, 76
prophesy, 42
protein
    aggregates, 24
    chains, 136, 157
    function, 140
    library, 138-139
    precursors, 53
    structure, 137, 139-141
proteinoids, 25
protocells, 47-50, 54, 56-57, 115-116,
    118, 143, 148, 150-152, 154, 157
protometabolic pathways, 57, 116
protometabolism, 54
protoplasm, 22-23
protoplasmic theory of the cell, 22-23
protozoans, 64, 166, 173
pseudo-success, 111
pseudofossils, 68
psychrophiles (Polaromonas

vacuolata), 50, 172, 178-179
psychrophilic origin-of-life explana-
    tions, 176
pulsars, 126
punctuated equilibrium hypothesis,
    91
purines, 48, 58
purple bacteria, 66
Pwyll (crater), 200
pyrimidine, 48, 58, 112
pyrite, 52, 54, 74
    formation, 52
    surfaces, 52
pyrophosphates, 53
pyrrhotite crystals, 187
pyrrhotite, 187
pyschrophilic pathways, 178

quality control, 224
quantum mechanics, 128, 243
Qur'an, 14

racemic mixtures, 124-125, 129, 131-
    132
radiation pressure, 23, 202-203
radiation, 23, 82, 97-99, 101, 126-
    128, 132, 174, 185, 194-196, 199,
    202-204, 207, 213
radiation-resistant bacterium
    (Bacillus subtilis), 203
radioactive decay, 48, 101, 215-216,
    245
radioactive elements, 216-217
radioactivity, 132
radioisotopes, 87
radiometric dates, 83
radiometric isotopes, 83, 198
Raman signature, 69
random processes, 23
random-sequence libraries, 139
Rea, John, 41
reactive oxygen species, 101
Reasons To Believe (RTB), 11, 16-18,
    35-36, 42-45, 60, 63, 72, 78-79,

90, 105, 120, 133, 140, 157, 161, 168, 181, 195, 204, 208, 216, 221
red blood cells, 156
reducing gases, 24, 51, 99
rehydration, 151-152
religious pluralism, 14
repeating structure, 135
repetitive condensation reactions, 53
replicator molecules, 94
replicator-first hypothesis, 117
reverse transcriptase, 119
ribose, 111, 113, 115, 118, 124, 129
ribosomal RNA (rRNA), 175, 177
ribozymes (RNA enzymes), 56, 119, 180
rings, 94, 96, 112, 130
RNA, 48, 50, 52-54, 58-59, 71, 78, 81, 93, 111-115, 120, 124, 129-130, 133, 136, 141, 151, 158, 161, 165, 175, 177-180, 194, 224
    ancestral molecules, 56
    chain reaction, 118
    molecules, 55-56, 89-90, 94, 102, 117-119, 152, 178
    systems, 135
RNA-world hypothesis, 55-56, 178
rock deposit, 64, 67, 69, 71-72, 77, 83
Rosetta spacecraft, 130
Ross, Hugh, 16, 225
rotation axis, 87, 194
rotation rate, 82, 87, 216, 220
RTB Model's predictions, 36, 42-46, 78-79, 90, 157, 160-161, 168, 181, 208
RTB testable creation model, 42
RTB testable creation research model program, 35
rubidium-strontium dating method, 186
rubidium-strontium dating, 184
runaway evaporation, 214
runaway freeze-up, 214

Sackmann, Juliana, 218
Sagan, Carl, 81, 98-99, 183
salt mines, 172
San Diego, California, 26
sand, 84, 214-215, 219-221
Santa Fe Institute, 91
Saturn, 18, 201, 203
Schenk, Paul, 200
Schopf, J. William, 68-69, 79
Schwartzman, David, 219
Science, 189
scientific orthodoxy, 40
Scripps Institute, 97, 190
Scripture, 15, 35, 37-38, 41-42, 225, 227
sea-floor vents, 52
Search for Extraterrestrial Life Institute (SETI), 33, 97, 150, 207
seas, 152, 193
seawater, 65, 220
second law of thermodynamics, 91, 131, 243
sediment groundwater, 131
sedimentary rocks, 73, 75, 84
sediments, 63-65, 73-75, 77, 131, 220
seeds of Earth's first life, 43
seeds of life, 37, 41, 204-206, 211
self-assembly, 105, 158
self-organization pathways, 54
self-organization, 54
self-replicating molecule, 24, 48, 55-56, 89, 115-116, 133, 148, 151
self-replication, 47, 54, 116-117, 135, 151
self-replicators, 49, 54-55, 57, 109-110, 112, 115-120, 151-152
sequence data, 160
serine, 97
Sermon on the Mount, 15
shallow water environments, 65-68, 72, 75
Shapiro, Lucy, 166
Shapiro, Robert, 112, 117-118, 205
Shark Bay, 64-67

shock melting, 185-186
short RNA chains, 53
"shotgun" sequencing strategy, 160
side-chain sequence, 135
silica sediments, 75
silica, 68, 75, 177
silicate erosion, 84, 215, 220
silicate rocks, 215
silicon, 94
single bilayer structures, 154, 156-157
single-celled
    microbes, 64, 171, 173
    microorganisms, 171
    prokaryotes, 79
    protozoans, 64, 166
sixth creation day, 44
skeletal remains, 64
soils, 171, 194, 219
solar and volcanic heat, 48
solar energy, 57, 214, 229
solar heat, 193
solar ionizing radiation, 82, 174, 213
solar luminosity, 215, 220
solar nebula, 50, 212-213
solar system, 25, 27, 40, 44, 49, 51, 72, 82-83, 86, 180, 186, 193-194, 197, 201-204, 206, 212, 221-222, 264
solar ultraviolet radiation, 82, 174, 196
solar wind, 218
solfatara, 171
soluble organic compounds, 95
solution salt level, 152
Song of Moses, 40
South Africa, 63-64, 67-70, 74-77
space debris, 95
space-time, 208
spark-discharge experiments, 24, 109, 112-114
spectrographs, 200
sphalerite, 266
Spirit of God, 37, 40-41, 233

spontaneous generation, 63
spores, 23, 27, 202-204
stable hydrogen fusion, 215-216
stable nuclear burning, 213
Stanford University, 140, 166, 176-177
stars, 101, 186, 203, 206, 212, 218
    companion, 207
    giant, 207
    neutron, 125-128, 264
    super-giant, 127-128, 204
    young, 207
    young solar-type, 82
starter proteins, 89
stellar radiation pressure, 203
stellar winds, 127
sterilization event, 83, 85-86, 99
sterilizing impact events, 174
stromatolites, 64-68, 70-72, 76-77, 236
    formation, 72
    fossils, 66-67, 70
    remains, 67-68, 71, 76-77
subunit molecules, 52, 117, 135, 151
sugar phosphates, 71
sugars, 26, 48, 52-54, 58, 78, 84, 93, 102, 113-114, 124-126, 129-130, 133, 162-163, 194, 215, 229, 252
sulfate-reducing bacteria, 74-75, 217, 266
sulfate-reducing microorganisms, 74
sulfate-reduction, 77
sulfide deposits, 70, 74-75, 77
sulfide, 52, 74, 103, 184, 187
sulfur isotope composition, 101
sulfur isotope, 74, 101
sulfur, 66, 93, 102, 217, 220
sulfur-32 isotope enrichment, 76
sulfur-32, 72, 74-75
sulfur-32-enriched hydrogen sulfide, 74
sulfur-32-enriched sulfide deposits, 70, 77
sulfuric acid, 200-201
sulfurous gas, 171

Sun, the, 39-40, 82, 84, 94, 101, 193-194, 203, 212-216, 218, 220-221, 261
sunlight, 65-66, 199, 201, 213, 229
SUNY Stony Brook, 103
super giants, 127
supernatural directed panspermia, 208, 221
supernatural explanations, 15, 17, 31-33, 115
supernatural intervention, 33, 133, 208
supernatural origin of life, 33, 208, 233
supernatural, 15, 17, 21, 30-33, 45, 63, 115, 133, 140, 157, 208, 212, 221, 223
supernaturalism, 29-30
supernaturalist, 35
supernova eruptions, 101, 212
supernova, 101, 126, 207, 212
superoxide, 101
Swaziland Supergroup, 64, 68, 70
Sweden, 73
Swiss Federal Institute of Technology, 139
synchrotron radiation, 126
synthetic routes, 26, 110

Tagish Lake meteorite, 96, 99, 131
Tagish Lake, 96, 99, 131
tectonic activity, 40, 43, 64, 67, 180-181, 216, 220
tectonics, 64, 84, 87, 212, 215-217
template, 54, 117
terrestrial contamination, 131, 150, 187, 190
Tesla coil, 110
Thaxton, Charles B., 17, 138, 149
The Institute of Genomic Research (TIGR), 160
theology, 32
thermal alteration, 69
thermal springs, 172

thermoacidophile (*Sulfolobus acido-caldaruis*), 172
thermophiles, 50, 172, 177-178
thermophilic window, 177
thioesters, 50, 54
third creation day, 43-44
thorium, 85, 101, 212, 245
thorium-232, 85-86,
threadlike microfossils, 68
three-dimensional solids, 64
three-dimensional structures, 136-137, 175, 178-180
tidal action, 53, 57, 65
tidal brake, 216
tidal heating, 197-199
tilt, 87, 194
time window, 43, 84-85, 194, 218
    for life's origin, 84-85, 194
Time, 109
timing of life's appearance, 42, 63, 76
Titan, 18, 201-202, 204, 263
tōhû wābōhû, 38-39, 41, 43, 90
top-down approach, 17-18, 159, 168, 171
transcendent causation, 29
transitional molecular system, 24
transport problem, 132
Treiman, Allan, 192
triglycerides, 144
trimetaphosphate, 53
tungsten-182 isotope, 84
Twentieth Lunar and Planetary Science Conference (Houston, TX), 203
two-dimensional imprints, 64
type I supernova, 212
type II supernova, 212
Tyre (crater), 200

UCLA, 68, 183
ultraviolet radiation, 23, 48, 82, 96-97, 101, 126-127, 194-195, 203
undermat, 66
United Kingdom, 68

United States, 73, 187
universe, 21, 23, 27, 30-32, 35, 37,
    49, 51, 91, 94, 124, 139-141, 164,
    183, 202, 206, 208, 211-213, 231,
    243, 263-264
University of Arizona, 204
University of California, Santa Cruz,
    150
University of Chicago, 24
University of Illinois, 173
University of New Mexico, 186
University of Texas, 186
upper stromatolite layers, 66
uracil, 95, 112-113
uranium, 85, 101, 212, 245
uranium-238, 85-86
Uranus, 203
urea, 112
Urey, Harold, 24, 110
Utah, 171

vascular plants, 219-220
vegetation, 37, 219
velocity of light, 207
Ventor, Craig, 159-160
Venus, 83, 86, 203
vesicles, 151, 155-156
Viking orbiters, 192
Viking, 192
vital poison, 266
volcanoes, 102-103
    activity, 40, 43, 171, 261
    islands, 40, 53, 57, 67, 72, 136
    lightning, 51
    pools, 172
volcanism, 87, 212, 215, 217
Volk, Tyler, 219
Von Helmholtz, Hermann, 23

Wächtershäuster, Günter, 52
Ward, Peter, 91
Warrowana Hills, 63
water
    flows, 191

molecule, 52-53, 179
vapor, 24, 48, 87, 99-100, 190,
    214, 216
world, 40, 174, 197
wavelength, 66, 101, 125-126, 128
Weber, Arthur, 149
West Virginia State College, 14
western Australia, 64, 67-68, 74, 76
western Europe, 187
western Greenland, 71-74, 76
Wickramsinghe, Chandra, 27
Wills, Christopher, 85
Wirtanen comet, 130
Woese, Carl, 56, 173

X- and gamma-ray radiation, 126,
    132

Yockey, Hubert, 92, 104, 140, 164
young-earth creationism, 232

Zimbabwe, 6
zinc, 212, 217, 221, 266
zircon crystals, 85
zircons, 85-86

ABOUT THE AUTHORS

FAZALE RANA is the vice president for science apologetics at Reasons To Believe. His research in biochemistry provided him with the initial evidence that life must have a Creator. A personal challenge daring him to read the Bible led him to the scriptural evidence that the Creator is the God of the Bible.

Dr. Rana attended West Virginia State College and then Ohio University, where he earned a Ph.D. in chemistry. His postdoctoral work was conducted at the Universities of Virginia and Georgia. He was a Presidential Scholar, elected into two honor societies, and won the Donald Clippinger Research Award twice at Ohio University. Dr. Rana worked for seven years as a senior scientist in product development for Procter & Gamble before joining Reasons To Believe.

He has published more than fifteen articles in peer-reviewed scientific journals and delivered more than twenty presentations at international scientific meetings. Dr. Rana also coauthored a chapter on antimicrobial peptides for *Biological and Synthetic Membranes* in addition to contributing numerous feature articles to *Facts for Faith* magazine. He appears weekly on the "Creation Update" webcast and gives frequent radio interviews.

Dr. Rana and his wife, Amy, have four daughters and a son. They live in southern California.

HUGH ROSS is founder, president, and director of research for Reasons To Believe, a nonprofit and interdenominational institute based in California. Reasons To Believe researches and communicates how God's revelation in the words of the Bible harmonizes with the facts of nature.

Dr. Ross studied physics at the University of British Columbia and earned a Ph.D. in astronomy from the University of Toronto. For several years he continued his research on quasars and galaxies as a postdoctoral fellow at the California Institute of Technology.

For two decades Dr. Ross has served on the pastoral staff at Sierra Madre Congregational Church. Today, in addition to managing the day-to-day operations of Reasons To Believe, he lectures around the world and hosts a weekly live webcast.

Dr. Ross is the author of *The Fingerprint of God*, *The Creator and the Cosmos*, *Creation and Time*, *Beyond the Cosmos*, *The Genesis Question*, and *Lights in the Sky and Little Green Men* (coauthored with Kenneth Samples and Mark Clark). He also coauthored *The Genesis Debate* and has contributed to other books, including *Why I Am a Christian* and *The Day I Met God*.

He lives in southern California with his wife, Kathy, and two sons.

ABOUT REASONS TO BELIEVE

Founded in 1986, Reasons To Believe is an international, interdenominational ministry established to proclaim compelling new reasons—from up-to-the-minute scientific research—for faith in Jesus Christ. Through books, articles, talks, tapes, and the Web, its scholars demonstrate how the latest discoveries add weight to the existing (enormous) body of evidence for the transcendent God of the Bible and for the authority of Scripture.

For more information about Reasons To Believe and its apologetics resources, call 1-800-482-7836, visit www.reasons.org, or write to this address: Reasons To Believe, P.O. Box 5978, Pasadena, CA 91117. For questions on faith, science, and the Bible, call the hotline (626-335-5282), which operates daily from 5 to 7 P.M. (Pacific Time). "Creation Update," a live interactive webcast, airs Tuesdays from 11 A.M. to 1 P.M. on RTB's website and at oneplace.com, where it is also archived.